Uncle John's Know It All Bathroom Reader

No. 38

Portable Press

San Diego, California

Portable Press / The Bathroom Readers' Institute
An imprint of Printers Row Publishing Group
9717 Pacific Heights Blvd, San Diego, CA 92121
www.portablepress.com • mail@portablepress.com

Correspondence regarding the content of this book should be sent to Portable Press / The Bathroom Readers' Institute, Editorial Department, at the above address.

Publisher: Peter Norton • Associate Publisher: Ana Parker
Editorial Director: April Graham
Art Director: Charles McStravick
Production Team: Beno Chan, Julie Greene

Creator: Javna Brothers LLC

Interior and Infographics Designer: Linda Lee Mauri
Cover Design: Linda Lee Mauri

Image credits: cheremuha/stock.adobe.com, lidiia/stock.adobe.com (page 22); GabiWolf/stock.adobe.com (page 52); Shanvood/stock.adobe.com, Good Studio/stock.adobe.com, Hennadii/stock.adobe.com, Paul Kovaloff/stock.adobe.com (page 112); GraphicsRF/stock.adobe.com, Sensvector/stock.adobe.com, Wahyu/stock.adobe.com (page 158); Valerii/stock.adobe.com (page 22); Vitaliy/stock.adobe.com (page 339)

"Words can be like X-rays if you use them properly—they'll go through anything. You read and you're pierced."
—Aldous Huxley

Library of Congress Control Number: 2025932323

ISBN: 978-1-6672-0848-0

Printed in Faridabad-Haryana, India

29 28 27 26 25   1 2 3 4 5

OUR "REGULAR READERS" RAVE!

It's full of interesting stuff to read while doing your business and you'll likely find yourself at times sitting a little extra to finish out new tidbits.

—Ben

After all, what else do you have to do while you're sitting there? You'll never get up without learning something either amazing or flat-out silly.

—Michael K.

Buy this book! I guarantee you will not be disappointed!

—Nancy V.

They are a great read whether sitting on the toilet. Or just relaxing in your favorite chair. Highly recommended.

—Steven L.

I am always amazed and entertained as well as learning something.

—Scott V.

I've been buying these yearly editions for 37 years, I actually look forward to them. Great reading!

—Jerry O.

If you thought pooping was great, just try it while reading this book. TERRIFIC.

—Anonymous

Every book in this series is great and has unique information and fun facts throughout. Fill your head while you fill the pot.

—Eric B.

Every new edition is filled with interesting trivia. Wife complains that I spend too much time in the bathroom.

—Steve

I'm not sure where all the facts keep coming from, but it sure is entertaining reading for all ages.

—Kelly

CONTENTS

Because the BRI understands your reading needs, we've divided the contents by length as well as subject.

Short—a quick read

Medium—2 to 3 pages

Long—for those extended visits, when something a little more involved is required

INTRODUCTION

Has anybody ever called you a "know-it-all"? I know that the term has a negative connotation—it's usually used to describe someone who eschews advice or assistance, or someone who is haughty about how smart they are. But I always thought, what's so wrong with knowing it all? Doesn't having as much knowledge as possible help me understand the world better? (Not to mention that it makes me more interesting at dinner parties! At least that's what I tell myself...)

One thing I know for a fact is that it's impossible to know everything. There's just too much information in the world, and the amount only keeps growing! But that hasn't stopped me from seeking out as much knowledge as I can about anything and everything that catches my attention. Poring over physical copies of *Encyclopedia Brittanica* may have morphed into falling down the metaphorical rabbit hole of the Internet, but the BRI staff and I still enjoy educating ourselves on the widest variety of topics we can—and sharing what we learn with you. That's why we want you to

KNOW IT ALL

We're now in our 38th year of publishing the Bathroom Reader, and we've covered a lot of ground! But we've made it our mission to keep unearthing the most interesting and entertaining (and occasionally random) stuff there is to know. Of course, because a lot of people *never* learn, it helps that every year we have a fresh crop of news stories to help with our favorite ongoing features: year after year, the world continues to be populated by dumb crooks, parents who give their kids funny names, and people who have embarrassing bathroom moments. Luckily, the world also has no shortage of people who do nice things, people who have lucky finds, scientists who engage in fascinating research, and plenty of other smart, entertaining folks whose exploits we love to, well, exploit! Here's just a sample of what *you* will know by the time you finish this year's Bathroom Reader.

STUFF YOU ALWAYS WANTED TO KNOW: The science behind all the goodies you used to order from comic books, how various dog breeds got their names, the reasons why people used to be admitted to psychiatric institutes, a primer on the six wives of Henry VIII, what makes your favorite cleaning products work, and what really happened to Elvis (according to some of his fans).

POP CULTURE: TV channels that went away as quickly as they came, the quirkiest game shows you won't believe actually exist, the strangest conspiracy theories that fans have formulated about movies and television shows, the origins of some of the ugly-but-trendy footwear we've worn recently, and nepo babies you didn't realize were nepo babies.

SPORTS: The most bizarre things to happen in America's favorite pastime, the most odd things to happen during pro sports drafts, what pickleball is and where it came from, and the kid who beat the Nintendo game everyone thought was unbeatable.

LAUGHS: Tongue twisters you'll have to twy out—er, *try* out for yourself, what the Victorians thought were clever puns, police departments honing their comedic chops on social media, unintentionally funny mistranslations, obituaries that truly celebrate the dearly departed, and our favorite pirate jokes.

LANGUAGE: A handy guide to understanding your Gen Alpha teen, another handy guide to translating government and business speak, common phrases coined on the big screen and the small screen, typos we're glad we didn't make, and literary genres readers used to love that don't even exist anymore.

HISTORY: How the U.S. military's World War II book campaign changed the publishing industry, the origins of hospitals, a few of the many attempts on the life of Queen Elizabeth II, etiquette of yore we're glad has been forgotten, fads and phases of facial hair, and the saga of how we reached our current measurement systems.

FOOD: Where our favorite casseroles came from, the history of Canadians' favorite foods, why vanilla is a big deal, the weirdest sandwiches we've come across, and the origins of some of our favorite processed-food treats.

STUFF YOU NEVER THOUGHT ABOUT: A deep dive into the questions surrounding the big purple weirdo who hangs out in McDonaldland, the toaster-inventor hoax that burned Wikipedia, carny slang, and everything there is to know about Pez.

And much, much more!

Of course, because I don't know everything, I have to solicit the help of other knowledge enthusiasts. Luckily, the Bathroom Readers' Institute is staffed by some of the smartest, most trivia-minded people around:

Gordon Javna	**Linda Lee Mauri**	**Bruce Langley**
Brian Boone	**Olin Shockley**	**Thomas Crapper**
Jay Newman	**Emilio Rissolo**	**Gordon Shumway**

And, as always, we must thank our loyal readers, who continue to support this annual endeavor. As long as you keep reading, we will continue in our quest to make sure that, eventually, you really will know it *all*!

Happy reading, and, as ever,

Go with the flow!

—Uncle John and the BRI Staff

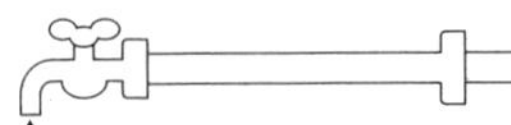

YOU'RE MY INSPIRATION

It's always interesting to find out where the architects of pop culture get their ideas. Some of these may surprise you.

JAMES BOND

Author Ian Fleming based his British spy character on his stepcousin (and friend and golfing partner), a tall, handsome, dapper man who'd served in the special forces for the Royal Air Force in World War II. Fleming's stepcousin never talked about those classified missions, but rumor had it he'd been a spy who hunted down Nazi war criminals. Just who was this dapper man with the mysterious past? Future *Dracula* and *Lord of the Rings* actor Christopher Lee.

HALSEY

"I didn't like being Ashley Frangipane," the alternative pop singer-songwriter ("Without You") has said. "It was a person I thought was weak and silly and sad." Born in New Jersey in 1994, Ashley was bullied at school before being diagnosed as bipolar, then tried to end her life at 17. To cope, she invented a stronger persona for herself while taking a New York City subway to the Halsey Street stop in Brooklyn. Bonus: "Halsey" is an anagram of "Ashley."

JUDY GARLAND

In 1922, Frank Gumm planned to name his next child Frank Junior (he already had two daughters). But his wife had *another* girl, so Frances (instead of Frank) it was. When Francie was a teenager, she and her sisters performed vaudeville as the Gumm Sisters. But that sounded "glum," so an emcee changed it to the Garland Sisters, because they were "prettier than a garland of flowers!" Frances was also called "Baby," but she didn't like either name, so she became Judy. Her inspiration? A popular Hoagy Carmichael song of the same name, with the lyric, "If she seems a saint but you find that she ain't, that's Judy." Four years later, Judy Garland starred as Dorothy in *The Wizard of Oz*.

CHARLOTTE'S WEB

In 1949, future children's book author E. B. White was in a barn on his Maine farm when a spider caught his eye. "I didn't like spiders at first," he later said, "but then I began watching one of them, and soon saw what a wonderful creature she was and what a skillful weaver. I named her Charlotte." From there, it wasn't a big leap in the author's head for Charlotte to be clever enough to spin the words "Some Pig" into her web, which really worked out for Wilbur.

Accidental 911 calls are on the rise due to people riding roller coasters—some rides' impact can initiate a crash detection feature.

LOCO GOVERNMENT

That title was going to say "Local Government," but this one is more appropriate.

NEITHER PARK NOR RECREATION

Michigamme (pop. 226) is an unincorporated community along Michigamme Lake in northern Michigan. For nearly 150 years, residents enjoyed the "pocket park," a 25-by-65-foot patch of grass along the lakefront at the end of Lake Street and Park Street. With a gazebo and a picnic table, it wasn't just the perfect spot for the mostly elderly residents to enjoy an afternoon on the lake (with calm waters suitable for fishing and swimming), it was the only public spot left: 99 percent of the lakefront land is privately owned.

Make that 100 percent. In 2019, the Michigamme Township Council voted to remove the gazebo, citing a request from a private buyer to purchase the land and a letter from the county Road Commission confirming that the pocket park was not an official park, so the sale was legal. Despite a public outcry, contentious council meetings, and several signed petitions, late one night in 2021, workers moved the gazebo to a new spot inland with no lake access. "I feel that this was done very secretively," said resident Tricia Martinez. "This was very underhanded, and we're going to get to the bottom of it." It got even fishier when they saw the full text of the Road Commission's letter, which "exercised its discretion to allow the gazebo to remain until further notice."

Neighbors held a candlelight vigil in the rain where their gazebo once stood, while news outlets around the world picked up the story, but it wasn't enough. At last report, the locals were in the process of recalling the township supervisor at the heart of the matter. A quick check on Google Maps shows that the Michigamme Pocket Park is "Permanently Closed."

ZIP IT

The San Diego City Council sure likes to issue proclamations—like "Jerry Coleman Day" (in honor of the late baseball announcer) or "In-N-Out Burger 70th Anniversary Day." San Diegans have had mixed feelings concerning these proclamations. According to the *San Diego Union-Tribune*: "Critics have said the practice often amounts to council members furthering their political careers by flattering key constituents with photo opportunities at City Hall." It got to the point where the public comment portions of city meetings were "overtaken by hecklers"—often with the honorees present.

The council's solution: disallow public comments before ceremonial proclamations. Their reason? Proclamations aren't technically considered policy, so

Only two people to play in the college basketball Final Four and baseball's World Series: Tim Stoddard and Kenny Lofton.

they don't fall under the Ralph M. Brown Act—which requires, by California state law, that all local government legislative sessions be open "to curb misuse of the democratic process by secret legislation."

A watchdog group, the Center for Local Government Accountability, filed a lawsuit against the San Diego City Council...and won it handily. Judge Timothy Taylor ruled that proclamations are indeed public policy because "choosing to support or honor an organization or individual is a policy decision." And, "by seeking to protect honorees from criticism, the City Council is also prohibiting public criticism of its decision to bestow the honor at a time when that public criticism is perhaps most important: before the action is taken." Not only was the council ordered to reallow public comments, it had to pay the watchdog group's legal fees. Honorees beware.

NIMBY

"If they'd consulted and said, 'We're going to put a 160,000-square-foot warehouse there that's going to block your view,' I would have obviously objected to it, but they didn't." Georgie Wallis was furious. So were all of his Hook Close neighbors in Corby, Northamptonshire, England—who all woke up one morning in February 2024 to find a "monstrosity" of a warehouse being constructed in their backyards...almost literally. The 60-foot-high wall was being built only a few feet behind their fences. Even worse, the residents didn't even know about the warehouse until *that morning*. "It's a nightmare," said neighbor Jose Cruz. "The building will leave our home in complete darkness." Neighbor Kieran Joseph reported that vibrations from the daily "bang, bang, bang" have cracked his roof, and now rain leaks into his kids' bedroom. "It's been pretty hellish."

Why didn't the council contact them beforehand, as required by law? Apparently, the council tried to, but they got the addresses wrong and sent the notice to homeowners half a mile away on Hubble Road. When those folks on Hubble Road learned of a warehouse being built over by Hook Close, of course they didn't object.

Once the council realized its mistake, they apologized to the residents "for the errors," but since the project had been approved by the city, it was deemed lawful. An internal review later confirmed that, in fact, it was not lawful, and recommended the entire planning improvement board be replaced. But that didn't change the fact the warehouse still went up...while the neighbors' property values all went down. "How can you get that so wrong?" asked Wallis.

* * *

"The moment I accept that there's an artistic, redeeming quality in puns, I have a horrible feeling I'll get hooked."

—John Oliver

Light reflecting off the moon can form a rainbow—or a moonbow, rather.

UNCLE JOHN'S PAGE OF LISTS

Random bits of information from the Bathroom Readers' Institute's bottomless files.

6 SONGWRITERS WITH THE MOST BILLBOARD HOT 100 NO. 1s

1. Paul McCartney (32)
2. John Lennon (26)
3. Max Martin (26)
4. Mariah Carey (18)
5. Lukasz "Dr. Luke" Gottwald (18)
6. Barry Gibb (16)

7 ANIMALS THAT GET LITTLE TO NO SLEEP

1. Dolphin
2. Fruit fly
3. Alpine swift
4. Bluefish
5. Orca
6. Jellyfish
7. Bullfrog

MERRIAM-WEBSTER'S "13 WORDS THAT DEFINED 2023"

1. rizz
2. deepfake
3. coronation
4. dystopian
5. EGOT
6. X
7. implode
8. doppelgänger
9. covenant
10. indict
11. elemental
12. kibbutz
13. deadname

11 AGES OF ACTORS WHO PLAYED TEENS

1. 23: Adam Brody, *The O.C.*
2. 24: Tom Welling, *Smallville*
3. 25: Rachel McAdams, *Mean Girls*
4. 26: Jon Heder, *Napoleon Dynamite*
5. 27: Andrew Garfield, *The Amazing Spider-Man*
6. 28: Taylor Kitsch, *Friday Night Lights*
7. 29: Sissy Spacek, *Carrie*
8. 30: Alan Ruck, *Ferris Bueller's Day Off*
9. 31: Bianca Lawson, *Pretty Little Liars*
10. 32: Ashleigh Murray, *Riverdale*
11. 33: Ingrid Bergman, *Joan of Arc*

6 ARTIFACTS FOUND IN KING TUT'S TOMB

1. Two iron daggers
2. Gold rings wrapped in a scarf
3. Mannequin for his garments
4. Sandals made of pure gold
5. Gold-plated leopard head
6. Board game called Senet

10 THINGS INVENTED IN A BAR OR A PUB

1. *The Guinness Book of World Records*
2. Southwest Airlines
3. The Pet Rock
4. The square typeface of credit card numbers
5. The Ironman Triathlon
6. The United States Marine Corps
7. Shark Week
8. Buffalo wings
9. NASCAR
10. The public library

"GERMANY" IN 7 LANGUAGES

1. *Alemania* (Spanish)
2. *Allemagne* (French)
3. *Deutschland* (German)
4. *Doitsu* (Japanese)
5. *Niemcy* (Polish)
6. *Saksa* (Finnish)
7. *Tyskland* (Danish)

7 FINALISTS OF MINNESOTA'S "NAME THAT SNOWPLOW" CONTEST

1. Taylor Drift
2. Clark W. Blizzwald
3. Dolly Plowton
4. Beyonsleigh
5. You're Killin' Me Squalls
6. Fast and Flurrious
7. Barbie's Dream Plow

Last country to get its first McDonald's location: Kazakhstan (2016).
Last country to lose all its McDonald's locations: Kazakhstan (2023).

JUST PLANE WEIRD

Are you reading this on a plane? Do yourself a favor and turn to another page before reading any further. Save this article for when you're back on solid ground.

AIRBORNE TOXIC EVENT

Have you ever had diarrhea so bad it forced a jumbo jet to return to its point of departure? Then you're luckier than the poor, unfortunate, and thankfully anonymous passenger on a September 2023 Delta Airlines flight from Atlanta to Barcelona. The Airbus A350 departed Hartsfield-Jackson Atlanta International Airport with 336 passengers onboard. Just around 1,000 miles into the trip, the plane turned around over Virginia. "It's just a biohazard issue," the pilot told air traffic controllers. "We had a passenger who had diarrhea all the way through the airplane so they want us to come back to Atlanta." "They" in this case meant the other passengers, who had to smell and see all that human waste in the cabin. After ground crews replaced the carpets, the passengers continued to Barcelona the next day, delayed by eight hours, and with no further biohazard issues.

UNSTABLE PASSENGER

An Air Atlanta Icelandic flight departed New York City's John F. Kennedy International Airport in November 2023, bound for Liege, Belgium. Only about 30 minutes after takeoff and just after the plane had reached a cruising altitude of 31,000 feet, the pilot of the 747 cargo plane told air traffic control that he needed to go back to New York on account of an inflight emergency—a loose horse. "We are a cargo plane with a live animal, a horse, on board. The horse managed to escape its stall. There's no issue with flying, but we need to go back to New York as we can't rescue the horse," the pilot told air traffic controllers. After dumping 20 tons of fuel over the Atlantic Ocean off the coast of Massachusetts to account for weight issues and asking for a veterinarian to meet them upon landing, the plane safely returned to New York. It was unclear how the horse escaped, but it hadn't been secured by the time the flight landed, still reportedly agitated and loose in the cargo hold.

FLOORED

Just about every reason there can be to delay a flight beset a single October 2023 EasyJet voyage from the Spanish island of Tenerife to London's Gatwick Airport.

After the flight didn't take off as scheduled, it was delayed further when EasyJet switched out the plane with a smaller one, bumping many passengers. Those who made it to the second plane, two hours later, had to wait on the runway another hour while luggage was unloaded because the craft exceeded weight limits. Finally, the pilot told passengers that their flight would depart in 20 minutes' time. "And that's when the incident happened with the defecation," passenger Aaran Gedhu told reporters. Gedhu saw one passenger on the still-grounded plane use the bathroom, and then another, and that's when the news quickly spread—as did the odor—pertaining to the human waste left on the facility's floor. A cleaning crew rushed on board to sanitize the bathroom while passengers waited and watched. Then they were told to deboard; after being put up in a hotel for the night at the airline's expense, passengers finally departed on a "rescue" flight the next day.

✈ AISLE DO IT MYSELF

A woman flying on a November 2023 Frontier Airlines flight out of Florida bound for Philadelphia desperately needed to use the plane's restroom. But the seatbelt sign was lit up, and flight attendants prevented the passenger from walking to the restroom. But when you've got to go, you've got to go. So, as captured in a phone video that went viral, the woman dropped her pants, squatted in the aisle, and went to the bathroom...not *in* the bathroom. "Sorry, everybody," she said as she started, but when people began yelling at her to stop, she proceeded to yell profanities. No word on whether she was apprehended by authorities at flight's end.

✈ A MARK OF COINCIDENCE

Mark Garland, a 58-year-old bus driver from Wiltshire, England, arrived at London's Heathrow Airport in March 2024 for his flight to Thailand. At the check-in counter, he encountered some trouble, arguing with an airline agent for 40 minutes who claimed that they'd already checked in Mark Garland for his flight. The source of the confusion: *another* Mark Garland, a 62-year-old construction worker, had signed in already. The two Mark Garlands met at the gate and had a good laugh because they also bore a striking resemblance to each other, even beyond their mutually shaved heads. Then the two Mark Garlands wound up with their assigned seats next to each other, and they spent the 11-hour flight chatting and finding all sorts of parallels and connections. They had mutual friends, lived 15 miles apart, and were both single fathers with four children each. The elder Mark Garland even rides the younger Mark Garland's bus. "It was crazy, I have never known anything like it," Mark Garland (the construction worker) told reporters.

Number of airports and train stations in Andorra: zero.

TOASTING UP A HOAX

Here's the story about the man who invented the electric toaster in 1893—a college student from the 2010s. Let us explain. This is the wild true story about the totally untrue story of Alan MacMasters.

A WIKI IDEA

While working toward his degree in engineering at a London university in 2012, Alan MacMasters listened to a lecture from a professor on the importance of not relying on Wikipedia as a reputable source for class assignments or professional research. While the free online user-generated encyclopedia—and the fourth-most-visited website in the world—requires every article to be thoroughly sourced, the professor pointed out flaws in the system. Users and editors can fix flagged incorrect statements and false articles, but only if they notice them. For example, he said, nobody noticed that some time earlier, his friend Maddy Kennedy had falsely and humorously claimed on the article about the history of the electric toaster that "Maddy Kennedy" had invented the kitchen gadget.

Slightly disturbed that this false information was being knowingly distributed on Wikipedia, where anyone could read it and cite it, MacMasters considered signing up for a Wikipedia editor account to correct the fake fact. But his friend and classmate, identified in reports only as Alex, beat him to the punch. And Alex didn't so much as *correct* the electric toaster article as he did perpetuate the prank. "I just changed it so that it said that my friend, who sat next to me, Alan MacMasters, had in fact invented the toaster in Edinburgh in 1893. We had no idea who invented the toaster," Alex said.

FAKE NEWS

Alex and MacMasters thought that surely *someone* would notice the inaccuracy in the article and come along to correct it shortly. But, as had been the case in the Maddy Kennedy era, nobody had noticed, cared, or changed it. It could be a labor issue—of the more than 6.5 million Wikipedia articles, fewer than 125,000 volunteer editors can alter them. This article never got flagged, and so there the name "Alan MacMasters" sat...for 10 years.

Wikipedia is clearly such a popular source of information—not all of which is double-checked or verified—that the phony assertion that Alan MacMasters invented the electric toaster in 1893 made its way into the collective consciousness as a known fact. About a year after the Wikipedia edit, and having forgotten about the whole thing in the months after, Alex saw an article about little-known Scottish inventors in

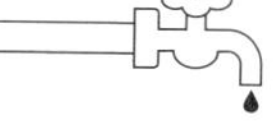

Fifth-largest employer in Mexico: cartels (175,000 workers).

a major U.K. newspaper that discussed MacMasters and the toaster. That's when he decided, in February 2013, to give Alan MacMasters, toaster inventor, his very own Wikipedia article.

BURNED

First, Alex realized, he'd need a photo of "Alan MacMasters" to make it all seem real. So he grabbed a photo of himself staring off into the distance, 1800s style, and edited it to give himself what he believed to the be the appearance of late 19th-century style, with sideburns that looked like era-appropriate mutton chops; he also made the photo look old, weathered, and yellowed. That sat at the top of the page for Alan MacMasters on Wikipedia, fooling everyone who saw it.

The hoax really took off from there. "Alan MacMasters" is named as the inventor of the electric toaster in at least a dozen serious textbooks. The Scottish government held him up as a paragon of Scottish ingenuity on a site devoted to business pioneers and inventors. One school in Scotland held a day devoted to this inventor of this very common and revolutionary kitchen gadget, where they painted pictures of toast, built pretend toasters, and wrote essays and listened to lectures about MacMasters. Edinburgh chef Scott Smith prepared a MacMasters-themed dessert on the BBC's *Great British Menu* cooking competition. In 2018, MacMasters was among the nominees for the next person to appear on the U.K.'s new £50 banknote. Museum exhibits opened up on MacMasters, and Alex consistently added new fake information to the Wikipedia article, asserting that MacMasters had helped create the lighting for the London Underground subway system. At one point, the father of the real Alan MacMasters wondered aloud to his son about whether they might be related to the 1890s inventor of the same name (who didn't exist)—"I had to disappoint him," MacMasters said.

ROUND AND ROUND

All the while, Alex didn't really think he was doing any harm. He wrote off the whole matter as trivial—literally. "If you get false information about who invented the toaster, the consequences might be that you get a question wrong in a pub quiz," he said. "It's a bit of trivia, which doesn't have a significant real-world impact." Except that the elaborate hoax says a lot about not being able to trust what one reads, and that in the age of user-generated content, misleading information can be easily and alarmingly distributed.

Wikipedia is well-sourced, and heavily policed by its users for just such a reason. An article must cite its legitimate sources for every claim, or the piece may be removed. Alex got around this thanks to what journalists and ethicists call *circular referencing*, a phenomenon that has become common in the Internet age. He would

Youth football pioneer Pop Warner coached Iowa State's team for four seasons...

simply make a claim about MacMasters in the Wikipedia article, wait for a legitimate news agency or book to lazily repeat the claim, and then he'd link to that item, allowing Wikipedia to present the journalistic claim as evidence. "I would cite them, and they would become fact," he explained.

OVER, DONE

The Alan MacMasters legend would've lived on as truth if not for a bored 15-year-old. In 2021, Adam, a student in Kent, England, used to enjoy reading Wikipedia when he was bored in class. One day, one of his teachers made a comment about the Wikipedia article about the inventor of the electric toaster. When Adam looked up the entry, something about it immediately seemed off to him—namely, the accompanying picture. It looked fake, or at least curiously edited.

Suspicious, Adam took to a Wikipedia-vandalism forum on the Internet message-board site Reddit. He wrote an explanatory post titled "The picture of the inventor of the toaster on Wikipedia was faked." It didn't even occur to him that the article was false, just that the picture seemed inaccurate. Adam's post sounded alarms in the Wikipedia editor community, who analyzed the article and found it far-fetched. Within 24 hours of Adam calling it out, the Alan MacMasters entry had been flagged for deletion. Within a week, it had been dismissed as a hoax, and listed on a Wikipedia article titled "List of hoaxes on Wikipedia." "You shouldn't just believe everything you read on the Internet," the real Alan MacMasters said with a giggle.

So who *did* invent the toaster? Frank Shailor, who worked for General Electric, filed the first electric toaster patent in 1909. His D-12 model is accepted as the first commercially available toaster. We promise.

* * *

TWO WEIRD SEWING MACHINES

- The four Steinlauf brothers emigrated from Austria to Chicago in the early 20th century and opened a bike shop. In 1939, they unveiled a novelty tandem bicycle that seated four people. One spot faced to the side and was attached to a small table that held a fully functional sewing machine, powered by the kinetic energy of the bike in motion.

- In 2000, Nintendo sold a series of three miniature sewing machines as accessories to its Game Boy Color. Each machine connected to the video game system via a cable, and users bought special software that told the machine what patterns to stitch.

...while simultaneously coaching Georgia's for two and Cornell's for two.

FAILED AND FORGOTTEN TV CHANNELS

There used to be just three major broadcast channels. Then cable came around and created the potential for an almost endless array of niche networks. More over-the-air channels debuted, along with lots of cable networks, all seeking a portion of that big TV audience. Here are some that came and went, or never even premiered.

UPI Newstime

Two years before CNN launched in 1980 and made the 24-hour-news network a viable concept, syndicated news outlet United Press, International developed its open all-day service, UPI Newstime. The format was simple and rudimentary: the channel aired a 15-minute block of news composed of black-and-white still images, which a camera would pan across and pause on before moving to a new image after eight seconds, accompanied by audio reporting from UPI's radio news feed. Commercials would air after the block, and then the same 15-minute segment would repeat for a total of four hours before UPI Newstime unveiled a new block. Unable to compete with CNN's full-color video news that changed more than every four hours, UPI Newstime went dark in 1981.

Daytime and Cable Health Network

In March 1982, a partnership between the Hearst newspaper conglomerate and ABC News resulted in Daytime, a newsmagazine-style cable channel. It broadcast for only four hours a day, five days a week, with programming aimed at female viewers. It was probably viewed more by people trying to find HBO than by people who tuned in intentionally—it shared space on the transponder (which beams out a cable channel's feed) with HBO, which, in the early 1980s, didn't broadcast 24 hours a day. In 1984, Lifetime, branded "Television for Women," launched, born out of a merger between Daytime and the Viacom-owned, short-lived medical channel Cable Health Network. Also debuting in 1982, the latter showed programs about healthy living, nutrition, and medical conditions. Lifetime would keep that channel's programming post-merger and into the early 1990s, airing shows like *Living with Diabetes* in an early Sunday morning block called Lifetime Medical Television.

The George Fox Network

The George Fox Organization was a small media company based in California that ran a handful of TV stations in the mid-1950s. In 1955, when television was taking off as a cultural phenomenon, company president George Fox told reporters that plans were in the works for a fourth national broadcast network to compete with NBC,

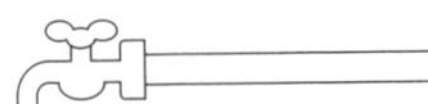

CBS, and ABC. Fox said that he had interest from 45 to 50 independently owned and operated stations around the U.S. seeking affiliation with his yet-to-be-named network. The bulk of the programming would come from licensing Hollywood movies to air around the clock, along with four original programs; those shows were called *I'm the Champ, Answer Me This, It's a Living,* and *Jack for Jill.* By May 1956, less than six months before the network's tentative launch, just 17 stations had signed affiliation contracts. Fox called the whole thing off.

Sumo.tv

When YouTube became instantly, phenomenally popular upon its debut in 2005, it proved that people would happily watch programming prepared by amateurs. That should have served as a wake-up call to the companies who distribute and produce old-fashioned, professionally prepared television. British media company Cellcast saw where the future of TV was headed and tried to create a curated YouTube for broadcast television, introducing Sumo.tv in 2006, an expansion of the Sumo.tv website. The first "user-generated" TV network, branches of Sumo.tv appeared on the dial or on cable networks in the U.K., Asia, Europe, and the U.S., airing locally made videos of all kinds sent in by viewers. Not only couldn't it compete with the fully on-demand nature of YouTube, but in the U.K., TV regulator Ofcom forced Sumo.tv to follow broadcast standards. Rather than censor content itself, the network made the people making videos do that. Submissions dropped off, so did the ratings, and Sumo.tv was gone by 2012.

Satellite Program Network

The installation and monthly fees for a satellite dish were double or triple that of cable TV in the late 1970s and early 1980s, but the possibility of being able to tune in to hundreds of stations from around the world—and to the commercial-free, internal feeds of broadcast and cable networks—was worth it for many subscribers. Debuting in 1979, the Satellite Program Network (SPN) was available on both satellite dishes and on cable systems, and served as a 24-hour-a-day ad for the joys of satellite dish ownership, with a programming lineup of the weirdest and wackiest greatest hits of what was available to watch on a dish. (The owner of SPN was Southern Satellite Systems Co.) The slate was all over the place, including the pre-MTV music video show *Video Concert Hall*, small colleges' football games, week-old minor league baseball games, *News from Home* (a news show geared toward Canadians living in the U.S.), *Nutrition Dialogue, Sewing with Nancy, The Shopping Game* (a staged auction that would set the prices for items viewers could call in and buy), public domain movies, and *Moscow Meridian*—a news discussion program produced by the government of the Soviet Union. Acquired by a rival company in 1985, the name changed in 1986 from the ultra-generic Satellite Program Network to the meaningless Tempo Television, after which NBC bought it and converted it into the CNBC news channel in 1989.

Two of President Lyndon Johnson's dogs died during his term. Her ate a rock and Him was hit by a car.

ACCORDING TO THE LATEST RESEARCH

Every new day brings some bold new study. Some are interesting, and some are weird. For example, did you know that science says...

Your Fists Were Made for Punching

Researcher: David Carrier, Professor of Biology at the University of Utah

What He Studied: The severed forearms and hands of dead men

What He Learned: *Homo sapiens* is the only primate species that can make a tight fist. Our shorter fingers and meatier thumbs make it "possible for the hand to be used as a club during fighting," Carrier wrote in the *Journal of Experimental Biology* in 2015. His controversial "pugilism hypothesis" (*pugilism* is a fancy word for "boxing") posits that the tight fist evolved to give our hominid predecessors—the male ones—an advantage when they got into fights. His reasoning: the metacarpals (finger bones) are protected within the fist during impact.

Achieving these findings wasn't easy. "You can't implant strain gauges on living subjects," said Carrier, so his team procured severed forearms from medical cadavers and then wired them up to wooden boards with fishing line. Then, by adjusting the tension on the strings with guitar pegs, the researchers could create loose fists, clenched fists, and open hands. They attached each forearm to a pendulum and then "punched" a padded surface. Sensors measured the strain on the metacarpals, revealing that a closed fist not only protects the hand, but it strikes with 55 percent more force than a loose fist. "It is a little macabre and strange," admitted Carrier, "but there was no other way to really get this data."

Carrier's critics argue that the human hand evolved primarily to make complex tools; the fossil evidence supports this, as the emergence of tools and the change in hand anatomy both occurred about three million years ago. Critics also argue that, even if the hand did evolve to punch faces, how come the face didn't evolve tougher bones to take those punches?

They did, says Carrier's "protective buttressing hypothesis." When *Australopithecus* roamed, a broken jaw usually led to starvation, so males with thicker cheekbones lived longer and reproduced more, making tough cheekbones a dominant trait...and still one of the more pronounced differences between modern males and females. Carrier also notes that the predominant theory—that big cheekbones evolved to chew hard nuts—doesn't hold up because *Australopithecus* ate fruit. The professor's theories have

Only time Heimlich maneuver creator Henry Heimlich used the technique: in 2016, when he was 96, to save a fellow resident of his nursing home.

been mocked as "bro science," but while he acknowledges there may be more factors at play, there's no denying that "aggression was very important" to our ancestors. He adds, "If our anatomy is adapted for fighting, we need to be aware we always may be haunted by basic emotions and reflexive behaviors that often don't make sense—and are very dangerous—in the modern world."

Your Dog Dreams About You

Researcher: Deirdre Barrett, clinical and evolutionary psychologist at Harvard Medical School

Who She Studied: Dogs' best friends (us)

What She Learned: "Humans dream about the same things they're interested in by day, though more visually and less logically," said Barrett, after spending years studying sleeping habits. She later noticed that dreaming dogs exhibit many of the same sleep behaviors as dreaming people—including rapid eye movement, moving around, and vocalizing—and therefore concluded, "Since dogs are generally extremely attached to their human owners, it's likely your dog is dreaming of your face, your smell, and of pleasing or annoying you."

We All Have an Unspoken Agreement to Not Try Our Hardest

Researchers: Gloria Origgi, a philosopher at the Jean Nicod Institute in Paris, and Diego Gambetta, a professor of sociology at Oxford University

Who They Studied: Event organizers and attendees in Italy, France, and England

What They Learned: We 21st-century people are under more pressure than ever before to "aim high," "be the best," "win the day," and so on. When someone we depend on—be it a loved one, friend, stranger, company, organization, or government—doesn't perform as expected, we become angry.

But, also, secretly relieved.

Why? "Sometimes all this rhetoric about efficiency is just unbearable, so people like to have a chance to just ease up," said Origgi. She and Gambetta call this principle "kakonomics." *Kako* is ancient Greek for "bad." As *The Guardian* put it, "Thus emerges a web of silent agreements to do a poor job."

In the short term, kakonomics can make us feel...well, not "good," but less bad about ourselves. In the long run, however, when systems begin to break down, it can make life a lot more difficult for everyone. This was most obvious in Italy, where the country's laid-back "la dolce vita" lifestyle impacted the conferences and workshops that Origgi and Gambetta attended. "[They had] twice or half as many people as they were told to expect; the time allocated to speak was halved or doubled; people

The ridges on the roof of your mouth are called *rugae.*

did not show up for meetings or showed up unannounced; messages got lost; and reimbursements were delayed, decreased, or forgotten altogether."

Origgi explained to the BBC that "kakonomists are not corrupted people. They do this because they want to live, as you say, in a sort of more relaxed way." (That was a quote from the beginning of the interview. In the spirit of kakonomics, we didn't listen to the whole thing.)

When You Die, You Know You're Dead

Researcher: Sam Parnia, director of critical care and resuscitation research at NYU Langone School of Medicine

Who He Studied: Rats and humans

What He Learned: When the electric currents that power the heart cease, blood is no longer feeding oxygen to the brain. That's called cardiac arrest, or more commonly, death. But some people who have been declared clinically dead due to cardiac arrest, and were later resuscitated, have reported that they were aware of what was happening in the room after they were "dead."

These "near-death experiences," or NDEs, are more common than you might realize. But how can the brain keep working without oxygen? Parnia studied rats right before and after death and found that there's a heightened period of brain activity prior to signing out for good. He then found that this occurs with humans as well. When the heart dies, says Parnia, "you lose all your brain stem reflexes—your gag reflex, your pupil reflex, all that is gone." But the brain still gets anywhere from two to 20 seconds of activity in the cerebral cortex—the last part of the brain to stop working, and the area responsible for processing information from our senses.

It might use that time to process sensory inputs from the room, or to send a rush of thoughts to the consciousness—the proverbial "life flashes before your eyes" moment. This rush could also explain the "bright light" that some NDE patients have reported. Brain activity is still detectible during this time, and that activity might not completely cease for hours. That activity is far too low to be measured, so who knows what we're "thinking" about during that time.

This is part of a larger experiment that Parnia and others are studying to find a scientific answer to the age-old question: is there an afterlife? "In the same way that a group of researchers might be studying the qualitative nature of the human experience of 'love,' we're trying to understand the exact features that people experience when they go through death." Not only can this improve lifesaving techniques by calculating exactly how much oxygen the brain needs to keep working, but the ultimate goal is "to understand whether consciousness becomes annihilated or whether it continues after you've died for some period of time."

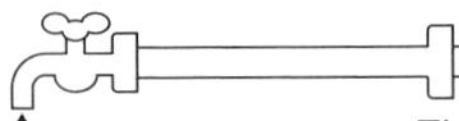

First *SNL* cast member to win an Oscar for acting: Robert Downey Jr. for *Oppenheimer* (2024).

WHAT'S IN THAT CLEANING THING?

We all use this stuff to clean our homes and offices every day. (Well, maybe not every day.) But what are all those cleaning products and tools really made of?

FEBREEZE

Introduced by household goods conglomerate Proctor and Gamble in 1996, Febreeze promises to literally clean the air of germs and impurities that lead to foul odors, rather than just mask the offending scent with fragrances. It really does do what it says, at least from a scientific perspective. The active ingredient in Febreeze is a carbohydrate called beta-cyclodextrin, created by an enzyme reaction in the starch found in corn. The molecule is doughnut-shaped, and when millions of them are sprayed out of a Febreeze bottle inside a solution of water, the H_20 makes the odor-causing particles bind to the hole in the beta-cyclodextrin. That deactivates the smell cells while the other element in Febreeze—an artificial fruity or flowery scent—replaces the bad scent in the air.

DAWN POWERWASH

Multiple dish-soap makers have released their own "miracle" cleaning product in the last few years: jacked-up soap that's sprayed on dishes and eliminates grease and caked-in food, and washes away with water after setting for a while. Is it some new kind of chemical permutation? Not at all—Dawn Powerwash and other, similar products are made up entirely of water, regular old dish soap, and isopropyl (rubbing) alcohol. The soap cleans as it always has but the addition of alcohol dissolves tough stains. Pushing it through a pressurized spraying mechanism concentrates the cleaning combo to make it more effective.

MAGIC ERASER

This Mr. Clean–branded product, available since 2003, looks like a white sponge, but made of a particularly porous material and with holes that are tinier and less visible to the naked eye. That's pretty much what the Magic Eraser is, manufactured from a patented material called Durafoam that can purportedly remove everything from soap scum to food stains to ink from hard surfaces with only the addition of a little water. The Magic Eraser is based on melamine foam, a porous sponge that acts as a mild abrasive, more like fine sandpaper. The brick is loaded with triangle-shaped air pockets that get activated with water, becoming hard as glass when wet and can scrape like sandpaper.

LET'S CALL IT BOSTON (OR NOT!)

For the most part, countries, states, and cities have been around for a lot longer than anybody walking around today has, so they've always just kind of...existed. It's strange to think that these familiarly named places could have had totally different names.

PLACE: AMERICA

Almost Called: Synonymous with the New World, and the large, continuous Western Hemisphere landmass stretching from the North Pole to almost the South Pole, the name America is a geographic designation rather than a political one. The title comes from Amerigo Vespucci, a Florentine navigator who voyaged to the New World in the 15th century and wrote extensively about it, helping to popularize the exploration and colonization of the area. It would be named in his honor, sort of—"Land of Amerigo" would technically be *Amerige*, a masculine form of *America*. But because Asia and Europe are feminine forms, so too did *Amerige* become America.

PLACE: NEW YORK CITY

Almost Called: British settlers named what's now the biggest city in the U.S. after one of the major cities in England: York. But before the British took it over in the 1600s, the city was established and populated by Dutch people, from the Netherlands, who gave it the name New Amsterdam. In 1673, in the middle of the Third Anglo-Dutch War, a Dutch contingent of ships arrived in what was then New York, seized control for around a year, and named the city New Orange in honor of the Netherlands' ruling family, the House of Orange.

PLACE: UTAH

Almost Called: Settlers from the Church of Jesus Christ of Latter-Day Saints, colloquially known as the Mormons, moved way out West in the 19th century seeking religious freedom and landed in what now comprises parts of Nevada, Arizona, New Mexico, and Utah. They established a provisional state they called "State of Deseret," a word from their holy text, the Book of Mormon, used by a tribe called the Jaredites and meaning "land of the honeybee." The portions of all the other states dropped out of the statehood push, leaving just the area of what's now Utah. The name "Utah" was chosen by the federal government, overruling the request for Deseret, when the government admitted the area into the union in 1896. It's derived from the Ute tribe, the indigenous people of the area.

There are 31 states with a Washington county, but Washington state isn't one.

PLACE: NEVADA

Almost Called: German explorer and geographer Alexander von Humboldt was the first European to map Latin America, and his acolyte John C. Fremont did the same for large swaths of the American West. Fremont's idea to name lots of things after Humboldt was accepted—the Humboldt River and Humboldt County, California, for example. So many things in the region bore that name that local leaders proposed it in 1864 for the moniker of a new state. But the government decided on the Spanish word for snowfall—Nevada—over Humboldt.

PLACE: WASHINGTON STATE

Almost Called: Officially recognized as a United States territory in 1853, the Washington Territory was formed out of what was left of the Pacific Northwest after the borders of Oregon were established, and it included portions of what are now Montana and Idaho. In 1889, the bustling home of lumber companies and a port industry became an official state, with the government dropping "Territory" to give it the name Washington. Some members of Congress thought this was confusing, given that the nation's capital was called Washington, D.C., and proposed that the new state be called Columbia—which is almost as confusing, considering that the C in "D.C." stands for "Columbia."

PLACE: PORTLAND, OREGON

Almost Called: The Oregon Trail, which brought so many American settlers west, ends in Oregon City, just outside of what is now Portland, the largest city in Oregon. Portland began as a 640-acre piece of land removed of its valuable timber that city founders Asa Lovejoy and Francis Pettygrove co-claimed and called "The Clearing." When looking to incorporate the city officially in 1845, Lovejoy and Pettygrove needed a better name, so they flipped a coin at a dinner party to decide on it. If Lovejoy won the toss, the city would be named after his hometown of Boston, Massachusetts, but if Pettygrove won, the city would be named in honor of his home in Maine. Pettygrove was the winner.

PLACE: ST. PAUL, MINNESOTA

Almost Called: At the place where the Mississippi and Minnesota Rivers meet, a military outpost called Fort Saint Anthony was established in 1819. That fort turned into a town, and one of the most thriving businesses in that frontier town was the tavern, run by an old fur trader named Pierre Parrant, nicknamed "Pig's-Eye." By the 1830s, the town, too, adopted the name of Pig's-Eye. That lasted until 1841, when a French Catholic minister arrived and built a chapel devoted to Saint Paul the Apostle. In 1849, the still-growing settlement was established as the capital of what was just the Minnesota Territory at the time, and by then the residents were calling the town St. Paul.

The shortest U.S. president, standing at 5'4": James Madison.

LOST IN NON-TRANSLATION

The U.K. and the U.S. share not only a language, but a lot of popular culture: their Beatles were popular stateside, while our Elvis did very well in Britain. But not every act works on both sides of the Atlantic. Here are some of the most overwhelmingly successful British acts who just didn't pop in the States.

BONEY M.

German songwriter and producer Frank Farian recorded the single "Baby Do You Wanna Bump" in 1975. He wasn't interested in being a performer, so he hired four session singers from the Caribbean to lip-synch to his studio creations. Billed as Boney M., a disco act with light R&B and reggae touches, the group was one of the most successful acts of the 1970s in Europe. "Daddy Cool," "Sunny," "Ma Baker," "Belfast," "Rasputin," and "Mary's Boy Child" all hit #1 in Germany. So did "Rivers of Babylon," a chart-topper in Austria, Ireland, the Netherlands, Sweden, Switzerland, and the U.K. The folk song with a disco beat became the fourth-best-selling single ever in the U.K. up to that point. Boney M. would rack up more hits in the U.K. well into the 1980s. In the U.S., "Rivers of Babylon" was a minor hit, reaching #30 on the pop chart in 1978—the only time Boney M. made the American Top 40. Farian would reemerge about a decade later, again writing and producing songs for a duo hired for their looks to lip-synch to studio singers' recordings: Milli Vanilli, who went to #1 in the U.S. four times before their miming routine was exposed.

SIMPLY RED

A melancholy, keyboard-driven pop band from Manchester, England, Simply Red—named for redheaded singer Mick Hucknall—reached #1 in the U.S. as well as in the U.K. with their first two hits. The slow, sad, and mournful "Holding Back the Years," a rebuke of Hucknall's father and a recollection of his miserable childhood, was followed to the top by a cover of the old Harold Melvin & the Bluenotes ballad "If You Don't Know Me by Now." After those smashes in 1987 and 1988, respectively, Simply Red quickly disappeared in the U.S. The band's last chart placement in America: "Stars" hit #44 in 1991. Back home in the U.K., however, the album *Stars* yielded five Top 40 hits, with the title track topping the pop chart. In the U.K., *Stars* sold 3.4 million copies—seven times its U.S. sales figures—and is the 16th best-selling album ever in Britain.

First universally ratified U.N. treaty: the ozone-protecting Montreal Protocol (1987).

TAKE THAT/ROBBIE WILLIAMS

Bubblegum pop songs performed by four or five young male singers with accompanying dance moves were a cultural phenomenon in the U.S. in the 1980s with New Edition and New Kids on the Block. By the early 1990s, these "boy bands" were passé...until the emergence of *NSYNC and Backstreet Boys at the end of the decade. Over in the U.K., however, boy bands never went away at all in the 1990s. Busted, Westlife, Dream Street, Five, East 17, and BBMAK were all popular, and Take That was the biggest British boy band of all. The five-guy group released three albums in the 1990s, and they hit #2, #1, and #1 on the U.K. album chart, respectively. On the singles side, Take That reached the Top 10 on 14 occasions in the 1990s. Their eight #1 songs included "Never Forget," "Sure," "Everything Changes," "Babe," and "Back for Good." The last is the only song that ever reached any chart in the U.S.: "Back for Good" hit #7 in America in 1995. Take That took a hiatus from 1996 to 2006, during which time members Gary Barlow and Robbie Williams launched very successful solo careers. Williams's first seven albums hit #1 in the U.K., spawning three dozen hit singles. But none of his solo material made an impact in the U.S.

SHAKIN' STEVENS

Shakin' Stevens (real name: Michael Barratt) found minor success as the lead singer of a band called the Sunsets. In 1977, he was cast as Elvis Presley in a major London production of the musical *Elvis!*. Promoted on numerous national TV programs and viewed by millions of Elvis fans in mourning, Stevens was unofficially accepted as a replacement King of rock 'n' roll in the U.K. In the 1980s, and while still halfway imitating Elvis Presley (and dressing like him, and wearing jet-black hair like him) along with other 1950s stars like Buddy Holly and Jerry Lee Lewis, Stevens sold more singles than anyone else in the U.K. He'd ultimately hit the Top 40 more than 30 times with songs that sounded like they came from the 1950s or with covers of songs that originated in the 1960s, like "Hot Dog," "Shirley," and "It's Late." Back in the United States, where 1950s rock 'n' roll was created and perfected, Shakin' Stevens managed just one minor hit—"Cry Just a Little Bit" topped out at #67 in 1983.

WET WET WET

A pleasant and lilting easygoing rock band from Scotland, Wet Wet Wet constantly brought songs to the top of the U.K. charts from 1987 to 1997. During that time, the group sold millions of records thanks to hit singles like "Wishing I Was Lucky," "Sweet Little Mystery," "Goodnight Girl," "Julia Says," and "Strange." Wet Wet Wet did particularly well when they covered well-known tunes, like the #4 version of

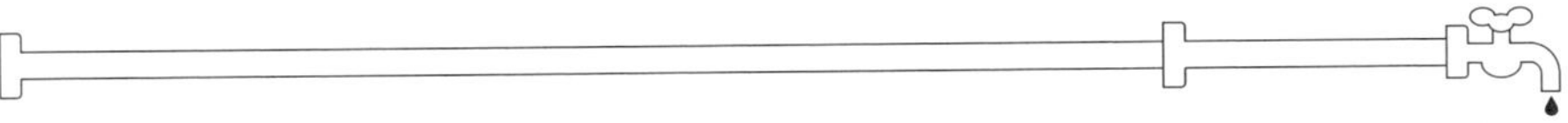

The Archi language of central Russia has more than 1.5 million verb forms.

the Beatles' "Yesterday," the #1 version of the Beatles' "With a Little Help from My Friends," and a cover of the Troggs' "Love Is All Around," released on the soundtrack of the 1994 romantic comedy *Four Weddings and a Funeral*. The Troggs cover spent 15 weeks at #1 in the U.K., setting a record for the time. *Four Weddings and a Funeral* was an Oscar-nominated box office smash in the U.S., but not even that could help Wet Wet Wet: the band's highest chart showing in the U.S. stalled at #41 on the Billboard Hot 100.

THE JAM

The punk rock movement started in the U.K. in the late 1970s, with abrasive and loud bands like the Sex Pistols and the Clash gaining commercial success and respectability around the world. The punk style gave way to bands presenting a more melodic and less aggressive sound. The Jam's songs, nearly always written by frontman Paul Weller, were politically charged diatribes against conservative prime minister Margaret Thatcher's policies, but they were catchy, guitar-driven, and often laced with horns that sounded like they came from 1960s American R&B records. The palatable songs of the Jam served the band well. Between 1977 and 1983, the group recorded 23 Top 40 hits. Four of those songs went to #1, including "A Town Called Malice" and "Going Underground." Probably because their sound seemed old-fashioned in the wake of keyboard-driven new wave and disco popular in the U.S., coupled with lyrics about very specific political concerns, the Jam never took off in the United States. "A Town Called Malice" made a brief appearance in the lower rungs of Billboard's Rock Chart in 1982, and that was it.

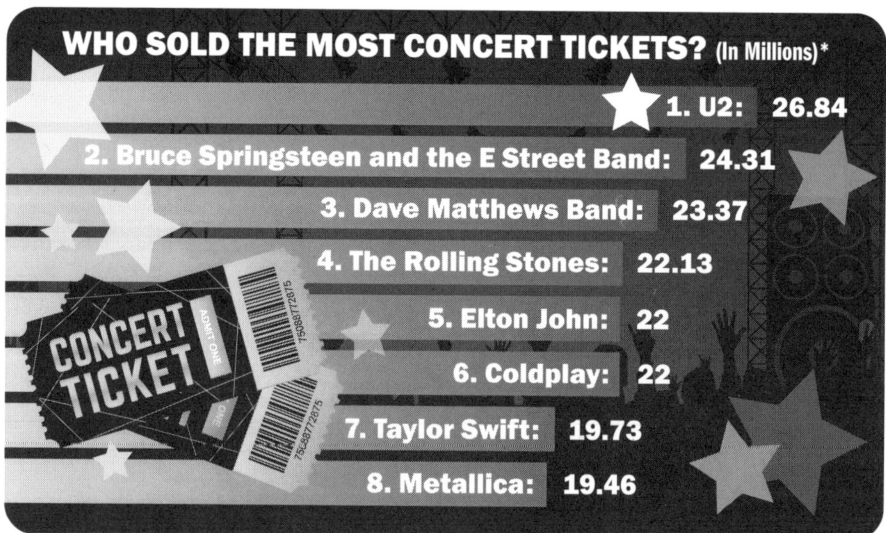

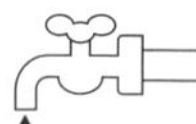

There's an outstanding balance of more than $1 billion in unpaid traffic violations in New York City.

MEDICAL MISHAPS

If you ever wonder whether or not you should go see a doctor when you're feeling curiously ill or experiencing random pain... let these stories help you err on the side of caution and go.

STICKING TO A STORY

In November 2023, an unnamed 35-year-old man in Vietnam checked himself into Cuba Friendship Hospital in Dong Hoi, citing severe headaches and fluid discharge. Over the previous five months, he'd suffered increasingly serious headaches that didn't seem to diminish with the use of medication. A CT scan led doctors to diagnose tension pneumocephalus, which was causing severe intracranial pressure and can be fatal if not treated. The corrective surgery revealed the source of the pressure: two chopsticks had entered his nose and pierced his brain. Presented with this information, the man remembered that five months earlier, he'd gotten into a drunken bar fight and thought that he was maybe stabbed in the face with something, but a hospital visit at the time hadn't revealed anything.

THE BITTER END

As discussed at the annual North American Clinical Congress on Toxicology conference in 2023, a 37-year-old Denver man survived the ingestion of a "sip" of assisted suicide drugs. In Colorado, physician-assisted suicide is legal, and the patient's friend, who had been diagnosed with terminal pancreatic cancer, opted to end his life with a prescribed concoction that included lethal doses of drugs designed to end consciousness and stop the heart. The man's ill friend drank it during an end-of-life ceremony with loved ones, and after mentioning that the drink tasted "bitter," the man in question had to taste it for himself. He was hospitalized for three days before he recovered.

PIG OUT

According to a 2024 story in *American Journal of Case Reports*, an unnamed 52-year-old man in Florida complained of migraine-grade weekly headaches that got gradually worse over a period of more than four months and wouldn't respond to medication or therapy. He had no other health issues or newly diagnosed problems, and hadn't traveled to any exotic locations where he may have picked up a parasite or virus. Doctors noticed just one weird thing in his diet: he liked to eat barely cooked floppy bacon and had regularly done so for decades. The man's migraines were diagnosed as cysticercosis, a condition resulting from a pork tapeworm, and one that's extremely rare in the U.S. The man was given antiparasitic and anti-inflammatory medication to treat his tapeworm.

Number of full-time skywriters worldwide: six.

LOCAL HEROES

You're going about your day, minding your own business, when all of a sudden—BOOM!—you're face-to-face with a life-and-death situation! What do you do? Do you freeze...and hope someone else comes to the rescue? Or do you step up and become a local hero?

WHAT THE PUCK?

An Ohio man named Andrew Podolak attended a Cleveland Monsters minor league hockey game in April 2024. Surrounding the rink is a clear plastic barrier, but it only goes so high. Fans sitting above it always have to keep an eye out for a wayward puck, which is harder than a baseball and can cause serious injury or even death (it's happened). Toward the end of the match, a player hit a puck that flew over the barrier...and was zooming right toward four-year-old Nasir Davis's head. He was oblivious to the danger, but Podolak, sitting nearby, saw it. "I was like, 'Oh God,'" he told a local news station. "The first thing I gotta do, first instinct, is protect the kid, jump in front of it." Podolak just managed to deflect the puck with his arm.

After the game, Nasir's mom, Asia, took to social media to thank the man who "literally saved my son's life." The team was able to track Podolak down, and gave all three of them tickets to their next game. The trio even got to go out on the ice, meet the team, and participate in a puck drop. "You're a really special person," Asia told her new friend.

ONE AT A TIME

In April 2023, Claudia Jimenez of Phoenix, Arizona, woke up at around 3:00 a.m. and smelled smoke in her second-story apartment. Then she saw flames. She gathered her two daughters—aged one and eight—but there was no way out of the burning apartment, so she ran to her window and yelled for help.

Sleeping nearby were Joe Hollins and his wife, who were homeless. Hollins saw right away how dire the situation was; standing underneath the apartment, he told Jimenez to drop her children. "I'm going to catch them!"

With no time to spare, Jimenez tossed down the one-year-old, and Hollins caught her. Then she tossed down the eight-year-old, and Hollins caught her, too. Then she tossed down her dog, and Hollins caught it. Then she tossed down her *other* dog, and Hollins caught it, too. Finally, Jimenez jumped, and Hollins caught her. A moment later, firefighters arrived; they would have been too late to save the young family. Hollins said he was happy to be in "the right place at the right time," and that anyone would have done what he did.

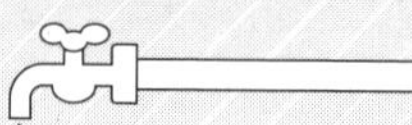

One of the oldest words in the English language (sixth century): *keel*. It means "ship."

LIFESAVERS

In August 2021, David Winner took a swim at Coalcliff Beach, south of Sydney, Australia. The 69-year-old former lifeguard had been swimming in these waters for 40 years, but this time, the strong waves pushed him away from shore and into the rocks. By the time other beachgoers found Winner, he'd been floating in the rock pool for several minutes, unconscious, with a broken back and a cracked skull.

It took five people to haul Winner's bloodied, limp body onto the rocks. One of them—Winner's friend and neighbor, volunteer lifesaver Andrew Massey—started administering CPR, but it wasn't reviving him. Then more people arrived, and they all took turns doing chest compressions. "I thought, 'I'm just going through the motions, he's dead to the world,'" said Massey.

But the rescuers didn't give up. For 15 minutes, 10 people kept Winner's blood pumping until a medical helicopter landed and paramedics took over. They detected a pulse, and airlifted Winner to a hospital.

He survived, but the accident cost him the ability to walk. "I drowned, went into cardiac arrest, and I passed away that day," said Winner, who vowed to pay the good deed forward. It just so happened that four of the 10 rescuers were trained to use CPR by Winner himself. Two years later, he announced his initiative to teach CPR to one million Australians by 2030. As he likes to say, "I teach CPR, because one day, the person being saved might be me!"

SHARP SHOOTER

Owen Burns of Northern Michigan owns a slingshot, but his mom didn't let the 13-year-old use it without supervision because he would sometimes "break things." Then, one afternoon in May 2023, Owen was inside when he heard his eight-year-old sister screaming from the back yard. He ran to the window just in time to see a strange teenager attempting to carry his terrified sister into the woods.

Owen got his slingshot.

After running outside, he loaded a marble into the slingshot, aimed, and hit the teen; then he grabbed a rock, aimed, and hit the kidnapper again. That did it! The kidnapper ran off, and Owen took his sister home. "It's alright," he told her. "He can't hurt you now."

Police discovered the kidnapper a few blocks away with injuries to his head and chest "consistent from getting hit with a slingshot," said Michigan State Police 1st Lt. John Grimshaw, who hailed Owen as a hero. "He really is the one that I believe saved his sister's either life or from something seriously bad happening to her."

In 1905, James Blackstone bowled a near-perfect 299.5. Why not 300? A pin broke in half during the last frame and the bottom half stayed put.

LOOK UP

Spanning the Detroit River, the Ambassador Bridge connects the United States and Canada. One afternoon in July 2023, a 27-year-old ironworker from Windsor, Ontario, named Spencer Baker was part of a crew replacing the suspension cables when the unthinkable happened: he fell. "I was just thinking this is it, man, my life is over. I'm never going to see my daughter again. My fiancée. My whole life flashed before my eyes." After falling nearly 150 feet, he hit the water so hard that he could barely move, much less keep his head above the surface. With his body bruised and broken, Baker had only a few minutes before he succumbed.

Thankfully, a few minutes was all it took for a rescue boat to arrive—actually a mail boat. "We're coming! We're coming!" yelled Captain Sam Buchanan. They got Baker onto the boat, "covered him up real good," and raced to shore, where first responders were waiting.

Buchanan wasn't even on his boat when the accident happened. He was in his office on the dock when a little girl named Tionne Bevelle started banging on his door and yelling that someone had fallen off the bridge.

Tionne (who'd begged her mother and grandmother to go the park that day) was actually looking up at the bridge—marveling at how tiny the workers looked—when it happened. "We were like, 'Oh my God, somebody has fallen!'" said her grandmother, Bernita Flowers. Tionne's mom, Terri George, said Baker was "doing cartwheels" in the air. "So we ran over, well [Tionne] ran, I tried to run. I knew she was faster than me, so I let her run ahead of me."

After a day in the hospital, Baker made it home to his family. He had broken ribs, a fractured cheekbone, and bruises covering his entire body. Captain Buchanan and Tionne Bevelle and her family were honored by the U.S. Coast Guard and Harbor Master Peter Berry, who explained just how fortunate Baker was. "In my 15 years in this position, unfortunately people have entered [the river] from the Ambassador Bridge. Mr. Baker is the only one I know who has survived."

* * *

WHERE IN THE NAME OF SAINT PAUL ARE WE?

In the Minnesota "twin cities" region made up of Minneapolis and Saint Paul, Minneapolis is seated to the west of Saint Paul. But they're so close together that what's called the West Side of Saint Paul is actually south of its downtown. And that's a different entity entirely from the separate town of West St. Paul, which is also south of Saint Paul's downtown. There's another city in the mix, South St. Paul, which can be found to the east of the town of West St. Paul. And then there's North Saint Paul, another town of its own, but at least that actually *is* north of Saint Paul.

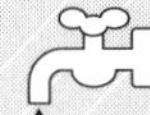

There's a large population of Luxembourgish people in Belgium, Wisconsin, and lots of Belgians in Luxemburg, Wisconsin.

JUDGE JUDGE

Aptronym *was coined by early 20th-century humorist Franklin P. Adams to describe the funny situation that occurs when a person's name perfectly suits, or is "apt" for, their passion or profession—like toilet manufacturer Thomas Crapper, for example. Here are some others.*

Chris Trimmer, tree nursery operator

Melanie Proffitt, business director

Matt Germino, U.S. Geological Survey research ecologist

John Laws, judge

Georgia Ball, pro golfer

William Payable, tax collector

Adrian Bloom, gardening book author

David Seaman, Fishing Republic ambassador

Mitchell Shippey, shipbuilder

Chris Moneymaker, professional poker player

Peter Goodnight, anesthesiologist

Tom Kitchin, chef

Richard Chopp, vasectomy surgeon

Carle Pace, cyclist and marathon runner

Karina DePiano, keyboard player

Andrew Drinkwater, water researcher

Michael Dadson, father-son relationship counsellor

Michael R. Lawyer, lawyer

Anna Smashnova, tennis player

John Judge, judge

Susan Stoner, drug researcher

Arthur Blessitt, Christian minister

Beth Chance, statistician

Kyle Anger, convicted murderer

Ted Shuffle, choreographer

Rich Fortune, entrepreneur

Assad Butt, gastroenterologist

Darren Sellwood, timber merchant

Sara Blizzard, weather reporter

Frank Fish, marine biologist

Richard Makepeace, peace negotiator

Nicola Lambe, sheep researcher

Duran Workman, recruiter

Henry Head, neurologist

Lauren Beers, pub keeper

Harold Charles Organ, organ player

Wally Wallington, wall builder

Hugh C. Dick, urologist

Matthew Hartman, cardiologist

HELLBOY, STARRING VIN DIESEL

Some roles are so closely associated with a specific actor that it's hard to imagine those people weren't the filmmakers' first choice. But it happens all the time. Can you imagine, for example...

Amy Schumer as Barbie (*Barbie*, 2023)

After a Barbie movie was first proposed in the 1980s, it took nearly 40 years for the iconic doll to finally land on the big screen. It finally looked like it was happening in late 2016 when Sony Pictures announced that raunchy comedian Amy Schumer would be starring, as well as cowriting the script. Then in 2017 Schumer released a statement: "Sadly, I'm no longer able to commit to *Barbie* due to scheduling conflicts. The film has so much promise, and Sony and Mattel have been great partners. I'm bummed, but look forward to seeing Barbie on the big screen."

Producers then considered Anne Hathaway, but the production didn't get off the ground fast enough before the rights transferred from Sony to Warner Bros. Interestingly, Margot Robbie was originally brought in to produce, and she wanted *Wonder Woman* actor Gal Gadot to play the living doll, but Gadot said no ("scheduling conflicts"). Robbie took the lead, and *Barbie* made a billion dollars and garnered a Best Picture nomination.

Most mentions of scheduling conflicts are actually scheduling conflicts, but sometimes they're "scheduling conflicts." Schumer later revealed why she left the project: "They definitely didn't want to do it the way I wanted to do it, the *only* way I was interested in doing it." How'd she want to do it? Barbie gets kicked out of Barbieland because she's not perfect enough.

Vin Diesel as Hellboy (*Hellboy*, 2004)

Mike Mignola, who made his mark illustrating comics for DC and Marvel in the 1980s, thought there weren't enough anti-heroes in comic books, so he created *Hellboy* in 1993 based on a character he initially drew in 1991. The Nazi-hating half-human, half-demon was a breakout hit for Dark Horse Comics. One fan was Spanish director Guillermo del Toro, who would go on to spend several years collaborating with Mignola on a *Hellboy* screenplay.

Initially, studio after studio turned them down. Then, after the runaway success of the first big-budget Spider-man and X-Men movies, Universal finally took interest in *Hellboy*. The studio wanted Vin Diesel, who'd recently become an action star

First Black female author to sell a million copies of a book: Ann Petry, with *The Street* (1946).

playing Riddick in the sci-fi thriller *Pitch Black.* In 2001, Diesel was officially attached to the upcoming *Hellboy* movie.

But that's not the name that del Toro and Mignola said when they decided to announce their first choice to each other simultaneously. They both said, "Ron Perlman." Del Toro had directed Perlman in *Blade II* and knew he could "deliver subtlety and nuance with makeup." The suits at Universal said Perlman wasn't famous enough to entice theatergoers: his best known role was the heavily made-up Beast in the 1980s syndicated TV series *Beauty and the Beast.*

Then Columbia greenlit the project, and offered the lead to future *Hawkeye* actor Jeremy Renner, who turned down "more money than I'll probably ever make" because he didn't feel a connection to the source material. Columbia wasn't sure about Perlman, either, but no other actor felt right for del Toro, so he stuck to his guns until the suits relented. Result: *Hellboy* was a sleeper hit and turned Perlman into a movie star. "I just think I'm really lucky that at the end of the day it was me," he said. "That Guillermo cared enough about his vision that he wouldn't compromise or do it any other way. I thought that was a battle he was going to lose, frankly, so I just relish the triumphant aspect of winning that fight."

James Corden as Charlie (*The Whale*, 2022)

In 2012, after watching Samuel D. Hunter's play about a morbidly obese shut-in who tries to reconcile with his estranged daughter, director Darren Aronofsky (*Black Swan, Requiem for a Dream*) decided to make it into a movie, but only if he could find the right actor. "[Charlie is] a very multifaceted, complicated character," said Aronofsky. "He's both incredibly giving and incredibly selfish. He's incredibly loving, but physically extremely hard to look at. So trying to find that actor who could kind of really bring this internal golden beauty to this character was just very hard."

Aronofsky was taking too long to find his perfect lead, so the directing job was offered to Tom Ford (*Nocturnal Animals*). He cast British sitcom actor James Corden (*Gavin & Stacey*) as Charlie, a few years before Corden landed his late-night American talk show job. Ford reportedly wanted too much creative control, so he was let go, as was Corden, who suspected he was too young for the role.

Then George Clooney got involved in the fim, but would only make the film if he could actually cast a 600-pound actor. The studio balked, and Aronofsky was back in the director's chair. And he still didn't have a lead...until one night in 2020 when he happened to see a trailer for a low-budget 2006 Brazilian movie called *End of the Night*, starring Brendan Fraser, whose star had somewhat faded after such 1990s hits as *Encino Man, George of the Jungle*, and *The Mummy.*

"I, like most of the world, had kind of forgotten about Brendan Fraser," recalled Aronofsky. "But a light bulb went off and I was like, 'Oh, wow, we haven't considered

The European Union has an anthem:
"Ode to Joy," a.k.a. Beethoven's Ninth Symphony.

Brendan. That's a really cool idea.'" An idea that won Fraser an Oscar. (And what if Corden had landed the role? Would he still have done his talk show?)

Michael Jackson as Eric Draven (*The Crow*, 1994)

The Crow is a story steeped in tragedy. A rock star named Eric and his fiancée are brutally murdered by a gang. A supernatural crow resurrects Eric, and he embarks on a bloody trail of revenge. American illustrator James O'Barr wrote the comic book in the 1980s while grieving the death of his fiancée at the hands of a drunk driver. The major movie studios weren't interested in adapting the violent graphic novel until the unlikely success of Tim Burton's *Batman* (1989).

Then, with only four days left of a 54-day shoot, star Brandon Lee was fatally wounded by a dummy blank in a gun, leaving behind his own fiancée. Coincidentally, Lee's father, acclaimed martial arts actor Bruce Lee, had died on a film set 20 years earlier...while playing an actor who gets murdered after real bullets are placed into a prop gun. Australian director Alex Proyas (*Dark City*; *I, Robot*) ultimately decided to finish *The Crow* as a tribute to its fallen star. He was so loyal to Lee that he declined to participate in any sequels of remakes. "Only Brandon is the Crow."

But it could have been much different. When Hollywood execs first called O'Barr in for a meeting, they told him they wanted to do *The Crow* as a musical starring Michael Jackson. O'Barr started laughing, thinking they were kidding. They weren't. "Some of the ideas the producers put out there," he later said, "were incredibly moronic. To this day, I'm still baffled by them. It's like, 'Did you read the book?'" O'Barr and Proyas were eventually able to convince the studio to take a more serious tone. They considered rock star Jon Bon Jovi and 1990s heartthrob Christian Slater, whom O'Barr said was "really hot to play it." But Brandon Lee, with his haunted expression and love of the source material, ultimately won his breakout—and final—role.

Jeff Goldblum as Doc Brown (*Back to the Future*, 1985)

One of the strangest movies ever made was the Peter Weller–starring sci-fi romp *The Adventures of Buckaroo Banzai Across the 8th Dimension* (1984). The cult classic featured early performances from Jeff Goldblum, John Lithgow, and Christopher Lloyd. When *Banzai* producer Neil Canton started working on his next movie, about a high school student who joins a middle-aged scientist on a time travel adventure, he recommended those three names to writer Bob Gale and director Robert Zemeckis. Goldblum auditioned for Doc Brown, but at only 32, he was deemed too young. He did *The Fly* instead. Lithgow would have played the part had he not already signed on to film the "Nightmare at 20,000 Feet" segment of the upcoming *Twilight Zone: The Movie*. The filmmakers also looked at Gene Wilder, Gene Hackman, Robin Williams, John Candy, and Danny DeVito. At one point, producer Steven Spielberg

World's smallest town: Hum, Croatia.
It's the size of a football field and has a population of 24.

and Zemeckis offered the Doc Brown part to Devo frontman Mark Mothersbaugh. He turned it town, saying that he'd rather score the movie than act in it.

That left the door open for 47-year-old Lloyd, who'd shown his range after playing a mental patient in *One Flew Over the Cuckoo's Nest*, a drugged-out cabbie on the sitcom *Taxi*, and a rogue Klingon in *Star Trek III: The Search for Spock*. While Lloyd was shooting a film in Mexico City, his agent sent him the *Back to the Future* script. "I scanned it," he said later, "but I wasn't terribly impressed." Lloyd wasn't interested in becoming a "movie star"; he was more excited about starring in an upcoming off-Broadway play as Hans Christian Andersen. He didn't even get back to his agent. But then, "A friend who was with me at the time said, 'My mantra has always been to never leave any stone unturned.'" So, on a whim, Lloyd flew to Los Angeles and read for the part that would turn him into a household name.

Sandra Bullock as Neo (*The Matrix*, 1999)

You know that scene in *The Matrix* where Morpheus tells Neo about the Matrix and offers him two pills? Imagine it if Neo were being played by Sandra Bullock, and Morpheus was Arnold Schwarzenegger. That almost happened. But in the end, "The casting process more often than not leads you to the right place," said producer Lorenzo di Bonaventura, who spent five years casting *The Matrix*.

Before deciding on Keanu Reeves, the filmmakers looked at every leading man in Hollywood, including most famously Will Smith, who would have starred as Neo along with Val Kilmer as Morpheus (a part that went to Lawrence Fishburne). Smith turned it down because he didn't understand the concept, and ended up making *Wild Wild West* instead, which flopped. Brad Pitt said no (he needed a break after *Seven Years in Tibet*), as did Leonardo DiCaprio (who wanted to do a smaller film after *Titanic*). The filmmakers were having such a tough time finding their male lead that at one point, "We went to [Sandra] Bullock and said, 'We'll change Neo to a girl.'" Di Bonaventura had worked with Bullock on *Demolition Man*, and thought she could do it. But, as he recalled, "It just wasn't for her at the time." They later offered Bullock the part of the love interest, Trinity, which she also turned down (Carrie-Anne Moss was cast). Instead, Bullock starred in *Miss Congeniality*, which was an enormous hit. She later said she regretted not taking the Trinity part but acknowledges that they found the right actors. "*The Matrix* was sexy and great because of Carrie-Anne and Keanu."

* * *

A FISHY GRAMMAR LESSON

The singular form of fish is *fish*. The plural form of *fish* is also *fish*, if you're talking about more than one of the same kind of fish. When you're talking about multiple varieties of fish, you should use *fishes*.

HOW TO SPEAK ANTARCTICAN

Isolated from the rest of the world for months at a time, the revolving collective of English-speaking scientists stationed in Antarctica research stations have developed a cross-national lingo all their own.

Great White South: Antarctica.

Usarp: An American, part of the United States Antarctic Research Program.

The crud: The assortments of colds, flus, and viruses brought in by new arrivals.

The field: Anywhere off base.

Wintering: To stay in Antarctica during the even-more-punishing winter months.

Tourist: An Antarctic summer-only worker.

Beaker: A scientist.

Scradge: Food.

Nutty: Dried and preserved meat granules to which ice or snow can be added to make a protein paste.

Freshies: The rare, air-dropped treat of fresh fruit or vegetables.

Slot: Dangerous and, often, unseen large ice crevasses.

Big eye: Insomnia.

Bronzy: Sunburned.

Ching: A "Dear John" letter sent from a partner back home.

Yikla: From Australian telegraphic code, it means "this is the life."

Snowquake: An avalanche.

Wolf of the sea: A whale.

Spell-o: A break or rest.

Toasted: Having gone a bit mad from the cold, ice, and isolation. When a worker gets toasted, they have to leave.

Country mice: Scientists that travel to various camps around Antarctica.

Turdcicle: Frozen animal dung.

Wov: An area for stowing personal effects on ships and in research stations.

Tongue: A long and narrow peninsula of ice attached to firm ground that extends into the sea.

Young ice: Thin ice, less than six inches thick, that's still settling and forming.

Yomp: To trek across the wilderness.

Try pot: To render whale and penguin blubber into usable oil. It's done in a round, deep cast-iron pot also called a try pot.

Weasel: An enclosed floating snowmobile, a unique vehicle suited to traversing Antarctic terrain.

Woolly: A windstorm that happens with little to no warning.

Wig: A male seal.

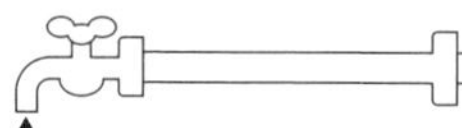

Nine Nobel Prize winners attended the Bronx High School of Science in New York City.

BEHOLD THE TURTLE, PART I

Turtles were roaming the planet before the dinosaurs, but what are these roundish enigmas really like? Are they merely creatures of instinct, or do they wonder and feel and dream? And how'd they get that shell? And can they really breathe out of their butts? Slow down there! It's Turtle Time.

SURVIVAL OF THE FITTEST

Herpetologists (researchers who study reptiles and amphibians) have been trying for years to find out what makes turtles tick, but perhaps 19th-century philosopher Ralph Waldo Emerson said it best: "All the thoughts of a turtle are turtle." Anyone who's spent time with these stubborn reptiles can verify this. When a turtle decides it wants to do something, it does it, and does it, and does it...

If you're unfamiliar with these animals, turtles are reptiles, along with snakes, lizards, and crocodilians. Unlike mammals, turtles are cold-blooded, and they hatch from eggs. But before we attempt to unlock the turtle's brain, we have to learn about its unique body. To do that, we'll go back about 260 million years, when an evolutionary adaptation gave a chubby lizard called *Eunotosaurus africanus* a crucial tool in a rapidly changing environment. The ribs of this lizard broadened, giving the *Eunotosaurus* a hard, scaly chest. That gave it stability while digging into the hard ground with its powerful front claws. Result: when Earth endured a prolonged drought that resulted in the Permian-Triassic extinction, which killed off 70 percent of terrestrial species, the *Eunotosaurus* survived. Thanks to its superior digging abilities, it could find food and shelter while so many other reptiles perished. From this prototurtle evolved the order Testudines—which comprises turtles, terrapins, and tortoises.

Until the *Eunotosaurus* was discovered, the prevailing theory went that the turtle's shell adapted on top from bony scales (as is the case with the armadillo) for protection against predators. But now we know that the shell evolved to give the turtle more stability while digging. The fact that the shell also provides protection is what's known as an *exoadaptation*.

SHELL GAMES

So, what exactly is—and isn't—the turtle shell? Contrary to what cartoons might have taught us, it's not a house that a naked turtle lives in. The shell is technically part of the animal's skeleton, but it's not an exoskeleton. Think of a turtle shell as a box with one opening in front for the head and two forelegs, and another in the back for the tail and two hind legs. The top (*carapace*) and bottom (*plastron*) of this box are made

of fused-together bones—fused to the ribs on the plastron, and to the spine on the carapace—connected by a bridge of bone on each side. The shell is composed of 59 to 61 bones covered by horny plates called *scutes*. They're made of keratin, the same substance as human hair and fingernails. But unlike hair and fingernails, turtle shells have nerve endings, which means they can really feel it when something damages their shell. And as pet turtle owners can verify, it feels good when their shells are petted. Some more shell facts:

- The shape and function of the turtle's shell depends on where it spends most of its time. In general, turtles that live exclusively on land have dome-shaped shells. That makes it easier to right themselves when they get flipped over.

- Turtles that spend most or all of their time in the water have flatter, more aerodynamic shells that allow them to swim faster.

- Though the shell's rigidity protects the turtle, it doesn't allow the lungs to expand and contract. To make up for this, the turtle's lungs are attached on top to the carapace; the abdominal muscles, which move food through the stomach and liver, also move air in and out of the lungs.

- The shell of the alligator snapping turtle, known as "the dinosaur of the turtle world," is covered with spikes, and its scaly skin has horns. Not surprisingly, it has no natural predators (and uses its worm-like tongue to lure in unsuspecting fish).

- The most clever shell belongs to the box turtle. When this forest dweller retracts its head, tail, and legs, its uniquely hinged plastron closes tight, turning the turtle into an impenetrable box.

OF TORTOISES, TERRAPINS, AND TURTLES

Three characteristics all turtles have in common: they have shells, they have beaks, and the females lay their eggs, in a group called a clutch, in a nest on dry land. Beyond that, there are vast differences between families, genera, and even species. Making it more confusing, there are two *suborders* of turtles, marked by how they retract their necks. Freshwater turtles, snapping turtles, tortoises, softshell turtles, and sea turtles are classified as Cryptodira because they pull their necks straight back into their shells. Less common are Pleurodira, which have longer necks and fold their heads to the side. Pleurodira include freshwater species that mostly dwell in the Southern Hemisphere, with one exception being the American side-neck river turtle. Now, let's take a closer look each one.

Tortoises: Like the prototurtle, *Eunotosaurus*, the 65 modern tortoise species live on dry land; many who live in hot climates burrow underground. Unlike turtles and terrapins, tortoises eat mostly plants, although some species are omnivorous, and some females will eat rocks or soil for calcium. They get their water from plants, grasses, and cacti.

The smallest tortoise species, the speckled padloper from South Africa, can fit in one hand. The largest, the Galapagos giant tortoise, can weigh up to 700 pounds.

Tortoises have round, stumpy feet (like elephants) to help them walk on the ground. And they certainly earn their reputation as slowpokes: according to Guinness World Records, the fastest tortoise clocked in at a whopping 0.63 mph. You don't need to be fast when there's little that can hurt you, and your food doesn't move.

Terrapins and Turtles: If you see a group of turtles sunning themselves on a log on a pond, those are terrapins: species of small turtles with webbed toes and flattened carapaces that make them speedy swimmers. The box turtle has both terrapin and tortoise qualities: it has webbed feet for swimming, but because it spends most of its time on land, it has a domed shell like a tortoise. The largest freshwater turtle species is China's Red River giant softshell turtle (also called the Yangtze). It can reach five feet long and weigh over 200 pounds. Make that *could*—as of 2023, after the last known female died, the species is functionally extinct. The aforementioned alligator snapping turtle is the heaviest turtle, weighing up to 200 pounds.

Sea Turtles: These creatures may almost seem like different animals altogether. Instead of feet, they have flippers. Their teardrop-shaped shells allow them to maneuver in the water like fish. But they have lungs like all reptiles. Still, they can stay underwater for several minutes while swimming, and up to two hours while resting. Only the females leave the water, to lay their eggs on the beach.

The smallest sea turtle species, the Kemp's Ridley, weighs between 70 and 100 pounds. The largest is the mighty leatherback, which can reach six feet long and weigh up to 1,500 pounds. (The only reptile that weighs more is the saltwater crocodile.) The leatherback also sets the turtle speed record, swimming at an impressive 22 mph. Their shells are leathery so they won't implode—but will instead contract—as the animals dive as deep as 4,000 feet.

WHAT DOES THE TURTLE SAY?

Despite their deaf and dumb reputation, turtles are quite the communicators. And they do have interior ears, located beneath the skin, allowing them to pick up vibrations.

- Lacking vocal cords, turtles expel air from their lungs to create a hissing or wheezing sound. (Some males make this unnerving noise during mating.)
- Some species create vibrations via their throats or shells; some have been recorded making purring-like noises.

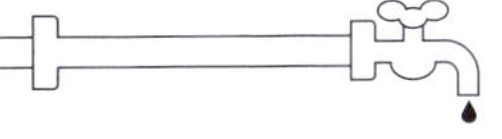

Only English word to end with *-mt*: dreamt.

- Turtles also click their beaks, grunt, chirp, and make squeaking sounds. One researcher reported that a common snapping turtle "sounded like Darth Vader."
- Sea turtles emit low-frequency sounds undetectable by human ears.
- Fetal sea turtles buried on the beach have been recorded squeaking to one another within their clutch of eggs, so they all hatch at the same time, increasing their chances for survival.
- Fetal freshwater turtles can also communicate within the clutch. Those on the top develop quicker, so as they're closer to hatching, they breathe more, which emits carbon dioxide. When the carbon dioxide reaches the lower turtles, their metabolisms speed up so they will all hatch together.
- Turtles also use body language—such as bobbing their heads, extending or retracting their necks, and staring intensely at each other—to assert dominance or show submission. They also use touch to communicate, rubbing their beaks together affectionately before mating.

But these scenarios are not the norm. Outside of mating and the occasional fight for territory, most turtles lead solitary lives—*long*, solitary lives.

OLD MAN TURTLE

Every living thing ages at a genetically predetermined rate. Turtles live so long because they are among the slowest agers. How slow? Sea turtles can live 50 to 100 years; smaller turtles, 10 to 50 years; and tortoises, up to 200 years. In fact, researchers haven't even determined the tortoise's true lifespan because the oldest ones just keep on living.

In the wild, there are three ways to die: succumbing to illness, succumbing to injury, and getting predated. Avoiding all three of these plays a crucial part in the turtle's secret to longevity.

- **Good Genes**. Make that, good *telomeres*. Every animal has them. Located on the ends of chromosomes, these noncoding strands of DNA keep the chromosomes safe during cell reproduction. As most animals age, telomeres wear out, leaving the genes vulnerable to cell degradation and tumors. Turtles' telomeres wear out at a much slower rate than other animals'. And scientists still don't know why. If they do figure it out, it could be a game-changer for humanity.
- **Apoptosis**. Even with the long, healthy telomeres, turtle cells can become damaged enough to grow tumors. When this does happen, they utilize a process called *apoptosis* that causes the compromised cells to self-destruct before they can

Women were able to serve as jurors in all 50 states for the first time in 1968.

cause problems. Giant tortoises are the masters of apoptosis, and thus enjoy the lowest cancer and aging rates in the animal kingdom.

- **Low Heart Rate**. In general, animals with lower heart rates live longer. The world's oldest known living land animal, a Seychelles tortoise named Jonathan estimated to have been born around 1832, has a heart that beats only 10 times per minute (compared to a human heart's 60 to 100 beats). Even small turtles have lower heart rates compared to similar-sized animals. This isn't due to them being cold-blooded, however, as most other cold-blooded reptiles and amphibians have higher heart rates and shorter lifespans.

- **That Shell**. Predators strive for efficiency: the less energy spent on the kill, the more reserves they'll have after the meal. That's why most predators leave turtles alone—that body armor is tough to penetrate. It also helps protect the turtle from injury.

Yet even with these advantages, if turtles were simply mindless automatons, they'd get themselves into trouble and die a lot sooner. It turns out that there's a lot going on in the noggins of Testudinidaes.

For more about the amazing turtle, clop...clop...clop...clop on over to page 216.

* * *

THINGS WITH DIFFERENT NAMES IN U.S. AND U.K. ENGLISH

U.S.	U.K.
ATM	Cashpoint
Checkers	Draughts
Wrench	Spanner
Acetaminophen	Paracetamol
Teleprompter	Autocue
Burlap	Hessian
Thumbtack	Drawing pin
Truck stop	Transport café
John Doe	Joe Bloggs
Crosswalk	Zebra crossing
Bullhorn	Loudhailer
Jumping jacks	Star jumps
Caboose	Guard's van

Tuna and mackerel sleep by shutting off half their brains at a time.

CANADIAN FOOD ORIGINS

Canada has lots of land, seven NHL teams, and a unique cuisine all its own. Here are the origins of some classic foods from the Great White North.

KETCHUP CHIPS

Ketchup and chips are both individually popular in the U.S., but in Canada, the combination is so popular as to be mundane—ketchup chips are the best-selling flavored potato chip in Canada. They don't taste entirely like potato chips dipped in ketchup—they've got a sweet, tangy, salty tomato flavor that would *almost* nail that ketchup sensibility, if it weren't for the abundance of vinegar. Only in the past five years or so have ketchup chips become available in the United States, and usually as a test-marketed product or limited-time offering. They're a novelty, which is how they began in Canada: In 1970, a potato chip manufacturer named Hostess—unrelated to the baked goods company that makes Twinkies and HoHos, and since sold to Frito-Lay—attempted to differentiate itself from the strong Canadian potato chip competition with strange flavors. Among its introductions: grape, orange, mint, and ketchup chips. Ketchup, intending to mimic the flavor combination of french fries dipped in ketchup, is the only one that didn't flop.

CANADIAN BACON

Most of the English-speaking settlers of Canada came from Ireland and the United Kingdom, and they brought with them pork as a dietary and farming staple. When the British Isles experienced a pork shortage in the 1870s, not long after the official establishment of Canada, importers brought in a specific kind of pork product from the new nation, giving the ham-esque food the exotic-sounding name of "Canadian bacon." In Canada, it's never been called Canadian bacon, but is known as "back bacon." Made from the lean eye of pork loin found on a pig's back—the same meat used in pork chops—it's cured, smoked, cooked, and trimmed along the way.

NANAIMO BARS

Similar to powerfully sweet, layered cookies like hello dollies and millionaire bars, the Nanaimo bar is also made with pantry staples. The original Nanaimo bar, and the one most commonly found in Canada, is made up of layers of cookie or graham cracker crumbs, custard, melted chocolate, and chopped nuts. The bars started popping up at bakeries and bake sales in the 20th century but the first person to make that specific combination of ingredients into a tray of no-bake cookies has been lost to history. All that food historians know is that the dessert first found popularity in the 1950s in and around the Vancouver Island port city of Nanaimo, British Columbia.

First American with a doctorate in computer science (1965): Sister Mary Kenneth Keller.

POUTINE

One might think that Americans would love a finger-food combining several fatty, salty favorites in a towering heap. Strongly associated with Canada, where it's found on the menu of most every bar, restaurant, and fast-food joint from coast to coast, a standard poutine consists of a pile of well-cooked french fries, a generous portion of cheese curds, and a whole lot of gravy. In the small farm town of Warwick, Quebec, in 1957, customer Eddy Lainesse swept into the L'Idéal restaurant and was in such a hurry he ordered two of the menu's á la carte snacks thrown together into a bag—fries and cheese curds. According to lore, owner Fernard Lachance looked at the unattractive combination and called it "un poutine," *poutine* being French Quebec slang for "mess." Le Lutin Qui Rit ("The Laughing Elf"), as the restaurant was later named, sold it that way for years, and the dish spread around the province. Gravy-topped fries were already common in Canada, a specialty of Le Roy Jucep in Drummondville, Quebec. After owner Jean-Paul Roy saw more and more customers ordering a side of cheese curds to mix into their gravy fries, he got the idea in 1964 to sell the dish preassembled. From there, the three-ingredient dish and its variants spread across Canada.

MAPLE SYRUP

That brown, super-sweet, woodsy pancake and waffle topping originated in the land that's now Canada, but long before the country was established by European settlers. According to the lore of the Iroquois, the Indigenous people who occupied what is now Quebec, a chief's wife discovered maple syrup by accident. On a cold winter's day, Chief Woksis threw a tomahawk at a maple tree. The next day, the heat of the sun had warmed the sap inside, and it flowed out of the tree. His wife took the sap home, thinking she would save herself a trip to get water and use the sap instead. It tasted sweet and pleasant, and the Iroquois adopted it into their diet. When Europeans arrived, the Iroquois taught them a method of drilling into maple trees (prevalent in North America but not Europe) to access their sweet sap. Before winter, maple trees pack away starch to survive, and they convert it into a sap. After it's collected, the sap is then boiled so the water cooks off, leaving a sweet, viscous syrup. There are so many maple trees in Quebec that the province is now the single biggest producer and exporter of maple syrup: about 70 percent of all syrup available worldwide comes from Quebec.

* * *

"Everything that needs to be said has already been said, but, since no one was listening, everything must be said again."

—André Gide

While serving as the elected sheriff and executioner of Erie County, New York, future president Grover Cleveland executed two people.

BOOKS! BOOKS! AND ADDITIONAL BOOKS!

Watch any episode of The Simpsons *from the last 30-plus years and you'll likely spot a quick shot of a store in the town of Springfield. This is another opportunity for* Simpsons *writers to throw in more jokes—here are some of our favorite store names from the series.*

Banana Monarchy
It Blows: The Air Conditioner Store
Restoration Bard Wear
Crazy E.T.'s Phone Home
Poverty Barn
Dr. Zitsovsky's Dermatology Clinic
The Ear Piercery
Girdles N' Such
Wee Monsieur
Bikini Atol
Crème de La Creams
Alternative Knifestyles
Bloodbath & Beyond Gun Shop
Armistead's Mopeds
Just Vinegar
Left-Mart
Just Rainsticks
Banana Dictatorship
Abercrombie & the Other Guy
Saks Fifth Grade
Boris' Car Loft
Royal Majesty for the Obese or Gangly Gentleman

The Copy Jalopy
Puttering Barn
Oedipus Rx
Nothing Under a Thousand
Neiman Mark-Up
Loose Chandeliers
J.R.R. Toykin's
Broken-Home Chimney Repair
Blowhole Republic
The Boob Tubery
Spiffany's
Snooze at 11
Book Cellar
Books! Books! And Additional Books!
Donner's Party Supplies
Cossacks Fifth Avenue
H.R. Muffin Store
Shell Shack
Linens-N-Such
Goody New Shoes
Miscellaneous, Etc.
All Creatures Great and Cheap
One Size Fits All Lingerie

THOSE BURMA-SHAVE BILLBOARDS

In the early 20th century / this toiletries company / blanketed the nascent highway system / with sequential, small billboards / that told a story or a joke. / Burma-Shave!

LOOKING FOR A SIGN

In 1925, the Odell family of Minneapolis started the Burma-Vita company. Its flagship product: a topical ointment or liniment, made with what at the time were exotic, scented essential oils with quasi-medical properties. Those ingredients were harvested in "the Malay Peninsula and Burma," according to the packaging. It proved too exotic, however, and was a complete flop, so the company reworked its formula into a shaving cream, one that—like fellow newcomers Barbasol and Noxzema—was scooped from a jar and slapped onto the face. This innovation was a game-changing alternative to the previous messier method of working shaving soap into a lather and spreading it about the face with a brush.

The newly rebranded Burma-Shave attempted a few marketing plans to set itself apart from the competition. In the "Jars on Approval" campaign, Odell men, working as product reps, talked their way into offices in major Midwestern cities and gave away jars of Burma-Shave. They'd return at a later date and if the recipient liked the product, he'd hand over 50 cents; if he didn't, he'd give back the rest of the jar. That only lost the company lots of money and lots of product, leaving sales manager Alan Odell the opportunity to pitch to his father another idea, an altogether brand-new method of advertising.

EARLY SIGNS

The highway system was in its infancy in the 1920s, with mostly state routes and country roads bisecting but connecting the entire United States. All of a sudden, there was a lot of unused roadside real estate, and it quickly became a place for outdoor advertising, or billboards. While driving back from a sales trip in Illinois, Odell spotted a series of small billboards for a service station. Each of the half dozen signs, placed 100 feet or so apart, touted a different service or product on offer.

Alan Odell passionately pitched the idea of similarly sequential billboards for Burma-Shave to his family. Each set of signs could tell a little story, or show a little humor; they'd consist of fairly run-of-the-mill advertising copy, just broken down into five or six segments, with drivers and passengers who spotted them keeping their eyes peeled to see the wordy cliffhangers resolve, or catch the punchline. The final billboard, per Alan Odell's instructions: the name and logo of Burma-Shave.

Bermuda has no native peoples.

GIVE ME A SIGN

One problem: Alan's father thought that fleshed-out, precise idea was a terrible one. Each time his son pitched the concept, he turned it down—he believed that Alan Odell's fixation on roadside advertising was a form of homesickness developed by so much time out on the road doing sales calls in far-flung cities. But in 1926, tired of the push, he relented, and allocated $200 to test out the idea.

The first signs were hastily placed on a section of U.S. Highway 65 outside of the city of Lakeville, Minnesota, for test-marketing purposes . The parameters for the first Burma-Shave signs pretty much became the rules the company would stick to for nearly 40 years. Alan's first stab consisted of just four signs, while Burma-Shave would later use five or six billboards, but the initial test pieces were each 36 inches long and placed 100 paces apart along the side of the road. (Alan personally figured out those 100 paces, determined to be the right amount to capture drivers' attention before they forgot.) The first message encouraged men to shave their facial hair as a celebration of the end of World War I, eight years earlier: "Cheer up / Face / The War is Over / Burma-Shave."

SIGNS, SIGNS, EVERYWHERE SIGNS

Sales increased, Burma-Shave received inquiries from the press, and the novel use of billboards was the company's primary method of advertising until 1963. In total, about 7,000 sets dotted sections of highway across America, adorned with 600 different lyrical sayings, usually rhyming and often informal, poking fun at men for the annoyance of shaving and suggesting that women preferred a clean-shaven guy. Burma-Shave copywriters composed the signs, although an annual national write-in contest generated new material. Sometimes Burma-Shave went off-message with public service announcements about safe driving, but the billboards generally stayed witty in their limited space of five or six related signs. The last entry in each series, invariably and inevitably: "Burma-Shave."

Those Burma-Shave billboards were easy to spot. Initially black text on an orange background, Burma-Shave went all in on a white-on-red scheme nationally (except in South Dakota—there was a state law that allowed red signs only for emergency signage, so Burma-Shave made South Dakota its own white-on-blue billboards). They appeared everywhere except Nevada, because there was a lack of traffic, and Massachusetts, where the protected foliage made billboard space rare and overly costly.

SIGN OF THE TIMES

When the newly built interstate freeway system had superseded the state-route network by the early 1960s, Burma-Shave's method of advertising was rendered obsolete, too. Cars traveled so much faster on the freeways that to place ads there would've been dangerous, if people could even see them. In 1963, the Philip Morris

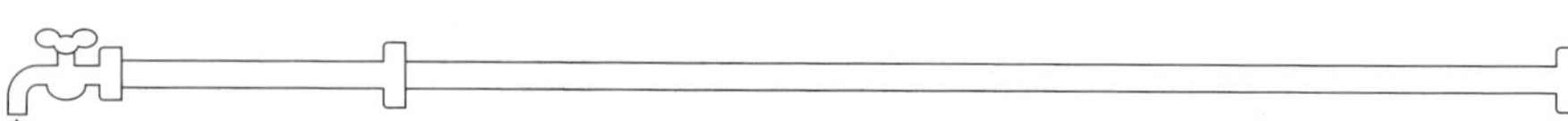

Coldest marathon: in Yakutia, Siberia, in 2022, runners raced in -63°F.

tobacco company acquired the slumping Burma-Shave and in its first order of business, killed the roadside ad campaigns.

Other forms of advertising, particularly television, also served to make the Burma-Shave method quaint. And the rise of affordable electric razors made sales fall, too. Burma-Shave faded into obscurity and was relaunched in the 1990s as a nostalgic product. But there was no return of the roadside sequential billboards—always the most famous thing about Burma-Shave anyway.

HERE ARE SOME / OF THE MOST MEMORABLE / OR CLEVER / OF THE SIGNS / USED TO PROMOTE / BURMA-SHAVE

Car in ditch
Driver in tree
Moon was full
So was he
Burma-Shave

He saw the train
he tried to duck it
Knocked first the gas
Then the bucket
Burma-Shave

Said Farmer Jones
Who's bald on top
I wish I could
rotate the crop
Burma-Shave

Diplomacy is
To do and say
The nastiest things
In the nicest way
Burma-Shave

You can beat
A mile a minute
But there ain't
No future in it
Burma-Shave

A peach looks good
With lots of fuzz
But man's no peach
And never wuz
Burma-Shave

Folks wouldn't feel
So much danger
If we still had
The ol' Lone Ranger
Burma-Shave

The one who
Drives when
He's been drinking
Depends on you
To do his thinking
Burma-Shave

Shaving brush
In army pack
Was straw that broke
The rookie's back
Use brushless
Burma-Shave

Proper
Distance
To him was bunk
Pulled him out
Of some guy's trunk
Burma-Shave

He lit a match
To check gas tank
That's why
They call him
Skinless Frank
Burma-Shave

His beard
Was long
and strong and tough
He lost his
chicken in the rough
Burma-Shave

Ashes to ashes
forests to dust
keep Wisconsin green
or we'll
all go bust
Burma-Shave

Don't pass cars
On curve or hill
If the cops don't get you
Morticians will
Burma-Shave

First TV family to own a computer: the Addams on *The Addams Family* (in 1965). The machine's name was Whizzo.

CREMAINS TO BE SEEN

Ashes to ashes, dust to dust / here are some stories about cremains that went bust.

ARTISTIC FLOURISH

Jocelyn Cronin wasn't sure what she wanted to do with the cremated remains of her husband of 32 years, John, a California firefighter who died in 2019. She kept some in a pendant around her neck and some in an urn, and in 2022 discovered an artist on TikTok who made portraits of deceased loved ones using their actual ashes mixed in with other art supplies. Cronin loved the idea and contacted the artist, who instructed her to send John's cremains to her in Woodstock, Georgia. A few days later, Cronin received an email purportedly from the customs department in Cambodia, telling her to pay $3,756 or she'd lose her husband's ashes. "And right there, I knew I had been scammed," Cronin told reporters. To date, she has still not determined the location of John's cremains.

THEY GOT THE WRONG GUY

Jim Allmon, the coroner of Sangamon County, Illinois, received a call from a local hospital to report that a body that was supposed to be picked up for cremation by Heinz Funeral Home and Family Care Creations was still in their possession. Allmon called the family of the deceased, who were confused—they'd already been given cremains by Heinz weeks earlier. Allmon launched an investigation and discovered a pattern. "Our investigation has discovered numerous incidents similar to this that involve Heinz Funeral Home or Family Care Cremations telling the family that their loved one had been cremated, that they were then provided with cremains when in actuality, a cremation never even took place," Allmon told reporters.

MAIL CALL

In 2023, the U.S. Postal Service Office of the Inspector General released a report on unclaimed packages, noting that it was sitting on 452 separate, unrelated parcels of unclaimed human cremains, the oldest eight years old. About half of the packages failed to reach their final destination because strict shipping rules about the material weren't honored, and so they were held back from the mail system. (Cremains must be marked with a special sticker that reads "Cremated Remains.") Unreadable addresses

Average Manhattan apartment size in 2013: 721 square feet. In 2023: 740 square feet.

were the other main problem. Unsendable packages wind up at the Mail Recovery Center in Atlanta, where they sit for 60 days, after which, if unclaimed and worth more than $25, they are sent to a government auction program. Human cremains, however, are held there indefinitely.

THE COMEBACK

Late one night in April 2024, a thief quietly absconded with a 2023 Dodge Charger SRT Hellcat parked in front of the Winter Haven, Florida, home of its owner, Larry Carter Jr. The sports car was especially important to Carter, because he purchased it in honor of his mother, who died in 2019. Carter commemorated her with a custom decal on the rear windshield that read "In Loving Memory of Lorena Leonard." She also occupied the car—Carter kept a container full of her ashes in a cupholder. Carter called police to report the stolen vehicle. They had no leads, but a day after the theft, Carter at least got the ashes back—they were in their original container, sitting inside of his mailbox. "Good thing they brought it back because that car was special for her. So, without having her ashes, I felt like I'm a failure," Carter told reporters.

NEAR DEATH AT A FUNERAL

Tryfan is one of the tallest mountains in Wales, and it's the final resting place, per request, of late local man Steve Parry. In a February 2024 ceremony conducted entirely on her own, Parry's daughter, Kitty Harrison, spread his ashes on the mountain's peak. Afterward, Harrison made it about a third of the way back down the mountain's notoriously tricky and tough terrain...and lost her footing. "My foot slipped on the loose shingle and I slipped quite a way and I landed on a tiny ledge," Harrison told reporters. "If I hadn't gone down that side, I'd have gone straight down the mountain and I'm not sure I'd be here today." She held onto a small ledge for more than three hours before she was rescued in a seven-hour effort by a 12-person rescue team and a coast guard helicopter, which spotted her hanging on the mountain.

STOPPING BY FOR A VISIT

In 2006, NASA launched the unmanned New Horizons spacecraft. Nine years later, it passed the celestial body Pluto, formerly classified as a planet. On board the craft at the time were the ashes of Clyde Tombaugh—the astronomer who discovered Pluto in 1930.

Rock band Mötley Crüe decided to add umlauts (also known as röck döts) to their name while they were drinking Löwenbräu.

THE CRAFT OF THE DRAFT

Every year, all the teams in all the big sports leagues jockey for position in player drafts, seeking to stock their rosters with the freshest and best new talent available. They don't always take it that seriously—here are some draft selections made as a joke, a lark, a prank, or a gesture of kindness.

JOHN WAYNE

The 1971 NFL draft extended into 17 rounds. Very few players selected that late had much of a chance of ever playing, and the Atlanta Falcons—with the last pick—didn't need anybody at that point. As a prank, coach Norm Van Brocklin drafted John Wayne, the tough guy actor famous for war and Western movies. Wayne—64 years old at the time of the draft—actually had played college football, at USC, but in the 1920s. (In later tellings of the draft tale, he was called an alum of "Fort Apache State," a reference to his 1948 film *Fort Apache*.)

BRUCE JENNER

Future reality TV star Caitlyn Jenner, known in 1976 as Bruce Jenner, had just won gold in the punishing Olympic decathlon, and, with it, the title of "best athlete in the world." Jenner hadn't played basketball since high school in the late 1960s, but was nevertheless selected with the 139th pick in the 1977 NBA draft by the Kansas City Kings.

TARO TSUJIMOTO

Punch Imlach, general manager of the NHL's Buffalo Sabres, found the annual draft to be an interminable affair. To make it more fun for himself, and to play a massive prank on the NHL, he used the Sabres' pick in round 11 (out of a record 25) of the 1974 draft to select Taro Tsujimoto from the Tokyo Katanas—a Japanese prospect from a Japanese pro league. The punchline: neither Tsujimoto nor the team existed. Imlach flipped through a phone book, found a name that sounded Japanese, and invented a team to go with it. It took a month for the NHL front office to notice that the draftee was invented and to mark the pick an "invalid claim."

CARL LEWIS

Among the best and most decorated track and field athletes ever, Carl Lewis won a total of nine Olympic gold medals, including four at the 1984 summer games in Los Angeles. They came in three short-distance running events and the long jump.

Oldest American civil rights organization: the National Association of the Deaf (1880).

Presumably, because running fast and jumping well are skills critical for basketball, the Chicago Bulls drafted Lewis in the 10th round of the 1984 NBA draft.

NORMAN HORVITZ

Who's Norman Horvitz? He was a pharmacist and the director of medicine for the Nutrisystem weight loss program. Horvitz was also a poker buddy of Philadelphia 76ers owner Harold Katz, who, as a joke, drafted the then 49-year-old with the 228th and final pick in the 1983 NBA Draft.

MIKE PIAZZA

The three-day-long 1988 Major League Baseball Draft finally ended on June 3, with the Los Angeles Dodgers using the final pick in the 62nd round, and the 1,390th selection overall, to take an obscure first baseman from Philadelphia who played at Miami-Dade Community College. His godfather and close friend of his father was a fellow Italian American and son of immigrants: Dodgers manager Tommy Lasorda. With such an irrelevant late-round pick, the Dodgers could afford to draft Mike Piazza as a sentimental favor for Lasorda's buddy. But then Piazza turned out to be good—really good. After working his way through the Dodgers' farm system and moving to catcher, Piazza was named the 1993 National League Rookie of the Year, played in 12 All-Star games, and was inducted into the Baseball Hall of Fame in 2016.

DENISE LONG

There was no WNBA in 1969, so that year the NBA's San Francisco Warriors picked high school phenom Denise Long with its pick in the 13th round—the first time the men's league selected a female player. Long had averaged 69 points per game in her senior season, so she was obviously skilled, but NBA commissioner J. Walter Kennedy made the Warriors' pick null and void, convinced that the team had tried to recruit Long as a sexist publicity stunt.

DERRELL ROBERTSON

In the mid-1990s, the Canadian Football League experimented with a handful of teams based in the United States. After the end of the 1994 season, the Las Vegas Posse ceased operations, and its signed players were made up for grabs to the rest of the CFL in a dispersal draft that took place in April 1995. The Ottawa Rough Riders selected Derrell Robertson, a defensive end from Las Vegas, with executives impressed by Robertson's stats and profile, prepared by the league. Nobody in the CFL front office, or on the Rough Riders, was aware that Robertson had died in a car accident in December 1994, just weeks after the season ended.

Annual sales of the Apple Watch are almost double that of the entire Swiss watch industry.

WE FORGOT OUR MANNERS

We can all agree that society has grown more informal if not a little crasser; there used to be common rules of etiquette understood by everyone. Maybe because they were so strict, or because there were so many, or because they were just ridiculous, a lot of these Victorian-era rules have been lost to time.

Arriving at or around the time that an invitation said the event would start? That's rude. It's customary and expected to show up one hour after the stated time.

A lady should take a bath every morning immediately upon waking up. She doesn't need to use more than a quart of water, which should be collected rainwater.

A lady should accept only one glass of champagne.

A woman's hair should be worn up, unless she is in her bedchamber.

It's vulgar for a lady to lift up her dress with both hands while crossing the street. She should use just her right hand, to limit ankle exposure.

When courting, a woman is forbidden from giving a man gifts, unless he gives her one first. And at that point, she must reciprocate, but only with something handmade.

It's rude to ask a direct question. Inquire about others with leading statements: instead of "How are you?" say "I trust you're well."

It is improper to hold a wedding after noon.

Gloves should always be put on inside the house, before stepping outside, and never put on in the street.

During post-dinner entertainments in the parlor, like the collective singing of songs around a piano, it's improper for one person to sing more than two tunes consecutively.

Gentlemen must not bow from a window to greet a passing lady on the street. However, if she sees him first, he should bow a little bit. Such recognition is best avoided altogether, though, to prevent gossip.

Marry for physical contrast. Someone with pale skin and red hair is expected to marry a person with black hair. An overweight person ought to marry a thin person.

Single women are required to avoid any behavior that may result in being kissed or handled by a man in any way. If a gentleman admires a woman's necklace and wants to look at it more closely, she must remove it first and hand it to him.

Never allow dinner conversation to shift away from chitchat. Anything more serious might interfere with digestion.

When traveling by train, anyone with poor eyesight should avoid reading, and anyone with weak lungs should stay quiet.

Women may never leave a party alone. A married woman must leave with at least one other married woman; a single woman must leave with her mother.

There are eight churches in Antarctica.

LET'S POO A STUDY

This very special episode of "Uncle John's Stall of Fame" celebrates those defecated–er, dedicated *scientists who dare to get down and dirty to shed some light where the sun don't shine.*

Honorees: Lawrence David, graduate student at Massachusetts Institute of Technology (MIT), and his mentor, professor of biological engineering Dr. Eric Alm

Notable Achievement: Creating the ultimate scata-log

Methodology: Your microbiome is comprised of the genetic material of all your body's microbes–including "friendly" bacteria, fungi, and viruses. In recent years, the gut microbiome as an indicator of health has become a major area of study. But little was known about how the biome changes over time. Then, one fateful day in 2013, Dr. Alm presented his grad student with a challenge: collect stool every day for an entire year. David rose to the challenge by collecting his own.

David didn't stop at his stool (which he placed in "little plastic hats"); he also collected his mouth bacteria and kept a detailed journal of when he pooped, what it looked like, what he ate, his mood, his blood pressure and weight, and more, with a total of 349 "health and lifestyle measures." Then, when the year was up, David and his mentor analyzed the gut bacteria and the mouth bacteria to see how they corresponded with his lifestyle measures.

Findings: "The gut microbiome remains stable for months, but some events, such as travel, illness or changing the fiber content of the diet, can rapidly change the mix of gut microbes," per reports. The data became the foundation for all of MIT's subsequent studies, bringing medical science one step closer to treating irritable bowel syndrome, heart disease, behavioral issues, and a host of other problems. Dr. David, who has since become a celebrated scientist and professor, calls his year of collecting his own poo "the most enjoyable thing I've done in science."

Honorees: Chaoran Ma, research fellow at Brigham and Women's Hospital and Harvard Medical School, and her professor, Dr. Dong Wang

Notable Achievement: Linking pooping to thinking

Methodology: Ma's team investigated the results of three earlier studies that collected data from more than 112,000 test subjects, data pertaining to their cognitive capacity and how frequently–or infrequently–they get to do some bathroom reading.

Findings: The more regular your BMs, the less likely you are to suffer from cognitive decline in old age. Conversely, test subjects with chronic constipation suffered

Former job of Jonestown cult leader Jim Jones: door-to-door spider monkey salesman.

"significantly worse cognition, equivalent to 3.0 years more of cognitive aging," Ma reported. Regular folks who enjoy one healthy bathroom visit per day fared the best, while those who had to go several times a day have a "slightly increased" risk of cognitive decline.

Ma and fellow researchers also looked at how the contents of the gut impact cognition, and warn that these are preliminary findings, with much more study required, but it's clear that gut health is crucial to brain health. "Our microbiome study found that individuals with specific microbial profiles in the gut, i.e., more bacteria that can cause inflammation and fewer bacteria responsible for digesting dietary fibers, had less frequent bowel movements and worse cognitive function." Dr. Wang's advice: eat more fiber.

Honorees: David Hu, associate professor of mechanical engineering and biology, adjunct associate professor of physics, and Patricia Yang, Ph.D. student in mechanical engineering at Georgia Institute of Technology, along with colorectal surgeon Daniel Chu, and undergrad students Candice Kaminski and Morgan LaMarca

Notable Achievement: Figuring out the physics of fecal matter

Methodology: In 2017, two undergrads, Kaminski and LaMarca, visited Zoo Atlanta to record the bathroom activities of 34 mammals...and collect their samples. Back at the lab, Hu and Wang measured the samples' density, viscosity, and aroma before placing them in a special blender called a "rheometer" to gather more data. Then the "fluid dynamicists" compared their results to data collected from studying the bathroom activities of human mammals.

Findings: The most surprising takeaway was that 65 percent of mammals—including elephants and humans—take the same average time to go (around 12 seconds), despite depositing decidedly different volumes of defecation.

Larger mammals create much longer leavings, but thanks to a hair-thin layer of super-slick mucus lining their large intestine, it exits the body a lot faster. For elephants, the rate is 6 cm (2.4 inches) per second; for humans, it's 2 cm (0.8 inches) per second. The researchers also determined that most herbivorous mammals produce "floaters," whereas large carnivores like lions and wolves produce "sinkers." They also learned that "in ideal conditions...feces extend halfway up the length of the colon from the rectum."

Grossed out? "Sure, it's uncomfortable to talk about," wrote Hu and Yan in "Physics of Poo" for the website The Conversation. "But that's where science comes in, because what we don't like to discuss can still cause harm." Their findings are influencing all kinds of applications, from how to better treat IBS and other gastrointestinal maladies to "an adult diaper for astronauts" that they created.

Count 'em: there are 352 quintillion gallons of water in the world's oceans.

"Astronauts want to stay in space suits for seven days, but are limited by their diapers. Taking advantage of the viscosity of feces, we designed a diaper that segregates the feces away from direct contact with skin. It was a semifinalist in the NASA Space Poop Challenge in 2017." Way to go!

Honorees: Gastroenterologist Anish Sheth, MD, and Josh Richman, coauthors of *What's Your Poo Telling You?*

Notable Achievement: Helping you achieve "poo-phoria"

Methodology: We all know that few things in life are more satisfying than a good ol' number two, but few know the science behind why—other than "lightening your load," that is. But the physical feelings might also be accompanied by a physiological reaction, in the right conditions.

Findings: Proper pooping is so integral to health and well being that it's the proverbial "canary in the coal mine" (sorry, little bird), indicating that when things go south down south, there might be something wrong all over. First, here's why letting one go can feel so good:

- Defecating stimulates the *vagus nerve*, which extends from the brainstem down to the colon. And what happens in the vagus doesn't stay in the vagus, which is good news. This nerve relaxes tense muscles after a sneeze, cough, vomit, or laugh. It also releases endorphins while lowering the blood pressure, heart rate, and breathing. "This stimulation," explains gastroenterologist Niket Sonpal, "is usually associated with having an orgasm." Size matters, however, as your log must be long enough to stimulate the vagus nerve.

- The pelvic floor is a group of muscles and ligaments that support the bladder and, in women, the reproductive organs. It's regulated by the *pudendal nerve*, which (among other things) tells you when you have to go to the bathroom by stimulating your sphincter and/or your urethra. Healthy, regular bowel movements help maintain the pelvic floor, and the pudendal nerve reacts by relaxing your pelvic floor after a successful evacuation. That's why "regular" people with healthy pelvic floors aren't just healthier, they're happier. Their digestion works as it should, with no speed bumps at the bottom.

- Serotonin, a.k.a. the "happy hormone," is stored mostly in your gut; it gets released when things are moving right along as they should.

- Psychologically, proper bowel movements make you feel more in control of your body, especially if you've been constipated. A successful sittin' session feels like a battle won.

Half of American record buyers don't own a turntable to play them on.

- On the flip side, if that battle was lost, you'll remain clogged, and your core will be robbed of its strength, leaving you with less serotonin and less control over your emotions.

Here's what you're striving for, according to experts: a stool that is neither too hard nor too soft. The Bristol Stool Chart is a handy reference that categorizes poo into seven groups. "Healthy stool types are type three, which are sausage-shaped with cracks on the surface, and type four stools, which are sausage-shaped but smooth and soft like a snake," says GoodRX medical editor Dr. Karla Robinson.

Achieving true "poo-phoria" (a term coined by Dr. Sheth) is different for everyone, but you can start by eating more fiber and less fat, staying hydrated, remaining active, and—this one is very important—never holding it in for too long.

Perhaps most crucially, don't be afraid to talk about your gut health. When Dr. Sheth was informed that 67 percent of Americans diagnosed with GI disorders like IBS waited more than a year to see a doctor after their symptoms started, he commented, "As a gastroenterologist, it's a little bit disheartening because you sort of feel like, this person unnecessarily suffered when we could have intervened earlier and maybe things would be better than they are now. And it just sort of speaks to the stigma, sometimes people feel that exists around things related to your gut." (We're proud to report that the stigma does not exist here at the BRI. We're never embarrassed to report on number two!)

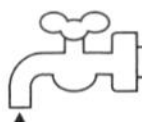

On October 3, 2010, Germany paid off their reparations debt from the 1910s World War I.

"DISSOLUTE HABITS"

Mental health in the late 1800s was no joke.

BACKGROUND

In 1864, a year before the U.S. Civil War ended, the West Virginia Hospital for the Insane opened in the town of Weston, and it remained in operation until 1994. For most of that time, the massive gothic building nestled in the Appalachian Mountains was known as the Trans-Allegheny Lunatic Asylum.

In the 2010s, a list began circulating called "Reasons for Admission: 1864–89." That title is a bit misleading, according to Snopes. The fact-checking website verified that the list is real, and that it was compiled from the asylum's log book in the 1890s; however, "its entries should not be considered as denoting things that were all considered symptoms of mental instability. Rather, among patients who were treated...for various illnesses such as chronic dementia, acute mania, and melancholia, these entries recorded the reasons or causes why those patients were said to have developed their underlying maladies."

The point is, everything on the list below affected the sufferer enough for them to get committed. The list also teaches us a bit about those times: folks referred to the Civil War as "the War"; they got just as riled up about politics as we do today; and most of these entries seem to apply to women. As *Time* magazine puts it, "According to 19th-century psychiatry, female independence *was* madness." Here's the unedited list (unless our editor edited the more explicit entries out).

REASONS FOR ADMISSION

Intemperance & Business Trouble
Kicked in the Head by a Horse
Hereditary Predisposition
Ill Treatment by Husband
Imaginary Female Trouble
Hysteria
Immoral Life
Imprisonment
Jealousy and Religion
Laziness
Marriage of a Son
Masturbation & Syphilis
Medicine to Prevent Conception
Menstrual Deranged
Mental Excitement
Novel Reading
Nymphomania
Opium Habit

Just go: you're more likely to develop Alzheimer's disease if you're frequently constipated.

Over Action of the Mind
Over Study of Religion
Over Taxing Mental Powers
Parents Were Cousins
Periodical Fits
Tobacco & Masturbation
Political Excitement
Politics
Fever and Loss of Law Suit
Fits and Desertion of Husband
Asthma
Bad Company
Bad Habits & Political Excitement
Bad Whiskey
Bloody Flux
Brain Fever
Business Nerves
Carbonic Acid Gas
Congestion of Brain
Death of Sons in War
Decoyed into the Army
Deranged Masturbation
Desertion by Husband
Dissolute Habits
Domestic Affliction
Domestic Trouble
Dropsy
Egotism
Epileptic Fits
Excessive Sexual Abuse
Excitement as Officer
Exposure and Hereditary
Exposure and Quackery
Exposure in Army
Fever and Jealousy
Fighting Fire
Suppressed Masturbation
Suppression of Menses
The War
Time of Life
Uterine Derangement
Venereal Excesses
Vicious Vices
Women Trouble
Superstition
Shooting of Daughter
Small Pox
Snuff Eating for 2 Years
Spinal Irritation
Gathering in the Head
Greediness
Grief
Gunshot Wound
Hard Study
Rumor of Husband Murder
Salvation Army
Scarlatina [Scarlet Fever]
Seduction & Disappointment
Self Abuse
Sexual Abuse & Stimulants
Sexual Derangement
False Confinement
Feebleness of Intellect
Fell from Horse in War
Female Disease
Dissipation of Nerves

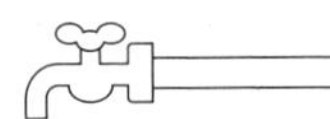

Second-biggest airport in Denmark: the private one built in 1961 by LEGO (but not *of* LEGO).

WEIRDLY COMPETITIVE

It seems like there's a contest or competitive event for just about everything. Take these, for example–they're all real. (We're holding out hope that this article is a winner at the Article Writing Awards.)

Since 2000, participants gather in Savonlinna, Finland, for the **Mobile Phone Throwing World Championships**. Official phones are provided for tossers, who compete in one of four categories: original (for distance), freestyle (creative throwing counts), team, and junior (for participants 12 and under).

Microsoft Excel is one of the most widely used office software programs in the world. The spreadsheet maker offers so many hundreds of functions that to master them all allows an office worker entry into the **Microsoft Excel World Championship**. Contestants have to use all the cells and rows to build and solve complex math problems the fastest. The contest gives away $15,000 in cash prizes and has been broadcast on ESPN.

The World's Biggest Liar Championship takes place at the Bridge Inn in Cumbria, England, every November. Conducted in honor of a local publican known for his long, elaborate, and blatantly untrue stories, participants have five minutes to tell an intricate full story that sounds true but is clearly not. (Politicians and lawyers are not allowed to compete, as they're considered "too skilled" at lying.)

Hundreds of industry-specific awards shows are staged in England each year. They're all staged similarly, and if the people who make them are deemed to be good at it by their peers, they just might clean up at the **Awards Awards**. They're given out each July in a London ceremony with categories like "Best Development of an Existing Awards Event" and "Awards Event of the Year (Up to 600 Attendees)."

Chitwan Elephant and Tourism Festival in Nepal hosts the annual **Elephant Beauty Contest**. It's open only to female elephants, and it's intended as a publicity stunt as well as to encourage understanding of elephants and to create bonds between the animals and their handlers. The 2023 winner, Selfiekali, was 17 years old and was notable for her vibrant skin color and fluid movements. Her handlers won the equivalent of $112.

France's Cannes Film Festival is among the most prestigious in cinema, where major filmmakers and studios debut their latest works of art or potential commercial hits. Awards for achievement in screenwriting and acting are given out, including the Palme d'Or for best overall film. Since 2001, it has also awarded the best onscreen performance by a dog, the **Palm Dog Award**. One recent winner: Messi as Snoop in *Anatomy of a Fall*.

World's smallest drawbridge: the 56-centimeter Somerset Bridge in Bermuda.

PHRASE ORIGINS

If you're going through a weird or tough phrase, Uncle John is here to help you make sense of it all.

Phrase: Cute as a button

Meaning: Adorable

Origin: "It was originally 'bright as a button,' which originated in British English and was used to show something tiny and shiny or adorable. The phrase morphed into 'cute as a button' sometime during the late 1800s, and other phrases popped up with the same, or at least similar meanings like 'cute as a bug in a rig' or 'cute as a bug's ear.' Funnily enough, 'cute as a button' never did refer to an actual button but a flower bud." (From Grammarist)

Phase: Have a bone to pick

Meaning: A grievance or issue to address

Origin: "This phrase originated with Sicilian marriage feasts. When the festive wedding dinner was over, the bride's father would hand the bridegroom a bone and say, 'Pick this, for you have taken on a difficult task.' Then, in the presence of the wedding guests, the groom would 'pick the bone' while the bride looked on in silence and humility. Through this ritual the groom would publicly establish his authority over his wife and household. By 'picking the bone,' the young husband was granted the right to be the final and sole arbiter of all differences that might arise between the couple during their married life." (From *Common Phrases: And Where They Come From*, Second Edition, by Myron Korach)

Phrase: Here's mud in your eye

Meaning: Used as a toast expression

Origin: "The expression is not a toast to another; it is a toast to yourself—for it means, 'I hope I beat you.' The allusion is to a horse race. If the track is at all muddy the rider of the losing horse is very likely to get mud in his eye from the horse that is winning." (From *Dictionary of Word Origins* by Jordan Almond)

Phrase: Beyond the pale

Meaning: Out of bounds; beyond reproach

Origin: "The 'pale' in 'beyond the pale' is not the familiar adjective 'pale,' meaning 'dim or lacking color.' This 'pale' is a noun. It comes to us from Latin *palus*, a stake, and denotes a stake, post, fence, or other marker indicating the perimeter

of a territory or district, historically one under the protection of some army or government. For example, in the fourteenth century, the Pale referred to the areas in Ireland colonized by the British, and that which took place outside the Pale was beyond British jurisdiction. It later came to have the figurative meaning." (From *What in the Word?* by Charles Harrington Elster)

Phrase: Mosh pit

Meaning: An area near the stage at concerts where fans can run around and slam into each other

Origin: It was coined at a concert by Washington, D.C., punk rock band Bad Brains. "There was the song 'Banned in D.C.'—at the end of which the Brains would switch the gears of their revolutionary sound, causing the whole house to drastically change their slam tempo. Well, it was at some point in either late 1979 or early 1980 that H.R. of the Bad Brains yelled a Rasta/reggae inspired 'mash it-mash down Babylon!' Add a little Jamaican accent to the mix and the untrained ear hears 'mosh it-mosh down Babylon.'" (From *White Riot: Punk Rock and the Politics of Race,* edited by Stephen Duncombe and Maxwell Tremblay.) Those parts of songs became known as "mosh parts," which came to describe the areas where the frenetic dancing took place: "mosh pits."

Phrase: The whole shebang

Meaning: The whole thing

Origin: "Whatever its origin (possibly the Irish word *shebeen*), Walt Whitman made it clear what the word meant in 19th-century American in his *Specimen Days* (1862): 'Besides the hospitals, I also go occasionally on long tours through the camps, talking with the men. Sometimes at night among the groups around the fires, in their shebang enclosures of bushes.' Hence a type of rustic dwelling. But its meaning had clearly widened 10 years later. Mark Twain in *Roughing It* (1872) was using the word to mean a vehicle. By the end of the century shebang meant 'anything and everything.'" (From *Common Phrases...and the Amazing Stories Behind Them* by Max Cryer)

Phrase: Pipe dream

Meaning: An elaborate but far-fetched fantasy

Origin: "This phrase first popped up in the 19th century, with the earliest known documented case coming from the December of 1890 issue of the *Chicago Daily Tribune*, in this case referring to aerial navigation: 'It has been regarded as a pipe-dream for a good many years.' Yet another reference in *Chicago*, in September of 1895, demonstrates the true origin of phrase in terms of meaning, namely, as a reference to the dreams experienced when smoking opium." (From Today I Found Out)

It would take you around 18 months to walk atop the entire Great Wall of China.

KILLER, QUEEN

Queen Elizabeth II reigned over the United Kingdom for longer than any other monarch. She survived on the throne for 70 years...and survived multiple near-misses at the hands of strangers.

ATTACK #1: AUSTRALIA, 1970

Queen Elizabeth II and her husband, Prince Philip, visited Australia in 1970; on April 29, their itinerary called for them to travel from Sydney to Orange, New South Wales, via a train trip through the Blue Mountains. Just outside the town of Lithgow, eagle-eyed engineer Albert Rowley noticed a large log on the tracks. As security forces had checked the tracks an hour before the queen was supposed to come through, investigators determined that the log had been placed there intentionally in an effort to fatally derail the train. Whatever the case, Rowley acted quickly and pulled hard on the train's brakes, safely stopping the vehicle just before striking the log. Royals, police, and the media all agreed to a code of silence over the matter. The event wasn't publicly revealed until 2009, after a detective who worked the case retired and talked to a reporter. As the news unfolded, it was also discovered that the queen quietly and privately awarded Rowley an Imperial Service Medal in 1974, "in recognition of the meritorious service you have rendered."

ATTACK #2: TROOPING THE COLOUR, 1981

The annual Trooping the Colour ceremony takes place in London every June, commemorating the British sovereign's birthday. The event involves marching soldiers, marching bands, a flyover from Royal Air Force planes, and many participants on horseback. Queen Elizabeth II, an avid equestrienne, rode a horse in the 1981 Trooping the Color. As the queen slowly guided her animal through the parade grounds, a 17-year-old named Marcus Sarjeant emerged from the crowd and fired six shots at the monarch. The queen wasn't hit by any of those bullets, and, not wanting to rile up her horse or cause chaos around her, barely acknowledged the attack. There were a lot of police in the area, and while Queen Elizabeth kept her horse calm, a few officers quickly subdued and arrested Sarjeant, who served three years in prison.

ATTACK #3: NEW ZEALAND, 1981

Trooping the Colour wasn't the only attempt on the queen's life in 1981. During a tour of New Zealand in October 1981, Her Majesty visited Dunedin with Prince Philip. As her motorcade slowly drove through the downtown area, with the streets

lined with waving well-wishers, 17-year-old Christopher John Lewis camped out in a stall in a bathroom on the fifth floor of a nearby building. It gave him a clear view of the festivities as well as a clear shot. When the queen and her husband emerged from their Rolls-Royce, Lewis opened fire with a stolen .22 rifle. The bullet sailed over the royal couple and landed somewhere away from the masses. The queen had no idea someone had taken a shot at her, and the media were assured that what they'd heard were firecrackers. Lewis was imprisoned on firearms charges and spent time in prison and in psychiatric hospitals—from which he tried to escape in 1983, hoping to assassinate Prince Charles on another New Zealand visit.

ATTACK #4: THE QUEEN'S BEDROOM, 1982

In the summer of 1982, a 32-year-old British man named Michael Fagan twice breached all kinds of security measures at Buckingham Palace, the queen's official London residence. The first time, in June 1982, Fagan snuck into the building through a maid's bedroom window. Terrified, she sought out security, who didn't find anyone in her room and thought she was making it all up. That left Fagan able to walk around Buckingham Palace, which he did for a few hours before leaving, unnoticed by security. (He insists he peed on some bins labeled "corgi food" because he couldn't find a bathroom.) Then on July 9, 1982, he managed to make his way into the bedroom of Her Majesty. Somehow, he scaled the 14-foot-tall barbed-wire-topped railings surrounding the palace, climbed up a drainpipe, and managed to find the queen's bedroom; along the way, he'd found a glass ashtray, smashed it, and wielded a sharp chunk of glass as a weapon. As he opened the curtains around the queen's bed just past 7:00 a.m., Her Majesty woke up and calmly talked to Fagan, and managed to call for assistance. Fagan was briefly imprisoned in a mental health facility.

ATTACK #5: SAN FRANCISCO, 1983

Queen Elizabeth II died in September 2022; eight months later, the FBI declassified documents that detailed the foiling of an assassination plot during Her Majesty's March 1983 visit to California. The FBI heard chatter that the anti-U.K., anti-crown, pro-Ireland-unification Irish Republican Army was looking to assassinate the queen to send a message. In February 1983, a credible threat came in, when a San Francisco police officer told the FBI that a man claimed he planned to kill the queen to avenge the death of his daughter, killed by a purportedly non-fatal rubber bullet in a riot in U.K.-controlled Northern Ireland. Federal agencies had enough time to change their already elaborate security measures: for example, the FBI opted to close the walkways of the Golden Gate Bridge to make sure no armed pedestrians could watch as the queen's yacht arrived in San Francisco.

There are 41 independent cities in the U.S. not claimed by a county, and 38 of them are in Virginia.

THE MONKEY SELFIE AFFAIR

The bar probably isn't too high, but get ready for the most exciting copyright-law story you've ever read. Why is it so interesting, and why would you want to read it? Because it revolves around a wild monkey that took a picture of itself. Really.

Setting Up the Shot

In 2011, professional photographer David J. Slater left his home in Gloucestershire, England, and ventured to the Tangkoko-Batuangus Nature Reserve, situated on the island of Sulawesi in Indonesia. His mission: photograph critically endangered species in their natural habitat, and then distribute those images to raise awareness of their frightening plight. Slater spent three days in the jungles of the nature reserve, along with a guide and plenty of gear.

One day he set up a tripod to prepare for a shot. Then he turned his back and walked away for a minute to grab a piece of equipment. When Slater returned, he discovered that a group of crested black macaques had commandeered his camera. They seemingly knew what they were doing, because they managed to press down on the shutter button while the lens could capture multiple images. But the prize of the set was one well-framed, in-focus photograph. A male macaque, named Naruto by the reserve staff, looked into the camera with his wide, amber-colored eyes and his mouth open, exposing his teeth, as if he were smiling. Naruto the crested black macaque had snapped the pic himself—the first time we know of that a monkey did a "selfie."

Coming into Focus

Slater sent the photo to Caters News Agency, the service that regularly syndicates his work, and there was a lot of demand for the picture because of the story that went along with it. The image of Naruto, and the tale of how he took the photo of himself, was featured in dozens of major media outlets both print and online in Europe and the U.S., including the *Guardian*, the *Telegraph*, *Huffington Post*, and the *Washington Post*.

Naruto instantly became the most famous crested black macaque on the planet, so much so that his image—the one taken with Slater's camera—became the representative image of all macaques. At the end of 2011, an anonymous user of Wikipedia—an audience-generated, self-policed, and forever-growing database of all knowledge—placed the Naruto selfie on the entry for "macaque," among other pages. Wikipedia is strict about what images can be used on the site, as are the operators of its photo bank sibling site, Wikimedia Commons: only public domain or explicitly

A dessert found in Heilongjiang, China: hasma, made from rock sugar and frogs' fallopian tubes.

free-use images may appear. No copyrighted photos are allowed—and Slater's Naruto photo was one of those.

Let's Get Another One

Or was it? In early 2012, Slater petitioned parent company Wikimedia to remove the image from all of its sites. They complied and the photo was taken down, but then it was uploaded again, and stayed up, on Wikimedia Commons. Once again, Slater requested the image that was credited and copyrighted to him be removed. This time, Wikimedia refused, and they had some legal standing to back up their position.

Thus began a legal quagmire—Slater didn't *really* own the photo, according to Wikimedia, because he didn't take the picture. It may have been made with his camera, based on his setup, but Naruto clicked the shutter on the image of Naruto. If anyone could stake a claim to the photo, it would be the macaque...but that would be absurd and a moot point, per Wikimedia. "Monkeys don't own copyrights," chief communications officer Katherine Maher told reporters. "U.S. copyright law says that works that originate from a nonhuman source can't claim copyright."

If that's true, then that means Slater didn't have the copyright, but then neither did the macaque. By default, the photo then falls into the public domain, and is a copyright-free product, which is totally fine to post on Wikimedia Commons or Wikipedia.

Say Cheese

Slater and Wikimedia reached an impasse in their disagreement. For the better part of three years, Naruto's selfie floated around the internet via quasi-legal distribution. But then in 2015, the People for the Ethical Treatment of Animals, or PETA, got involved. The aggressive international animal rights organization filed a lawsuit—on behalf of Naruto.

While acknowledging that it was legally original and would set a precedent to have an animal claim copyright on media material, PETA's lawyers also tried to assert that at question was a simple case of intellectual property, and they were merely the first to ever argue that animals were entitled to intellectual property.

After two years of legal wrangling, the parties reached an out-of-court settlement. Courts couldn't find any basis in the law for giving rights to the photo over to the macaque, so the rights reverted to Slater, the photographer whose equipment was used to take the image. To settle the suit with PETA, however, he agreed to donate 25 percent of whatever revenues the Naruto selfie generates to Indonesian macaque protection charities.

* * *

"I wish I could see what my skull looks like. I bet it's crazy."

—Willem Defoe

Best-selling individual car in a single year in U.S. history: the 1965 Chevrolet Impala, with 1,074,925 sold.

BEHIND THE HITS

Another edition of a longtime Bathroom Reader favorite–the secret stories behind popular songs.

The Song: "Joy to the World" (1970)
The Artist: Three Dog Night
The Story: Country singer-songwriter Hoyt Axton was also a composer for hire, and in the 1960s, he was asked to write a song for a planned animated television special called *The Happy Song*. The production fell apart, so Hoyt was left with an anthemic pop-rock song he didn't think was right to record himself. But then he was asked to be the opening act on a tour with pop group Three Dog Night. That band employed a unique setup for the early 1970s—three lead singers who took turns performing covers or songs written entirely by outside songwriters. Axton offered "Joy to the World" to singers Chuck Negron, Danny Hutton, and Cory Wells, who didn't love it, but agreed to record it because they had an album due to Dunhill Records that was one track short. *Naturally* was released in 1970, with "Joy to the World" the tenth and final track and "One Man Band" selected as the lead-off single. "Joy to the World" took off only after Seattle disc jockey Larry Bergman played the song for a "deep cuts" hour, after which his station, KISW-FM, fielded dozens of appreciative phone calls. Within weeks, it was the #1 song in Seattle, and by the spring of 1971, it was #1 in the rest of the U.S., too.

The Song: "All That She Wants" (1993)
The Artist: Ace of Base
The Story: Consisting of three Berggren siblings and leader Ulf Ekberg, Ace of Base formed in Sweden in 1987. After scoring some local hits, the group wanted a new sound, just like the one behind a song called "Another Mother" by the singer Kayo. They figured out that a producer who called himself Denniz PoP had made the song, so in 1992 Ekberg sent him a demo of a song called "Mr. Ace." PoP habitually listened to demos on his car's tape deck during his daily commute to his studio, and upon listening to "Mr. Ace" didn't like it. But then the deck broke, and the tape wouldn't eject. PoP had to listen to "Mr. Ace" over and over, every day, to the point where he grew to actually love the song. He brought Ace of Base to his studio and had them rewrite and rerecord "Mr. Ace" as "All That She Wants," a hypnotic electro-pop song about a love 'em and leave 'em kind of woman. By the end of 1992, "All That She Wants" hit #2 in Denmark, and throughout 1993 it topped the charts across Europe. In the U.S., the song reached #2 and was the first of four smash singles from Ace of Base's dance-pop album *The Sign*, the top-selling disc of 1994.

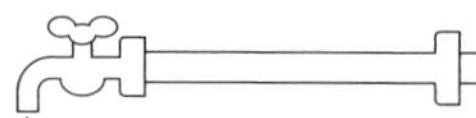

The Song: "Right Here Waiting" (1989)
The Artist: Richard Marx
The Story: In the afterglow of the success of his first hit single, 1987's "Don't Mean Nothing," singer-songwriter Richard Marx found himself painfully lonely for his then-fiancée and future wife, Cynthia Rhodes, thousands of miles away in South Africa filming a movie. "I had not seen her for a few months. But my visa application was rejected and when I came back I wrote this song which was more of a letter from me to her," Marx later said. It took him all of 20 minutes to write, and not much longer to record so he could send it to her. Months later, Marx received a request from Barbra Streisand. She wanted him to write her a surefire soft rock hit. He sent her a copy of "Right Here Waiting," because he found it too personal to ever release himself. Marx sent a tape to Streisand, who called him the next day and left a voicemail message—with some notes. While she thought the song was "beautiful," she requested a lyric change, insisting that she would never "be right here waiting for anyone!" The rejection made Marx realize he should record the song himself, and he did. Appearing on his second album, *Repeat Offender,* "Right Here Waiting" went to #1 in the summer of 1989.

The Song: "Wake Me Up When September Ends" (2004)
The Artist: Green Day
The Story: Jazz drummer and truck driver Andrew Armstrong died from esophageal cancer in September 1982. He left behind six children, including the youngest, 10-year-old Billie Joe Armstrong. In the midst of his profound grief, young Billie Joe dreaded the idea of returning to school so quickly after his father's death—he didn't want to be stared at as "that kid with the dead parent." He spent the first few weeks after the death in his room; when his family tried to get him to come out, he said, "Wake me up when September ends." The anniversary of his father's death more than 20 years later inspired Armstrong to write a rare ballad for his band, the mega-bestselling pop-punk group Green Day. "That song, I feel, was sort of a new breakthrough for me. I started thinking about how September is just really hard for everybody. The summer's over, a lot of people are going back to school, vacation's over, it's the beginning of the fall, everything is changing, it's getting colder out. And I think that's what that song means to me," Armstrong said. The fourth single off Green Day's *American Idiot,* "Wake Me Up When September Ends" peaked at #6 on the pop chart, a rare crossover hit for the rock band.

The Song: "These Boots Are Made for Walkin'" (1965)
The Artist: Nancy Sinatra
The Story: One of the original show business "nepo babies" (see page 283), Nancy

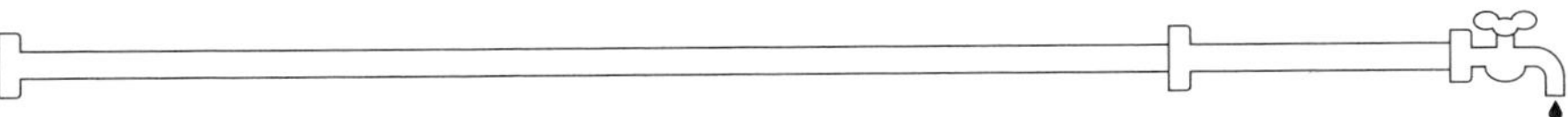

What did ancient Romans call the Colosseum? Nobody knows.

Sinatra was pushed hard by her father, beloved crooner and powerful music-industry figure Frank Sinatra. When he cofounded his own label, Reprise Records, in 1961, he signed his daughter and took out a full-page ad in *Billboard* to tout her first single. "Cufflinks and a Tie Clip" flopped, as did her next 15 singles; only "So Long Babe" charted, at a lowly #86 in 1965. Later that year, Sinatra connected with Lee Hazlewood, a gravelly voiced songwriter who wrote and performed dark and seedy country-tinged, drug-addled songs (notably "Some Velvet Morning"). Sinatra's pop sensibilities smoothed out Hazlewood's edges enough that he was able to write bubbly singles. Sinatra finally scored a hit in 1966 with "These Boots Are Made for Walkin'," a song written and produced by Hazlewood that referenced and helped popularize go-go boots while also serving as an anthem of female empowerment. Not so coincidentally: the titular line comes from *4 for Texas*, a 1963 Western in which Frank Sinatra's character says, "They tell me them boots ain't built for walkin'." The tune spent a week at the top of the charts.

The Song: "Sailing" (1980)
The Artist: Christopher Cross
The Story: Cross spent a lot of his summers as a teenager in San Antonio, Texas, messing around on a sailboat with a friend, which he found to be a relaxing and centering experience. A decade or so later, he thought it might make a nice meditative song. "I was just at home sitting in this cheap apartment, sitting at the table. I remember coming up with the verse and chorus, and the lyrics to the first verse of the chorus all came out," Cross later said. But then—nothing. It took him two years of thinking and experimentation for the rest of the song to come together. By that time, he'd been signed by Warner Bros., and he finished "Sailing" (and its complicated, classical-esque bridge) just in time to include it on his debut, self-titled album. "Sailing," a very smooth and laidback song about being on a boat, went to #1 in 1980 and propelled Cross to instant mega-stardom. At the 1981 Grammys, he won all four major categories—Album of the Year, Best New Artist, and both Song and Record of the Year—for "Sailing."

* * *

A TRAGIC ORIGIN OF A SILLY THING

"Mooning," the practice of exposing one's rear end to others in a comical manner, gets its name from the fact that most people pull the prank at night, showing off their bare behind to the moon. The first recorded incident of mooning, unnamed at the time, came in AD 80. While Jewish pilgrims had gathered in Rome-controlled Jerusalem to celebrate Passover, a Roman soldier standing guard nearby exposed his bottom to them in derision. This created outrage, which turned to panic, which turned to a military crackdown on the city that left 30,000 people dead.

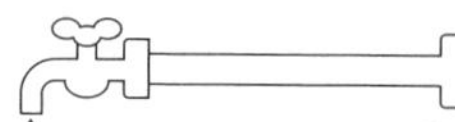

Only legal ban on driving without shoes in the U.S.: motorcycle riders in Alabama have to wear them.

HOLES IN THE STORY

There are holes in all of these stories. All of these stories are about the ill-advised digging of dangerous and unnecessary holes.

LAND HO

Police in Ledyard, Connecticut, answered a call one Saturday morning in January 2024 from a family complaining that a neighbor had dug several large and deep holes in their front yard and wouldn't stop or leave the premises. Authorities arrived to find 62-year-old Mark Uterstaedt using a rock rake to clear dirt, which he then swung at the resident who called the police on him. Uterstaedt explained that he owned the entire neighborhood and that he was preventing the family from installing an unauthorized water line. But he'd previously told the residents that he believed them to be pirates, and that he wanted the treasure he suspected they'd buried in the yard. Uterstaedt was charged with risk of injury, second-degree threatening, fourth-degree criminal mischief, breach of peace, and trespassing.

WHAT A GAS HOLE

In 2018, a seemingly bottomless hole appeared virtually overnight in Russia's Siberia. Local news footage of the ominous hole went viral around the world, and social media users proposed many theories about the origins of the crater, with the most common ideas being that it was from an alien attack, or a meteor that hit the Earth without any sort of space-monitoring agency noticing. Both are unlikely, but at any rate, it felt apocalyptic or a sign of the end times to many—it didn't help that the crater was located just outside the village of Yamal, whose name translates to "end of the world." Since that time, eight total holes have been discovered in the same Siberian region. Scientists' most plausible theory is that the holes are caused by gas explosions beneath the permafrost.

FALL IN BUFFALO

During the 2023–24 NFL season, the Buffalo Bills played their home games at Highmark Stadium. Right next to that venue was the site of the Bills' future home, New Highmark Stadium, which was under construction. The two properties were separated by a fence, and in September 2023, a few hours before the first Bills game

Fastest gun in Hollywood in the golden age of Westerns: Glenn Ford. He could draw and shoot in 0.4 seconds.

of the year, a 29-year-old male fan (who understandably remained anonymous in news reports) showed up and jumped the fence to explore the active construction site. Then he fell into a 40-feet-deep hole. It took authorities 20 minutes to extract the man, who called for help and was heard by passersby. He suffered only a forehead cut and was found to be under the influence of alcohol, LSD, cocaine, and marijuana. The individual was also nude and covered in human waste, which he attributed to mismanaging a portable toilet he found on the construction site before his accidental descent.

IT'S GOING DOWN

Conceptual artist Anish Kapoor created *Descent into Limbo*, an optical illusion installation at the Serralves Foundation museum in Porto, Portugal, in 1992. Intended to make viewers contemplate nothingness and the mysteries of life, the piece consists of an eight-feet-deep hole painted over with black pigment to create an optical illusion that looks exactly like a big cartoon circle—something that Elmer Fudd or Wile E. Coyote would be tricked into walking into and hurting themselves. And that's what happened to a 60-year-old Italian man who took in *Descent into Limbo* in 2018. He literally and momentarily descended into limbo when he somehow walked up to the pit, set off with caution signs and watched over by a security guard. He then fell into the hole, was removed, and then briefly hospitalized to treat his injuries.

SHAFT: CAN YOU DIG IT?

João Pimenta da Silva, a 71-year-old resident of Minas Gerais, Brazil, spent the entire calendar year of 2023 digging a massively deep shaft through and underneath his kitchen floor. Why? He was convinced by a dream that valuable stores of gold ore were buried there, just waiting to be found. He spent whole days digging the shaft, and he paid local workers to help him excavate using homemade tools that Silva built himself out of the few repurposed household objects he didn't sell to fund the project. By January 2024, Silva's hole had become a tunnel, about three feet wide and stretching 130 feet underground. A neighbor advised him to stop digging, but Silva carried on, stopping only when he fell off the access seat—made from a child's swing—while trying to remove mud and groundwater from the shaft. Authorities retrieved Silva's corpse, then complimented the deceased man on his work. "This tunnel looks like something alien, with the perfection with which he dug it: very small diameter, very perfect cylinder," fire brigade sergeant Luís Filipe de Miranda told reporters.

Most-recorded Christmas song: "Silent Night," with 137,000 versions.

Q&A: ASK THE EXPERTS

More questions and answers from the world's top science and trivia experts.

ALL THERE IN BLACK AND WHITE

Q: *Why do salt and pepper come as a pair?*

A: "Salt and pepper were fated to end up together inevitably, but it was a Frenchman, François Pierre La Varenne, France's first celebrity chef and a royal chef to Louis XIV, who encouraged folks to combine the seasonings in the 17th century. It was said that King Louis XIV was a picky eater and didn't want seasonings to overpower the taste of his food. The pairing was a smash hit because pepper was the only spice that complemented salt and didn't dominate the taste. The use of salt and pepper as tableside condiments has since spread throughout Europe and the Americas, though it's quite uncommon in Asia where soy sauce, fish sauce, and oyster sauce are predominantly used as a sodium source." (From *Allrecipes*)

HEAR YE, HEAR YE

Q: *Why do so many newspapers call themselves "Post"?*

A: "'Oyez, oyez, oyez!' It would however have been a common cry on the streets of medieval England. 'Oyez' (pronounced 'oh yay') comes from the French *ouïr* ('to listen') and means 'Hear ye.' The town crier would begin his cry with these words, accompanied by the ringing of a large hand bell to attract attention. It was the job of the crier or bellman to inform the townspeople of the latest news, proclamations, bylaws, and any other important information, as at this time most folk were illiterate and could not read. Having read out his message, the town crier would then attach it to the door post of the local inn, so 'posting a notice,' the reason why newspapers are often called 'The Post.'" (From *Historic UK*)

CUTE AS A BUTTON

Q: *Why are the buttons on men's shirts and women's shirts sewn into different sides?*

A: "In the Renaissance and through the Victorian era, women—particularly wealthy women—wore elaborate items and often enjoyed the luxury of being dressed by a servant. In that case, it was easier for the assistant to have the buttons on the right side (when facing the woman being dressed) with the assumption that the servant was right-handed, as most people were believed to be. Men usually dressed themselves, hence the buttons on the other side." (From *Mental Floss*)

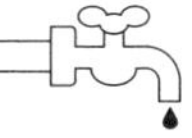

If you're a Buddhist monk and a woman, you're not allowed to eat garlic.

MELLOW YELLOW

Q: *Why is urine yellow?*

A: "Urine is the finale of our body's natural drainage system. It's made out of excess water and waste products filtered out of our blood via the kidneys. Some of these waste products are created when our cells reach the end of their life cycle, including the red blood cells that use hemoglobin to deliver oxygen throughout the body. An important compound produced by red blood cells is *heme,* the precursor to hemoglobin, and the eventual degradation of red blood cells and their heme results in a chain of events that causes urine to be yellow. When red blood cells degrade after their six-month lifespan, a bright orange pigment called bilirubin is produced as a byproduct. Once in the gut, the resident flora can convert bilirubin into a molecule which can turn yellow if exposed to oxygen. This molecule, urobilin, is a major reason why urine is yellow." (From *Gizmodo*)

DRYLY STATED

Q: *Why is it considered unlucky to open an umbrella indoors?*

A: "In 18th-century London, when metal-spoked waterproof umbrellas began to become a common rainy-day sight, their stiff, clumsy spring mechanism made them veritable hazards to open indoors. A rigidly spoked umbrella, opening suddenly in a small room, could seriously injury an adult or a child, or shatter a frangible object. Even a minor accident could provoke unpleasant words of a serious quarrel, themselves strokes of bad luck in a family or among friends. Thus, the superstition arose as a deterrent to opening an umbrella indoors." (From *Panati's Extraordinary Origins of Everyday Things* by Charles Panati)

BURNING QUESTION

Q: *What happens to the rubber that gets worn off tires?*

A: "The amount of rubber whittled off by the friction between tire and pavement: about a third of an inch of tire every 40,000 miles. Where does all this rubber actually go? After these particles become airborne, one of two things might happen to them. In their tireless search for a second home, the newly formed pieces of rubber are either ground into the road or deposited in street gutters and eventually washed into the nearest river or sewage treatment plant." (From *Why Do Men Have Nipples?* by Mark Leyner and Billy Goldberg)

WE STAN IT

Q: *Why do the names of so many countries end in "-stan"?*

A: "The *-stan* suffix, and also *sta* and *-istan,* occur in various languages as markers of

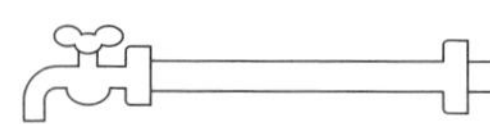

The military makes $100 million each year from slot machines used by its personnel overseas.

place. In Persian and Urdu, *-stan* means 'where one stands' or 'place of.' The Indo-European root word *sta* is used to signify 'stands' and 'settlement' and this root still appears in Russian. The construction *-istan* appears in Persian and means 'land.' So, the word Tajikistan means essentially 'land of the Tajiks.'" (From *Encyclopedia Britannica*)

A FRESH ANSWER

Q: *Why does mint taste and feel "cold"?*

A: "Our nervous system is built to sense changes in temperatures—a whole set of nerves running from our skin to the brain is dedicated to conveying just that information. The receptor protein that senses the change in temperature is called TRPM8 and it is found in all cold-sensing nerve cells. Falling temperatures is not the only factor that switches on TRPM8, though. A waxy crystalline organic chemical, called menthol, found in peppermint and other mint oils, can somehow bind to TRPM8 directly and activate it. Peppermint drops fire up TRPM8 in cold-sensing nerves and make your mouth instantly feel cool." (From The Conversation)

UNDERNEATH IT ALL

Q: *Why do boxer shorts just have a small opening while men's briefs have a more complex series of pull-apart folds?*

A: "Even though most briefs and boxers sold in the U.S. are made out of the same material (cotton-polyester blends), briefs are knitted and boxers are woven. The two techniques yield different wear characteristics. Boxers are built for comfort and won't stretch unless elasticized bands are added. Briefs are intended as support garments and are designed to stretch. Without all the reinforcements, the opening on briefs would tend to gape open at embarrassing and unfortunate times." (From *Are Lobsters Ambidextrous?* by David Feldman)

THIS IS THE END

Q: *Why do Americans call the final letter of the alphabet Z but other English-speaking countries call it "zed"?*

A: "Zed is the eldest. It comes from the Greek and Latin 'zeta,' meaning 'z,' and the French word for the same letter, 'zède.' It appeared in print for the first time in the early 1400s in a Middle English manuscript. Zee, on the other hand, entered English as a 17th-century variant of zed. Its first known appearance is in the 1677 textbook, *A New Spelling Book*. The book eventually made its way to the British colonies in America. This pronunciation was thought to be influenced by the *bee, cee, dee, eee* pattern of the rest of the alphabet. When the 'Alphabet Song' was copyrighted in Boston in 1835, 'zee' was used to rhyme with 'me.' Since then, zee has become the American standard." (From Ellii)

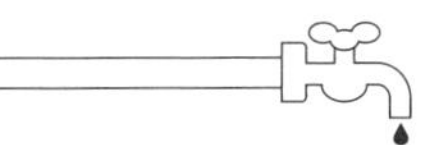

In the 1920s, Theodore Roosevelt's sons became the first Westerners to shoot a panda.

WHERE ARE ALL THE ALIENS?

What's the biggest thing in the universe? Space. It's full of billions of planets stretching out in every direction, and yet we've never encountered any definitive evidence of other advanced civilizations or even any life. Various scientific disciplines—and some obscure communities, too—all have their theories as to why we haven't yet made contact.

Aliens, or life-forms from other planets in microbial- or bacterial-type forms, are buried deep within oceans. Sound crazy? Many of the moons of the other planets in the solar system may contain oceans beneath their surfaces, and those could very well be a place where some kind of life once did, or continues to, thrive.

In astronomy, a super-Earth is any planet with a mass as much as ten times that of Earth. Studies indicate that some may have liquid water, and if other Earth-like conditions are met, they could foster life. The problem with these planets is that they're so large that they'd have an escape velocity nearly twice that of Earth—making it nearly physically impossible for any alien astronauts to leave.

A contingent of futurists thinks that there's a reason why human instruments have picked up mysterious radio signals from deep space—the aliens out there are electronic beings, or robots created by long-ago disappeared biological races. This theory also holds that if all aliens are robots, then they don't live on planets habitable like Earth, but on planets closer to galaxy centers, because those have the most energy (and robots *love* energy).

On Earth, we know from survival of the fittest that those bent on expansion and survival continue on that path unabated. Some scientists theorize that the same thing could happen on a cosmic level. As humans explore space, we get closer to finding other races who are also exploring space, and that's a collision waiting to happen. Or, possibly, we haven't even noticed that we've always destroyed relics and representatives of other civilizations as our machines float through space and explore distant worlds.

Earth is potentially facing climate change issues that could one day end all life. Some astrophysicists theorize that other alien races already met this fate. If climate change

World's oldest casino: the Casino di Venezia in Venice, Italy, opened in 1638 and remains operational.

were an end result of a technologically advanced population, then any others out there somewhere could have eradicated themselves with climate change on their own planets.

While scientists have discovered lots of potentially habitable planets, those planets may have experienced life come and go. There may have once been aliens on those planets but they evolved, lived, and died out well before we humans back on Earth could find them and make contact.

According to a fringe scientific theory called the panspermia hypothesis, the aliens have already arrived, and they are us. Theorists hold that all life on Earth didn't originate here, but was seeded and left to grow millions of years ago accidentally from bacteria that found their way onto meteors that crashed here.

In 1973, an MIT astronomer published an essay stating that the lack of alien evidence isn't because there aren't any aliens, but because the aliens out there are so much more advanced than us that they are respectfully, patronizingly, leaving us alone. We're like pets or zoo animals to them, and our part of the universe is off-limits to at least one advanced race who watch us like Earth is some kind of zoo.

A 2022 essay by Hebrew University of Jerusalem researcher Amri Wandel suggests that there's a large interplanetary community somewhere out there that may be receiving our signals, but doesn't have the technological capabilities to respond. Despite how advanced their technology may be, those alien civilizations still have to deal with the same boring problems we do here on Earth, like energy storage and time management. It's easier to receive a transmission than it is to send one back, so the aliens may be hearing us, but aren't able to send any messages in return.

Similar to Wandel's theory is one published in 2023 by the Laboratory of Statistical Biophysics at the École Polytechnique Fédérale de Lausanne in Switzerland. There are aliens out there, and they may have the technology to receive our transmission—and they may be responding. However, these advanced worlds might have been keeping up alien communications stations for centuries. Humanity has only been broadcasting into space for about 60 years, and we may not yet have the technology to receive alien transmissions, let alone understand them, so we're currently in a silent "bubble" where we can't hear back.

The most likely and logical theory is perhaps the obvious one. Sure, in a massive, ever-expanding universe where things are getting farther and farther away, there are many planets where life is possible and probable. We may just not have found them yet in this universe-level needle-in-a-haystack style of searching—or they're so far away we might *never* get close.

A single bear in Yellowstone National Park can eat up to 40,000 moth grubs every day.

WEIRD MEDICAL CONDITIONS

It's amazing—and sometimes creepy—what can happen to the human body. Here are some strange-but-true tales from the BRI's medical files.

The Bionic Girl

Patient: Olivia Farnsworth, a teenager from England

Symptoms: Olivia's mother, Niki Trepak, knew something was off when Olivia never cried as a baby. Nor was she interested in breastfeeding, and she slept less and less as she entered toddlerhood. Trepak finally decided to take Olivia to a doctor to figure out why she doesn't feel pain, she's never hungry, and she rarely sleeps.

Diagnosis: Specialists eventually diagnosed Olivia as one of only about 100 people in the world with a genetic abnormality known as "chromosome six deletion," marked by "a missing copy of the genetic material located on the short arm (p) of chromosome six." Olivia is the only known patient who has all three symptoms together.

As with all sufferers of this disorder, Olivia was developmentally delayed, which made it difficult for her mom to raise her: "She had no sense of danger." In 2016, when Olivia was seven, she was run over by a car and "dragged about 10 car lengths down the road," said Trepak. "It was horrendous. I don't think it's something I will ever get over." Not only did Olivia not complain; she barely got hurt—just a few scratches and tire marks on her chest. Doctors chalked it up to the fact the "bionic girl," as the press had dubbed her, didn't tense up when the car first hit her.

Outcome: There's no cure for chromosome six deletion, so Olivia's condition can only be managed. She has trained herself to eat, and she takes medication to help her sleep. Perhaps under the right set of circumstances, she'll become a superhero.

Taylor Didn't Know

Patient: Marie Trainer of Canton, Ohio

Symptoms: In May 2019, a few days after returning from a Caribbean vacation to the Dominican Republic, Trainer started feeling too bad to go to work. She had nausea, soreness in her back, and her body temperature was fluctuating. When she began to get disoriented, she was taken to the emergency room. There, her skin became a "purplish-red color" and started to show signs of gangrene. Then Trainer fell into a coma.

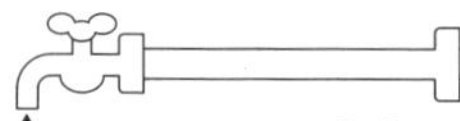

Diagnosis: The medical team knew she had an infection, which they first assumed she'd brought back from the tropics, but a series of tests revealed that the culprit was a lot closer to home: her dog, Taylor. The German shepherd puppy greeted Trainer with licks, one of them over a "slightly infected open wound" on Trainer's arm. The resulting bacterial infection, *Capnocytophaga canimorsus*, found only in dog and cat saliva, is extremely rare, with fewer than 500 confirmed cases since the 1960s. Because the bacteria had spread so quickly, Trainer's family was informed that she could either lose her extremities...or her life. A second opinion by another doctor came to the same conclusion.

Outcome: After 10 days in a coma, Trainer awoke with her husband, Matt, at her side. Through tears, he told her that her legs had been amputated just above the knees, and her arms just below the elbows. All she could say at first was, "Why did you let me live?"

But with the strong support of her family and the Canton community where she owns a hair salon, along with financial help from a GoFundMe campaign, within eight months Trainer was learning to walk on prosthetic legs, with prosthetic hands on the way. Even though the surgeon, Dr. Ajay Seth, couldn't save most of Trainer's legs, he concentrated on her arms. After removing 40 to 50 blood clots, "I was able to save every nerve, every muscle so she can literally put on prosthetics, and she'll be able to move her fingers just like she normally did."

As of last report, Trainer was well on the road to recovery. And she doesn't blame Taylor—the dog even got to visit her at the hospital. "That just put the biggest smile on my face."

Pearls of Wisdom (Teeth)

Patient: Ravindran, a seven-year-old boy from southern India

Symptoms: For four years, Ravindran had swelling in his mouth, but dentists were having a tough time figuring out why because the boy wasn't being "cooperative," according to reports. The boy's pain kept worsening. Then, in 2019, the swelling in his jaw increased and a large lesion formed in his mouth. Fearing cancer, his parents took him to a dental college where he received X-rays and a CT scan.

Diagnosis: The swelling wasn't cancer: it was teeth. Due to a rare condition called *compound composite odontom*, a five-inch-long "bag-like tumor" full of teeth had been growing inside Ravindran's jaw—"small, medium, and large teeth," said the surgeon, Dr. P. Senthilnathan, who described them as "reminiscent of pearls in an oyster."

Outcome: Ravindran is pain free, with a normal set of chompers. A few similar cases have been documented but never with that many teeth—526 in total. That nearly doubles the previous record holder, a Mumbai 17-year-old who had 232 teeth removed in 2014.

Afraid of your mother-in-law? That's called *pentheraphobia.*

Ghost Boy

Patient: Martin Pistorius of South Africa

Symptoms: Imagine being aware of your surroundings but not being able to move or speak. Everyone thinks you're a "vegetable," but you can hear them talking to you and about you! Now, imagine that going on for more than a decade.

It all started in 1987, when Martin was 12 years old. He came down with the flu, or so doctors thought, but it kept getting worse. He began to lose motor function and eventually fell into a coma.

When Martin was 16, he began to regain awareness, but he couldn't move or speak. It took about three years to fully regain consciousness. He'd later describe it "like when you are trying to wake up from a dream, but can't." Martin could see and hear people in his room but couldn't speak to them. As the years passed, he was aware of everything going on around him, without any way to express himself. Because the special care center where Martin spent his days assumed he was in a vegetative state, he spent much of his time parked in front of a television playing episodes of *Barney & Friends* on repeat. But he was awake, and miserable. "I cannot even express to you how much I hated Barney."

Then, when he was 25 and had spent nine years without anyone realizing his mind was active and aware, a caregiver finally noticed that his eyes were reacting to her words.

Diagnosis: Doctors had originally diagnosed Martin with a neurodegenerative disease that left him unaware of his surroundings, but after being assessed at a specialized communication center, Martin was upgraded from "vegetative state" to "total locked-in syndrome."

Outcome: Within a year and a half of the communication assessment, he'd improved to the point where he could "speak" using a computer. After a few more years, Pistorius gained most—but not all—of his functions back. He still requires a wheelchair and speaks through a computer. But he's a happily married computer scientist living in England. He cowrote a book about his experience called *Ghost Boy*. "I was lost in the land where dragons lie and no one could rescue me."

* * *

#UNFORTUNATE_HASHTAG

Way back in 2012, when people were still getting the hang of hashtags, British singer Susan Boyle's record label promoted an album release party with #Susanalbumparty. If you can't see how that could otherwise be read, you're in the minority ("Su's Anal Bum Party"). The hashtag was swiftly changed to the much less funny #Susanboylealbumparty.

BETTER EATING THROUGH SCIENCE

Here are the origin stories of some very popular foods that wouldn't even exist were it not for breakthroughs in modern science and engineering.

HOT POCKETS

In the 1970s, brothers Paul and David Merage fled their home nation of Iran and settled in Colorado, where they created Chef America, a company that would make frozen convenience foods. It was such a successful venture that they'd only ever need to make two products. After a false start with a flop called Toaster Pizza, the Merages devised the Tastywich. A handheld, rectangular calzone-style sandwich, its dough was specially formulated to cook in the newfangled breakthrough kitchen gadget called the microwave. The turnover-like pastry, filled with pizza ingredients or with ham and cheese, was encased in a paperboard sleeve lined with metallic film called a susceptor, which absorbs the microwave's electromagnetic energy and converts it into infrared thermal radiation, quickly heating the food. (The industry name for the device: a microwavable crisping sleeve.) Capitalizing on the wide adoption of microwaves, the Tastywich didn't really become a blockbuster until the Merages changed the name of the product to Hot Pockets. In the 1980s and 1990s, they introduced more than 50 kinds of Hot Pockets (plus a variant with pretzel bread, breakfast versions, and lower-fat Lean Pockets), selling the whole company to Nestlé in 2002 for $2.6 billion.

POP ROCKS

In 1953, General Foods acquired the rights to Kool-Aid. Three years later, the company tasked staff scientist William Mitchell with improving the powdered drink mix—to make it carbonated, so that when water and sugar were added, it would instantly make soda. To do that meant inserting and stabilizing carbon dioxide (the substance that makes the bubbles) into powdered, solid granules. Mitchell couldn't crack it, however, and his experiments consistently wound up taking the form of tiny, crystal-like rocks. He decided to eat the stuff, along with some sugar, and realized he'd made a candy that popped and sizzled as it dissolved on the tongue—the water in saliva heating the carbon dioxide to cause a chemical reaction. After adding sugar into the recipe, Mitchell perfected what would come to be called Pop Rocks. General Foods received a patent in 1961 but didn't release Pop Rocks on the market until 1976. It was so new and different that it flopped, with sales hurt by an urban legend

Eat up: there's no federal law against cannibalism, and only Idaho has a state law prohibiting ingesting human flesh.

that the mysterious new candy was responsible for the death of "Mikey," the young Life cereal pitchman. Pop Rocks went off the market in 1983, before candy company Zeta Espacial licensed the name and tech in the late 1980s and brought it back.

DIPPIN' DOTS

Microbiologist Curtis Jones was supposed to be formulating a way to use enzymes and flash-freezing technology to make a more nutritionally dense and efficient cattle feed. But at a lab in Paducah, Kentucky, in 1988, he stumbled on a new and novel way to present ice cream. After he plunged cattle feed into a liquid nitrogen–cooled vessel at a temperature of –350°F, he found that the treatment turned the fodder into pellets. A big ice cream aficionado, Jones wondered what would happen if he tossed a couple of scoops into the liquid nitrogen. It also emerged in the form of rock-solid beads, which, when placed into the mouth, instantly melted. After tweaking the recipe and the preparation, and realizing that the pelletized ice cream functioned best when created at –40°F, Jones started a company out of the garage of his parents' home in Illinois to make Dippin' Dots. Because Dippin' Dots require ultra-low temperatures for storage and transport, grocery stores and ice cream parlors weren't equipped to sell the treat, so Jones approached outdoor locations where special, standalone freezers could keep his product intact. The first of many amusement parks to carry Dippin' Dots, in 1989, was Opryland USA. Eventually sold in thousands of locations, Jones's company went bankrupt in 2011, and it's now operated by J&J Snack Foods.

COOL WHIP

In 1966, General Foods executives asked William Mitchell (yep, the same guy who invented Pop Rocks) to create an alternative to whipped cream. At the time, home cooks who wanted whipped cream had to prep cream by hand or via an expensive electric mixer, and research suggested Americans wanted a more convenient option—one that was more transportable, durable, and shelf-stable than heavy whipping cream. After tinkering in a lab for months, Mitchell devised the recipe for what would be marketed as Cool Whip, an artificial whipped cream–like dessert topping made up of chemicals to approximate the dairy product. It's a careful combination of water, corn syrup (for sweetness), hydrogenated oils (mimicking the fat from dairy), polysorbate 60 (to keep everything mixed), xanthan and guar gum (thickening agents), sorbitan monostearate (to keep everything in solid form), and sodium caseinate (to prevent the oils and water from separating). While marketed as a non-dairy product, Cool Whip always contained the milk protein called casein, and since 2010, it's made with skim milk and a trace of cream. Sold frozen and intended to be defrosted before use, 200 million tubs of Cool Whip sell each year.

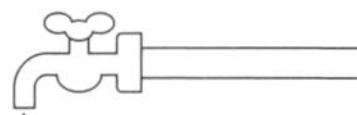

Until post-9/11 rules were changed, a four-inch knife could be present in a carry-on bag.

CAKE, ZAMPS, AND HOOP-LA

Step right up and win a prize! (The prize is this page of carnival worker slang.)

The show: What carnival workers call the traveling carnival.

24-hour man: The worker who moves on early to the next show spot to put up advertisements and directional arrows to guide the many carnival trucks where to travel.

Arch: The front entrance of a carnival.

Backyard: Where the carnival workers keep their tents, trailers, and personal living spaces.

Carny: A derisive term for a carnival worker—they call themselves "showmen"—used to denote untrustworthy ride operators.

Ride jock: A ride operator.

Talker: A worker who yells an elaborate spiel to get people into a ride or attraction is called a talker, not a barker. If he talks inside the ride or attraction, the talker is a lecturer.

Roughies: Carnival managers.

A&S man: An age-and-scale operator, or the "guess your age and weight" guy.

Butcher: A refreshment salesperson who wanders around the carnival selling sodas, candy, and pretzels.

Bozo: The person who sits in the dunk tank and yells insults at potential customers to try to get them to pay to dunk him.

Mark: A customer or carnival victim about to be cheated out of their money.

Mooch: An especially dumb or easy-to-fool mark.

Cake: Money made specifically by shortchanging customers.

Cowboy: A local ne'er-do-well who shows up at the carnival to make trouble.

Peek his poke: When a carnival worker tries to get a glimpse of a customer's wallet or bankroll to see how much money they can cheat the customer out of.

Punks: Children.

Eli: The Ferris wheel, which used to be made by the Eli Bridge Company.

Zamps: Kiddie rides, which used to be made by the Zamperla Rides Company.

Glass house: A hall of mirrors.

Jenny: The merry-go-round.

Hanky-pank: A midway game where every player always wins a prize—with prizes so cheap that the attraction still makes a huge profit.

Handle: The specific method by which a game is rigged.

Hoop-la: The ring toss game, where players throw hoops over a prize atop a wooden block—and the ring is always smaller than the block, making it impossible to win.

Shake machine: A ride designed to get loose change to fall out of customers' pockets, which the ride operator gets to keep.

Flukum: Snow cone syrup.

Rag: The cheap prizes customers actually win, which aren't displayed.

The Earl of Sandwich restaurant chain was founded by the 11th Earl of Sandwich, direct descendant of the man who popularized the food.

DEAD LITERARY GENRES

What people like to consume as entertainment is always changing. Collective taste in everything evolves, even books. (Except for Uncle John's Bathroom Reader. We've been here forever and always will be.) Here are some of the most popular genres of books from the past 200 years...that have been largely forgotten and just don't sell anymore.

Genre: Robinsonade
Details: Daniel Defoe's *Robinson Crusoe* (1719) was one of the first novels written in the English language, and it proved so popular that it helped establish long-form fiction as a viable style of book. *Robinson Crusoe* was so original and captivating that it launched a cottage industry of other writers telling much the same story. *Robinson Crusoe* is a high-seas, first-person adventure about an Englishman who gets shipwrecked on a desert island and wills himself to survive by living off the land. He also exploits the natives, and the survival story and romanticization of colonization proved irresistible for the readers of hundreds of exotic island-set "Robinsonades" in the 1700s and 1800s.
Examples: *The Swiss Family Robinson* by Johann David Wyss (1812); *The Mysterious Island* by Jules Verne (1875)

Genre: Travelogue
Details: In the 1880s, Robert Louis Stevenson became a popular adventure novelist with classic works like *Treasure Island* and *Kidnapped*. His fictional stories were informed by his actual travels around the globe in the previous decades, experiences he turned into several best-selling travelogues. Not dissimilar from today's travel TV shows, long-form printed travelogues detailed the life and looks of faraway lands and cultures, before the advent of practical photography rendered such thorough and descriptive books obsolete. Stevenson's first book, *An Inland Voyage* (1878), breathlessly describes the author's unique trip through France and Belgium—in a canoe—and *Travels with a Donkey in the Cevennes* (1879) recounts a voyage through a large national park in France (with a donkey).
Examples: *Travels in America* by Thomas Ashe (1808); *Recollections of the Last Ten Years* by Timothy Flint (1826)

Genre: Social novel
Details: The Industrial Revolution rapidly altered the reality of life in England in the early 1800s. Factories presented job opportunities and urban living for millions, but the suddenly overcrowded and polluted cities made humanists and writers of

the time take notice. The social novel developed in the 1830s and 1840s as a way to expose social ills, such as the plight of the working poor, child labor, child abuse, and pollution. These melodramatic, harrowing, fictionalized depictions of real-world issues raised awareness for these causes and inspired people to lobby for governmental and factory reform.

Examples: *Alton Locke* by Charles Kingsley (1850) shows the brutal life of sweatshop workers; *Shirley* by Charlotte Brontë (1849) details a worker rebellion in a textile mill; Charles Dickens became one of the best-selling writers and most famous people in the world thanks to his novels' depictions of bleakness and strife, including *Oliver Twist* (1838), *Bleak House* (1852), and *Hard Times* (1854).

Genre: Biblical epic

Details: Historical novels have been consistently popular with readers for a century. They make history come alive by telling the stories of fictional characters set against a backdrop of real and important events. In the late 19th century, one of the top-selling fiction styles was an offshoot of the historical novel: the biblical epic. At a time when the United States was predominantly Christian and churchgoing, readers loved novels that took place during events chronicled in the Bible. Main characters were usually fictional, but they interacted with figures familiar from history or who are prominent in the Bible. Not long after its release in 1880, *Ben-Hur: A Tale of the Christ* surged past Harriet Beecher Stowe's *Uncle Tom's Cabin* to become the best-selling novel in American history, and would later be adapted into a blockbuster 1925 silent film and a 1960 Oscar-winning remake. *Ben-Hur* follows the life of a 1st-century Jewish slave turned champion chariot racer named Judah Ben-Hur whose life runs parallel to that of Jesus.

Examples: *Quo Vadis* by Henryk Sienkiewicz was the best-selling book in the U.S. in 1897, and the fifth best-selling in the U.S. in 1898.

Genre: Edisonade

Details: Before science-fiction was established as a genre with its own known tropes, a quirky precursor sprung up, inspired by a wildly popular, prolific, and influential inventor whose work must have felt magical to the world at large in the late 19th and early 20th centuries. The work of Thomas Edison, creator and perfector of so many technologies, gave rise to a collection of novels that critics decades later would label Edisonades. Cheaply produced and sold for a nickel to an audience of kids and teenagers, Edisonades almost exclusively star a young male American inventor who uses his grit, determination, and uncanny engineering skills to create devices big and small with which he saves himself (and the world) from nefarious Europeans.

Examples: *The Steam Man of the Prairies* by Edward S. Ellis (1868); the Tom Edison Jr. books by Philip Reade (1891–92).

First sci-fi movie—and last X-rated movie—to earn an Oscar nomination for Best Picture: *A Clockwork Orange* (1971).

50 SHADES OF GREEN

According to Kermit the Frog, it ain't easy being green. But that's OK, he sings, because green is "the color of spring"; it's "cool and friendly-like" and "big like an ocean, or important like a mountain, or tall like a tree." Here are some verdant facts about this versatile color.

- Our prehistoric ancestors ate plants to survive, but distinguishing between similar-looking leaves could be difficult...and deadly. Natural selection favored the early primates that had a third cone cell in their eyes that could distinguish the red-green spectrum, which helped them deduce which plants were poisonous. That's why, even today, we *Homo sapiens* can detect more shades of green than of any other color.
- Here are 25 shades of green (how many can you picture?): asparagus, avocado, British racing green, chartreuse, emerald, fern, forest, grass, harlequin, jade, khaki, lime, malachite, mint, moss, olive, pea, pear, pine, pistachio, sage, seafoam, teal, turquoise, viridian.
- Why do night-vision goggles make everything look green? Because of our heightened sensitivity to that color, the eye detects more shades, giving a clearer view.
- The color green is mentioned in 49 Bible verses, none more grand than the vision of God in Heaven that the apostle John receives in Revelation 4:3: "And the one who sat there had the appearance of jasper and ruby. A rainbow that shone like an emerald encircled the throne."
- When England's King Henry VII declared Ireland a kingdom in 1520, its official color was blue. It wasn't until the early 19th century that green came to be associated with Ireland.
- What do Adele, Jennifer Lopez, Julianne Moore, and George Washington have in common? Their favorite color is green.
- The second-most popular favorite color in the world—after blue—is green.
- In L. Frank Baum's highly symbolic *Wonderful Wizard of Oz* books, the Emerald City represents "greenbacks," or money. It is a stand-in for Wall Street.
- Green represents a rise in stock prices in North America; in Asia, green represents a drop in stock prices.
- In 1970, a group of activists were planning a protest at a nuclear test site in Alaska. At the end of the meeting, the organizer raised two fingers and said,

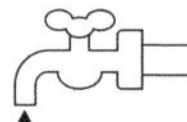

Protein shakes and human blood have a similar protein content—about eight grams per 100 milliliters.

"Peace!" Then a younger attendee declared, "Let's make that a *green* peace!" And that's how Greenpeace got its name.

- Having trouble concentrating? Try surrounding yourself with green. It's been scientifically proven to help people both relax and stay focused.
- The original scrubs: Dr. Harry Sherman, an American surgeon during World War I, used color theory to replace the glaring white hospital environment—including walls and gowns—with what he called "spinach green." We now call it "hospital green."
- Wedding dresses were green in 16th-century England because of the color's association with fertility.
- The origin of the term "green room"—where performers relax backstage—is lost to history, but the first known room to be called such (and that was actually green) was in London's Blackfriars Theater in 1599.
- The ancient Greek words *khloros* ("pale green") and *phyllon* ("leaf") comprise the word *chlorophyll*, name for the pigment in plants and algae that not only makes them green, but provides the means by which they absorb energy from light.
- The origin of the red-and-green traffic signal goes back to the Industrial Revolution, when early factory machines displayed green to indicate that they were in use, and red when they were turned off. In the 1840s, when British railroads enacted a standardized flag signal system, they adopted the same color scheme.
- Ever seen an old penny that's turned green? That's what happened to the Statue of Liberty. She was originally shiny brown, because her outer surface was made from hundreds of shiny copper sheets. But after Lady Liberty moved from Paris to New York City in 1886, the oxygen in the air reacted with the copper to form a thin green layer called a verdigris, or patina, rendering her green by 1906.
- Why a *green* screen? It could be any color that the camera's chroma key device is told not to record, but green won out because it's not usually a skin color. (If it is, seek help immediately.) That means skin won't be cancelled out. But if any clothing is green, it *will* be cancelled out, leading to some hilarious footage online that you can watch on your phone now that this article is over.

* * *

"A blade of grass is a commonplace on Earth; it would be a miracle on Mars. Our descendants on Mars will know the value of a patch of green. And if a blade of grass is priceless, what is the value of a human being?"

—Carl Sagan

First celebrity product endorsement: British actor Lillie Langtry was featured on packages of Pears soap (1893).

LEAVING ON A JET PACK

While science and society have fulfilled many promises of futurists past—space travel, robots, pocket computers—we still don't have personal jet packs. Advances have been made, but progress tends to get impeded when the greatest minds in a particular discipline wind up dead. Here's the very strange story of the murders surrounding viable jet pack technology.

FIRST IN FLIGHT

Personal aviation devices, contained within backpack-like enclosures and thus earning the nickname "jet pack," started popping up in science-fiction stories in the 1920s, which inspired lots of scientists to try making one for real. It would prove difficult to create a practical model that could fly for any length of time because the fuel to make them work would be too heavy to lug around in a backpack along with all the necessary machinery. The Nazis tried to build one during World War II, NASA's Project Apollo failed to produce one in the 1960s, and by 1961, only Bell Aerosystems engineer Wendell Moore had built a workable jet pack. His "Rocket Belt" could fly for 21 seconds on compressed nitrogen. The army was funding the project but declined to develop it further, citing impracticality. So Bell, with the help of test pilots Harold Graham and Bill Suitor, occasionally trotted out the jet pack for special occasions. Most notably, Suitor flew one in the 1967 James Bond movie *Thunderball*, and into the opening ceremony of the 1984 summer Olympics from above.

An insurance salesman named Brad Barker became obsessed with jet packs as soon as he saw *Thunderball*. In the early 1990s, he worked on the ground crew for stuntman Kinnie Gibson, who flew prototypical jet packs at air shows and amusement parks. When Barker found out that Gibson made $25,000 per jet pack flight—which lasted all of 20 seconds each—it inspired him to make his own.

BRING ME THE ROBOSAURUS GUY

In 1992, Barker formed the American Rocket Belt Corporation. He had some engineering know-how, but as a salesman, he knew that good things could come from collaboration and glad-handing, so he recruited the necessary teammates to bring his dream to fruition. He'd leave most of the science of the jet pack to Doug Malewicki, an engineer and inventor best known for creating and building Robosaurus, a gigantic robotic dinosaur whose schtick was picking up cars and "eating" them at the monster truck rallies so popular in the U.S. in the late 1980s and early 1990s. He also contracted with Bill Suitor, the best-known jet pack operator in the world (one of only 11 people who had ever flown one).

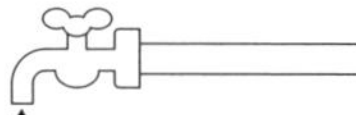

Barker brought in two business partners on American Rocket Belt Corporation. Larry Stanley, a wealthy Houston-based businessman and owner of a hot-air balloon rental company, would fund the entire expensive (though potentially lucrative) operation. Joe Wright agreed to provide the extensive amount of real estate for testing and construction facilities in exchange for a share of the profits.

WE HAVE LIFTOFF

Amazingly, within just two years, the American Rocket Belt Corporation had a working prototype of a jet pack. The Rocket Belt 2000 (or RB-2000) was lighter and stronger than previous versions, including Gibson's. The size of a large, overstuffed backpack, the RB-2000 ran on two tanks filled with hydrogen peroxide and a third with nitrogen. When the operator squeezed the throttle, it combined those into high-pressure steam out of nozzles that provided lift and thrust, enough for a flight as long as 30 seconds—the most ever achieved by jet pack engineers.

By late 1994, American Rocket Belt Corporation was ready for some public demonstrations of its breakthrough technology, but the company, and the relationships among its participants, was rapidly falling apart. Stanley suspected that Barker was cheating him—he believed that Barker had requested reimbursements on parts and machinery for amounts at least twice what they actually cost, then pocketed the rest. Stanley confronted Barker about it, who took such offense that he started a fistfight. The altercation escalated, and during a physical struggle, Barker reached out for a four-pound lead hammer, which he used to strike Stanley twice in the back of the head. That left Stanley dazed enough to where Barker could flee company headquarters for parts unknown—and he took the one RB-2000 with him.

Meanwhile, hemorrhaging money over his other professional and personal interests—a cratering car stereo business and an addiction to crystal meth—Joe Wright placed a lien on the jet pack in order to force Stanley to pay him the fortune he owed in back rent.

HOUSTON, WE HAVE A PROBLEM

Meanwhile, for the next year, nobody knew what happened to Barker and the RB-2000. Then Stanley was watching a Houston Rockets basketball game in 1995 that featured a special halftime entertainment: jet pack pilot Bill Suitor would fly over the Houston Ship Channel. It was touted as the first public debut of the most advanced jet pack the world had ever seen to that point—the RB-2000. Barker had set it all up, of course, without the knowledge, involvement, or financial participation of Stanley and Wright.

Just after the broadcast, Barker, and the aviation device he'd started calling the Pretty Bird, had already skipped town. Stanley was livid—he was still out hundreds of thousands of dollars, and to recoup his investment, he needed the jet pack back. So, he filed a lawsuit in Houston seeking full and solo ownership of the device.

Out of the more than 300 identified types of headaches, only 10 percent have a known cause.

FIGHT TO THE DEATH

Various legal maneuvers delayed the start of the trial for years. At one point, Stanley agreed to drop his complaint against Wright entirely if the latter could sus out where Barker and the belt ran off to. Wright never found his old business partner or their coveted piece of technology, so the lawsuit remained on the table and earned a spot on the docket of a Houston judge in July 1999.

But just 11 days before opening statements, Joe Wright died. Or, rather, Joe Wright was murdered. An unidentified assailant went to Wright's home in Houston, knocked on the door, and, when Wright opened it, beat Wright to death with a blunt item so viciously and violently that the victim was "unrecognizable as a man or woman from the waist up," according to police reports. The prime (and only) suspect in the alleged murder: Brad Barker. While neither Stanley nor Wright had been able to find him in four years, the Houston police did. They arrested and questioned him, but finding there wasn't enough evidence to charge him with any crime, released him after 72 hours. Once more, Barker—and the RB-2000—disappeared.

THE VERDICT IS IN

When Barker didn't turn up for the civil trial in the RB-2000 case, the judge issued a default judgment. Stanley won, and, in absentia, Barker was ordered to pay $10 million and to return the jet pack. This would have been the end, had Barker done what a court ordered him to do. A year later, he hadn't paid any money to Stanley or handed off the jet pack, so Stanley tried to get what was his with some violence, intimidation, and vigilantism. He set up an elaborate sting, contacting Barker and pretending to be a Hollywood producer who wanted to use the jet pack in a movie. Fooled, Barker agreed to a meeting place, where he was kidnapped by four thugs hired by Stanley. They placed him in a box, made up to look like a SCUBA gear container dumped in coastal areas, and Stanley told Barker he planned to drop the whole thing into the Gulf of Mexico—drowning him—if he didn't tell him where the jet pack was hiding. A week of torture culminated in Stanley holding a gun to Barker's head and forcing him to sign paperwork giving Stanley full and sole ownership of the jet pack.

CRASH

After eight days captive, Barker managed to escape his captors. He stumbled into an FBI field office and explained what happened. Suffering cuts in his arm that exposed bone and having lost 23 pounds in his ordeal, he helped authorities arrest Stanley. Stanley was sentenced to life in prison, later reduced on appeal to eight years.

The murder of Joe Wright was never officially solved. Barker never paid Stanley (who died in 2022) his $10 million and never surrendered the RB-2000. The whereabouts of Barker and the jet pack remain unknown.

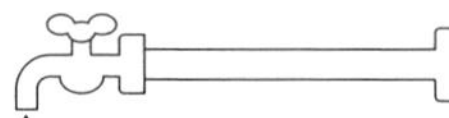

The long e sound can be spelled seven ways. "Please be brief, people. Caesar sees deceivers."

WEIRD SANDWICHES

Danny DeVito once said, "I've been to the Leaning Tower of Pisa. It's a tower, and it's leaning. You look at it, but nothing happens, so then you look for someplace to get a sandwich." Look no further, Mr. DeVito!

Toast Sandwich (U.K.): A piece of toast—which may or may not be buttered—between two pieces of bread.

Pineapple Sandwich (U.S. South): Mayonnaise, pineapple, and white bread. (Optional: cheese or ham.)

Peanut Butter and Raw Onion (Pacific Northwest): With sweet Walla Walla onions.

Pop-Tarts and Cheese (Iowa): American cheese between two (toasted) Pop-Tarts.

Banana and Mayo (U.S. South): Add optional peanut butter.

DNE Chicken Sandwich (New York): "Ghost pepper–seasoned onion strings, Carolina Reaper sweet chili sauce and Carolina Reaper smoky aioli [with] a homemade hot sauce composed…of Reaper, Ghost and Arbol Chilis…served on a bun that's been doused and glazed with Carolina Reaper extract." DNE stands for "do not eat."

Chow Mein Sandwich (New England): Chinese vegetables, fried noodles, and gravy in a hamburger bun.

Toast Hawaii (Germany): One slice of toast topped with ham and melted cheese beneath a pineapple slice with a maraschino cherry placed in the center.

The PBJ Burger (Florida): A burger with peanut butter and jelly.

Spaghetti Burger (Pennsylvania): The bun is "baked spaghetti pasta."

Maggot Melt Sandwich (Arizona State Fair): A cheeseburger with grilled maggots in place of the patty.

Snickers, Apple, and Custard (Germany): Make sure the Snickers bar is melted and the custard is cold.

Lasanwich (U.K.): Cold lasagna and white bread.

The 52-Ingredient Sandwich (Connecticut): Developed by Certified Master Chef Ron DeSantis for Hormel, this sandwich is made with pizza bianca, mayo, provolone cheese, salami, dried oregano, pickled onion, black olives, banana pepper, grilled eggplant, smoked paprika, black pepper, salt, spinach wraps, spicy brown mustard, ham, pickle chips, iceberg lettuce, porchetta, avocado spread, ricotta salata, grilled peppers, grilled onions, salsa, almond butter, hummus, fresh rosemary, lemon zest, butter, focaccia, extra virgin olive oil, Havarti cheese, grilled zucchini, sambal olek, SPAM, fried eggs, roasted tomatoes, fresh basil, fresh thyme, flatbread, tapenade, smoked Gouda, pulled pork, corn chips, roasted sweet potatoes, romesco sauce, spinach, bacon, cranberry mostarda, sliced turkey breast, artichoke spinach dip, cucumbers, and watercress.

MISUNDERSTOOD HITS

The Beastie Boys' highest chart-topper, "Fight for Your Right," was written to make fun of "frat boys," so imagine the band's dismay when the rap song became a frat boy anthem. Here are some other hits that missed their marks.

RANDY NEWMAN: "SHORT PEOPLE"

The prolific singer-songwriter-composer has penned hit songs for everyone from the Animals to Frank Sinatra. His *Toy Story* anthem, "You've Got a Friend in Me," earned him a new generation of fans (and his first Oscar). But the hit with which Newman will forever be associated was on his 1977 album (his fifth), *Little Criminals*, and begins with the line, "Short people got no reason to live." How come? "They got little hands / and little eyes. / And they walk around." How dare they? Later in the song, Newman sings that "short people are just the same / as you and I / (a fool such as I)."

The blowback came immediately. Despite the song reaching #2 on the Billboard Hot 100, many radio stations refused to play it. Newman was labeled a bigot and even received death threats. "I was surprised by the reaction," he recalled. "Because it was a hit, the song reached people who aren't looking for irony. For them, the words mean exactly what they say. I can imagine being a short kid in junior high school. I thought about it before I let the record get out. But I thought, 'What the hell?' I know what I meant—the guy in that song is crazy. He was not to be believed."

A lot of people did believe "that guy," and Newman has spent the past 40-some years either defending "Short People" or trying to change the subject. He laments that the song is his one big hit, because it was a "novelty record like the Chipmunks." He's stated, "I like other ones on the album better but the audiences go for that one."

PAULA COLE: "WHERE HAVE ALL THE COWBOYS GONE?"

This misunderstood hit really ruffled the folk-rock singer-songwriter's feathers. One of two chart-topping singles (the other was the *Dawson's Creek* theme, "I Don't Want to Wait") from her 1996 breakout album, *This Fire*, "Where Have All the Cowboys Gone?" is a feminist lamentation decrying men that are all talk and no compassion. But it doesn't start out that way. The early verses include lines like, "Oh, you get me ready in your '56 Chevy," and, "I will do the laundry / if you pay all the bills." And then there's the refrain: "Where is my John Wayne?...Where is my Marlboro Man?"

Apparently, a lot of listeners didn't listen to the second half of the song, where Cole sings, "I am wearing my new dress tonight / But you don't, but you don't even

Shortest Oscar-nominated performance: Hermione Baddeley appears in *Room at the Top* (1959) for two minutes and 19 seconds.

notice me." And he goes to the bar nearly every day while she's at home raising the new baby (that they had to sell that Chevy to afford).

"It was so bizarre," Cole observed later. "You put out a piece of work and *you* know what it means, but then you let it go out into the world and it's like... an anthropological study. You learn about people. It was one of Rush Limbaugh's favorite songs; he'd play it on his radio station!" But Europeans understood it. "I remember in Spain especially, they loved the irony and the laughter—like, the 'shiny gun' is a phallic reference, totally tongue-in-cheek. Whereas this 'shiny gun,' America didn't get that."

OUTKAST: "HEY YA!"

You couldn't be blamed for not jibing with the lyrics of this 2003 #1 hit written and performed by André 3000. With its upbeat mood and tempo, this catchy combo of electro, funk, and soul has become a staple at parties, dance clubs, and weddings—any place where people go to have a good time. But when you read the lyrics without the music, they're anything but upbeat. "Why, oh, why, oh, why, oh / Are we so in denial when we know we're not happy here?" And, "Separate's always better when there's feelings involved."

André 3000 was commenting on the fragility of love and relationships—though not necessarily his own. "The song isn't autobiographical," he explained, "It's more like fantasies or tangents based on real life....The story was set in the '50s, so the song was me trying [to] do a Woody Allen kinda thing, a humorous kind of honesty." But few people got the joke. As one Redditor commented, "I bartend a lot of weddings, and at least half the time they'll play 'Hey Ya!,' and I always wonder why. Yeah, it's catchy as s***...but [the lyric] 'if nothing is forever, then what makes love the exception?' really isn't the best note to start your marriage."

The least surprised person that "Hey Ya!" was misunderstood? André 3000 himself. One of the song's lyrics even predicted it: "Y'all don't want to hear me, you just want to dance."

MICHAEL NESMITH: "DIFFERENT DRUM"

This misunderstood hit was among the highest-charting songs of Nesmith's storied but overlooked career. But it wasn't a hit for Nesmith. He'd written "Different Drum" in 1964, two years before he beat out hundreds of other singers and actors to join *The Monkees*, a made-for-TV band (in the spirit of the Beatles) that was a huge hit for NBC in 1966 and 1967. Nesmith lent his songwriting chops to the Monkees—as much as music supervisor Don Kirshner would let him. The two didn't get along, and for whatever reason, Kirshner turned down "Different Drum."

Nesmith sold the song to a new group called the Stone Poneys, who were originally going to record it as a stripped-down acoustic ballad. But in the end, they went with a more upbeat arrangement. "Different Drum" became the first hit single for the band and its lead singer, 21-year-old Linda Ronstadt, who would go on to sell over 100 million records.

Here's the misunderstood part: the song is about two lovers who no longer see eye to eye. "I'm not saying you ain't pretty / All I'm saying's I'm not ready." That's because, "You and I travel to the beat of a different drum." So, basically, it's a break-up song, or as Nesmith described it in his autobiography, *Infinite Tuesday*, "It's this sad song, full of melancholy, about a couple that can't seem to get together. Who are on a different page. He likes different things than she likes. And I have people come up to me and say, 'That's our song. They played it at our wedding.' This is a song about two people breaking up! Of course, I never say that. But what do you do?"

R.E.M.: "THE ONE I LOVE"

Released in 1987, R.E.M.'s first hit song almost never saw the light of day because frontman Michael Stipe thought his lyrics were "too brutal." This scathing takedown of a significant other "just came up from somewhere and I recognized it as being really violent and awful," he said. "But it wasn't directed at any one person. I would never write a song like that." Stipe assumed the lyrics should have made its darker meaning obvious: "This one goes out to the one I love / This one goes out to the one I've left behind / A simple prop to occupy my time."

But when the band started playing this "savagely anti-love" song live, as guitarist Peter Buck remembers, "I'd look into the audience and there would be couples kissing." Were they not listening? "People told me that was 'their song.' *That* was your song?"

Stipe is equally baffled, but conceded long ago, "Now it's a love song, so that's fine."

* * *

WHAT EXOTIC MEATS REALLY TASTE LIKE (SAY THOSE WHO KNOW)

- **Rattlesnake:** bland or mild chicken.
- **Iguana:** mild duck.
- **Beaver:** lean, herbaceous beef.
- **Jellyfish:** almost flavorless, with a gelatinous texture akin to rubber bands.
- **Tarantula:** crab.
- **Human flesh:** pork with a little bit of veal, but gamey.

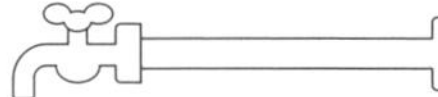

There is an annual award given to those who make the best hold music.

ORSON WELLES VS. EVERYONE

Welles was revered as an actor and director for such classics as Citizen Kane *and* The Third Man. *Actors and directors loved him, but he didn't love them back.*

(On *Rear Window*): "To discover that Jimmy Stewart can be a bad actor. Even Grace Kelly is better than Jimmy, who's overacting."

(On Laurence Olivier's *King Lear*, of which Welles watched only two scenes): "The worst things I ever saw in my life."

(When asked while in a restaurant if he wanted to meet Elizabeth Taylor): "No. As you can see, I'm in the middle of my lunch."

(On Elizabeth Taylor's husband Richard Burton): "Burton had great talent. He's ruined his great gifts. He's become a joke with a celebrity wife. Now he just works for money."

(On Spencer Tracy): "I'm having a hard time trying to think of a great Tracy performance."

(On Norma Shearer): "One of the most minimally talented ladies to appear on the silver screen."

(Calculating Joan Fontaine's acting tools): "Two expressions, that's it."

(On Alfred Hitchcock): "I've never understood the cult of Hitchcock. Particularly the late American movies. Egotism and laziness. And they're all lit like television shows."

(On John Landis): "The a****** from *Animal House*, a real s***. Kill him. Won't leave me alone. Keeps phoning me and giving me advice on how to make the movie. In a very patronizing way. Everything he says is dumb!"

(On Jean-Luc Godard): "His message is what he cares about these days, and, like most movie messages, it could be written on the head of a pin."

(On Jerry Lewis): "He really has a way of coming on like a great thinker. Which really should be stopped."

(On *Anna and the King*): "I couldn't stand Irene Dunne, who had already been cast. That's why I turned down *Gaslight*, too."

(On Jennifer Jones): "Hopeless."

(On Bette Davis): "I can't look at her."

Country with the most islands: Sweden lays claim to 267,570.

WEIRD CANADIAN MUSEUMS

Museums: they're not just for paintings and old bones anymore. There's a museum out there for almost any interest—even (and especially) up in Canada.

 The Anne Murray Centre

Location: Springhill, Nova Scotia

Details: In the 1970s, the country-inflected easy-listening musical stylings of Anne Murray were everywhere. The sensible soft-rock singer sold millions of albums, won four Grammys, and topped the charts in the U.S. and Canada with ballads like "You Needed Me." She's easily the most famous person to ever come out of Springhill (population 2,654), and the town's Anne Murray Centre pays appropriate tribute. The museum plays Murray performance videos on a loop and displays the real instruments used on her recordings and the costumes she wore in TV appearances, along with childhood photos and other personal and career memorabilia.

Can't-Miss Highlight: Visitors can step into a small studio and record a "duet" of themselves singing with Murray.

 World Famous Gopher Hole Museum

Location: Torrington, Alberta

Details: Technically, the animals honored and on display here aren't the common garden pests, but a similar, native-to-Canada species called the Richardson ground squirrel. No matter what you call them, they feature in 47 different taxidermy dioramas. The animals are real, stuffed, and dressed up like people in little costumes depicting snapshots of human life ranging from the mundane to the special—like a trip to the beauty salon, kissing under the stars, a hockey game, and a wedding.

Can't-Miss Highlight: The tableau of criminal gophers robbing a gopher bank.

 Canadian Potato Museum

Location: O'Leary, Prince Edward Island

Details: It may be the nation's smallest province, but Price Edward Island is home to more than 100 varieties of potato—and home to the nation's museum celebrating all things about spuds. Among the museum's offerings are the world's largest collection of antique potato-farming implements, a potato-themed gift shop, and a restaurant specializing in baked potatoes.

Can't-Miss Highlight: The world's largest sculpture of a potato.

Hold on: the Earth moves around the sun at a rate of 18.5 miles per second.

 Sign Post Forest

Location: Watson Lake, Yukon Territory

Details: In 1942, an American soldier was sent to this remote outpost just over the border from British Columbia to fix directional signposts. Missing home and having little to do in the sleepy town in the middle of nowhere, he added a new signpost to his project, pointing to his Illinois hometown several thousand miles away. As other visitors passed through Watson Lake, they added signposts pointing to their hometowns and other points of interest. Over the years, more than 80,000 entries have been added to the site, a mazelike outdoor structure since dubbed Sign Post Forest.

Can't-Miss Highlight: There are supplies out for you, the visitor, to add your own signpost.

 Diefenbunker: Canada's Cold War Museum

Location: Ottawa, Ontario

Details: In 1957, at the height of mounting Cold War tensions between the West and the Soviet Union, Canadian Prime Minister John Diefenbaker authorized the secret construction of an underground facility where the government could continue functioning in the event of nuclear war. Operational in 1962, the 30,000-square-meter bunker was never put to its intended use, so in 1994 it was decommissioned and became Diefenbunker, a museum commemorating the Cold War experience in Canada. It's essentially a monument to fear and dread, with all of the offices and living spaces preserved in their early 1960s glory along with exhibits on the nuclear arms race and spy technology.

Can't-Miss Highlight: Inside the underground nuclear bunker is another underground bunker that's been turned into a nuclear bunker–themed escape room attraction.

Sam Waller Museum

Location: The Pas, Manitoba

Details: Situated in the town's old, disused courthouse in its downtown area, the Sam Waller Museum houses the personal collection of late resident Sam Waller. A self-identified "pack rat," he collected strange things in his travels and had a thing for taxidermy. Today the collection—which Waller himself called a "cluttertorium"—is divided into a "Main Gallery" and "Sam's Gallery." The former is replete with relics of the Canadian fur trade, old steamboats, and the local lumber industry. The latter includes thousands of animals preserved in taxidermy, including a preserved albino alligator.

Can't-Miss Highlight: A typewriter with a keyboard featuring Cree characters instead of English letters.

Neutral Switzerland was accidentally bombed 70 times during World War II.

TWUNG TISTERS

Tongue twisters aren't just silly—they're used by speech therapists, by people learning English, and by vocal performers as warm-up exercises. But they're also fun.

Happily hoping a hopping hiccupping hippo is hiccupping and hopping happily.

Give papa a cup of proper coffee in a proper copper coffee cup.

Cross a coarse cross cow across a crass cow crossing.

Through three cheese trees three free fleas flew.

A loyal warrior will rarely worry why we rule.

Top chopstick shops stock top chopsticks.

We surely shall see the sun shine soon.

You know you need unique New York.

Irish wristwatch. Swiss wristwatch.

Pad kid poured curd-pulled cod.

He threw three free throws.

Nine nice night nurses nursing nicely.

Six slick sick hicks nix six slick bricks.

Intent Tic Tacs kick intact Kit Kat tactics.

Can a clam clan cram a camel in a chasm?

A synonym for cinnamon is a cinnamon synonym.

Great Greek grape growers grow great Greek grapes.

Whisking the risky whiskey river with quivering whiskers.

The sea she saw was a saucy sea, a sort of saucy sea saw she.

An estranged strange astronaut strained to train strained trains.

Moses supposes his toes are roses, but Moses supposes erroneously.

Eleven benevolent elephants evenly enveloping eleven benevolent elephants.

This black bug bled blue-black blood while that black bug bled black-blue blood.

Last American-made car with a front bench seat: the 2013 Chevrolet Impala.

THE REAL AND FAKE WORKS OF NORVAL MORRISSEAU, PART I

Norval Morrisseau is one of the most important painters to come out of North America in the 20th century. How he was exploited and used to perpetuate the most substantial and brazen fraud in art history is a maddening, shocking, and remarkable story.

EARLY WORKS

The First Nations of Indigenous tribes collectively known as the Anishinaabe once flourished in the Great Lakes area, particularly in what is now Canada, in the northern part of Ontario. Ojibwe artist Norval Morrisseau was born in 1932 on a Bingwi Neyaashi Anishinaabek reservation. After spending his first six years being raised by his grandparents, he then—like many Native American children in early 20th-century Canada—was forcibly sent to an abusive government boarding school, where staff set out to remove all Indigenous heritage and culture from its charges. Morrisseau turned to drawing to help cope with his experiences.

As a teenager in the late 1940s, he took up painting, an act that defied both his traditional and European-influenced culture. He created canvases representing Anishinaabe myths and oral traditions; such visual representation was forbidden by his tribe, and, until 1951, practicing Indigenous culture in any way was against the law in Canada. Morrisseau kept painting into adulthood, developing a unique and eye-catching style: his work was visually bold and vibrant, loaded with bright and inviting colors, held within thick lines, and depicted humans, animals, and foliage through the lens of Anishinaabe history and folklore.

A STAR IS BORN

In 1962, Morrisseau became one of the first celebrity Indigenous artists—and one of the first famous Canadian painters overall—when Toronto art gallery owner Jack Pollock discovered him and featured his work in his gallery. That marked the first time an Indigenous painter's work was shown in a contemporary Canadian gallery. All of Morrisseau's paintings sold within a day, and his work began popping up in major galleries around the world, including in England, Norway, Germany, and the U.S. Morrisseau enjoyed a solo exhibition at the National Gallery of Canada, and around that time, began signing his works as Copper Thunderbird, a sacred name given to him in a shamanic healing ceremony.

Not just a celebrity in the art world, Morrisseau was nicknamed "the Picasso of the North" and was a purveyor of a strikingly new, Indigenous-meets-European style. This came to be known as the Woodlands school, a Canadian art movement that brought international attention and acclaim to many other indigenous artists who hailed from the same region as Morrisseau. But he remained the best-known name in that movement, and in Canadian art. Over the next 40 years, the prolific Morrisseau turned out thousands of works that were routinely sold at auctions for hundreds of thousands of dollars.

Personally, Morrisseau struggled with the fame his works brought him. As he tried to keep his culture and traditions alive, he had to cope with his childhood traumas suffered at the residential school. Seeking to escape the pain and stain of rampant physical, mental, and sexual abuse, Morrisseau fell into drug addiction and alcoholism in adulthood. By the late 1980s, he'd blown through the substantial money he'd made and was living on the streets. Meanwhile, as is common in the world of high-level art trading, Morrisseau's works commanded huge sums from dealers and auctions. He didn't see any of that money but enjoyed a reputation as one of Canada's most important artists.

SIGN HERE, PLEASE

There's a seedy underbelly to the art world. Expensive paintings serve as legally gray-area tax shelters, and forgeries of the works of even moderately famous and popular artists are extremely common; organized crime syndicates have been known to engage in all of those pursuits and more. In 1978, Morrisseau himself reportedly participated in a fraudulent art-trading operation. Some antiques-dealing mobsters working out of Toronto moved into fine art and enlisted a very broke Morrisseau to get the operation up and running. Not only did the mob pay Morrisseau a flat fee to create a number of paintings, but the criminals gave Morrisseau counterfeit copies and rip-offs of his own work, and he signed them for a fee.

Morrisseau also crowded the market for his own work further by going into business for himself, apart from the organized crime connections. When his half-brother, Wolf, needed money for eyeglasses, Norval asked his relative to throw together some paintings, which the more famous artist then signed and claimed as his own, and traded to the optometrist in lieu of payment. He also taught art classes around Canada, and swiped students' paintings and the credit for them, putting his name on them and selling them as authentic Morrisseau creations. Pollock was aware of Morrisseau's fraudulent activities and ominously warned the artist that such behavior could hurt the market for his work, and not only flood it with fakes that drive down the price of the originals, but also invite criminal activity with which he had no control, involvement, or financial benefit.

FAKE IT 'TIL YOU MAKE IT

And that's exactly what happened. In 1991, Morrisseau attempted a comeback, and a Toronto art gallery hosted a retrospective of his works. In the run-up to the event, Morrisseau spoke with *Toronto Star* art critic Christopher Hume and told him of the rampant forgery of his work. By this point, it wasn't just in shady criminal channels, but in the legitimate art market. "He says he has been ripped off time and time again yet refuses to lay blame or get angry," Hume wrote.

While he remained calm and accepting that fakes were going to happen, Morrisseau approached various Canadian law enforcement channels, who were too overburdened or inexperienced with art crimes to launch a proper investigation. If Morrisseau was going to stop the art fraudsters that he'd once helped out, he'd have to take the law into his own hands. Teaming up with a couple of lawyers, Morrisseau kept close track of when Canadian galleries and auction houses were displaying or offering his works up for sale. He'd go over the catalogs and carefully pinpoint exactly which pieces were fakes, or ones that he had nothing to do with painting. Then he'd let the institutions know they were selling fakes and would face an injunction or lawsuit if they continued to operate in such a fashion. Each and every time, Morrisseau's pleas were ignored.

MORE THAN ONE MAN COULD DO

In 2001, Morrisseau's gallery agent in Toronto sent him photos of some works credited to the artist that had sold at an unrelated auction. Morrisseau didn't recognize any of the 23 acrylic-on-canvas paintings and began correspondence with the auction house, which had marketed the paintings as coming from an obscure seller. The auctioneers didn't think anything of it, as it had previously sold 800 other "Morrisseau paintings" (that definitely were not authentic) without incident.

For the volume, and the direct involvement of Morrisseau, the story made headlines in art-world publications. Auctioneers and art dealers across Canada—most of whom had sold paintings credited to Morrisseau but that were now being called into question—emerged to publicly discredit the artist. His decades-long struggles with alcoholism and drug addiction had left him with brain damage so severe he couldn't differentiate his own works from fakes, some suggested; others believed his diagnosis of Parkinson's disease gave him a tenuous grasp on reality. One dealer told the *National Post* that Morrisseau had devalued his own work because he'd been so prolific, hence the abundance of Morrisseau-credited paintings out in the world. "You give him acrylic paint and a canvas and tell him you'll take him out for dinner and give him some liquor, and he'll paint."

THAT'S CLEARLY NOT RIGHT

Morrisseau and his associates struck back, maintaining that the artist was lucid and

Last country to adopt the modern Gregorian calendar: Turkey (1926).

offering up some damning evidence that could almost completely and immediately prove that the questioned pieces of art were phonies.

- Morrisseau signed his authentic works with his shamanic name, Copper Thunderbird, in Cree syllabics on the front of the canvas. The ones that the artist claimed were fakes were signed "Norval Morrisseau," in English, and on the back, some with a handwritten "copyright" symbol.

- The bold, thick lines indicative of the painter's style were made with regular paint on authentic Morrisseaus. The fakes likely got their lines quickly and cheaply with black permanent ink marker—some accused fakes gave off the telltale noxious smell of those pens.

- The titles of poems on the backs of canvases were frequently misspelled.

- The Indigenous myths and stories were frequently depicted incorrectly; figures that never interacted would be seen together, or the tales would lack thematic elements that needed to be there or had acquired inaccurate ones: "the paintings don't make sense."

Between 2001 and 2005, Morrisseau filed 15 official affidavits attesting to auctions and galleries selling fakes wrongly attributed to him in the name of making money. His lawyers also delivered cease-and-desist letters to gallery owners ordering them to stop selling frauds. He probably would've kept going, ordering museums, galleries, and auctions to remove phony works, except that Norval Morrisseau died in December 2007 at age 75.

WHO'S AT FAULT?

But the legal and moral battles Morrisseau started late in life raged on after his death. The old cliché that an artist's work is worth more after death held true, with the value of Morrisseau's paintings potentially skyrocketing in 2008. With possible financial windfalls in jeopardy due to Morrisseau's tireless, yearslong campaign to expose the counterfeiting network to which they were a party (if only unwittingly), auctioneers, galleries, and private collectors sued Morrisseau's estate, as well as his dealer and lawyers, accusing *them* of fraud: the artist and his team's persistent message that many valuable Morrisseaus were fakes constituted slander and libel.

In response to the suit, the FBI-like wing of the Royal Canadian Mounted Police opened an investigation into the Morrisseau black market, but couldn't build a case. "Investigators did not identify nor obtain the requisite evidence necessary to support the allegations of criminal activity," the RCMP said in a statement. But the investigation was only beginning, however.

Turn to page 270 for the next chapter of this very artsy crime story.

The speed of light and the speed of gravity are the same.

ROBOTS IN THE NEWS

Before the inevitable day comes in which the robots rise up and kill all humans, we can at least read about their ridiculous and increasingly alarming antics.

JAM-BOTS

Due to its proximity to the technologically fruitful area of Silicon Valley, San Francisco enjoys a high volume of driverless, robotic cars. In August 2023, the state of California approved expansion of the legal use of autonomous vehicles as taxis in the Bay Area city. At about 11:00 p.m. on the day after the rule changes went into effect, traffic on two streets in the city's lively North Beach nightlife district became impassable due to 10 robo-taxis that stopped working and simply became motionless right where they were. All the cabs, operated by a company called Cruise, stalled in the middle of the road with lights flashing for 15 minutes. Then, all at once, they awoke and starting driving again. The next day, a Cruise representative told reporters that the robot cars lost their internet connectivity because of an overload of cell phone connectivity from a music festival in nearby Golden Gate Park.

MOON-BOT

Working with a $2 million grant from NASA, teams from five institutions, including the Georgia Institute of Technology, USC, and Oregon State University, formed the LASSIE Project. "LASSIE" is an acronym for Legged Autonomous Surface Science in Analog Environments, but it also cheekily describes their product: the teams build and test robot dogs to study the surface of the moon. The first bot built in 2024, Spirit, traverses Mount Hood outside of Portland, Oregon, because the mountain mimics the lunar landscape. "With every step that the dog robot takes, it's able to sense mechanical resistance with its leg, kind of similar to the way that we walk on uneven surfaces as humans," said Cristina Wilson, a LASSIE Project cognitive scientist. The program will serve as the basis for developing more robotic dogs to be used as explorers on the moon and other planets, as a viable substitute for human space travel.

WATCH-BOT

What's that metal creature about the size of a large headless dog that looks like a fancy vacuum cleaner? It's the prototypical, skinless version of Aurora, a robot put into use by the Alaska Department of Transportation and Public Facilities to patrol the outer reaches of Fairbanks International Airport to "enhance and augment safety and operations." In other words, it will climb up on rock formations near the airport's runways to scare off and, if necessary, chase away migratory birds to dissuade them from hanging around where planes land and take off. To keep the birds on their

Actor who dies on-screen the most: Danny Trejo (65 times).

toes and not too used to Aurora, airport employees will change Aurora's appearance, employing a series of lifelike skins to disguise the robotic exoskeleton with blade-like appendages, making Aurora resemble a fox or coyote.

GROPE-BOT

DeepFest, held most recently in Riyadh, Saudi Arabia, in March 2024, calls itself "the premier meeting place for the global artificial intelligence ecosystem." In other words, it's a trade show and show-off gathering for cutting-edge robots and A.I. technology. A television reporter named Rawya Kassem was covering the event, taping a news segment while standing in front of Mohammad, a robot made by Saudi Arabian firm QSS. Billed as "the latest marvel in robotics," Mohammed introduced himself to the crowd in Arabic and stood by as Kassem spoke. Then, slowly, his arm rose up and patted Kassem's rear end, a moment captured on video and that briefly went viral. QSS absolved itself of all blame, claiming that Mohammad is a "fully autonomous" robot that acted of his own accord, operating "independently without direct human control."

CONDUCTOR-BOT

For the first time in South Korean history, a robot conducted the country's national orchestra. In July 2023, EveR 6, an android robot developed by the Korea Institute of Industrial Technology, led the prestigious collective at the National Theater of Korea in Seoul. A two-armed humanoid blue and white robot attached to a sleek white column, EveR 6 bowed to the audience, then directed the musicians with a baton while maintaining its blank expression, providing an ultra-precise, unfaltering tempo. "Movements by a conductor are very detailed," the orchestra's human leader Choi Soo-yeoul said. "The robot was able to present such detailed moves much better than I had imagined." EveR 6 probably won't be replacing Choi anytime soon, though—it has some flaws, specifically that it can't hear or respond to cues or other stimuli. "It seemed there was some work to be done for the robot to do the job," said Lee Young-ju, an audience member and expert in traditional Korean music.

KILL-BOT

A pepper processing plant in South Korea was planning on implementing an assembly line of robots in November 2023. Due to sensor issues, the rollout was delayed, and human staff were running another check of the robots before they were put fully into use. One robot, responsible for picking up boxes of the vegetables and placing them on pallets, confused a human inspector for one of the boxes. The robot grabbed the unsuspecting employee and pressed him into a conveyor belt with such force that the man's face and chest were crushed. The man later died from injuries suffered in the accident, his death attributed to the robotic arm.

BLIND MISCONCEPTIONS

An estimated 43 million people worldwide are blind, including one million Americans. Another 12 million Americans over 40 have uncorrectable vision loss. Due to higher rates of chronic diseases like diabetes, those numbers will skyrocket in the coming years. While it's impossible to understand exactly what vision loss is like, a little knowledge goes a long way.

CHALLENGED

Here's an actual post from a Reddit forum called "No Stupid Questions": "How do I communicate with blind people? Like, obviously there's Braille, but is there some form of clicking I can do with my tongue to simulate Braille verbally? (Edit: never mind you can just talk to them.)"

Hmm.

Remember the *Bird Box* challenge from early 2019? Inspired by the Netflix movie about a mother and her two kids who must travel blindfolded so they won't see an evil entity, social media influencers started donning blindfolds and walking through their houses, or around their neighborhoods, or, if you were Jake Paul, into traffic. The fad got so out of hand that Netflix was forced to tweet: "Can't believe we have to say this, but: PLEASE DO NOT HURT YOURSELVES WITH THIS BIRD BOX CHALLENGE." People *were* hurting themselves...and others, like those mentioned in this CNN article: "Blindfolded Utah Teen Crashes Her Car while Doing the Challenge."

The challenge wasn't merely dangerous—it was yet another step back in the ongoing quest for blind people to get sighted people to really "see" them. A blind writer and musician named Ria Andriani explained it this way in the *Guardian*: "After being blindfolded for a short stint, people feel it as a more debilitating condition than it really is; they underestimate the adaptive capability of blind people and end the experiment more likely to agree with statements such as: 'If I were blind, I would do anything to get my sight back.'"

Andriani further explains that "most blind people don't make like Jake Paul and immediately walk blindly into a busy Los Angeles street." It takes time to learn how to navigate a world designed for the sighted, by the sighted. Blindness forces one to adapt. "Take body protection, for starters," she says. "If you can't see what's in front of you, you do the next best thing: protect yourself from collision. This means shielding yourself with your arms or twisting your body away from the object you're trying not to run into."

Let's take a look at what it is, and isn't, like to be visually impaired.

About $1.6 million worth of coins are tossed into the Trevi Fountain every year.

MYTHS AND FACTS

The three most common misconceptions, per Rutgers University: being blind means you can't see anything at all, you can't operate "most technology," and an independent life is impossible.

Some facts: complete blindness is rare. According to the National Federation of the Blind, "We encourage people to consider themselves as blind if their sight is bad enough—even with corrective lenses—that they must use alternative methods to engage in any activity that people with normal vision would do using their eyes."

Christine Hà is a restaurateur, author, and TV host who rose to stardom by winning *Master Chef* in 2012, even though she was declared legally blind in 2007 due to an autoimmune disease. "It's a very common misconception that people think blindness is all or nothing," she said in response to criticism that she wasn't "100 percent blind." She explains, "From a medical standpoint, doctors call my vision 'counting fingers.' If you hold your hand 10 to 12 inches from my face, I could count your fingers as long as the lighting isn't too dark or glaring. The way I often describe it is that it's like if you take a really hot shower and then you look into the foggy bathroom mirror, where you only see vague shapes and shadows."

EVERYDAY LIFE

Hà and Andriani are just two of the growing voices of blind writers who are more than willing to share their experiences to dispel the notion that they can't live on their own. They can, eventually, thanks to a growing number of programs that offer vision-loss rehabilitation treatment and basic skills training from occupational therapists.

Hà certainly hasn't let her disability hold her back, as is evident in this 2023 *Houstonia* magazine profile where the topic of blindness hardly came up while she discussed earning her master's degree, writing a memoir, and owning a restaurant. "In my home kitchen, everything's completely organized." However, "When it comes to the restaurant...I know my limitations. I've built a team I trust to execute my menu...Customers ask, 'Is Christine back there cooking?' and my staff is laughing, 'No, she's busy doing other things.' I don't want them to feel stressed knowing their blind boss is around and they have to worry about safety."

As Andriani points out, living independently takes some extra steps: "Most people don't need to break down preparing dinner into sizeable goals such as food preparation, operating the stove, and checking whether the food is done." But for those like her, who've been blind since birth or an early age, "these tasks might not come naturally." That's where the training comes in.

But first, let's look at...

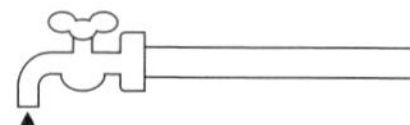

THE TYPES OF SIGHT LOSS

- **Visual impairment** occurs when vision loss reaches the point where it's unable to be corrected back to "normal vision," even with eyeglasses or surgery. Symptoms include blurred vision, cloudiness, spots or waves in the central vision, low peripheral vision, and impaired night vision.
- **Blindness** is a blanket term that simply means "unable to see." There are numerous causes and degrees. *Preventable blindness* is caused by disease, like untreated diabetes or hypertension, or injury, like staring at the sun or running with scissors. (You were warned.)
- **Legal blindness**, also called "statutory blindness" by the Social Security Administration, is defined as "central visual acuity of 20/200 or less in the better eye with the use of correcting lens." Someone with 20/200 must be 10 times closer to an object to see it clearly than a person with 20/20 vision. You can also be declared legally blind if you have less than 20 degrees of peripheral vision.
- **Congenital blindness**, sometimes incorrectly referred to as "childhood blindness," is blindness from birth due to a genetic condition or a physical defect that can occur from the prenatal stage to just after birth. If caught early, congenital blindness can sometimes be treated with gene therapy.
- **Complete blindness**, also called total blindness, it is the inability to distinguish between light and dark. This accounts for only about 15 percent of blind people, but even they can lead productive, fulfilling lives. Here's how.

THE BLIND LEADING THE BLIND

You know the old adage: when one sense diminishes, the others take up the slack. This isn't to say they improve; you just learn to use them better. This has been proven scientifically and anecdotally—most incredibly by Daniel Kish. Born in 1966, Kish lost his eyes as a baby due to cancer and then grew up to become the first person with complete blindness to become a Certified Orientation and Mobility Specialist. At a young age, Kish developed a knack for *echolocation*—when you make a clicking sound and listen for it to bounce off nearby objects to detect where they are. Kish learned it so well that he can navigate cities without a cane, even on a bicycle! In 2000, he founded World Access for the Blind in California. From its mission statement: "Barriers to functioning associated with blindness arise more from poor interaction between blind people and society than from intrinsic deficiency."

Another cutting-edge school is the Colorado Center for the Blind, where the mostly blind faculty train people who have recently lost their vision, or will in the imminent future. After three months of students learning how to dress, cook,

The soft dip in your arm where it bends is called the *cubital fossa.*

clean, use power tools, and more (while wearing blindfolds if they still have some vision), the final exam comprises three challenges: produce a professional-looking presentation, cook a meal for 60 people, and tackle the "independent drop" challenge: the student is driven in circles around Denver and then dropped off at a mystery spot, then must find their way back to the center on their own.

BAG OF TRICKS

Making it back safely is possible thanks to a bevy of tools at their disposal, and not over-relying on one at the expense of the others. Take echolocation, which Andriani explains is not as "simplistic" as *Bird Box* makes it seem: "Most hard materials such as walls amplify echoes, while soft ones like a hedge absorb them."

That's why it's also important to stick to a routine and learn the "sounds" of that routine to detect any changes. And, of course, there's using a guide dog or a cane, and learning braille. This tactile reading system was invented in 1824 by French teenager Louis Braille, who'd gone completely blind in early childhood. Braille did more than just make reading accessible; the life-long teacher was among the first blind people to advocate for more inclusion in society. "Access to communication... is access to knowledge, and that is vitally important for us if we are not to go on being despised or patronized by condescending sighted people. We do not need pity, nor do we need to be reminded that we are vulnerable. We must be treated as equals—and communication is the way we can bring this about."

EQUAL ACCESS

Throughout history, unless you were wealthy, if you were blind, you were probably screwed. It wasn't even until 1990 that the Americans with Disabilities Act was passed, in which "a public accommodation shall...ensure that no individual with a disability is excluded, denied services, segregated, or otherwise treated differently than other individuals because of the absence of auxiliary aids and services."

There are more of these "auxiliary aids" than ever: braille on ATMs, in elevators, on computer keyboards; crosswalk signs that click (for echolocation); and an array of fancy tech gadgets like audio labelers that announce an object's identity; AI-assisted glasses that read text, locate objects, describe the scene, and even translate; and "bone-conducting headphones" situated in front of the ear so the wearer can also hear what's happening around them.

Yet despite all these advancements, many people with blindness feel left out of society as a whole. According to the National Industries for the Blind, "About 70 percent of blind people are unemployed, reflecting not so much their abilities as the limited vision of potential employers." We can only hope that the coming years see advances in this area, as well.

He doesn't speak now, but silent Teller of Penn & Teller used to teach high school Latin.

DOG NAMESAKES

Many pet owners give people names to their dogs. These familiar breeds are named after real-life human beings.

BOYKIN SPANIEL

Plantation owner and land appraiser L. Whitaker "Whit" Boykin organized hunting trips outside of Camden, South Carolina, in the late 1800s and early 1900s. He and his hunting buddies, members of the prominent Cantey family, tried to selectively breed dogs to assist them, seeking something tough but also small enough to help track and fetch gamebirds, and able to swim after waterfowl. Around 1905, Boykin landed on his ideal dog, bred several generations out from a stray dog of unknown lineage who wandered onto his property one day. He began breeding that dog and its descendants with water spaniels, cocker spaniels, springer spaniels, and Chesapeake Bay retrievers to create a medium-sized brown dog with furry, floppy ears. He named it the Boykin spaniel after himself, and it's the official state dog of South Carolina.

GORDON SETTER

Originally called the Gordon Castle Setter, this breed that originated in Scotland in the 1600s technically gets its name from a castle and a lordship, which were named after people. The 4th Duke of Gordon and his grandson, the 6th Duke of Gordon, resided in and near Gordon Castle. Gamebird-hunting dogs called setters were common in those Scottish highlands, and the 4th Duke of Gordon actively bred them, developing an animal that was black and tan. When his grandson, the 6th Duke of Gordon, gained control of the noble kennels in 1835, he incorporated other breeds to make for better hunting dogs with a more regulated and standard look. Those dogs are recognized today as looking like hounds with black bodies and heads but dark brown legs.

DOBERMAN PINSCHER

A late 19th-century German tax collector named Karl Friedrich Louis Dobermann needed protection on the job, particularly to guard against robberies and hold-ups as he traveled through the country. He wanted a guard dog that was loyal and smart, but also vicious when necessary, and he went about breeding short-haired shepherds with rottweilers and German pinschers, and likely also muscular and thin dogs like

Weimaraners and Greyhounds. Dobermann's new dogs so resembled a new spin on the pinscher that he called them Doberman pinschers, dropping the second *n* in his name. The dogs were registered as an official German breed in 1900.

JACK RUSSELL TERRIER

A divinity student at Oxford and then a practicing minister in the early 1800s, Parson Jack Russell did so much hunting in the area that he became known as "The Sporting Parson." As such, he set out to create the perfect hunting dog, small and fast like a terrier, but assertive enough that it wouldn't hesitate to root foxes out of their hiding spots. One day, he saw a milkman walk by with a dog that matched his vision—it was a female white-furred terrier of some kind, likely a mixture of a bull terrier and a beagle. Russell convinced the milkman to sell him the dog, named Trump. That dog became the first of a family of dogs that Russell selectively bred into small fox hunters. Those dogs came to be known as the Jack Russell terrier; a similar breed, with slightly longer legs, is called the Parson Russell terrier.

SAINT BERNARD

Saint Bernards are one of the most instantly recognizable dogs out there—they're absolutely massive (in height and weight), and their thick brown, black, and white fur hangs over their kind-looking droopy faces. Commonly depicted in books and movies as mountain rescue dogs, they're often shown with a barrel of brandy around their necks, for the comfort of the humans they successful locate. This is all based on real history and a real breed originator. In 1050, Catholic monk Bernard of Menthon built a small hospice and relief center in the French Alps to serve religious pilgrims braving the treacherous, snow-filled mountains to visit Rome and other holy sites in Italy. Menthon was also motivated to help travelers before they got lost or stuck in snowbanks and avalanches. The monk bred two different breeds of mastiffs—large, muscular livestock-guarding dogs—to make a new dog. He trained them to find missing people in the mountains and rescue them, because they have an incredible sense of smell. Once called Bernard dogs, the monk's legacy animals became known as Saint Bernards after he was canonized as a saint in the 17th century.

* * *

There's only one internationally recognized dog breed named after a fictional character: the Dandie Dinmont terrier. Small and low to the ground, with a flop of hair on top of their heads, they resemble the unidentified dogs that accompany farmer Dandie Dinmont, a character in Sir Walter Scott's popular 1815 novel, *Guy Mannering: or, The Astrologer.* And that's how the breed got its name.

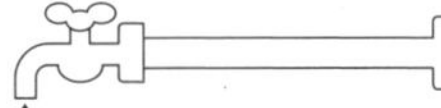

What's a panty gusset?
The tiny pocket in the crotch of women's underwear.

BOOK NATION

In the 1990s and 2000s, it seemed like every other nonfiction book had the word nation *in its name, and the trend continues to this day. (We get it—the word* nation *lends grandeur or implies a significant cultural shift.* Uncle John's Nation *has a nice ring to it...) Here are just a few of these very creative books with very uncreative titles.*

Prozac Nation
Fast Food Nation
Prison Nation
Rogue Nation
Dopamine Nation
Poker Nation
Roadtrip Nation
Nutcracker Nation
Bungalow Nation
Free Agent Nation
Credit Card Nation
Hellfire Nation
Asphalt Nation
Cornbread Nation
Chili Nation
Redneck Nation
Database Nation
Bloodbath Nation
Dangerous Nation
Bacon Nation
Hot Sauce Nation
Shame Nation
Ecstatic Nation
Corporation Nation
Translation Nation
Fat Nation
Fit Nation
Throwaway Nation
Improv Nation
Passionate Nation
Jackpot Nation
Parent Nation
Pet Nation
Barbecue Nation
ADHD Nation
Whistleblowing Nation
Tattoo Nation
Shed Nation
Litigation Nation
Salmon Nation
Gunfighter Nation
Fresh Food Nation
Dam Nation
Airbrushed Nation
Bully Nation
Gamer Nation
Occupy Nation
Wireless Nation
Slave Nation
Celebrity Nation
Suburban Nation
Bailout Nation
Custom Nation
Sugar Nation
Radical Nation
Wolf Nation
Apprentice Nation
Integration Nation
An Inflammation Nation
Smuggler Nation
Pantsuit Nation
Crude Nation
Invisible Nation

The first pair of soccer shoes was owned by King Henry VIII.

MORE LIKE DARKHOUSES

During the 18th and 19th centuries and beyond, lighthouses jutted out from the rocky coasts of the U.S. and western Europe to guide ships through dark and stormy seas. Despite all the light, they're a source of a lot of dark history—and some spooky ghost stories.

GET THE LEAD OUT

Before electricity and light bulbs, the light in a lighthouse tower came from old-fashioned fire. Those flames could easily grow out of control, something that happened in 1755 at the lighthouse at Eddystone Rocks off the southern coast of England. As 94-year-old lighthouse keeper Henry Hall noticed a spark travel up and ignite the tower—made of pitched-coated wood and lead paint—it was too late to do anything. Molten lead rained down on his face and into his throat. He died 12 days later, with 200 grams of solid lead in his stomach.

MERCURY RISING

Isolation in a tiny building where they had to remain all day and all night for weeks was part of the job for lighthouse operators, and they earned a reputation as being strange individuals. The effects of a solitary life left them desocialized—or so went the conventional wisdom at the time. But their mental-health problems were more likely the result of mercury poisoning. Until the mid-20th century, when lighthouses embraced electricity and automation, keepers had to maintain the 2.5-ton rotating lenses that flashed light and helped the ships at sea. The lenses spun more easily and for longer in liquid mercury, and long-term exposure to that toxin leads to hallucinations and depression. One example: British Columbia's Ballenas Island lighthouse operator William Brown was committed to a mental-health facility in 1905 after exhibiting violent behavior toward his wife. He got better during his stay, and then got worse immediately upon returning to work.

CAUSE OF DEATH: TAKE YOUR PICK

Ullman Owens ran the Holland Island Bar Light, a lighthouse on Chesapeake Bay in Maryland, from 1911 until his mysterious death in 1931. When fellow lighthouse keeper Henry Sterling across the bay noticed that Owens's light had gone out, he hailed a passing ship, whose first mate agreed to check in. The first mate and another sailor discovered a grisly scene: Owens lay dead next to a butcher knife in a kitchen splattered with blood, but he had no stab wounds or other non-superficial injury. His death was ruled the result of a "fit" related to a recent illness. But an autopsy showed he had a cracked skull, and there were witnesses who saw a dark boat moving away from the lighthouse at the time of Owens's demise; Owens also had a couple of girlfriends who

had left their husbands for him, suggesting one of the spurned husbands was at fault. The autopsy also indicated he died of a heart attack, and that was considered that.

ACCIDENTAL FINAL RESTING PLACE

Tillamook Rock Lighthouse, or "Terrible Tilly" as it's known to locals in northwestern Oregon, was built out of necessity in 1881. Two ships crashed on the rocks near the lighthouse during construction, including one just a week before the lights turned on. Terrible Tilly stands at an isolated nexus point of awful storms, including one in 1934 that caused boulders to crash into and damage the lighthouse. Deactivated in 1957, it was sold in 1980 to Eternity at Sea, a columbarium, or mausoleum for the storage of urns full of human cremains. After accumulating the ashes of 30 people who wanted Terrible Tilly to be their eternal resting place, Eternity at Sea went out of business. The urns remain, while the structure becomes increasingly hard to access as the rock it is built on slowly erodes into the ocean.

GHOSTS OF PRISONERS PAST

The lighthouse at Point Lookout in Maryland was built in 1830; in 1862, it became the site of the nation's largest Civil War prison. Up to 8,000 Confederate soldiers ended up dying there under deplorable conditions. Paranormal researchers say they've recorded a total of 24 different voices at the Point Lookout Lighthouse, which they believe to be coming from the spirits of deceased prisoners and that of Ann Davis, wife of the first keeper. Visitors and staff have also claimed to witness the ghost of Ann, whose spectral voice can be heard referring to "my home."

DUST TO DUST

Built in 1875, the White River Light Station in Whitehall, Michigan, overlooks Lake Michigan. Its first keeper died on the job in 1919, but his spirit apparently never left. A curator at the lighthouse museum claims to have frequently heard steps going up and down the stairs in the middle of the night, and sometimes with another pair of feet—those of the keeper's wife. That same contemporary curator says the ghosts are actually quite helpful—they once helped her dust the lighthouse-turned-museum.

CATS OFF

According to lore, the keeper of the Fairport Harbor Lighthouse on Lake Erie tended to his bedridden wife on the premises, bringing her a succession of cats to improve her mood. One gray cat still reportedly wanders around the lighthouse in a ghostly form. At the Cape Hatteras Light Station in North Carolina, a cat that supposedly once belonged to a keeper hung around more than a century after its death. The black-and-white cat, which looks like it weighs about 25 pounds, doesn't weigh anything at all—after it approaches visitors and rubs up against their legs, begging to be petted and picked up...it disappears.

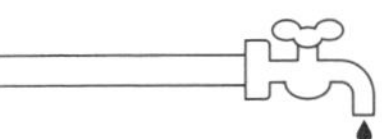

BELL LABS' GREATEST HITS

Many of the gadgets and technology you use today wouldn't be possible without a scientist dreaming up at least one of their components at a certain building in New Jersey. Here's a look at a century of innovation at Bell Labs.

Background

Originating from the Western Electric Engineering Department of the 19th century, Bell Telephone Laboratories was formed in 1925 as a joint venture with American Telephone and Telegraphic (now AT&T), at one point the one and only phone company and the corporate successor to the Bell Telephone Company, created by phone inventor Alexander Graham Bell. AT&T poured millions procured from its telephony monopoly into Bell Labs, making it a sophisticated think tank, or research-and-development facility.

At first the organization, at the time staffed by some of the world's most cutting-edge scientists, aimed to develop and improve phones and the phone system. Then it became a hotbed of scientific research, development, and innovation, working across disciplines—including computing, aeronautics, and electrical engineering—for AT&T and other clients. The result: Bell Labs had a major role in creating the technology that shaped the modern world and that we now take for granted. It's since changed hands, to other phone companies like Alcatel-Lucent and Nokia, but Bell Labs remains in operation at a top-secret state-of-the-art facility in Murray Hill, New Jersey.

Transistor

Full basic telephone service was installed and operational coast to coast by 1948. That completed one goal for AT&T, but left it needing to address the next issue: millions of new telephone users could easily overburden the primitive technology that had been used to build the nationwide telephone network. For more than three decades, vacuum tubes had been used to carry voices and signals. They were expensive to make and install, broke easily, had to be warmed up to work correctly, and were prone to moth infestations. Bell Labs put engineers William Shockley, Walter Brattain, and John Bardeen on the problem, tasking them with finding a modern, more sophisticated alternative.

During World War II, the U.S. military had asked Bell to explore ways to improve radar reception; while they hadn't gotten very far, engineers had stumbled on solid-state technology—materials that in their natural state effectively conducted and amplified electrical signals. The best substance was silicon, and Shockley, Brattain, and Bardeen fashioned it into triodes, tiny tubes made of pure, extremely durable

silicon that worked like vacuum tubes, but more effectively and at 1/100th the size. Within a decade, and beginning with a Sony-produced radio in 1955, transistors replaced vacuum tubes in most consumer electronics and in telephony. The Bell Labs team won a Nobel Prize for this development of the transistor.

Unix

A computer alone is just a bunch of wires and boards—it needs an operating system, or user interface software, to get it to do what you want it to do. Some of the most widely used operating systems are Mac OS for Apple Computers and Microsoft Windows for PCs. The first operating system was born at Bell Labs in 1965, designed for room-size mainframe industrial computers, which were really the only computers available at the time. Only a few facilities had them, including General Electric, MIT, and Bell Labs, and these organizations pooled their funds and engineers to write software both to share data among one another and make the computers easy to use. Programmers Dennis Ritchie and Ken Thompson created Unix, which organized stored computer data like a virtual filing cabinet, represented on monitors as such. Unix was easily transferable to other computer hardware systems, and it became the operating software of choice during the first wave of PC adoption, by hobbyist computer owners, in the 1970s.

Speech Synthesizer

Bell Labs acoustic engineer Homer Dudley was supposed to figure out how to compress and encrypt the human voice so that it could be transferred via copper wire—something that other engineers theorized would make telephone calls crisper and transmit faster. Instead, Dudley explored so much about the science of the human voice, and how the vocal tract works during speech, that he was able to synthesize sounds to create the first artificial human voice. At the 1939 World's Fair in New York, Dudley unveiled the Voder (short for Voice Operation DEmonstratoR). Rigged up to a set of electrified piano keys, Dudley used foot pedals to play the machine, which utilized 10 circuits to approximate 20 distinct human speech sounds. The Voder was first used by the Allies in World War II to encrypt voice-over-radio communications; it would later inform the development of the keyboard, the synthesizer, and the robotic voice used in sci-fi movies and electronic music.

Solar Power

The single most powerful and inexhaustible energy source is the sun, and in 1941, Bell Labs technicians made the first discoveries into how to harness and store its energy and convert it into usable electricity. Engineer Russell Ohl led the team that created the first solar cell, patented as a "light sensitive device," which was woefully inefficient, able to catch just 1 percent of the sunlight to which it was exposed. But

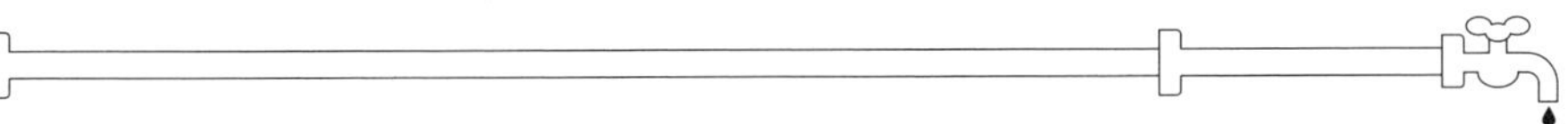

First chain restaurant to offer free soda refills: Taco Bell (1988).

Ohl laid the groundwork for a later Bell Labs project. In the mid-1950s, engineers Gerald Pearson, Daryl Chapin, and Calvin Fuller set out once more to build a solar cell. After testing out conductive metals and elements, they took a page from the transistor team and tried out silicon, which worked as a conductor. The team created a simple electrical circuit out of three strips of silicon the size of a razorblade, then put them in the sun; the silicon acquired free electrons, which were then converted into electricity. The Bell Solar Battery went into use in Georgia in 1955 to provide the electricity to power a rural telephone network.

Radio Astronomy

In 1931, Bell Labs engineer Karl Guthe Jansky was examining the mechanics of short-wave radio signals when he encountered three separate sources of unidentified interference. To get a better, all-around sense of where the static could have originated, he placed his radio antenna on a turntable, and the receiver pointed in the direction of incoming thunderstorms. Another came from somewhere in the Milky Way galaxy—in other words, from space. That basic, quickly rigged-up technology of a microphone on a rotating surface was the first radio telescope, and was essentially how NASA and other space-research agencies would build more sophisticated models. Radio telescopes are now parabola shaped and the size of a small building, and not only detect signals but communicate with space probes and satellites that beam signals back to Earth via radio waves.

Wi-Fi

A modem sends and receives data from the Internet, and a router relays the signal via low-power radio waves to your computer, phone, and other devices, connected by a wireless local area network, or LAN. This system is commonly known as Wi-Fi, and it was perfected at Bell Labs in 1988. The first Wi-Fi service, WaveLAN, was a product offered by Bell Labs' then-parent company AT&T when the internet was just beginning to be adopted by businesses and homes in the early 1990s, presenting an alternative to fully wired internet service delivered by phone lines.

Laser

A laser is a concentrated beam of light. It was an improvement on an earlier technology called the maser, an acronym for "microwave amplification by the stimulated emission of radiation." The maser came about at Bell Labs in 1954, after engineers Arthur Schawlow and Charles Townes converted a high concentration of radio and other forms of waves into an intense beam of energy. Their coworker Gordon Gould figured the method could be used to make beams of energy in the form of visible light—or, by making a maser into a laser. Bell Labs physicist Theodore Maiman built the working prototype of Gould's idea. Maiman wrapped a ruby crystal

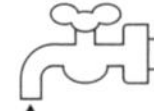

New York's Long Island is a peninsula, according to a 1985 Supreme Court ruling.

with a flash tube, which pulsed with high-voltage energy. Each pulsation delivered trillions of light particles, or photons, to the ruby, creating a beam of concentrated red light. Like every laser that came after, this one could cut right through biological material, metals, or plastics, or be used to read data.

Nuclear Reactor

In 1939, Bell Labs superiors asked William Shockley and James Fisk to look into the practical, energy-based applications of nuclear fission, which is defined as making uranium neutrons collide with larger atoms, which splits the smaller particles and releases powerful bursts of energy. Scientists in Europe had enjoyed some breakthroughs in the area in the 1930s. While Shockley and Fisk made most of their developments at the Bell Labs facility in New Jersey, Shockley had a revelatory moment in the shower at his home—if the uranium was delivered in distinct chunks rather than in a large amount, it would set up a chain reaction in which the neutrons don't get destroyed or swallowed up in the reaction, releasing more energy in the form of Uranium-235. In the span of two months, Shockley and Fisk had figured out the scientific principle to make nuclear reactors possible, thus rendering safe, controlled nuclear energy a viable concept. Their research was sent to the federal government and immediately classified. (Bell Labs was barred from patenting the technology: the scientists weren't aware at the time that the similarly nuclear-minded Manhattan Project, tasked with creating nuclear weapons as part of the World War II effort, was secretly underway.)

Cellular Phone Call Transmission

Motorola developed the first mobile phones in the 1970s, which transmitted voice calls wirelessly or cordlessly by using specific radio frequencies, or "cells." That worked fine until millions of people bought cell phones in the late 1980s and early 1990s, filling up all of the allocated radio waves. Somebody had to find a way to allow one frequency to handle countless calls simultaneously, without them interrupting one another and while maintaining privacy. Bell Labs developed the technology—time-division multiple access (TDMA)—to make it possible: signals from different phones would be sent one by one, in rapid succession, to a cell tower, where they'd be routed individually to the proper destination. That opened up the airwaves by 20 percent. But the TDMA system was exhausted by 1994 as cell phones grew more popular, leading Bell to reintroduce to the cell phone industry a World War II–era technology called code-division multiple access (CDMA). With CDMA, a cell phone call is broken down into bits of data, which are transmitted in different parts across multiple frequencies all at once, then reassembled on the other end. That opened up 20 times the amount of call capacity on the airwaves.

In Iceland, they call driving to go get ice cream *isbiltur*, which literally translates to "ice cream road trip."

Early Digital Computing

During his employment at Bell Labs in the 1930s, electrical engineer George Stibitz experimented with uses for electromagnetic relays—a component that can control multiple circuits with a single electricity source. The circuits alternate in an on-off, or binary, fashion, and Stibitz's research made binary digital computing possible. He was able to make one of the world's earliest simple computers, which could perform mathematical equations in that on-off fashion, or 1 vs. 0 binary code. In 1940, Stibitz demonstrated the Model 1 Complex Calculator, which could perform eight-digit division in under 30 seconds, to the American Mathematical Society. He operated the Complex Calculator remotely, sending commands to the society's computer at Dartmouth University in New Hampshire from Bell Labs in New Jersey. The system converted data into electric pulses and then back into data. The demonstration was the first public act of digital computing as well as the first remote computer operation.

THE BARE FACTS

Here at the Bathroom Readers' Institute, we're devoted to covering all that is uncovered—meaning all these weird news stories involve nakedness, nudity, and bare skin.

THE RIGHT TO BARE ARMS (AND EVERYTHING ELSE)

One night in April 2024, police in St. Petersburg, Florida, discovered 35-year-old Wyly James Weeks sitting inside of a trash can on a sidewalk. As if that wasn't odd enough, Weeks was also totally nude. When questioned by officers about how he found himself in his present situation, Weeks told police he "was allowed to be drunk and disorderly and sit naked in a trash can on the public sidewalk." He wasn't, however, as all those things are technically crimes. After the wobbly, booze-scented Weeks refused to provide his name to the police who helped him out of the trash can and onto his feet, he was convicted on a charge of disorderly intoxication; no public nudity counts were filed.

PINS AND NUDIES

If you hate to wear clothes and you're ever in Pittsburgh in late April, you just might want to check out Balls Out Bowling. Each year, the Pittsburgh Area Naturalists—a local society committed to the advancement of nudism—meet at Crafton Ingram Lanes to bowl in the buff. Full nudity (except, we assume, those special bowling shoes) is a requirement for men; women may wear something to cover their bottoms. All nude bowlers must be at least 18 years of age, and they're not allowed to initiate any kind of sexual behavior. They're also not allowed to bring along their phones—photos and videos are prohibited. (Where would a nude bowler put a phone anyway?)

BAD NUDES

For more than 1,000 years, the Kokusekiji Temple in Oshu, Japan, was the site of Somin-Sai, an annual event held on the seventh day of the Lunar New Year and commonly called the "naked man festival." Men wearing only loose-fitting, completely unhelpful loincloths converged at the temple and then wrestled, with the grand champion awarded a sack of religious talismans that have been blessed by the head priest of the temple. The festival of nudity, wrestling, and spirituality was held for the last time in February 2024, when chief priest Daigo Fujinami announced on the temple's website that the naked man festival had reached its end. "The decision is

due to the aging of individuals involved in the festival and a shortage of successors," he wrote.

THE NAKED CITY

The first Saturday in May is World Naked Gardening Day, a holiday started by a group that encourages embracing body positivity and embracing nature. In conjunction with the holiday in 2024, lawn care company LawnStarter examined 497 American cities and ranked them on which are the best for home gardening in the nude. Utilizing a metric that factors in population density, local indecent exposure laws, weather, sex offender density, and access to waxing salons, LawnStarter determined that sunny Miami is the best overall place for naked gardening, followed by Philadelphia, New York City, and Austin, Texas. Ranked at the bottom (pardon the pun): Billings, Montana, and the cities of Provo, Orem, and Layton in Utah.

IT'S A NUDE WORLD, AFTER ALL

The Sunday after Thanksgiving is one of the busiest and most crowded days of the year at the Disneyland theme park in Anaheim, California. In November 2023, during a full run of the It's a Small World attraction in which animatronic robots dressed in traditional clothes from cultures around the world sing the attraction's titular song over and over for almost 10 minutes, one park guest went a little mad. While his boat was in motion, the man stripped off some of his clothes, got off, and went to sit by and examine the animatronic robots representing India. As other guests shouted "please stop" and "sit down," he continued to check out the props while removing the rest of his clothes. Park personnel stopped the ride (which remained shut down for an hour) and the man was apprehended, escorted off the premises, and booked by the Anaheim Police Department.

EVERYONE COULD SEE HIS BASS

In January 2024, an adult male (not named in news reports) crashed his car near a Bass Pro Shop sporting goods outlet in Leeds, Alabama. Then he took off his clothes, ran into the store, and dove right into the Bass Pro Shop's onsite giant aquarium. The man entered the water with a cannonball-style dive and then stood under a waterfall, according to witnesses who also called police to the scene. After spotting the authorities, the naked man emerged from the water to yell at the police, then got back in to swim some more. Once the man was out of the aquarium, police arrested him and charged him with public lewdness, criminal mischief, resisting arrest, and disorderly conduct.

First movie based on a comic to earn an Oscar nomination for Best Picture: *Skippy* (1931).

JACKPOT!

Think all your problems would be solved if you won the lottery? Maybe... maybe not. Win or lose, a world with a lottery in it is still a weird one.

GOOD DOG

A woman identified in news reports only as Lin was shopping with her golden retriever in the Chinese province of Guangdong when the dog broke free of its leash and ran into a store. While in the shop, the dog managed to grab a scratch-off-style lottery ticket with its mouth, leaving it so covered in tooth marks that the store couldn't sell it. The clerk made Lin purchase the ticket, so she scratched off the rest of the boxes, just to see. The dog picked a good one—Lin won the equivalent of $139. The next day, Lin returned to the store where she'd been forced to buy the winning lottery ticket and had her dog pick another ticket. That one won $4. Appropriately, Lin spent some of her winnings on dog treats.

VERY BAD LUCK

John Cheeks bought a Powerball ticket in Washington, D.C., in January 2023, selecting his own special numbers. The next day, he checked his ticket on the D.C. Lottery website—and they matched, meaning Cheeks was the winner of the $340 million jackpot. "I got a little excited, but I didn't shout, I didn't scream. I just politely called a friend. I took a picture as he recommended, and that was it. I went to sleep," Cheeks told reporters. Then he went to the office of lottery and gaming to claim his prize, where staff told him that his winning ticket was not *actually* a winner, and that he ought to just throw the ticket away. Later, Cheeks was informed that he indeed hadn't won, and that he'd checked his numbers at a time when the lottery's website provider was running tests and posting dummy numbers—it was those numbers that matched the ones on his ticket. (Cheeks filed a lawsuit; stay tuned.)

SECRET STASH

The Guangxi Welfare Lottery awarded a player the equivalent of $30.6 million in a November 2022 jackpot drawing. The winner, identified only by the fake name Li, had played the same numbers regularly for about 10 years, and they finally paid off. But when the time came to collect his prize, which the Guangxi Welfare Lottery awarded with a large novelty check and press photographers present, Li opted to show up in a disguise: he wore a large mascot-style yellow bird costume to completely obscure his identity. The reason: he didn't want his family to know he'd just come into a huge amount of money. "I have not told my wife or children," "Li" told lottery officials. "I am concerned that they might feel superior to other people and will not work or study hard in the future."

CHAIN GANG

In the summer of 2021, a man identified in news reports only as Jamal won $30,000 after matching some of the numbers in a Michigan Lottery drawing. He used some of his earnings to purchase a $20,000 glitzy gold chain necklace. Not long after the lottery win and purchase of his necklace, Jamal entered a gas station in Detroit and had his new chain stolen.

SMALL PRIZE, BIG REACTION

The lottery that consistently doles out the most jackpots in the world is the national Christmas lottery in Spain. In 2019, the total pot was €2.24 billion (about $2.4 billion), with prizes of various sizes awarded to hundreds of participants, from €5,000 up to €400,000. When state run TV station RTVE announced the winners, reporter Natalia Escudero recognized one name: her own. "I'm not coming to work tomorrow!" she yelled into the camera. Escudero thought she'd won the "Fat One" jackpot—but she'd really won a mere €5,000. Escudero took to Twitter to apologize for her televised overreaction.

THE JUICE IS LOOSE

On May 1, 2018, Tayeb Souami made a quick stop at the ShopRite grocery store in Hackensack, New Jersey. He paid $5 for a bottle of orange juice, but when he got home, his wife asked him to go back to the store and get his money back—the same juice was on sale for half the price at another supermarket. So Souami returned to the ShopRite, and after getting his money back at the customer service desk, he noticed the nearby sign stating the Powerball jackpot had reached $306 million. Souami later told reporters that he'd thought to himself in the moment, "I like the number." With the $5 he'd just been refunded, he bought two tickets, and then immediately forgot about it. It wasn't until the next day, after the drawing, when a Powerball sign at a 7-Eleven he passed caught his eye, so he went inside and checked his numbers. Souami won the number he "liked"—$306 million.

Forgotten fast-food mascot:
Phil A. O'Fish, who promoted McDonald's Filet-O-Fish.

MYTHOLOGICAL BATHROOM CREATURES

And here we thought Uncle John was the only supernatural being obsessed with toilets! Many cultures from around the world harbor myths and legends about ghosts and monsters who prefer to lurk in waste facilities.

- According to ancient Babylonian medical texts, a demon called Sulak lurks in places where he can get his victims alone—such as pit toilets and latrines. He takes the form of a lion walking on hind legs and lashes out when a person is at their most vulnerable: on the toilet. Because it was so easy to contract a virus or infection from toilets at the time, Sulak was thought to be the reason for disease. A form of Sulak shows up in the sacred Jewish text the Talmud as Shed Bet ha-Kise, or the "Lurker of the Latrine" or the "Demon of the Privy." After using the toilet, the user must walk half a mile away or more before sex, or else the Lurker will ensure their children will get epilepsy.
- In the ancient Roman mythological canon—which was "overflowing" with toilet deities—Crepitus was the god of both the latrine and of farting. He could be called upon to help out during periods of distressing irregularity, be it constipation or diarrhea. When other things were backed up or overflowing, such as their first-in-the-world sewer system, Romans would invoke the power of the sewer goddess Cloacina. Stercutius was the Roman god of poop, but he was viewed as more of an agricultural god (dung is crop fertilizer, after all).
- In Japanese folklore, Izanami, the goddess of both the Earth and darkness, produced poop, from which the toilet god Kawaya no-kami was born. Kawaya no-kami provides protection for people using the toilets, a dangerous place. People decorated toilets as shrines and kept their bathrooms clean, lest Kawaya struck and made their children born ugly. Kawaya no-kami was rendered as a blind man who hid in toilets with a spear, just asking for a reason to attack—so users had to cough to make him aware they were present before sitting down. (What, you want to *look* down there?)
- Chinese lore speaks of the toilet goddess Zi-Gu. Once a beautiful woman, she was married to an actor during the Tang Dynasty, around the seventh century. But then a government official fell in love with Zi-Gu, killed her husband, and kidnapped her as his mistress. His jealous wife, Li-Jing, hid behind a stack of toilet

Vlad the Impaler—the real-life "Dracula"—had a rare condition that caused him to cry blood.

paper and killed Zi-Gu while Zi-Gu was using the bathroom. The stall in which she was killed supposedly became haunted, and she'd moan and wail at anyone who tried to use it. Today, she is worshiped on the 15th night of the first lunar month during the Lantern Festival; if you properly pay tribute to her, she will keep your bathroom protected.

- The ancient Middle Eastern culture of the Moabites worshipped a creature called Belphegor on Mount Phegor. Belphegor is a demon of laziness who appears on Earth as a beautiful young woman and lures unsuspecting innocents to their doom with promises of wealth—thus creating greed and selfishness. The pure of heart see him in his true form: a horned and bearded demon who sits on a toilet throne. Rabbis in the area said he could be invoked and called upon only while a worshipper was defecating. He could be worshipped by showing off bodily holes and offering poop as a sacrifice. Essentially, he sits on a toilet all the time eating human waste, offering wealth as a thanks.
- Dating back to 17th-century Japan is a spirit or *yokai* named Akaname. Depicted in old prints as a blue-green humanoid lizard with long black hair, he also has a long, intimidating forked tongue. While it may look frightening, it serves a valuable purpose in sanitation. Akaname reportedly uses that strong tongue to lick away accumulated scum, filth, and waste left behind on toilets and bathtubs. (*Akaname* translates to "filth licker.")
- Another ghost said to lurk in Japanese bathrooms has a history dating back only as far as the early 20th century: accounts of Akai-Kami go back to around 1930. He lurks in public bathrooms, waiting to ask those using the facilities what color of toilet paper they would like to use. Answer carefully—if you say red, Akai-Kami will flay you alive, while blue indicates your preference to be strangled to death and drained of your blood. Yellow is a little more obvious—choose that and the bathroom demon will pee on you or drown you in the toilet.
- Many animals boast some kind of natural and threatening defense mechanism to protect themselves from predators and danger. The bonnacon is just such an animal, except it's completely mythical, written about in the first century AD by ancient Roman author Pliny the Elder. The beast sported a bull's head, a horse's mane, and inward-bending horns to assist it in goring its enemies. But a fight with the bonnacon never got that far, according to Pliny the Elder. The creature, supposedly spotted in what is today North Macedonia, would spray its attackers with its own feces while running away. It hit them like a ton of bricks, and from several hundred feet away. The poop could reportedly scorch any living thing upon contact.

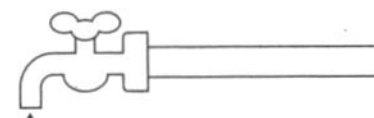

Only living monarch who can speak Czech: Norodom Sihamoni, the king of Cambodia.

THE DARWIN AWARDS

Famed evolutionary biologist Charles Darwin (1809–82) died of heart disease, making him ineligible for a Darwin Award.

BACKGROUND

"The Darwin Awards commemorate individuals who protect our gene pool by making the ultimate sacrifice of their own lives. Darwin Award winners eliminate themselves in an extraordinarily idiotic manner, thereby improving our species' chances of long-term survival." That's the official mantra of this macabre collection of strange-but-true stories. They were started in 1993 by a Stanford University biochemistry researcher named Wendy Northcutt, who "found dumb deaths in newspaper articles from around the world, rewrote them to bring out the humor, and sent them to a small email list of friends." That small list grew into a large list, then into a website and books, and is still going strong today.

Note: actual geneticists are quick to point out that this is neither how genetics nor natural selection works. Large groups or entire species—not individuals—evolve over time in response to their environment. As such, Darwin Awards should be viewed only as cautionary tales. And they should never be used to claim that someone—or the label they happen to belong to is "less evolved" just because, let's say, they got crushed to death by the very same vending machine they were trying to steal from (true story). So, as you read these ill-fated swan songs from the BRI's bottomless files, Uncle John reminds you that a lot of us have a "that time I almost died" story. These unfortunate folks will never get to tell theirs.

AWARD WINNERS

- In 2002, trying to prove to his friends that he had "a way with electricity," a 22-year-old Philippines man (who'd been drinking) grabbed an exposed live wire with his bare hand after claiming that doing so would have no effect. It did. The young man shrieked and shook violently. With third-degree burns to most of his body, he died on the way to the hospital.
- One night in 1523, a baker from Cambridge, England, had a bit too much to drink. While attempting to use the cesspit out back, he fell in and drowned.
- A 24-year-old delivery driver from India had some help from his 25-year-old friend. In 2023, the younger man took his two-wheeler in to be washed at a bike service center where his older friend was employed; afterward, the two friends were "playing" with the electric air hose that dries the vehicles. According to the police

What's the Confusion Bowl? A football game between the University of Miami and Miami University of Ohio.

report, the service-center employee shot a blast of air at his friend's face, then at his back, and then "filled his rectum with hot air." The young man collapsed and was rushed to the hospital, but doctors were unable to save him due to "massive damage to [his] intestines." His friend was arrested for "culpable homicide."

- In 2021, a New York dad-to-be constructed an explosive device for his baby's gender reveal party. While he was "tinkering" with the device beforehand, it detonated, killing him instantly.
- There's a staggering number of accounts of people dying in vain attempts to retrieve their smartphones—from cliffs, buildings, outdoor toilets, and more. But this Darwin Award goes to the 26-year-old man who was looking for the phone that he'd dropped while riding a roller coaster at Cedar Point in Ohio. According to the amusement park, "At approximately 5:00 p.m., a guest entered a restricted, fenced area of the Raptor roller coaster and was struck by the ride." He died.
- One night in 2024, a Buddhist monk and his 49-year-old friend took some meth in a temple. The friend went on a violent rampage and barricaded himself inside. When police finally reached him, it was a grisly scene. After trying to climb up a large Buddha statue, the man slipped and fell backwards onto the "sharp end" of a smaller Buddha statue below, impaling his heart and lungs.
- Wearing a neck pendant with a knife blade might make you look cool, just be careful not to trip and fall in a restaurant parking lot (or anywhere else). That's what happened to a 42-year-old Massachusetts man in 2023. At first, police thought he'd been attacked, but forensics concluded that when he slipped and landed on the pavement, his knife pendant pierced his neck. (Maybe try wearing a spork instead.)
- In 2015, a 37-year-old actor and fitness guru was filming a commercial for an energy drink...while running on active train tracks in Burbank, California. According to the police report, he misjudged which track an oncoming train was using (there was a curve) and failed to yield to it, even though its horn was blaring.
- The thermal hot springs for which Yellowstone National Park is famous are not the kind of hot springs you can soak in. That's why there are fences and signs galore warning visitors that it's illegal to leave the surrounding trail. In 2016, a 23-year-old man and his sister left the boardwalk area, which is the only space open to visitors, surrounding the park's Norris Geyser Basin. While his sister filmed with her phone, the man reached down the rocky edge to check the temperature of the boiling sulfuric acid...and slipped and fell in. When rescuers attempted to retrieve his body the next day, there was no longer a body to retrieve. "In a very short order," a park ranger told reporters, "there was a significant amount of dissolving."

The cremains of an adult human being amount to 3.5 percent of the person's weight at the time of death.

GENERATION ALPHA SPEAKS!

This page will probably be outdated two weeks after you read it, but for the time being, here's a handy guide to understanding the mystifying slang words the kids these days (born around 2010, give or take) are using.

Ate. Did something very well.

Sus. Short for "suspicious," meaning something is untrustworthy.

Snacks. Used to describe an attractive person.

Bffr. Abbreviation of "be for real," used to express disbelief; essentially the same as "seriously?"

Bae. Term of endearment for a romantic partner, short for "before anyone else."

Stan. A big fan of something.

Fam. Close friends.

Thirsty. Desperate for attention.

Ghosting. Abruptly ending all contact with someone, usually in a dating context.

Fanum tax. When friends sneak a bite or a fry from each other's food. It refers to Fanum, a person who plays video games live on the internet, and he steals food a lot.

Rizz. Charm, charisma, or style.

Basic. A person or thing that is ordinary, unoriginal, or bland.

Bussin. Very good. Used especially to describe food.

Vibe. Overall feeling or mood of a place or person.

Ratio'd. When a social media post receives more responses, usually negative ones, than it gets "likes."

Finna. Preparing (to do something).

Extra. Embarrassingly over the top behavior.

Clapback. To reply with wit to criticism or insults.

Cringe. Embarrassing or uncool.

Ohio. A loser; a person who does something poorly.

GOAT. Greatest of all time.

Fleek. Perfect in appearance or execution.

Drip. Great style or fashion sense, or a particularly stylish ensemble.

Fit. The clothes someone is wearing (short for "outfit").

Kicks. Shoes.

Jelly. Jealous.

Bruh. An all-purpose interjection, it came from *bro* and means the same thing as "oh man."

Yeet. An exclamation used to express enthusiasm.

Bet. To be in agreement. Short for "you bet."

WHAT A CROWD!

As we were finishing this book in the autumn of 2024, the world population was approaching eight billion people. From that perspective, these records for the largest crowds ever gathered don't seem that impressive. Unless you're in one of them!

LARGEST ANCIENT GATHERINGS

- The earliest evidence of tens of thousands of people coming together goes all the way back to the Neolithic Age, more than 7,000 years ago, when the Cucuteni-Trypillia culture built a megacity in present-day Ukraine. The city housed an estimated 29,000 residents; during festivals, that number rose to up to 46,000.
- Ancient Rome's Colosseum held up to 50,000 people. About a mile away was a stadium called Circus Maximus, where 300,000 spectators could cheer on the chariot races.

LARGEST RELIGIOUS EVENTS

- The largest gatherings in the world are religious pilgrimages. Currently in the top spot is the 2019 Ardh Kumbh Mela, a gathering of 50 million Hindus in Prayagraj, India. The event happens in that location every 12 years.
- The largest annual gathering is the Arbaeen pilgrimage in Karbala, Iraq. In 2017, more than 30 million Shia Muslims walked to the shrine of Imam Hussein, grandson of the Islamic prophet Muhammad.
- The largest Catholic gathering took place in 2015 when Pope Francis held mass in Manila, Philippines, to as many as 7 million people.

LARGEST FUNERALS

- C. N. Annadurai, or Anna, was a former teacher, playwright, and actor who was Chief Minister of the state of Madras before he died in February 1969. Anna's funeral was attended by an estimated 15 million people.
- After President Abraham Lincoln was assassinated in 1865, his body was sent by train from Washington, D.C., to his childhood home in Illinois. Millions of people—including two future presidents—lined up along the 1,700-mile route to pay their respects.
- After President John F. Kennedy was assassinated in 1963, a million people lined the streets of his funeral procession, and at least 250,000 viewed his coffin in the U.S. Capitol rotunda.

Butyric acid is used as a preservative in some chocolate bars. It's also the chemical that gives vomit its distinctive taste.

LARGEST MASS PROTEST

- The Business & Human Rights Resource Centre reports that, throughout 2021, an estimated 250 million Indian farmers, workers, and family members took to the streets to protest the country's working conditions.

LARGEST ANTI-WAR PROTESTS

- Guinness World Records recognizes a February 15, 2003, demonstration in Rome, Italy, as the "largest anti-war rally in history." There were 3 million protesters.
- An estimated 10 to 15 million more people held coordinated demonstrations on the same day in 600 other cities, making history's largest worldwide anti-war protest.

LARGEST CONCERTS

- Would you believe the record for the largest concert crowd in U.S. history was for classical music? In 1986, an estimated 800,000 people listened to a free performance by the New York Philharmonic in Central Park.
- The largest ticketed U.S. concert record was held by the Grateful Dead—with 107,019 in attendance at a 1977 show in New Jersey—until George Strait broke it in 2024 when he played in front of 110,905 country music fans in Texas.
- The biggest musical draw in history goes to Rod Stewart, who performed for 3.5 million fans on Copacabana Beach in Brazil in 1994.

LARGEST PARADES

- In 1951, an estimated 7.5 million New Yorkers held a ticker tape parade to honor World War II hero General Douglas MacArthur.
- In 2016, after the Chicago Cubs won their first World Series in 108 years, upwards of 5 million fans gathered in the Windy City to celebrate the team.
- Argentina'a 2022 FIFA World Cup win brought out about 4 million soccer fans to a parade in Buenos Aires.

LARGEST SPORTING EVENTS

- Every year, millions of people line up along the French countryside to watch the three-week-long Tour de France bicycle race; 2019 had up to 12 million spectators.
- Motor sports' biggest draw is the Indianapolis 500: an estimated 345,000 attended in 2024.
- The only time a Major League Baseball game broke the 100K mark: 115,300 watched a 2008 preseason game between the Boston Red Sox and Los Angeles Dodgers at the Los Angeles Memorial Coliseum.

Only living animal related to the giraffe: the okapi.

VICTORIAN PUNS

If you feel the need to make a need *pun whenever someone says "knead," don't think of yourself as unoriginal; you're keeping alive a "dad joke" that dates at least as far back as England's Victorian era (1837–1901). Queen Victoria, despite the common saying attributed to her, was very much amused...by these real jokes from Victorian joke books.*

Q: What is the best way of making a coat last?
A: Make the trousers and waistcoat first.

Q: Why are birds melancholy in the morning?
A: Because their little bills are all over dew!

Q: When does a sculptor explode in strong convulsions?
A: When he makes faces and—and—busts!

Q: Why is a man who never lays a wager as bad as a regular gambler?
A: Because he's no better.

"I have the best wife in the world," said the long-suffering husband. "She always strikes me with the soft end of the broom."

Q: When do we possess a vegetable time-piece?
A: When we get up at 8:00 o'clock (get a potato clock).

Q: What sort of tune do we all enjoy most?
A: For-tune, made up of banknotes!

Marriage is an institution intended to keep women out of mischief and get them into trouble.

Q: Why is a four-quart jug like a lady's sidesaddle?
A: Because it holds a gall-on.

Q: Why will seeing a schoolboy being thoroughly well switched bring to your lips the same exclamation as seeing a man lifting down half a pig, hanging from a hook?
A: Because he's a pork-reacher (poor creature)!

Q: What is the difference between a sycophant and a lover of hot condiments?
A: One curries favor, and the other favors curry.

There's a man at Camberwell so fat that they grease the omnibus-wheels with his shadow.

Q: Why is a baker a most improvident person?
A: Because he is continually selling that which he kneads himself!

Q: If you put your head between your legs, what planet do you see?
A: Uranus.

A lady wrote the following letters at the bottom of her flour barrel: O I C U R M T.

Q: Why is it easy to break into an old man's house?
A: Because his gait is broken and his locks are few.

Q: Why should a candlemaker never be pitied?
A: Because all his works are wicked, and all his wicked works, when brought to light, are only made light of.

Q: Why is a manuscript always called a MS.?
A: Because that is the state in which the editor finds it.

"Why didn't you put on a clean collar before you left home?"

"Because your mother hadn't sent home my washing."

THE SCIENCE OF COMIC BOOK JUNK

If you ever wanted to send away for some novelty advertised in the back of a comic book or magazine when you were a kid, here's what you actually would have received in the mail. And if you did pay your few cents or a buck to get these things, this is how they worked.

ITEM: X-RAY SPEX (ALSO KNOWN AS X-RAY SPECS AND X-RAY GOGS)

Description: Plastic horn-rim glasses that allow the wearer to see through skin, organs, and flesh and into another person's bones (or just underneath people's clothes), like an X-ray machine, all for $1 or less.

Science: Instead of lenses, the glasses housed cardboard discs decorated with hypnotic red-and-white circles. Those fake lenses consisted of two pieces of thin paperboard glued together with a quarter-inch hole cut all the way through in the center and a bird feather embedded in each hole. As the wearer looks at objects or people through the holes, the thin veins in the feathers diffract light, making the image being viewed appear offset and slightly overlapping and in shades of gray. Hold up your hand and you'll see a dark hand with a light-colored barrier. It's an optical illusion of penetrative vision—you can't really see your bones (or anything else).

ITEM: VENTRILO VOICE THROWER

Description: The ads never suggested how the system actually worked—they just showed a child confusing an adult by making his voice seem to come from across the room.

Science: With a name that suggests the baffling technique of ventriloquism, the Ventrilo Voice Thrower cost 25 cents and manufacturers still made a profit because the technology is simply a swazzle: two squares of cheap and flimsy metal tied together with a ribbon. When placed in the back of the mouth and held in place by the tongue, air moves through it when the user speaks, resulting in a high-pitched sound reminiscent of some kind of combo of Donald Duck and a kazoo. It makes the wearer's voice sound different and weird, which is plenty of fun—but it doesn't remotely work for "throwing" the voice. (Not to mention that a swazzle presents a choking hazard even for adults.)

ITEM: SEA-MONKEYS

Description: They were the first thing almost resembling a pet for millions of kids. Harold von Braunhut marketed Sea-Monkeys to multiple generations of kids

...but they're 21 hours apart in time zones because the International Date Line runs between them.

with elaborately illustrated ads that promised a family of tiny, regal, and beautiful humanoid sea monsters. Two parents and some kiddie Sea-Monkeys, looking more like mermaids with legs than like fish, posed proudly in front of an underwater castle. Kids who sent in their $1 in the 1960s and 1970s received a small plastic "tank" and a few packets—one packet was fish food and the other was the Sea-Monkeys themselves. (Sea-Monkeys are still available today, and sold the exact same way.)

Science: Barely visible to the naked eye, Sea-Monkeys are just brine shrimp, dehydrated and in a state of suspended animation. They are reborn when dumped into water. Scarcely a millimeter or two in length when fully grown, brine shrimp look like shellfish or bugs and they swim around the tank; they are about as interesting as goldfish, but nearly microscopic. They certainly couldn't "be trained," as the Sea-Monkey ads promised.

ITEM: POTATO CLOCK

Description: It's a common choice then and now for the not-particularly curious elementary schooler who has to come up with a science fair project. Sold via mail order or in toy stores, a potato clock kit comes with a bunch of wires, a galvanized nail, and a small digital readout; kids provide their own potatoes and harness the electricity inherent in the spud to make everything work together and operate as a functional clock.

Science: The galvanized nail is made of zinc, and when it's inserted in the potato, zinc reacts to the naturally occurring phosphoric acid. That leads to a loss of electrons, which are transferred to a penny stuck into the other side of the potato. This creates an electrical charge transferred by wires and alligator clips to the cheap little clock display.

ITEM: "EVERLASTING HEALTH AND STRENGTH"

Description: Bodybuilder and fitness champion Charles Atlas, who claimed to be "The World's Most Perfectly Developed Man," offered sale of his secrets for peak physical fitness via an ad disguised as a short comic strip. For decades in the mid-20th century, comic book readers stumbled on the illustrated story of a slender boy (a "wimp") whose beach date with a girl is ruined when a muscle-bound bully kicks sand in his face, humiliating him. The boy sends in for Atlas's book of secrets and in no time, he's strong enough to beat the snot out of that beach bully.

Science: Kids who sent in for Atlas's bodybuilding secrets received a small booklet detailing nutrition recommendations (Atlas believed the key to fitness was drinking up to five quarts of milk every day) and various exercises in his "dynamic tension" regimen. Those exercises really could help develop muscles (though not

to bodybuilder levels, like Atlas himself) by using household objects like chairs and tables or simply relying on resistance from the exerciser's own body.

ITEM: 7-FOOT-TALL MONSTER GHOST

Description: The copy for this supposedly scary toy was irresistible to kids, promising a "Scary and Life Size" ghost puppet that could be controlled by the operator "secretly hiding as far as 100 feet away." Somehow, it could "rise, jump, dart, float in air" with minimal direction, and it cost about $1 in the 1960s.

Science: While it sounded like some kind of robot or radio-controlled gadget, the ghost was actually a large white balloon with a ghostly face painted on it. You could blow it up with helium or regular air and then leave it around to rise, jump, dart, and float in the air, because it was a balloon and that's what balloons do. As for the element of control, that came from tying the ghost to one end of the spool of near-invisible fishing line and holding the other end.

ITEM: IRON-ON TRANSFER SHEETS

Description: Novelty T-shirts bearing the image of favorite TV or cartoon characters first came to prominence in the 1970s. Kids who wanted to get in on the fad could enter at a lower price point by buying the design they wanted from an array advertised in comic books, then applying the design to a blank T-shirt they supplied themselves. The chosen image came as a transfer sheet, which would stick to the fabric after being applied under heat and pressure via a common household iron.

Science: The images were printed on special heat-sensitive paper. The application of heat caused the ink to move over to the cloth of the T-shirt. But it was cheap paper, and the heavy plastic of the "ink" on the transfer when applied to the T-shirt tended to flake and chip off after just a couple of washes.

* * *

INSPIRATION COMES FULL CIRCLE

In 1939, a nine-year-old boy from Miami named Jerry Parr watched the movie *Code of the Secret Service*, which starred Ronald Reagan as a brave Secret Service agent named Brass Bancroft. That instilled in Parr a dream of one day joining the elite government agency responsible for, among other things, protecting the sitting U.S. president. By 1962, 32-year-old Parr was working as a lineman in Florida when a Secret Service recruiter offered him a chance to apply—Parr took it, and was successful. After stints watching Presidents Kennedy and Johnson, and Vice President Walter Mondale, Parr was security director for actor-turned-politician President Ronald Reagan. When Reagan was shot (but only injured) in 1981, Parr, inspired to join the Secret Service by that old Reagan movie, was credited with saving the President's life.

According to a 2024 study, toddlers have a flower-like odor, and teenagers smell like goats or cheese.

UNHEARD ALBUMS

Some of the most famous and popular musicians in the world have recorded albums that, for one reason or another, were never shared with the public.

Artist: The Supremes

Album: *Promises Kept* (1971)

Story: Motown Records tried a lot of things in the early 1970s to keep the Supremes going after Diana Ross's 1970 departure. A few albums showcased new singer Jean Terrell, some were recorded in collaboration with the Four Tops, and the planned-for 1971 LP *Promises Kept* consisted primarily of soul covers of recent and contemporary hits. A total of 19 tracks were recorded, including the Supremes' takes on Bread's "Make It With You," the Jackson 5's "Never Can Say Goodbye," the Beatles' "Eleanor Rigby," and Carole King's "It's Too Late." Motown executives just didn't like the record and didn't think it helped establish the Supremes in a post–Diana Ross era, so they rushed the group back into the studio to record the 1972 LP *Floy Joy* under the production of superstar singer Smokey Robinson. The title track would be the vocal trio's final top 20 hit.

Artist: Barry Gibb

Album: *The Kid's No Good* (1970)

Story: More than a decade before they dominated 1970s disco, the Bee Gees were a pop-rock band. The group of three Gibb brothers scored a bunch of hits in the late 1960s, including "To Love Somebody," "I Started a Joke," and "I've Gotta Get a Message to You." The Bee Gees were so popular that lead singer Barry announced his departure for a solo career in late 1969 and hit the studio to record 12 songs for an album tentatively titled *The Kid's No Good.* "I'll Kiss Your Memory" was released as an advance single to test the market for solo Bee Gees material. The song flopped, failing to make the pop chart in the U.S., U.K., or Australia. Record label Atco reacted by destroying its pressing of follow-up single "One Bad Thing" and then canceling the album altogether. By mid-1970, Gibb had reunited with his brothers and they'd recorded their biggest hits to that point, the #3 song "Lonely Days" and the #1 "How Can You Mend a Broken Heart."

Artist: Van Halen

Album: An untitled 1999 LP

Story: After alienating lead singer Sammy Hagar as well as David Lee Roth—who had returned to the band after being replaced by Hagar in 1986—Van Halen hired vocalist Gary Cherone. Cherone was the former lead singer of rock band Extreme, who had a #1 hit in 1991 with "More Than Words," and together they recorded the

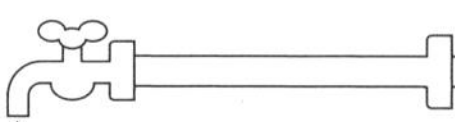

1998 album *Van Halen III*. It sold 500,000 copies, making it the worst-selling Van Halen record to that point. Nevertheless, the new configuration of Van Halen nearly completed a second Cherone-era album, writing two dozen songs and recording demo versions of seven of them. "I look back on some of those demos and I go, 'You know what? *This* should have been the first record,'" Cherone later said. The album would have been released in 1999 had Van Halen finished recording it, but personal differences drove Cherone and guitarist Eddie Van Halen apart before that could happen. Cherone was fired from the band, and the album never materialized in any form. Van Halen wouldn't release another album until 2012—*A Different Kind of Truth*, featuring (again) the vocals of David Lee Roth.

Artist: Marvin Gaye
Album: *Love Man* (1979)
Story: Reeling from a cocaine addiction, a divorce, tremendous tax debt, and the commercial failure of *Here, My Dear*—a double-length concept album about the dissolution of his marriage whose royalties were court-ordered to go to his former wife—Marvin Gaye retreated to a studio in Hawaii in 1979 to record an album he planned to ironically title *Love Man*. Gaye believed that 1960s- and 1970s-style soul was dying, as was his status as the "love man," a balladeer of smooth and sexy songs including "Let's Get It On." The LP was reportedly all over the place; some of the songs were free-form cries for help and calls for the return of his estranged new wife, while "Ego Tripping Out" was a seven-minute funk-disco song featuring Gaye doing as much talking as singing. A minor hit on the R&B chart that completely missed the pop chart, "Ego Tripping Out" helped lead Gaye to rethink the entire album because it was an exercise in non-authenticity. He wouldn't let his label, Motown, release it, much to Motown's chagrin. "I was holed up in Hawaii telling them the love man was dead. He was. The love man was me and I needed to stop that s***," he later said.

Artist: Lady Gaga
Album: A companion piece to *ARTPOP* (2014)
Story: As much of a performance artist as she is a dance music diva, Lady Gaga embraced the former with her experimental 2013 album *ARTPOP*. In contrast with the singer's previous efforts, *ARTPOP* sold more than two million copies in the U.S. and didn't generate any major hit singles, but the project was always supposed to last for at least two albums. In 2012, before the release of the first *ARTPOP*, Gaga mentioned she was recording an even more experimental sequel to the forthcoming record, and during a concert at the 2014 South by Southwest festival, she proclaimed that the still-unnamed LP had been written, recorded, mixed, and was ready to ship to stores. Then she never mentioned it again, making, in rapid succession, the standards album *Cheek to Cheek*, the intimate pop album *Joanne*, and the movie *A Star Is Born*.

George R. R. Martin's *A Song of Ice and Fire* (*Game of Thrones*) books include more than 2,000 named characters.

ASK UNCLE JOHN

Some questions have no answers. Others, like these, do.

Don't Say Cheese

Dear Uncle John, why are runway fashion models so grumpy?

A: Keep a smile on your face for 30 seconds, and see how long it takes for that smile to feel awkward and creepy. (The BRI staff average: 7.66 seconds.) Now, try perma-grinning while you're walking down a thin runway, wearing uncomfortable shoes and an elaborate, expensive outfit from a famous fashion designer. Also, there's makeup all over your face, and flashbulbs are trying to blind you. Remember to keep smiling as your try not to trip and fall onto the elites of your industry.

But the discomfort and awkwardness aren't the only reasons for the dour expression; in fact, if the models were instructed to smile, they'd give it their all to make it convincing. And there have been a few runway shows featuring smiling models, but only a few—which *New York Times* fashion editor Vanessa Friedman described as "almost always...terrifying." In addition to the creepiness factor, she says, "Smiling can make one seem like a supplicant, and fashion is supposed to make you feel powerful in your skin." Backstage at fashion shows, the models are instructed to project confidence and attitude. Tyra Banks instructs her runway models to "smile with your eyes"—not with their mouths, which just ends up weird.

EYE, MATEY!

Dear Uncle John, why did pirates wear eye patches?

A: Pirates *didn't* wear eye patches. Well, they did if they lost an eye, or were suffering from some kind of eye-related malady. But nothing in the historical record indicates that pirates wore eye patches in a greater ratio than the general public. That's one of many pirate myths likely created by pop culture, going back to Robert Louis Stevenson's 1883 novel, *Treasure Island.*

You may have read—or seen a meme—explaining that pirates with perfectly good eyes wore the patches so that when they went to and from the brightly lit deck and the dimly lit galley, they'd switch the patch from one eye to another to better adjust to the light or the darkness. A clever idea, but again, there's no actual record of this happening. In 2007, the TV show *MythBusters* proved, with the help of an

Experts say there are millions of mammoths stuck in the permafrost in the Arctic tundra.

ophthalmologist, that the wear-a-patch-to-adjust-to-the-light theory is sound. But if any peg-legged, parrot-shouldered, treasure-burying, *arr*-saying scallywag of a pirate did wear an eye patch for that reason, there's no record of it. (Pirates didn't do those other things, either.)

GOING DUTCH, PART I

Dear Uncle John, why are people from the Netherlands referred to as Dutch, and why is the Netherlands also called Holland?

A: Modern Dutch call their country *Nederland*, which means "low land" (it's 30 feet above sea level). Romans 2,000 years ago called the region *Germania Inferior* (the higher inland region, which included parts of modern-day Germany, was called *Germania Superior*); 600 years ago, the language that was spoken in the region was called *Nederlandsch*. When the Kingdom of Belgium declared independence in 1830, splitting off from the rest of the country, it went by the name *Belgica* (Latin for "low countries"). And the northern section—which for a few hundred years had been called Nederduytsch—officially became *Nederlandsch*.

Nederduytsch described the "lower people" who lived in the lowlands; *duytsch* came from a Proto-Germanic word meaning "of the people." (Germany's name in German is *Deutschland*, which means "land of the people.") Today, the language spoken in the Netherlands is called Nederlands, as are its citizens.

However, it's only English-speaking countries that refer to the language and the people as "Dutch," which can be chalked up to stubbornness. Traders had long referred to the "low Germans" who lived there as "Dutch," and they continued to do so even after the Kingdom of the Netherlands adopted its official name after the defeat of Napoleon in 1815.

Stubbornness is also why the name *Holland* stuck around: travelers from Great Britain mostly frequented the three largest cities in the country—including Amsterdam—which are located in the provinces of Noord-Holland and Zuid-Holland (from the Old Dutch *Holt Land*, meaning "wood land"). The nation has 11 other provinces, but the British were so insistent on calling the entire country Holland that the Netherlands government didn't try to stop them; they even encouraged them, all in the pursuit of tourism dollars. That's why people from the Netherlands are still called Hollanders. In 2020, the Netherlands government eliminated *Holland* from its nomenclature. Its official English-language website is still Holland.com (as of 2024), but the landing page says "Welcome to the Netherlands." And there's a photo of a windmill.

GOING DUTCH, PART II

Dear Uncle John, where is Old Zealand?

A: There is no "Old Zealand." But there is a place in Europe called Zeeland: it's the westernmost province of the Netherlands, on the North Sea, about 100 miles south of Amsterdam. The sparsely populated province got the name Zeeland—or "sea land"—for its numerous islands.

In 1642, Dutch navigator Abel Tasman sailed past two large islands in the South Pacific. Believing he was off the coast of South America, he named the islands *Staten Landt*, or "Isle of the States." Later, when the Dutch government realized that Tasman's calculations were 6,000 miles off, the islands were renamed Nieuw Zeeland. And the large landmass to the west was called Nieuw Holland, after the northern region of the Netherlands. When the British colonized that larger landmass in the early 19th century, they named it Australia and anglicized Nieuw Zeeland to New Zealand.

The Dutch—thanks to the globe-trotting Dutch East India Company—named a lot of places after their homeland, including Tasmania (after Tasman); Zeeland, Michigan; Zeeland, North Dakota; New Netherland (which the British changed to New York State); New Haarlem (now Harlem); and New Amsterdam (which the British changed to New York City). And the Queens neighborhood originally named after the Dutch city of Vlissingen was anglicized to Uncle John's favorite place name of them all: Flushing.

GOING DUTCH, PART III

Dear Uncle John, where does the phrase "going Dutch" come from?

A: The rivalry between England and the Netherlands to decide which nation could colonize the most places led to three naval wars and a lot of insults. English sailors joked that their enemies required "Dutch courage"—or alcohol—to fight. A "Dutch uncle" wasn't a nice man.

But that's not the source of "going Dutch." The Pennsylvania Dutch were 19th-century German and Swiss immigrants who settled in the eastern U.S. and were known to bring their own food and drink to gatherings. From there, the phrase "Dutch treat" came to describe a situation where everyone pays their own way. "Going Dutch" showed up around 1914.

A LOAD OF MALARKEY

Dear Uncle John, who came up with those collective nouns for birds, and are they official?

A: A collective noun is any noun that represents a group, as in, a *team* of players, a *squad* of cheerleaders, and a *murder* of crows. That last one seems a bit odd, but bird collectives like it have become a bona fide fad (especially for trivia hounds like us).

The modern origin of these terms dates back to 1968, when author (and future *Inside the Actor's Studio* host) James Lipton listed some in his lighthearted book, *An Exaltation of Larks*. The practice itself began centuries earlier in Medieval England when aristocratic hunters came up with imaginative names for groups of animals—like a "murder" of crows (perhaps due to their association with death), a "parliament" of owls (most of whom appear wise), and a "gaggle" of geese (because geese gaggle). In 1486, dozens of these clever quips, called "terms of venery" (*venery* meaning "hunting") appeared in one of the first popular books of the nascent printing industry, *The Boke of Seynt Albans*. Containing essays on hunting and hawking, this sophisticated tome allowed gentlemanly aristocrats to display their superiority with fancy phrases that ordinary people didn't know, like "an ostentation of peacocks."

The *Boke* didn't stop at birds: also listed were "a melody of harpers," a "superfluity of nuns," a "gaggle of women," a "giggle of girls," a "blush of boys," and a "blast of hunters." Bang! This naming convention remained popular for another century or so, and *The Book of Saint Albans* (as it's now called) has never been out of print.

However, in the 18th century, when biologists began giving scientific names to animals, they didn't include any terms of venery. The only scientifically accepted collective noun for birds is a "flock."

Nevertheless, some terms of venery have hung on, including a pride of lions, a herd of deer, a pack of wolves, a pod of dolphins...and an annoyance of ornithologists who are tired of laypeople always exclaiming, "Did you know a group of crows is called a *murder*?"

* * *

STAR TREK TRIVIA

Gene Roddenberry wasn't necessarily a fan of science fiction (he liked Westerns and cop shows). So, why did he create *Star Trek* in 1966? To get controversial storylines past the sensors. According to his wife, *Star Trek* actor Majel Barrett, "You put funny people in funny costumes and paint them green and we could talk about anything we wanted to, because that was the only thing that fascinated Gene about this particular genre."

Attention remote-plane-crash survivors: there's about 75 pounds of edible meat on the average adult human.

VANILLA FACTS

This page isn't "vanilla" meaning bland–it's vanilla because the BRI staff agrees vanilla is awesome, full of flavor and history alike.

- Priced about $200 per pound, vanilla is the second-most-expensive spice in the world, behind only saffron (at $5,000 per pound).
- First culture to cultivate vanilla: the Aztecs. At its peak in the 15th century in what is now Mexico, the Aztec empire cultivated, harvested, and cooked with vanilla plant seeds. The region is home to the Melipona bee, which pollinates the vanilla flower.
- The Aztecs got the idea from a small culture it conquered called the Totonacs. They took the Totonacs' minor crop and used it to flavor the popular Aztec chocolate drink called *xocolatl*. When Spanish conquistador Hernán Cortés overthrew the Aztecs in the 16th century, he brought vanilla back to Europe via hot chocolate.
- While cultivation techniques have been perfected, it's been found that vanilla can thrive only in tropical climates located within 20 degrees of the equator.
- Today, more than 70 percent of all vanilla comes from Madagascar, specifically the Plainifolia variety. That type is also grown in Indonesia, Uganda, Tanzania, India, and Mexico, while another variant, Tahitensis, is grown primarily in Papua New Guinea.
- The vanilla plant is a variety of orchid. Commercial vanilla is hand pollinated using a toothpick-sized implement. This results in pods or beans that take nine months to fully mature and ripen. They're then handpicked and cured for months, losing 75 percent of their moisture, which intensifies the vanilla flavor.
- How to create vanilla extract? Beans are chopped and left to percolate in a solution made up mostly of alcohol. Similar to making drip coffee from coffee beans, the vanilla flavor compounds move through the liquid and are collected.
- There are 250 different chemicals identified in vanilla extract, including vanillin.
- Vanillin is the main ingredient in imitation vanilla extract, made in a lab with chemicals derived from the petroleum production and refinement process, and taken from wood.
- About 90 percent of vanilla-flavored products are made with the fake stuff.
- How did "vanilla" come to mean "bland"? Because the ingredient is so ubiquitous that it's not considered special, exceptional, or unique.
- What's the difference between vanilla and French vanilla? It initially referred to a particular style of ice cream production, not the flavor or type of vanilla used. French vanilla ice cream uses a base made with egg yolks; regular vanilla ice cream doesn't. The end result tastes richer and more like a custard, which is the promise made by latter-day items bearing a French vanilla flavor, such as coffee creamer.

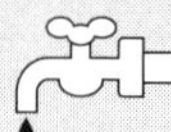

Longest-running sitcom with no Christmas episode:
Mad About You **(170 episodes).**

DUMB CROOKS

Here's proof that crime doesn't pay.

FOOL ME TWICE

In 2018, Anchorage police had no trouble finding Michael Gale Nash after he robbed a branch of First National Bank of Alaska because his name and birthdate were on the back of his demand note. Not that they had to go far, anyway—Nash was sitting on a curb outside the bank counting the $400 he'd stolen. After serving a year in prison, Nash robbed the same bank *again* in 2023. Rather, he would have, but he got there too early, so he slipped the demand note under the door and waited for the bank to open at 10:00 a.m. The cops showed up first and took Nash back to jail.

WHAT A GENIUS

There's an old *The Far Side* comic featuring a "Midvale School for the Gifted" student pushing on a door that says "PULL." (Get it?) The grown-up version of that kid—Matthew Leshinksy of Long Island, New York—was already a scientist by age 23. He even had his own facility, Quantitative Laboratories LLC, which analyzes legal cannabis. Late one night in June 2023, Leshinsky called 911 to report a burglary in progress at the lab. When officers arrived, they didn't find a burglar, but they did find, according to the *New York Post*, "100 items of lab equipment, chemical reagents and solvents that go into meth...along with over 3 ounces of meth, 625,000 milligrams of pure ketamine, and 20 plastic jugs of gamma-butyrolactone (GBL), which is similar to the 'date rape drug' GHB...[and] $40,000." Leshinsky's lawyer argued that his "brilliant" client was not a drug dealer, but was studying drug addiction "for the public good." The sketchy study, and his ill-advised 911 call, landed Leshinksy a four-year prison sentence.

LACKING HINDSIGHT

In 2016, a 23-year-old "serial burglar" named Christopher Atherton was arrested near Liverpool, England, for handling stolen goods. How'd police find out he was a serial burglar? After they handcuffed him and put him in the back of the police van, he retrieved a small phone from between his butt cheeks and somehow managed to take a selfie. The cops discovered the phone and (hopefully wearing gloves) scrolled through photos of Atherton's previous crime scenes, including the home of a sleeping elderly women. He was sentenced to 21 months behind bars.

Update: A few years later, police found an unopened, blood-stained safe in a shopping cart in the middle of the road. A DNA test revealed the blood belonged to

Most common model of little car driven in parades by Shriners: the Rupp Monza SS Chevy Jr.

Atherton, who was out on release. He claimed that he merely "found" the stolen safe, but later pled guilty and got another 26 weeks.

AMBASSADORS AT LARGE

In 2024, a 32-year-old singer named Cecilia Selina Mercado (who goes by the stage name Sessi) was driving her Audi in Sunny Isles Beach, Florida, when she was pulled over for a traffic violation. Mercado told the cops she can do whatever she wants to because she has "diplomatic immunity." It says so right on her license plate. Not really—it says, "ambassador at large." Two problems: 1) the plates were fake novelty plates; 2) Mercado was born in New York, and diplomatic immunity pertains only to non-U.S. citizens. Providing only a passport and no driver's license, Mercado refused to step out of her car, so officers dragged her out and arrested her. The next day, when she was released, her boyfriend picked her up in a car that also had fake diplomatic plates...and guns. He was arrested. "This is not funny," complained Mercado. "This is messed up."

TESTY DRIVE

The Memphis, Tennessee, car salesman (unidentified in news reports) knew something was off with Joshua Garvins, 26, who wanted to take a vehicle for a test drive. The apprehensive salesman refused to hand over the keys, and his suspicions were proven correct when Garvins threatened to kill him. The two men got into a tussle, during which Garvins pulled out a gun and somehow shot himself in the neck. He ran away but didn't make it too far before the police apprehended him. The salesman wasn't injured and said he just wants to "move on" from the experience.

THE DUMB SIDE OF THE FORCE

The Darth Vader of the movies wields a red lightsaber. This Darth Vader wielded a silver handgun, but he was no match for a jar of ranch dressing. The incident occurred at the 8 Till Late convenience store in Jacksonville, Florida, in 2015. The wannabe Sith Lord walked in—wearing a hoodie, a black Darth Vader face mask and chest plate, and dark jeans—and demanded all the cash. Not falling for the Jedi mind trick, the clerk went for the gun and, in the ensuing battle, threw a jar of ranch dip that smacked Vader in the face. A bottle of wine also fell and shattered on the floor. Breathing heavily, Vader ran outside and removed his mask in front of witnesses, who saw the bleeding robber jump into a getaway car that the cops quickly located in a nearby driveway. They arrested Anakin Sky...er, Jacob Jeremy Mercer, 32, without incident. "That was killer," said one witness.

* * *

"There is still no cure for the common birthday."

—John Glenn

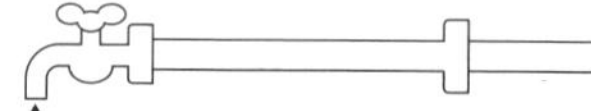

In Spanish, an avocado pit is called a *hueso*, which means "bone."

OOPS GOES TO WAR

War. What is it good for? Absolutely nothing! (Although these true stories of military blunders do make for good bathroom reading.)

DON'T KILL THE MESSENGER

The Setup: In 1218, a caravan of traders arrived in the city of Otrar in the Khwārezm empire (in present-day central Asia). But the local governor thought they were spies sent by a neighboring emperor, so he executed the members of the caravan. Only one trader escaped. When the neighboring emperor found out, he sent three emissaries to the sultan of Khwārezm, Shah Alā ad-Dīn Muḥammad II, reiterating that they just wanted to open a trade route. The shah didn't trust them, either, beheading the messengers and returning one of the heads to the neighboring emperor.

The Oops: That neighboring emperor was none other than Genghis Khan. Despite the ruthless Mongol's reputation, he really did want to open a new trade route. Not any more, though. In retaliation for Khwārezm's offenses, Khan sent more than 100,000 soldiers to obliterate the empire.

THE LONG KISKA GOODNIGHT

The Setup: It's a little known fact that a World War II military campaign took place in North America. It happened on the Aleutian island of Kiska near the territory of Alaska. In 1942, Japan invaded the sparsely populated island and set up a base there. In August 1943, after repeated bombings from Allied planes failed to take the island back, a force of American and Canadian soldiers attacked.

The Oops: By the time Allied troops landed on Kiska, the 5,000 Japanese soldiers that had occupied the island were long gone. They'd snuck away in the night a few weeks earlier after destroying their base. Not knowing that, Allied troops scoured the island, but in the confusion and fog, there were still 24 casualties resulting from friendly fire. Another 71 troops were killed when a navy destroyer hit an underwater mine. The Japanese won the battle without even being there to fight it.

"ABNORMAL DESCENT"

The Setup: In April 2023, a year after Russia invaded Ukraine, a Russian Su-34 fired a missile at the town of Belgorod, damaging a building and injuring two women.

The Oops: Belgorod is in Russia, a full 25 miles from the Ukrainian border. After trying to blame the goof on Ukraine, a Russian Defense Ministry spokesperson

described it as "an abnormal descent of aviation ammunition." And as *Business Insider* reported, this wasn't Russia's first "humiliating blunder" of the war: "In January, one of its sergeants accidentally detonated a hand grenade in a barracks, killing three of his comrades. Ukrainian and Western observers have also recorded multiple instances of Russian troops firing on their comrades."

DRINK ME

The Setup: By 1625, England's power and standing had diminished in Europe. So the Duke of Buckingham, Lord High Admiral, decided to invade Spain: 100 warships with 15,000 troops, commanded by Sir Edward Cecil, landed on the Spanish city of Cádiz. Finding it too heavily fortified, Cecil decided it would be better if they invaded the countryside. His army marched into Andalucía.

The Oops: Andalucía is known for its wine. Short on food, Cecil gave his men permission to raid the ample stores of the beverage. By the time the Spanish army showed up, the British soldiers were so drunk that the last thing 2,000 of them saw was the wrong end of a Spanish sword.

MISSED THE POINT

The Setup: During the Crimean War in 1854, when Great Britain teamed up with France and the Ottoman Empire against the Russian Empire, British Field Marshal FitzRoy James Henry Somerset saw something alarming during the Battle of Balaclava: Russian soldiers were raiding Ottoman artillery holds and stealing their cannons. Somerset dictated orders to Captain Louis Nolan to deliver to George Bingham, who was in charge of the cavalry. The orders were to send a "light brigade"—minimally armored horsemen who rely on speed—to protect the guns.

Nolan rode his horse to Bingham's position and relayed the order to "attack the guns." Then he pointed in the general direction of the Ottoman artillery stores, and Bingham ordered 600 members of the Light Brigade to ride there as fast as they could.

The Oops: Either Nolan pointed in the wrong direction, or Bingham misunderstood the pointing. Instead of the Light Brigade riding to the minimally guarded Ottoman artillery stores, they rode straight into the heart of the heavily guarded *Russian* artillery stores. The Russians opened fire, forcing the Light Brigade into a swift retreat. More than half of them made it back to safety, but 278 ended up dying—all thanks to sloppy pointing. (The Russians assumed their invaders were drunk.) Alfred, Lord Tennyson immortalized the fallen soldiers in his poem "The Charge of the Light Brigade," which calls to "Honour the Light Brigade" even though, "Someone had blundered. / Theirs not to make reply, / Theirs not to reason why, / Theirs but to do and die."

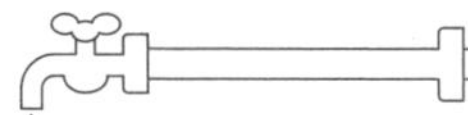

Most common form of murder among primates: infanticide.

WORDPLAY Q&A

Some conundrums for your cranium. Answers on page 341.

1. What do the words described here have in common: "an up-and-down toy," "more yellow than white for breakfast," and "a short exclamation of delight"?

2. Can you add one letter to *fast* to make it its own antonym?

3. Which English words are derived from the Japanese for "empty orchestra," from the Latin for "my own fault," and from the Arabic for "body-eating spirit"?

4. Try not to get winded thinking of this condition that begins and ends with the same vowel and has four different consonants between.

5. This five-letter word begins and ends with different vowels. The first letter is a word that means the same thing as the last four letters...and the same thing as the last three letters. What is this singular word?

6. This six-letter word has two pronunciations: one is a noun for "a small unit of time"; the other an adjective for "a small amount of anything." What is the word?

7. What do an island and the letter *t* have in common?

8. What's so special about *forty*? You won't find it in *four*, *fifty*, *one*, *eight*, *thousand*, *million*, or any other number.

9. What's the only word that becomes smaller when you add two letters?

10. Two states have six. Four states have five. What are they? And what are the states?

11. The seven letters that comprise this small European country's name are the most commonly used seven letters in English. What is the country?

12. Don't have a cow, man, but can you think of a common word that contains six consecutive consonants? If not, you are the weakest link! That's what she said. D'oh!

13. Good luck figuring out which two-digit number contains the most syllables.

14. Chances are you can't figure out which one-syllable word becomes a three-syllable word with the addition of a single letter (the same letter as the first).

15. Which nourishing word becomes its own past tense when you rearrange the letters?

16. Which common English word comes from the first two words of the Greek alphabet?

17. What do the New York Giants have in common with the Towering Yanks?

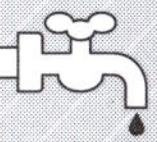

Only state with an official state nut that isn't the pecan: Oregon, with the hazelnut.

TOILET TECH

Better living through bathroom technology.

THE HEAT IS ON

Product: LumaWarm
How It Works: The toilet seat can be one of the coldest places in a home, and it's certainly an unpleasant and uncomfortable surprise when you're not expecting your bare bottom to make contact with something seemingly ice-cold. Enter the LumaWarm, a sophisticated electronic heated toilet seat with several luxurious features. At the push of a button, the LumaWarm heats to one of three preprogrammed temperature settings in about five minutes' time. It also comes equipped with a stay-on blue night-light to help navigate a middle-of-the-night bathroom trip—when the toilet seat would otherwise be at its absolute coldest.
Cost: $119–$159

FAMILIAR BATHROOM SOUNDS

Product: Talking TP: Talking Toilet Paper Roll Holder
What It Does: Manufacturer Spitfire Ventures markets this item as a prank-ready novelty and a communications device to spread secret messages. The unsuspecting victim, after doing their business, pulls on the toilet paper mounted on the gadget, which activates a hidden sound chip. A tiny speaker emits whatever six-second message you record yourself—you can make it say "Hey, don't pull so hard!" or "Will you marry me?" or a variety of preloaded movie or television sounds.
Cost: $15.95

ON THE GO

Product: Carloo
What It Does: The Carloo is designed for people who need to make frequent bathroom stops during long car trips or tooling around town but have "pee anxiety" about using public restrooms. The Carloo allows them to comfortably urinate (and only urinate—Carloo is explicitly not for number two) in the relative privacy and comfort of the car. Resembling a Tupperware-encased bed pan, because that's what it is, the Carloo consists of a round plastic tub into which fits a metal collection bowl with a seat on top. Simply do your business, put back on the locking airtight lid to prevent spills, and put it under a seat or in the trunk to dispose of later.
Cost: $49.99

Country that reads the most: India. The average resident reads for nearly 10.5 hours per week.

YOUR DAILY PAPER

Product: Toilet Paper Printer
What It Does: We're big fans of reading in the bathroom (in case you hadn't figured that out), but even we didn't think of printing reading material directly onto TP. This printer puts text onto small sheets—even linking to the Internet to print Tweets, social media posts, and RSS feeds—so you can get all your online content in nontoxic, rear end–safe ink. Simply read, then wipe and dispose of properly.
Cost: $300

WAD, DON'T WIPE

Product: The UnWipe
What It Does: Popular in Europe and Japan, the bidet is a cleaner, less wasteful alternative to toilet paper. It shoots a spray of water onto one's rear to clean things up; no wiping or flushing of TP or thick, pipe-clogging wet wipes required. But bidets are expensive, bulky, and require a special water line and an electrical outlet. The UnWipe is a super-low-tech alternative. It's a plastic mesh container that's filled with water, onto which you press a wad of toilet paper. It gets the paper just the right amount of wet, and then you use that mushy toilet paper to clean yourself up.
Cost: $34

KNOW BEFORE YOU NEED TO GO

Product: DFree
What It Does: The DFree is a medical device that tells you when you need to go to the bathroom before you go to the bathroom. Designed for people with incontinence issues, the device consists of a sensor that's attached to the lower abdomen. It notices when the bladder is getting full and notifies the wearer's phone that it's time to evacuate in a nearby toilet, before they get the sensation or potentially suffer an accident.
Cost: $399

TRICKLE-DOWN ECONOMICS

Product: Roca Connect
What It Does: Roca makes a variety of high-tech bathroom fixtures and toilets, and they want their customers to know just how much water those products use, or save. Roca Connect is a smartphone app that communicates with a bathroom toilet, sink, shower, bidet, or bath to determine how much each fixture uses daily. It can even be programmed with multiple users, so homeowners can get a handle on which person in the house uses the most water, and where.
Cost: Free (for Roca-branded high-end smart toilets and automated showers)

In 1777, Prussia's Frederick the Great officially decreed that his people start the day with beer instead of coffee.

PICKLEBALL, ANYONE?

A delightful fad has captured Americans' hearts since the early 2020s: pickleball. A gentler form of tennis that almost anyone with arms and legs can play, the game has been around for decades but only recently became a sensation outside of its Pacific Northwest birthplace. Here's the story of the origins, and very slow rise, of pickleball.

- Washington state House of Representatives member Joel Pritchard maintained a weekend home on upscale Bainbridge Island, situated in Puget Sound near Seattle. In the summer of 1965, he returned home after a round of golf with his friend Bill Bell, and both men's families complained about the lack of entertainment options on Bainbridge. Pritchard told his particularly bored teenage son Frank that when he'd gotten bored as a kid, he'd made up new games and played them; 13-year-old Frank sarcastically challenged his father to make up a game right there and then.
- Pritchard and Bell thought about just stringing up a badminton net over a disused tennis court on the property, but they couldn't procure enough rackets for everyone who wanted to play. What they did find was a box of table tennis paddles, along with a wiffle ball—the hard plastic kind covered in holes. The guys started volleying the plastic ball across the net with the wooden paddles. When the ball loudly but satisfyingly cracked on the pavement with every missed shot, they decided to make the game more tennis-like and lowered the net from 60 inches high to 32 inches, with a dip in the middle. By the end of the weekend, the Pritchard and Bell families had completely fallen in love with this new, still-unnamed game.
- All the adults went back to their jobs but returned to the Pritchard house on Bainbridge Island the next weekend, along with Pritchard's neighbor, Barney McCallum. They codified the rules about court size and game play, combining elements of tennis, badminton, and table tennis. McCallum, who ran a manufacturing company, dedicated himself to making paddles specifically for the sport: flat like a Ping-Pong paddle, but bigger and harder.
- There are two competing stories as to how this ramshackle racket game was named after pickles. The Pritchard family had a dog named Pickles, and for years it was rumored that he was the inspiration for the sport's moniker. But Frank's mother, Joan Pritchard, told reporters that they didn't get that dog until the early 1970s, years after pickleball was invented. The name actually comes from a rowing term. In competitive crew-style rowing, a craft staffed by available second-stringers

Makes sense: the noun *luggage* comes from the verb *lug*—as in, to lug things around.

from a bunch of other teams is called a pickle boat. Joan Pritchard coined the term because this sport combined random bits of other games, in the same way a pickle boat crew combined random rowers.

- Pickleball became a regional pastime in Washington state. That's where the Pritchard family incorporated Pickleball Inc. in 1972 and where the first pickleball tournament took place: in Tukwila, Washington, 60 people competed to be the first pickleball champion.
- The first time pickleball was mentioned in the press outside Washington: the *National Observer* ran a human interest story in 1975, playing up the quirkiness and telling readers that the official uniform for pickleball was an orange bodysuit, sunglasses, and a floppy hat. (It wasn't.) That same year, *Tennis* profiled the Pritchards and called pickleball "America's newest racket sport."
- The first composite, dedicated pickleball paddle rolled out of a factory in 1984. Industrial engineer Arlan Paranto made it, and it's still the standard and prototypical pickleball racket. Also in 1984, USA Pickleball formed, standardized rules, and introduced a ranking system.
- By 1990, pickleball was played in all 50 states, tournament play began, and it was adopted into the physical education curriculum in numerous schools on the West Coast.
- In 2001, the Arizona Senior Olympics welcomed it as an event. More than 100 players competed at a tournament in Surprise, Arizona.
- The first time a major or non-sports media outlet covered pickleball: *Good Morning America* ran a segment on the growing sport in 2008 in advance of the first national pickleball championship tournament.
- The Pickleball Hall of Fame was established in 2017. The first inductees: Joel Pritchard, Bill Bell, and Barney McCallum, the three people who invented pickleball over a couple of weekends in 1965.
- From 2019 to 2021, pickleball became a major fad; it was played by as many as five million people nationwide in 2022, a 39 percent growth rate since 2020.
- In 2022, pickleball was declared the official state sport of Washington.
- Pickleball took off in part because it's easy to play on preexisting tennis courts, available for use by the general public across the U.S. But to play pickleball by the official rules, one should mark out the boundaries for the smaller regulation playing area. A tennis court is 60 feet wide and 120 feet long; pickleball courts are just 20 feet wide and 44 feet long.

Casting director of the 1997 movie *Jackie Brown*: Jaki Brown.

"GOOD MORNING, DRAGON"

Millions of people use Duolingo (and similar smartphone apps) to teach themselves a second language. The program often throws up strange sentences for users to translate or recite, which Duolingo engineers say make an impression on the brain that helps the new words stick. But to the user, they're just strange, funny... and probably not entirely useful if you're ever in a foreign country.

"The Loch Ness monster is drinking whisky."

"Without a doubt, I want to eat ham."

"When I was young, I was not allowed to wear pants."

"Excuse me, I am an apple."

"Your cat has a beautiful profile picture."

"Owen is eating parsnips in the rain."

"The scream cuts the silence."

"Whose robot ate my cake?"

"I am crying and the onion is laughing."

"Does a toothbrush have feelings?"

"I do not hear you since I have cinnamon rolls in my ears."

"The baby wants to drink beer."

"I am not a person."

"My dog is unemployed and only has one eye."

"The horse cooked for the cows."

"I am the cheese."

"What is tea? What is water? Who am I?"

"The bride is a woman and the groom is a hedgehog."

"My uncle is a broken man."

"The man eats ice cream with mustard."

"I eat that in the bathroom."

"Tell the truth or I will throw your cell phone."

"I have 28 hairs."

"This blond has stupid ideas."

"Good morning, dragon."

"Why is the government giving so much false information to the public?"

"She wants to swim in a sea of sauce."

"Dogs do not write newspapers."

"My horse is not an artist but an architect."

"The teachers are screeching and running away."

"Are there stupid cats in Asia?"

"Who is the man in the bathtub?"

"This knife wants to visit Switzerland."

"I have this onion and I'm going to use it."

"The green owl is trying to come up with some new sentences."

"Spiders often sit on their beds and cry."

"There is a hand coming out of the toilet."

"Crime fell after the chicken became prime minister."

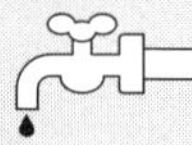

Don't let your eyes deceive you: the Gateway Arch in St. Louis is 630 feet tall and 630 feet wide.

SO WHO REALLY WROTE THAT POEM?

Some poems are such a part of our collective cultural DNA that it's hard to believe somebody once sat down to write them. But someone did, and some poems have origins so shrouded in mystery that multiple parties claim to have composed them. Here are three of the best-known poems in the English language for which it's tough to identify authorship.

Poem: "Mary Had a Little Lamb"

Premise: Mary had a little lamb (little lamb), and everywhere that Mary went? That lamb was sure to go.

Origin: The poem and, later, nursery rhyme "Mary Had a Little Lamb" has been recited since at least 1830, when Sarah Josepha Hale first published it in Poems for Our Children. And it was evidently a biographical tale. Hale had worked as a teacher at the one-room Redstone School in Sterling, Massachusetts, and one day in the 1810s, her student Mary was followed to school by a pet lamb, whom she couldn't shake and who hung around the schoolhouse all day. The memory of the event inspired Hale to write a poem about it in her book of child-friendly verses.

But Wait: Decades later, in 1876, 70-year-old Mary Tyler came forward to claim that she was the Mary who was featured in "Mary Had a Little Lamb": as a child she'd had a pet lamb she'd raised by hand who had become her constant companion, and one day her brother encouraged her to allow the lamb to follow them to school. Tyler became a minor celebrity for inspiring what had become a well-known poem and song, but she also created a scandal when she suggested that her former teacher was not the true author. Tyler recalled that a young man named John Roulstone had recently come to town, and he witnessed the lamb incident at the school. According to Tyler, Roulstone returned to the school and gifted her the three stanzas that comprise "Mary Had a Little Lamb." No physical evidence has ever surfaced pertaining to Roulstone's authorship, and Hale's version of the poem has an additional three stanzas, but Tyler maintained her version of events until her death.

Poem: "A Visit from St. Nicholas"

Premise: Also known informally after its first line—"'Twas the Night Before Christmas"—the rhyming story poem, told from the point of view of an agog father, details a visit from Santa Claus as he delivers presents to a home on Christmas Eve.

New Zealand high schools may legally possess a pound of uranium as a teaching aid.

Origin: On December 23, 1823, New York's *Troy Sentinel* devoted an entire column to the poem under the headline "An Account from a Visit of St. Nicholas." It was published anonymously, a decision explained by editor Orville Holley: "We know not to whom we are indebted for the following description of that unwearied patron of music—that homely and delightful personage of parental kindness, Santa Claus, his costumes, and his equipage, as he goes about visiting the firesides of this happy land, laden with Christmas bounties; but from whomsoever it may have come, we give thanks for it." A fun holiday novelty, the poem reappeared in the *Sentinel* and showed up in other papers in and around New York for the next decade or so before disappearing. In 1844, it began its ascent into the Christmas literature canon when New York City–based divinity and classical languages professor Clement Clark Moore published *Poems*, a collection of light and frivolous verse. The poem, now titled "A Visit from St. Nicholas," appeared in its pages, with Moore claiming to have been the original author of the hit regional newspaper feature. Ever since, his name has been associated with "A Visit from St. Nicholas," a poem that introduced enduring elements of Christmas mythology including the names of Santa's flying reindeer.

But Wait: Moore likely didn't send the poem to the *Sentinel* in 1823. One theory is that its submission to the paper was the work of Harriet Butler, daughter of his friend David Butler, who heard Moore recite it on a Christmastime visit and dutifully copied it down; no attribution was given because a serious man such as Moore would have been embarrassed to have his name associated with a children's poem. Moore's descendants could never produce an original manuscript, which called the authorship into question. A competing theory is that the true author was Henry Livingston Jr., whose family claimed it was their Christmas tradition to read the poem each December, starting as early as 1807. After Moore published "A Visit from St. Nicholas," Livingston's children reported that they'd seen their father's written version, with notes and annotations, but that it burned up in a house fire. The main proof that Livingston supposedly wrote the piece? His mother was Dutch, and there are traces of the language in the work. The poem gives names to Santa's reindeer, and Livingston's descendants remember the names Dunder and Blixem used, the Dutch terms for "thunder" and "lightning"; Moore anglicized the names as "Donner" and "Blitzen" for his 1844 version. In the 1990s, a study by a Vassar University professor strongly suggested that Livingston was the true author, as his analysis found that "A Visit from St. Nicholas" matched Livingston's writing style more than Moore's.

Poem: "Footprints"

Premise: An inspirational Christian poem, a man dreams of walking on the beach with God. During the toughest parts of his life, only one set of footprints appears

Old world, new food: ciabatta bread was invented in 1982.

in the sand; the rest of the time there are two sets, left by him and the Lord. When asked why God abandoned the man when he needed Him most, God explains that the single set of footprints were His, because He was "carrying" the man.

Origin: After a back-to-back discharge from the Navy and a split with his girlfriend in 1958, Burrell Webb was feeling hopeless and alone. That's when he says he felt a burst of supernatural inspiration, and the words of "Footprints" arrived in his brain, fully formed. He sent it to a small Oregon newspaper that published it anonymously, per Webb's request—he didn't want to take authorial credit when he felt he was merely a conduit for the word of God. In the ensuing decades, "Footprints" marched far and wide, and grew ubiquitous when reprinted in countless anthologies and appearing on inspirational merchandise, including posters, calendars, cards, and coffee mugs.

But wait: "Footprints" was usually credited to "unknown," but sometimes to Mary Stevenson, Margaret Fishback Powers, or Carolyn Joyce Carty, all of whom registered copyrights for slightly different versions of the poem. All claim to have written it, and in circumstances similar to Webb's: Stevenson says she was inspired by the sight of a cat's footprints in the snow in 1936 when she was dealing with the deaths of her brother and mother. Powers, who ran a children's ministry for a Baptist church, wrote in her memoir that the words came to her at the end of a life marred by tragedies but through which she maintained her faith; she's the one who licensed the use of "Footprints" the most, to more than 30 companies including Hallmark and Lenox Gifts. Carty, who sends cease and desist letters whenever she comes across "Footprints" online or in print when it's not credited to her, says she came up with the verse in 1963 when she was six years old, adapting a similar poem written by her Sunday school–teacher aunt.

But all those claiming authorship might have subconsciously pulled the poem from a frequently reprinted and well-distributed 1880 sermon by prominent Baptist minister Charles Haddon Spurgeon. In his essay, he speaks of a metaphorical "lonely desert island" where one sees footprints, which weren't those of a man but of God carrying a man in his time of trouble.

* * *

YOU'RE MY INSPIRATION: *DEATH PROOF*

One night, Quentin Tarantino and Sean Penn were getting drunk at a hotel when Tarantino said he wanted to buy a Volvo—a car known for its safety features—because, "I don't want to die in some auto accident like the one in *Pulp Fiction*."

"Well, you could take any car and give it to a stunt team," replied Penn, "and for $10,000 or $15,000, they can death-proof it for you." No word if Tarantino bought a Volvo, but he liked that phrase so much that he turned it into the exploitation actioner *Death Proof*.

When bees knock into each other, they emit a tiny "whoop" sound.

SCARY BATHROOM NEWS

The bathroom is supposed to be a place of peace, solace, and absorbing fun facts from a giant book–not one of harrowing mishaps, explosions, and fist-fights.

AMERICA RUNS FROM DUNKIN

A Dunkin Donuts customer named Paul Kerouac used the restroom at an outlet in Winter Park, Florida, in January 2023. As he wrapped up his business, he said, an explosion erupted from deep inside the toilet, sending gallons of water, various forms of human waste, and debris into the air and soaking Kerouac from head to toe. When he sought help from staff, he was told that they were aware of the "problem with the toilet" because there had been similar incidents already. Claiming to suffer from "severe and long-term injuries," Kerouac sued Dunkin for more than $100,000.

THE PITS

During a day of fun on Dixon Lake in northern Michigan in September 2023, a woman (unidentified in press reports) used an outhouse-style toilet in a boat launch area. While utilizing the facilities, her Apple Watch slipped off her wrist and into the latrine. She climbed into the waste-filled pit to retrieve it and got stuck. Hearing her cries for help, bystanders called 9-1-1. Michigan State Police troopers and Otsego County EMS workers combined their efforts to remove the toilet off of the pit to access the trapped woman, whom they pulled to safety with a strap. Michigan State Police warned people against retrieving objects in confined spaces, particularly outhouses. (No word on whether the woman found her watch.)

WINGING IT

Papa Bees, a chicken wing joint in Longwood, Florida, was the victim of a bathroom vandalizing incident in August 2023. The manager knew that five female customers were to blame because she saw them emerge from the restroom, and they were also the only customers present when a toilet was discovered intentionally clogged with wads of toilet paper "in excess." An employee cleaned the toilet, only for the toilet to turn up clogged anew. After calling police to report the vandalism, the manager tried to get the five women to leave, but that only made them angry: one of them punched the manager in the face and the others joined in with hitting, kicking, and pulling hair. The manager endured cuts and bruises, while another employee trying to intervene was accosted, too. A third employee broke up the melee and the women left, but ran into arriving police. The five were arrested and charged with battery, criminal mischief, and disorderly conduct.

The word *daisy*—a flower that opens in the morning and closes at night—is a contraction of "day's eye."

PIT STOP!

We interrupt your pit stop with some inside info on exactly what goes on during a NASCAR pit stop.

The World's Speediest Ballet

Despite what the naysayers believe, car racing is a sport, and the drivers are athletes—and so are their pit crews. Why have pit stops at all? Because North American Stock Car (NASCAR) races can run for as long as 500 miles, so both the cars and their drivers will need to stop several times to recharge and refuel. Successfully executing these pit stops is as crucial as the driver successfully navigating the race track. "It all relies on teamwork," says NASCAR driver Bubba Wallace. "We could be running fifth all day, and we come down pit road for the last stop and the pit crew messes up, then we all go down." Here's who does what.

The Driver: The driver is in constant communication with the crew chief, reporting on track and weather conditions, along with how he and the car are doing. When a driver decides it's time to pull in to pit road—a short spur on the inside of the race track where each team has a "stall"—he can't change his mind and return to the race once he passes the Commitment Line.

The Crew Chief: The crew chief is in charge of executing the team's strategy. This is worked out in advance with the driver, and they determine the number of pit stops to make. The 42 NASCAR tracks in the U.S. and Canada vary wildly from one another—from 2.66-mile "Super Speedways" to short oval tracks, to winding roads through cities—so creating a winning strategy for each is crucial. Every second the driver is on pit road, he falls more and more behind in the race. (The crew chief might decide that one extra stop will actually save time because they won't have to add as much fuel, so the car will be lighter and faster.) Only in extreme circumstances can the driver override the crew chief's orders.

The Car Chief: As the name implies, the car chief is in charge of everything related to the state of the vehicle, so the crew chief and the driver can stay focused on strategy. In the sport's early years, the pit crew members were all the car's mechanics. Today, each is a highly trained specialists who focuses on his individual job and his job only. But not the car chief—he's a master mechanic. If there's an issue with the car, it's his job to fix it.

The Jackman: For safety reasons, the pit crew wears protective clothing and helmets—just like the drivers—and they have to stay behind the pit wall (a few feet high) until the approaching stock car is within the stall; they can't start work until it's completely

stopped. The lone jackman runs to the far side with a special jack that lifts the car almost instantly.

The Tire Changers: Close behind the jackman are two tire changers armed with "pit guns" that remove the lug nuts and make that familiar "wheeez" sound. One tire changer starts with the front left, the other with the back right. They throw on the new tires, tighten the lug nuts, run to the other side of the car, do it again, and run back over the wall.

The Tire Carrier: He carries the tires. NASCAR allows only one tire carrier per pit crew; the strongest of them can carry two tires at once. Then they remove the old tires and get them back over the wall.

The Fueler: He runs out carrying a tall gas can, which can weight up to 90 pounds, on his shoulder. Often, a second can is required to fill a car's 18-gallon tank, so the fueler must run back to the wall and reach over for it for the other can. That's why stock cars' fuel tanks are on the side closest to the pit wall.

The Utility: Per the rules, the sixth member of the pit crew, the utility, cannot work on the car. It's his job to hold out the flag that alerts the driver where to stop. Then the utility tears off the transparent (but dirty) windshield covering. He might also hand the driver a new water bottle or a snack.

Back on Track

Just like a football team executing a play, or a dance troupe performing a musical, every single step of a pit stop has to be carefully choreographed, and the pit crew members have to practice exhaustively. But they also have to be able to improvise when conditions change. If the tire changers fumble when they remove the lug nuts, or the fueler has trouble with his nozzle, or the jackman doesn't place the jack just right, it could lead to a loss...or a crash.

A botched pit stop can also penalize the driver. Points are taken off if he doesn't park all the way within the stall, if he drives over an air hose, if any debris is left behind, or if the car exceeds the pit road speed limit (ranging from 30 mph to 55 mph depending on the track).

But the majority of the time, every NASCAR pit crew performs like a well-oiled machine—from the moment the stock car stops to when the jackman drops the jack for the second time and the driver speeds off again...all of which takes between just 10 and 16 seconds.

* * *

"Only the paranoid survive."

—Andrew Grove, CEO of Intel

PIRATE JOKES

These here jokes be clean...but also rated "Arrgh!" (Get it?)

Q: What did the pirate say on his 80th birthday?
A: "Aye matey!"

Q: How much do pirates pay to get their ears pierced?
A: A buccaneer.

Knock-knock!
Who's there?
Impatient pirate.
Impatient pirate wh—
Arrrrrr!

Q: Where do South American pirates come from?
A: Arrr-gentina.

Q: What does a pirate say when he's urinating in a sea filled with dead men?
A: "R.I.P."

Pirate: Argh, I've got all these moles on me back!
Doctor: Don't worry. They're benign.
Pirate: Argh, there not be 9, there be 10!

Q: What instrument did the pirate play in the orchestra?
A: The loot.

Q: What happened to the pirate who couldn't pee?
A: He became irate.

Q: Why are pirate parties so dangerous?
A: Because they always go overboard.

Q: Why do pirates have a hard time getting through the alphabet?
A: They always get lost at *c*.

Q: What do pirates do on vacation?
A: They travel around in an *arrrr*-V.

Did you hear about the pirate who covered his eye with sandpaper? He was in a bit of a rough patch.

Q: Why didn't the pirate take a bath before he walked the plank?
A: Because he figured he'd wash up on shore later.

Q: What has eight arms, eight legs, and eight eyes?
A: Eight pirates.

Q: What did the pirate say when his wooden legs fell off during a blizzard?
A: "Shiver me timbers!"

Q: Why couldn't the pirate play cards?
A: He was sitting on the deck.

Pirate #1: What a nice wooden peg ye got thar, and such a shiny hook, too! How much did they cost?
Pirate #2: An arm and a leg.

Q: Why do pirate captains always sing tenor in the choir?
A: They can hit the high c's.

Q: Why won't the pirates fire their weapons on Saturdays?
A: They only cannon Sundays.

Pirating is addictive: once you lose your first hand, you get hooked.

Q: Where would you find a pirate who has lost his wooden legs?
A: Right where you left him.

Q: What do you call a pirate with two eyes and two legs?
A: New.

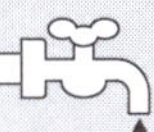

Queen Victoria survived eight assassination attempts.

MYTH-CONCEPTIONS

"Common knowledge" is frequently wrong. Here are some examples of things that many people believe...but according to our sources, just aren't true.

MYTH: Surfaces made with stainless steel don't stain—they're *stainless.*

TRUTH: "Stainless" doesn't mean the surface is free from stains; it means that it stains *less* than other metallic materials. It can still get marred, scraped, damaged, soiled, or rusty—it's just less likely to do so, and it won't be as bad as it otherwise might.

MYTH: Canada is a bilingual nation.

TRUTH: Federal law requires all signage to be listed in both English and French, the two official languages of Canada. But only 20 percent of the population can fluently speak, read, and write in French, and the only province that's officially bilingual is New Brunswick. But the province with the most bilingual people is Quebec—just over half the population can speak both languages, although the sole official language there is French.

MYTH: When you pay money to download a book to your phone or e-reader, you own a copy of the book.

TRUTH: You never actually purchase an e-book. When you "buy" a digital copy from Amazon, Apple, or Barnes & Noble through one of their proprietary devices or apps, you pay a fee that allows you to access the copy of the book on that platform. You're technically leasing the content, not purchasing it.

MYTH: A three-line poem, in which the three lines consist of five, seven, and five syllables, respectively, is called a *haiku.*

TRUTH: The Japanese poetry form of *haiku* uses a 5-7-5 syllable structure, but typically describes nature and refers to one of the four seasons. A poem with that syllable usage that covers any other topic is another form of Japanese poetry, *senryu.*

MYTH: The Statue of Liberty was given as a gift to the United States by France to celebrate the 100th anniversary of U.S. independence and its founding as a nation.

TRUTH: The Statue of Liberty arrived in 1886, just 20 years after the abolition of slavery—the celebration of that is why France commissioned and delivered the massive piece of art.

MYTH: Earth has only one celestial satellite in its orbit: the moon.

TRUTH: First identified in 1986, the bean-shaped asteroid 3753 Cruithne technically orbits the sun, but it follows Earth and takes the same amount of time to make its revolution, so it resembles and behaves like a moon. There's also asteroid 2002 AA29, which moves around the sun and Earth in a horseshoe pattern that takes 95 years for one full trip.

MYTH: Twinkies are made up of so many artificial ingredients that the shelf life for one of these processed snack cakes is indefinite.

TRUTH: Up until the 2010s, a Twinkie would stay fresh for just 26 days. Then Hostess changed some of the ingredients and added more preservatives, extending the life of the product to 45 days.

MYTH: The Australian shepherd dog breed originated in Australia.

TRUTH: The Basque region of Spain is historically a major sheep-raising area, and shepherds there developed the breed. When those Basque shepherds moved to Australia in large numbers in the 1800s, they brought their dogs. Then they emigrated to the United States, and brought the friendly long-haired dogs with them, where breeders honed the dog further until it became the modern notion of the Australian shepherd.

MYTH: *The Simpsons* setting, Springfield, isn't located in any particular state.

TRUTH: The ambiguity and impossibility of Springfield's exact location has been one of the major running jokes on *The Simpsons* across its 35-plus seasons. Creator Matt Groening was raised in Portland, Oregon, and initially intended for the Springfield of *The Simpsons* to be Springfield, Oregon. After he developed the show, he thought it would be funny to not name the state, so the series never has.

MYTH: The Mississippi River is the longest river in the United States.

TRUTH: It's the "Mighty" Mississippi and a major shipping channel through the U.S. with many major cities situated on its banks. But just because it's the busiest doesn't mean it's the *longest*, as is often claimed. According to recent and more precise measurements, the Mississippi is 2,340 miles long. The Missouri River is a little bit longer, at 2,540 miles.

About two out of every three of the world's geysers can be found at Yellowstone National Park.

MYTH: Kiwi comes from New Zealand (where *kiwi* is a nickname for locals).

TRUTH: The kiwi, or kiwifruit, was first cultivated centuries ago in what is now China, and it was known as *yang tao.* It was brought to New Zealand in the early 1900s. The fruit tasted like gooseberries, so they took on the name Chinese gooseberry. Because the fruit was small, round, and fuzzy like the kiwi bird, native to New Zealand, growers started marketing them as kiwi, or kiwifruit, in the 1950s.

MYTH: William Shakespeare had a profound effect on the English language, coining or inventing more than 1,700 words in his plays.

TRUTH: Almost all of the words the Bard popularized were already widely used in England when he put them in his plays in the late 1500s and early 1600s. The first history books that cited Shakespeare as the originator of so many words did so because they couldn't find any *printed* mentions of those words prior to Shakespeare's plays.

MYTH: The story of Aladdin takes place in the Middle East.

TRUTH: The folktale was Chinese in origin, but was popularized when it was included in 18th-century European translations of the Middle Eastern story collection *The Thousand and One Nights*, also known as *Arabian Nights.*

MYTH: Telltale and common symptoms of the degenerative neurological condition Parkinson's disease are a constant shaking and wobbly walking.

TRUTH: Parkinson's manifests in symptoms like a stiff body, slow movements, balance problems, and a slight tremor. The medication levodopa is a commonly prescribed for Parkinson's disease patients. It's a stimulant that increases dopamine production, which slows the progression of Parkinson's but also causes side effects: pronounced shaking and difficulty walking.

MYTH: Often done as an act of revenge or as a savage prank, pouring sugar into a car's gas tank will destroy the engine.

TRUTH: According to common lore, sugar added to gasoline results in a viscous mess that clogs and ruins the motor. But sugar doesn't dissolve in gas—it retains its granular nature. That sugar will sink to the bottom of the gas tank; if it doesn't, any car's fuel filter is designed to prevent materials much smaller than grains of sugar from making their way into the engine. A bag of sugar, at worst, would mess up the fuel pump, which can easily be replaced. (We still don't recommend this prank.)

A BRIEF HISTORY OF FUN

Having fun for its own sake is a relatively modern concept. If you told someone from 500 years ago that one of your goals in life is to "have more fun," they'd look at you kind of funny.

THE SCIENCE OF FUN

Researchers haven't come to a consensus as to why some species of mammals, birds, and even a few fish like to goof off for no apparent reason. "It's not like I can point to a place in the brain and say, 'Here's what happens when you have fun,'" says neuroscientist David J. Linden, author of *The Compass of Pleasure*. He links having fun to other dopamine-releasing activities like eating a delicious meal, working out, being altruistic, or making love. Our ancient and prehistoric ancestors received a similar "high" from performing activities that ensured their survival (especially that last one). But even finding a perfectly ripe, vitamin-packed piece of fruit was enough for their prehistoric brains to reward them with a little hit.

Modern humans can't seem to get enough of that dopamine. As sociology professor Thomas Henricks writes in *Psychology Today*, "Fun at its most fully realized has an effervescent, burbling quality." In these busy and uncertain times, reaching peak bubble can be quite the process, requiring "fun seekers" to enter "a special life-world, marked by its own spatial dimensions and meanings of time" that includes "exotic equipment...strange clothing, and accepted rules that would [be] silly in other settings." If that's too much work, there are shortcuts to fun: 62 percent of U.S. adults drink alcohol at least a little, and 25 percent admit to using illicit drugs. It's all for the same basic reason: dopamine. Of course, there are healthier ways to find that high, like running, but, like having fun itself, exercise for its own sake is a modern concept—as seen here in this historically accurate exchange from *Back to the Future Part III* when Doc Brown tells some Old West cowboys about the life in the 20th century:

> Doc: "Of course we run. But for recreation. For fun."
> Jeb: "Run for fun? What the hell kind of fun is that?"

THE ORIGIN OF FUN

No one knows if cavemen ran for fun—or what else they did for fun. Prehistoric cave paintings and ancient record keeping tended to stick to more serious subjects like hunting and bylaws. That's why researchers prefer the word *play*, a more observable behavior that's consistent across the young of most complex animal species. But even why kids play is disputed. The most widely held theory is that mock-wrestling among siblings serves a purpose: it hones skills and agility, and teaches boundaries. The other school of thought says that play is merely a way to pass the time when there's lots to eat and little to fear. That doesn't explain why this playful behavior usually stops at maturity (not always, though, as demonstrated by videos of fully grown bears frolicking on a trampoline, or cackling crows sliding rocks down a metal roof).

When it comes to humans, playing games and having fun don't always go hand in hand (as anyone who's played Risk can attest). This held true in the distant past as well, when early dice games—played with the ankle bones of sheep (or humans)—were mainly used for divination, or telling the future. Children's games, like marbles, along with board games, like the Royal Game of Ur, first showed up around 5,000 years ago. A little later, Indigenous cultures in the Americas played ball games like lacrosse and soccer (often with a human skull as the "ball"), but not necessarily for fun—games were often used in place of war to settle scores.

Finding ancient evidence of fun and games is skewed toward those who had the means to bury their favorite toys with them. Did the "common folk" get to play, too? Who knows? Evidence of ancient humor is even harder to find, as the world's "oldest joke"—cracked by a Sumerian circa 1900 BC—is neither that old nor that funny, but it's bathroom humor, so we give it a pass: "Something which has never occurred since time immemorial; a young woman did not fart in her husband's lap."

THE NORMALIZATION OF FUN

In Medieval England, only the well-to-do could afford the luxury of enjoying themselves. Before the printing press was invented in 1440, the few peasants who could read didn't have much to choose from, save for Bibles. Most writers catered to the tastes of the nobility, who still preferred to read the classics in Anglo-Norman French and Latin. Then came bureaucrat-by-day and writer-by-night Geoffrey Chaucer (c. 1343–1400), who dared to not only create content for the common folk, but to do so in what we now call Middle English. Due to the popularity of Chaucer's works, most notably his exaggerated character studies in *The Canterbury Tales*, the new language began to be used for writing in England. Just like with the book you're reading right now, you can open *Tales* to any page and start reading, and usually find a bathroom joke, like this one from "The Miller's Tale" about a thunderous fart:

> This Nicholas anon leet fle a fart,
> As greet as it had been a thonder-dent.

(Chaucer spends several more lines describing said fart.)

Though not widely distributed in Chaucer's lifetime, *The Canterbury Tales* became one of the first bestsellers when the printing press showed up a few decades later, earning Chaucer the title "Father of English Literature." Result: he normalized the

Editor of Muhammad Ali's memoir *The Greatest* (1975): Nobel Prize winner Toni Morrison.

concept of having fun for fun's sake...and fun would become hard to come by in Tudor England. The stuffy royals banned football, claiming that the sport interfered with military training, when the games got too noisy and violent for their tastes. Gambling was also outlawed, reportedly for the same reason

But players gonna play, and boy did they ever during the Renaissance era in the 15th and 16th centuries—which normalized, among other things, the concept of leisure time, without which having fun would not be possible.

THE ETYMOLOGY OF FUN

Of the 2,000 or so English words that made their first appearance in Chaucer's works, *fun* was not among them. Nor was it available to Shakespeare in the late 1500s, leading to lines like this one from *Love's Labour's Lost*: "Welcome, Mercade, / but that thou interrupt'st our merriment."

Exactly how *fun* made its way to English is unknown. It might have come from a similar-sounding Scandinavian word, first showing up in 14th-century Middle English as *fonnen*, used to describe a deranged person or someone who cheats. Its first English dictionary definition comes in 1699: "a Cheat or slippery Trick." That more negative connotation of *fun* is still in use today, as seen in the phrase "to make fun of."

The word's more lighthearted definition—where everyone is in on the fun—showed up in the early to mid-1700s. Then, according to the Merriam-Webster.com article "The History of Fun," "Fun made its way to the Americas as London's petty criminals, convicted of injurious fun, were shipped to her shores."

Not long after, the brand new United States—the South, specifically—coined a new adjective: *funny*. Within a few decades, *funny* would take on even more meanings than *fun*: humorous (a funny joke), strange (a funny look), ill (a funny feeling), dishonest (funny money), and whatever Joe Pesci is getting at in this famous *Goodfellas* scene: "I'm funny how? I mean, funny like I'm a clown? I amuse you? I make you laugh, I'm here to f***ing amuse you? What do you mean funny, funny how? How am I funny?"

THE DEATH OF FUN

On December 23, 2023, the *Washington Post*'s Karen Heller declared: "Fun is dead." It started back in 2004, she writes, when "Americans forgot to have fun, true fun, as though they'd misplaced it like a sock." How so? That year saw the emergence of YouTube, and right on its heels, social media. Since then, fun has "evolved into work," making it "often emphatic, exhausting, scheduled, pigeonholed, hyped, forced, and performative."

The stats back this up. According to one recent poll, 97 percent of respondents agreed that having fun "is important" (those other 3 percent must be a real riot at

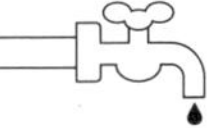

parties), but barely half reported having fun on a regular basis. That "fun gap" is not good for our collective mental and physical health, both of which have been shown to improve with regular fun. That poll, by the way, was conducted by Chase Bank, which concluded that the key to having more fun is to use credit cards more: "Our new Freedom Unlimited card gives people 1.5 percent cash back on everything they buy and they can use their cash back for little things like coffee or save them up for a larger event like a spa day."

Nice try, Chase, but everyone knows that money can't buy you happiness. But it can buy you time, and *that* is what the experts say you really need in order to have fun. You can learn all this on your own by hiring a "fun coach" or by following "fun influencers" or by listening to "how to be happy" podcasts.

Uncle John's advice: fun is wherever you can find it, even it's just for a few minutes a day—like when you can finally retreat to the throne room, open your Bathroom Reader, and read a fart joke that's actually funny: *Do you know why Uncle John's jacket smells like a fart? Because it's a windbreaker.*

ODD GAME SHOWS

Game shows are a perennially popular TV institution. But they don't all hit the way that Family Feud *or* Jeopardy! *do. Here are some of the weirdest game shows to ever air.*

Child's Play (1982)

In a gamified version of *Kids Say the Darndest Things*, producers taped children providing made-up definitions to big words they didn't know. Then two teams of adult contestants had to correctly guess what word the kids were attempting to describe. The kids came from a repertory company of wannabe child actors, and many went on to later success, including Tara Reid (*American Pie*), Breckin Meyer (*Clueless*), and Adam Richman (*Man vs. Food*).

Russian Roulette (2002)

It wasn't *really* Russian roulette, because no one is going to televise people putting a gun up to their heads and chancing a trigger pull, but this game show reflected the spirit of the game—a one in six chance of "dying," or losing. Contestants stood on a revolving table in one of six zones. If they answered a trivia question incorrectly, they had to pull a lever, which *might* send them plunging violently through a trap door.

Awake: The Million Dollar Game (2019)

This Netflix original was one part game show, one part cruel psychological experiment. Contestants compete in counting games, trivia tests, and mechanical feats—like threading needles—all after having been kept awake for 24 full hours and then released into a game show set covered with confusing lights and screaming audience members.

Labor Games (2015)

On this show on cable network TLC, brand-new parents could win a $10,000 scholarship for their child by answering rapid-fire questions about babies, childbirth, and parenting. And we mean brand-new parents—host Lisa Arch asked trivia questions *while* the mother was in labor.

Amnesia (2008)

The questions on this show, hosted by comedian Dennis Miller, were hyper-specific to the contestant, but also extremely hard. They were tasked with remembering obscure details about their own lives. They might be asked to name roads near the house where they grew up, the names of coworkers from decades prior, or to pick their mother's homemade cooking out of a lineup.

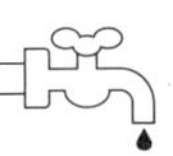

Shoes were rationed during WWII.
Americans could buy three pairs per year.

The Bum Game (2018)

The premise of this risqué, adults-only game show from Japan: male contestants had to identify their wife's or girlfriend's rear end when it was sticking out of a hole in the wall alongside the rear ends of other women—all nude. The men could determine the correct bum on *The Bum Game* by looking, of course, as well as touching or squeezing or whatever else they wanted to do.

Repo Games (2011)

Hosted by two repossession agents, whose job it is to go to someone's home and reclaim property due to lack of monthly payments, the stakes of *Repo Games* were high. If the "contestants" could answer enough trivia questions correctly when two repo men showed up to take their car, they'd get the car paid off; if not, the car was impounded.

Unnamed Sleeping Game (2022)

Unofficially retitled *Be Cute or Get Pie* for international viewers, this Japanese show implores female contestants to look as objectively adorable as possible upon being awakened abruptly. It takes most people a few minutes to be functional and presentable in the morning, but the contestants on this show had a fraction of a second to arise from a nap and do something "cute." The consequence, if they didn't, per judges' ruling? A pie in the face.

The Chair (2002)

Hosted by retired, and famously angry, tennis star John McEnroe, contestants were strapped into a chair outfitted with a heart monitor. Then they were faced with stressful situations (like having a hungry alligator being brought out on stage). If they were able to keep their heart rate down, they won prizes.

Hellevator (2015)

Conceived by horror movie filmmaker Jason Blum, each episode of this game show made terrifying horror movie scenarios into reality for teams of unlucky contestants. They'd go into a haunted house and fight off a "killer" modeled after a movie villain, urban legend, or real-life serial or mass murderer. The actor playing the murderer had free reign to touch, grab, and attack the contestants, and much of the show was shot in extremely dark rooms.

Oh Sit! (2012)

Like *American Gladiators* or *American Ninja Warrior,* contestants had to endure a gigantic, punishing obstacle course, albeit one made up entirely of hard-to-navigate inflatable apparatuses. All the while, a live band on stage played loud and frenetic music to keep the contestants moving—because they were all trying to get to the finish line and claim a place to sit. Yes, this was all an elaborate game of musical chairs.

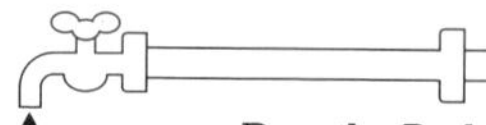

Dorothy Parker willed the rights of her work to Martin Luther King Jr.; after his death, they went to the NAACP.

TURN ME ON, ACIDHEAD

With every new generation comes new slang (see page 121 for some in use today), most of it fading away with the moment. But some endures, man.

We present to you this list compiled in 1967 during the "Summer of Love" by the women's magazine *McCall's* and published under the header "How to Talk to Your Kid, the Hippie." Try not to blow your mind. (A note included on the original article: "Now that you know how they talk, find out how they live in 'I'm not on your trip.' Page 56. September *McCall's*. If you get turned on, there's nothing wrong with an old hippie." Indeed.)

Acidhead: LSD taker.

Blow Your Mind: an overwhelming revelation.

Bread, Gold: money.

Bringing Me Down: taking off a high.

Cat: guy.

Chick, Bird: girl.

Cop Out: forsake things or people.

Crib, Pad: home, apartment.

Flower Power: carry and give flowers for love.

Grass, Pot, Mary Jane, Acapulco Gold: marijuana.

Groovy: great.

In Gear: with it.

It's Not My Bag: not for me.

Nitty Gritty: down to brass tacks.

Out of Sight: really good.

Sock It to Me: give it to me straight.

Taking Off a High: sobering up.

Turn Me On: excite me.

Up Tight: nervous, insecure.

What a Trip: an experience.

Where It's At: how things are.

Only person awarded both the Medal of Honor and a Nobel Peace Prize: Theodore Roosevelt.

3,000 YEARS OF CHOCOLATE FEVER

It's been driving people to chocoholism for millennia. Here's the story of how chocolate went from a bean on a South American tree to one of the world's favorite flavors, treats, and motivations.

1500–1200 BC The Olmecs of southeastern Mexico cultivate the cacao tree, native to that region and only that region. The Olmecs call the plant they learn to domesticate the *kakawa*, origin for the word *cacao*. Cacao beans are the tree's seeds, found surrounded by a gloopy white pulp inside the fruit, or pods. One tree produces around 2,000 pods each year, harvested about every six months. After picking, the Olmecs ferment beans in pits or wooden boxes covered with banana leaves. As fermentation progresses over a couple of weeks, the beans get darker and lose some of their natural bitterness, at which point they're dried in the sun for a week to make for better grinding. The Olmecs, like many subsequent cultures who will utilize cacao, take their chocolate as a drink—mixed with water into a very bitter, very hot beverage.

500 BC After the Olmecs die out—environmental issues cut them off from their water supply, and they can't grow crops—the Mayans take over the culture's Central American homeland. They also take up the cultivation of cacao and use the beans to make a beverage, mixing it with honey, water, and chilis and enjoying it at most meals. (Women in the Mayan culture prepare the chocolate drink, and they are considered high status if they can generate more foam in their beverages than others are able to.) This is the only way the Mayans consume chocolate, but they also use beans for currency and in religious rituals.

AD 1200 The growing Aztec empire conquers the already declining Mayan empire around AD 1200 and acquires its love of and uses for chocolate. For a period of 300 years, the Aztecs similarly use cacao beans for currency and frequently enjoy the chocolate drink, although in that culture it is served cold, not hot. The Aztecs also streamline the process for making chocolate drinks. First, the beans are roasted and then ground on a heated stone called a *metate,* then mixed with native spices. The Aztecs froth it with a *milnillo,* a wooden tool covered in rings that aerate, blend, and smooth out the liquid chocolate to bring out its complex flavors.

Emperor Montezuma II is a big fan, reportedly consuming 50 cups of the stuff each day.

1519 Montezuma II personally shares chocolate with Hérnan Cortés, leader of the contingent of Spanish explorers that would conquer the Aztecs. Cortés doesn't like the chocolate at first, finding it unpalatable because it is so bitter. Sensing he has something valuable, however, Cortés brings chocolate back to Spain in 1528, where chefs discover that chocolate drinks taste quite good if they are mixed with a fair amount of sugar, cinnamon, and vanilla. This also marks the arrival of caffeine in Europe, with chocolate hitting the continent years before coffee or tea. From Spain, chocolate spreads throughout Europe as an expensive luxury item reserved for royals and elites, prepared by court-appointed chocolate houses.

1641 Cacao, or *chocolate* as it becomes known in Europe, makes its way back to the New World from whence it came. A Spanish cargo ship carrying beans and chocolate-processing equipment departs Central America and makes an emergency stop in St. Augustine (now part of Florida). Some of the goods make their way into colonial trading and by 1670, pubs in Boston are importing finished chocolate made in Europe from Central American cacao beans.

1643 Chocolate is a hit at the very influential court of Versailles in France. Spanish princess Maria Theresa is betrothed to King Louis XIV and gifts him Spanish chocolates in a gilded chest. Louis is such a fan that he appoints Sieur David Illou to be the first royal chocolatier. French elites follow Louis's lead and bring in as much chocolate as they can, particularly after the spread of a rumor that it is the aphrodisiac of choice for a king who reportedly takes his wife to bed twice a day.

1650 Chocolate makes its way to London shops. It's such a hit that by decade's end, England has traveled to Jamaica, conquered it, and converted most of the Caribbean island into cocoa plantations.

1700 Irish naturalist Hans Sloane decamps to Jamaica in the late 1600s to study the flora and fauna. He notices that the local cocoa plantation workers enjoy a beverage of chocolate mixed with water. Sloane hates it—it is extraordinarily bitter—but thinks it might taste better with the addition of something creamy and something sweet. He mixes chocolate with sugar and milk, thus chocolate milk is born. (Hershey won't introduce chocolate syrup until 1926; Nestlé Quik chocolate milk mix hits stores in 1948.)

What's the difference between a grilled cheese sandwich and a melt? A melt contains anything else along with the cheese.

1710s–1730s As the European superpowers sail the world and colonize it, they establish large-scale cocoa farms on their newly acquired lands. The British, Dutch, and French all take cacao tree cuttings from Central America and propagate the plants in territories with a hot tropical climate similar to where cacao originated. The idea works, and soon, rampant commercial production of chocolate is underway in places like Sri Lanka, Venezuela, the Caribbean, Africa, and what is today Indonesia.

1741 Carl von Linne, the father of modern taxonomy, gives cacao its official botanical name: *Theobroma cacao*, Latin for "cacao is the food of the gods."

1755 Benjamin Franklin, who helped introduced chocolate to the colonies by selling it out of his Philadelphia print shop in the 1730s (and earning a fortune doing so), arranges to have the makings for chocolate drinks sent to troops fighting in the French and Indian War to bolster spirits. Those troops return from the war with a taste for chocolate. Many colonists want chocolate at the time—in 1758, George Washington orders 20 pounds to serve to guests at his Mount Vernon estate, and he'll regularly acquire large quantities of the stuff until he dies in 1799.

1800 Dutch chemist Coenraad van Houten invents the cocoa press. It separates the cocoa butter, or fat, from chocolate, leaving pure, rich, cocoa behind, allowing for more precise industrial production and opening up its uses. Van Houten also devises a method for washing the resultant cocoa. When treated with an alkali bath, chocolate's chemical structure changes, rendering it more mixable with water. This is still known today as "Dutch cocoa," and it's the first major development in transforming chocolate from a drinkable-only product into a solid food.

1824 Birmingham, U.K., quaker John Cadbury opens an anti-liquor store, selling mostly tasty drinks to dissuade people from drinking alcohol. His most popular offering is drinking chocolate, which he prepares for customers himself with a mortar and pestle. That sets him on the path to be the U.K.'s dominant name in chocolate, and his company distributes most British chocolate by 1849. In 1875, the first Cadbury Eggs appear in stores. Not exactly today's Easter candy, these first "eggs" are barely sweetened dark chocolate filled with sugared almonds.

1850 While experimenting, British chocolate company J. S. Fry & Sons find that adding extracted cocoa butter back in with the cocoa, along with sugar, can make a solid chocolate bar. Thus the method for creating the chocolate bar is discovered.

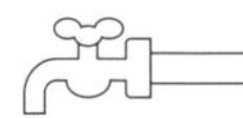

1875 It's not *really* chocolate because it doesn't contain any cocoa solids—the most chocolatey part of chocolate—but white chocolate first emerges in the kitchen of Swiss confectioner Daniel Peter. He adds sugar and milk to the separated cocoa butter to make an ultra-sweet, bright white candy that has a texture similar to chocolate.

1876 In the 1870s, German inventor Henri Nestlé, working out of Vevey, Switzerland, markets a baby formula of milk, flour, and sugar. He befriends Daniel Peter, who is interested in the chemical properties and commercial applications of chocolate. Peter, after inventing white chocolate, theorizes that if he adds the powdered milk (as well as sugar) that Nestlé developed to chocolate, the result would be a smoothly textured, solid chocolate bar. He is right. Peter invents milk chocolate. By the end of the century, Peter and Nestlé have teamed up to form the Nestlé company. Because they can use less actual chocolate in the process, Nestlé can sell bars for a lower price, bringing chocolate to the middle class.

1893 Bertha Palmer, wife of the owner of the Palmer House Hotel, asks one of her pastry chefs to make a dessert for socialite ladies attending the World's Columbian Exposition, a world's fair, in Chicago. Tasked with making something smaller than a slice of cake that can be put in boxed lunches, Palmer House staff create the Palmer House Brownie, made from chocolate, walnuts, and an apricot glaze.

1893 The World's Columbian Exposition also marks a turning point in the career of unsuccessful Pennsylvania cough drop maker and semi-successful caramel producer Milton Hershey. He sees a demonstration by a German chocolatier, who, instead of paying a huge fee to ship his processing equipment back home, sells it to Hershey for a low sum. Intending to make chocolate-covered caramels, Hershey instead sells sweetened, solid chocolate bars. The first Hershey Bar, the gold standard for American chocolate, hits stores in 1900, and Hershey will come to dominate the burgeoning chocolate-candy market.

1904 Some of the most enduringly popular new foods at the 1904 World's Fair are new and innovative chocolate delivery methods. Among the items to debut at the St. Louis exposition: chocolate mousse, chocolate ice cream, and chocolate pudding. Recipes for all three foods are well distributed because they're included in the official World's Fair cookbook.

1911 Frank Mars starts up his chocolate business out of his Tacoma, Washington, kitchen. His enterprise quickly rivals Hershey's, and over the

Biggest thing in the universe: the Hercules-Corona Borealis Great Wall measures 10 billion light years wide.

decades will introduce some of the best-selling candy bars in the world, including Milky Way, M&M's, Twix, Dove, 3 Musketeers, and Snickers.

1919 Iowa ice cream parlor owner Christian Nelson gets the idea to dip ice cream in liquid chocolate, thus inventing the chocolate-covered ice cream bar. At first called the I-Scream Bar, the product hits stores in 1921 under the name Eskimo Pie. (Today it's known as an Edy's Pie, after its parent ice cream company.)

1925 Chocolate is such an important commodity at this point that the New York Cocoa Exchange is established to facilitate wholesale transactions between buyers and sellers.

1927 Girl Scout troop leader Loretta Scott Crew probably isn't the first person to make "some mores," or "s'mores," but she's the credited creator of the campfire classic. In 1927, the Girl Scout guide book *Tramping and Trailing* features the first published recipe for the treat of a chocolate bar and marshmallow between graham crackers—and says they were Crew's idea.

1928 After Harry Burnett Reese is laid off from Hershey, he starts his own candy company, buying the chocolate he needs wholesale from his ex-employer. In 1928, he debuts Reese's Peanut Butter Cups. They sell poorly during the Depression and World War II, then take off in the mid-1940s, and are bought out by Hershey in 1963. Reese's Peanut Butter Cups are the best-selling candy "bar" in America today.

1938 Ruth Wakefield, chef at the Toll House Inn in Whitman, Massachusetts, gets the idea to roughly break up a chocolate bar into little pieces and add them to a standard sugar cookie mix. The result: Toll House cookies, or chocolate chip cookies.

2007 A trade group, the Chocolate Manufacturers Association, tries to get the Food and Drug Administration to change the legal definition of what can be sold and labeled as chocolate. Hershey leads the charge, as it wants to sub out the cocoa butter in its products in favor of much cheaper and heavily processed fats, like hydrogenated vegetable oil. The FDA denies the request. In 2008, cost-cutting Hershey revamps its formula in the most significant way in a century, replacing cocoa butter in the Hershey Bar with hydrogenated vegetable oil. The FDA in turn tells Hershey that because its candy doesn't contain cocoa butter, it isn't legally or technically chocolate. From that point, Hershey labels its iconic bars "chocolate candy" rather than "chocolate."

Gunmaker Samuel Colt raised funds for his firearms company by throwing laughing-gas parties.

GETTIN' POOED ON

Some animals relieve themselves wherever they want.

THE FOX AND THE FERRARI

A fox made headlines in London in April 2024 for leaving its droppings on the rear window of a Ferrari 488 GTB—worth around $250,000—and then coming back and doing it again four nights later. Security footage shows the fox unapologetically doing its business under the veil of darkness, and then the annoyed owner discovering the mess in the morning. As *Road & Track* pondered, "Perhaps the fox comes from a Lamborghini family?"

THE COW AND THE FARMER

In 2019, an Iowa dairy farmer named Karter Kilburg shared security footage of one of the hazards of raising cattle. He's in the barn, sweeping out the stalls, when a cow doesn't want to move, so she squirts a bit of mess in Kilburg's general direction. It just misses. Thinking that's the end of it, he starts sweeping the stall as the cow walks away. But then (brace yourself), from about five feet away, the cow shoots a projectile load directly at Kilburg and ends up soiling Kilburg's face, arms, and white T-shirt. "I didn't even stand a chance," the farmer wrote. "Direct line of fire. Typical Monday." The video is online. We don't recommend it.

THE PIGEON AND THE SOCCER PLAYER

Did a bird poop in Ashley Young's mouth? That was the big question after an English Premier League football match between Manchester United and Swansea in 2014. "Early in the match," reported Yahoo! News, "Young looked to be the victim of a laser-guided shot of bird poop directly to his mouth." But the bird in question was never spotted. And the poop looks like it could have whizzed right behind him at the exact moment he spits, making it appear as if the stuff is splattering off his lips. Debates raged online. Young's teammates mocked him relentlessly. But did it happen? Young didn't know, but he was clearly traumatized by the prospect of it: "I couldn't tell you," he told Sky Sports. "I need to put it out there, I don't actually know. I don't know what happened. You would have seen a reaction from me. I've seen the video about 100 times. I don't know what it was. I need to get to the bottom of it." Whether it happened or not, his teammates were happy to tease him: "Above my locker there was a pigeon put up. I walked in and thought 'oh no.' And that was it, everyone started taking pictures of it."

The golf comedy *Happy Gilmore* was nearly titled *Hole in Fun*.

THE BIRD AND THE GOLFER

Viktor Hovland wasn't upset that a bird dropped a turd on his arm during the first round of the 2023 Open Championship in Hoylake, England. The Norwegian pro hoped the dollop was a "good omen." (This was after the microphone picked him up saying, "What was that? I just got s*** on.") Believing bird crap is good luck is not an uncommon superstition, but it didn't prove lucky for Hovland, who came in 13th place.

THE WHALE AND THE DIVERS

There have been witness reports of "defensive defecation" in dwarf and pygmy sperm whales, possibly to thwart predators, but no one recorded this coming from an adult sperm whale until 2015, when Canadian diver and photographer Keri Welk and three colleagues happened upon one in the pristine Caribbean waters off the island of Dominica. Welk swam in for a close-up. It started slow, "like a regular bowel movement...but rather than continuing its dive down, [the whale] remained at the surface and continued to defecate for a startling length of time." The divers waited for the whale to finish. And waited. And then, "The whale bobbed up and down, spun in circles, and waved the poo in every direction," acting "like a bus-sized blender" and leaving the divers in the middle of what they dubbed a "poonado." Wilk only had on goggles and a snorkel—and no scuba equipment—so he wouldn't "disturb the whales." He said the water resembled "chocolate milk," and that whale poop got "in my eyes, mouth, wetsuit, everywhere, and I was soaked in it from head to toe." It's still unclear why the sperm whale did this; the divers weren't really posing any danger, so maybe it was just messing with them (and on them).

THE PIGEON AND THE POLITICIAN

In September 2019, a pigeon saw fit to drop a load onto the head Jaime Andrade Jr., an Illinois state senator. He was at the Irving Park Blue Line train station, giving a live television interview to CBS Chicago. "I think they just got me," he interrupted himself to say as he touched his head to verify. "I'll just have to go clean up." The lawmaker might have been targeted because he was there to discuss the perpetuating problem of pigeons pooping on trains, and the transit authority not cleaning it up. "That's what happens to my constituents," he said as he left. "They get s*** on all time."

* * *

"The more we're governed by idiots and have no control over our destinities, the more we need to tell stories to each other about who we are, why we are, where we come from, and what might be possible."

—Alan Rickman

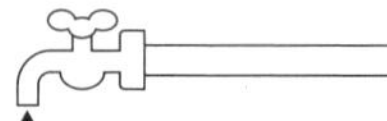

Sushi refers to the rice; a roll of rice, veggies, fish, and seaweed is *makizushi.*

UNSEEN TV

Here are some ill-fated TV shows that were interesting enough for a single episode... but too strange (or awful) to be picked up and made into a regular series.

1994 Baker Street (CBS, 1993)

Brilliant detective Sherlock Holmes (Anthony Higgins) helps the police solve the most baffling mysteries—except he's in San Francisco (not London), he's assisted by Dr. Amy Winslow (not Dr. John Watson), and it's the year 1994. That's because Sherlock was stuck in suspended animation but he's been awakened by an earthquake.

17th Precinct (NBC, 2011)

Created by *Battlestar Galactica* reboot producer Ronald D. Moore, it's a police procedural set in an alternate modern reality where magic is real but science and technology never really developed. The city of Excelsior runs on plants that are burned to release their magic, while the police try to stop terrorists who want to destroy all magic.

The Adventures of Superpup (Syndicated, 1958)

The popular *Adventures of Superman* TV series ended production in 1958, and producer Whitney Ellsworth tried to keep the franchise going (and reuse his sets) by reimagining the world of Superman with all characters as dogs. Superman became Superpup, and his alter ego, reporter Clark Kent, was thus Bark Bent; newspaper editor Perry White was now Terry Bite; and Lois Lane became Pamela Poodle. All roles were played by actors with dwarfism wearing dog suits.

The Oaks (Fox, 2008)

A complex and confusing family drama and supernatural series, *The Oaks* depicts three different families who all live in the same house but in different eras—the 1960s, the 1980s, and the 2000s. And the house is haunted, by one main ghost and then all the previous tenants of the house.

Anonymous Rex (Fox, 2004)

A strange cult called the Voice of Progress is taking hold in American society and wants to put an end to what it thinks is a shameful procedure that robs citizens of their identity and cultural heritage. What the VOP wants to end is a phenomenon where bipedal talking dinosaurs who live among humans disguise themselves with elaborate appearance-masking holographic technology.

Rex Is Not Your Lawyer (NBC, 2010)

Doctor Who star David Tennant plays Rex Alexander, a terrifically skilled lawyer who never loses his clients' cases. However, he's struck with unbearable anxiety attacks that prevent him from being able to argue in person, so instead he trains his oddball clients to defend themselves.

SEAL Team Six was the Navy's second elite unit, not its sixth; the name was chosen to instill fear in the Soviets by making them overestimate the size of U.S. forces.

Mermaids (PAX, 2003)

After a couple of guys use bombs to increase their commercial fishing yield and kill their father, three mermaids swear to hunt down the fishermen and avenge the death. What the mermaids have going for them? They all have incredible superpowers. Their problem? None of them can ever leave the water.

Without Breasts There Is No Paradise (NBC, 2007)

ABC found such success with 2006's *Ugly Betty*, an hour-long comedy based on a Colombian soap opera or *telenovela*, that NBC tried the same thing: adapting and translating a Colombian show with a hard sell of a premise. A 17-year-old girl lives in a violent slum and decides the only path to a good life is to acquire gigantic breast implants and win the love of a cocaine kingpin. To earn the money for the cosmetic surgery, she embarks on a career as a prostitute.

Jerks of All Trades (ABC, 1949)

The Three Stooges—the slapstick comedy trio consisting usually of Moe Howard, Curly Howard, and Larry Fine—made nearly 200 theatrical short films from the 1930s to the 1950s, which found a second home as filler for early television networks. In 1949, ABC tried to make a sitcom starring the trio in which they try and fail at a different job each episode. A pilot was taped, but Columbia Pictures, which owned the rights to all the Stooges films, cited breach of contract, and the show didn't enter production.

Blackjack (USA, 1998)

Jack Devlin (action movie star Dolph Lundgren) is a retired U.S. Marshal who works as a freelance fixer, hitman, and bodyguard. Devlin's only weakness: during a botched kidnapping attempt, a grenade explodes in a flash of light, leaving him with a crippling phobia of the color white.

Island City (1994, Prime Time Entertainment Network)

Science has created a wonder drug that makes everyone who takes it look and feel youthful. A troubling side effect, discovered after the drug has been widely distributed and consumed, is that whoever takes it turns into a monstrous caveman-type person. Those who don't take the drug or are immune to its effects live, work, and date inside a gleaming walled utopian city, sending researchers out into the wastes to collect the mutants to study and cure them of their affliction.

Crossroad Avenger (Syndicated, 1953)

Created and directed by B-movie king Ed Wood, *Crossroad Avenger* is a Western about a mysterious figure who calls himself the Tucson Kid (Tom Keene). He wanders from small town to small town, dispensing justice. But he isn't a sheriff or a gun for hire—he works for an insurance company and investigates claims before he authorizes payment.

The biggest ranch in the United States, King Ranch (in Texas), is larger than Rhode Island.

IRONIC, ISN'T IT?

There's nothing like a good dose of irony to put the problems of day-to-day life into perspective.

IRONY THROUGH THE CAT DOOR

Early one morning in August 2022, a young fur seal wandered away from the beach in Mount Maunganui, New Zealand, and found its way to the Ross family home. After a confrontation with the Rosses' cat (which fled to the neighbors' house), the seal made its way through two cat doors before coming to rest in a hallway. That's where mom Jenn Ross found it when she returned from the gym. Startled, the seal lolloped into a spare room and hopped up onto the couch. Jenn woke up her two kids to introduce them to their houseguest, whom she described as "polite company." However, after she shooed the seal out the front door, it wouldn't leave the yard, so a Department of Conservation ranger came and took it back to the sea. Not long after, dad Phil Ross arrived home. And he was sad. Why? "The big joke is that this is really the only family emergency where it would be useful to have a marine biologist in the house," commented Phil, who *is* a marine biologist, and was the only family member *not* at home. "I really missed my time to shine."

RECKLESS IRONY

- Why was Milwaukee Police Chief Jeffrey Norman sitting on a sidewalk while wearing a neck brace one afternoon in November 2023? Because his car had just been hit by a dump truck that had failed to stop at an intersection. And where was Chief Norman just coming from at the time of the accident? A press conference to discuss the Wisconsin city's growing problem of reckless driving.
- South Australia Police Minister Joe Szakacs witnessed an empty car—that had just been hit by a stunt car—go wildly off course and crash into a fence 150 feet away from impact. The initial accident was planned as part of filming for a road safety advertisement, but nobody had anticipated the car would roll all the way to a nearby Habitat for Humanity Re-Store, narrowly missing the store and additional cars. The Re-Store manager complained, "It could have driven into the shop." Luckily it didn't. Despite the mishap, the film crew got the shot they needed for their PSA about traffic safety.

WARNING: IRONIC SIDE EFFECTS

In 2024, after medical researchers determined that 25 patients who'd been treated with CAR-T therapy developed a rare type of blood cancer, the U.S. Food and Drug Administration ordered pharmaceutical companies to add a warning label that it can increase the risk of cancer. CAR-T therapy is used to treat...cancer.

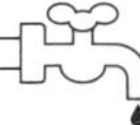

Only U.S. place with an aristocracy: the territory of American Samoa elects only members of the Matai native nobility to its senate.

DRAMATIC IRONY

- In January 2024, during a pivotal scene in the Missoula (Montana) Community Theater's stage production of the musical *Rent*, the cast was singing "La Vie Boheme" as the smoke on stage was getting thicker and thicker. Right after the character of Mark sang the line, "The Christmas tree goes up in flames," a fire alarm started blaring and a recorded voice came over the theater's PA system ordering everyone to evacuate. Because this particular play happens to take place in a condemned New York building that had caught on fire, audience members assumed it was all part of the show and remained rapt in their seats—even after a crew member rushed onto the stage and announced that the fire alarm was real and that the evacuation order had been for the audience. As smoke quickly filled the room, everyone made it out safely. Turns out, there hadn't been a fire—the overzealous smoke machine set off the alarm. Had there been an actual fire...let's just say they still would have (probably) made it out.
- *The Holdovers* is a movie about a grumpy prep school teacher who gets stuck on campus during Christmas break with a couple of students. The point is: they can't leave their location. After a late-night screening of *The Holdovers* in February 2024 in Rio de Janeiro, theatergoers tried to exit the theater, but the door was locked. And the staff had all gone home. After desperately calling out to people on the street from behind the theater's gates, they all made it out thanks to the fire department. As one of the "holdovers" (a grumpy teacher, no less) said later, "We didn't know how to proceed. It was like we were orphans there. Look, what drama, right?"

WHAT'S A FIVE-LETTER WORD FOR "IRONY"?

Since the 1940s, the terms "crossword puzzle" and "*New York Times*" have gone hand-in-hand. But before that, no newspaper was more critical of the "primitive form of mental exercise" than the *Times* itself, which had previously written that the crossword fad was "dying out fast."

CAUSE OF DEATH: IRONY

- In 1964, Douglas Tompkins founded the cold-weather clothing company North Face. In 2015, Tompkins, 72, died after a kayaking accident, but he didn't drown. His cause of death? Hypothermia.
- In 1974, 48-year-old British scientist Basil Brown became so obsessed with his health that he found the healthiest drink he could find—carrot juice—and drank gallons of it for weeks...until he died of cirrhosis of the liver caused by all the vitamin A in the carrot juice. Even his skin turned orange.

THERE'S SOMETHING ON YOUR FACE

One constant throughout history is how guys manipulate all the hair that springs forth from their face, upper lip, and neck. Here's a razor-sharp trip into the history of beards and mustaches.

Of Burnsides and Sideburns

In the mid-19th century, being clean-cut wasn't just fashionable, it was viewed as morally superior. Burly unkempt beards were something only self-identified revolutionaries or rabble-rousers wore, like abolitionist John Brown and Communist agitator Karl Marx. That all changed, at least in the U.S., during the Civil War of the 1860s. With the supplies and time required for shaving now a luxury, men grew out their beards, which, owing to the circumstances, became associated with manliness. During the war and after, one new style took off, an imitation of the way General Ambrose Burnside wore his whiskers—the sides of the hair on his head stayed bushy and came down into a beard that covered his cheeks. The sides connected via a large mustache, while the chin was shaven. This came to be called a Burnside, and when the fad for this elaborate creation passed, men who kept the sides of their hair long in front of their ears were said to be sporting long "sideburns," a play on "Burnside."

Looking Presidential

Men of the 1860s who didn't want the overwhelming and visually striking Burnside could opt for a style retrospectively named the chin curtain. It's also known as an Abraham Lincoln beard, after its progenitor; presidents were among the only frequently photographed people of the 19th century, so they became trendsetters. The style consisted of a long beard cut along the jawline, with everything else kept shaved, including the mustache. After Lincoln's assassination in 1865, imitating his style of beard felt too sad for most men to keep up, and they looked to successive presidents for facial hair cues. At this point, the full beard—imposing and just a little bit wild—worn by Rutherford B. Hayes and James Garfield came into mainstream fashion.

Fitting the Mask

Full beards remained commonplace until World War I in the 1910s. All that hair on their faces prevented soldiers from properly wearing gas masks during combat—facial hair puffed out and didn't allow for a safe seal around the nose and mouth. So men started shaving off their beards, but found that they could leave their mustaches and still get a good mask fit. The trend continued after the war, with modification: the

Moon temperature during the Apollo 11 landing (1969): 200°F (93°C).

handlebar style, flipped down and up at each side and left alone until it grew away from the face, was worn by countless men, notably its popularizer, President William Howard Taft.

Thinning It Out

In the 1920s, mustaches remained the standard for facial hair, but earlier burly and handlebar varieties went away in favor of smaller, thinner, more subtle styles. Agatha Christie's detective character Hercule Poirot, the basis of numerous best-selling books and popular stage productions starring Charles Laughton, inspired men in the U.S. and the U.K. to grow an ultra-thin, barely there mustache that appeared pasted on. The style grew in popularity into the 1930s when the most celebrated movie stars of the day—Ronald Colman, Errol Flynn, Clark Gable—adopted the facial hair choice, known in the U.S. as the pencil mustache. Gable's pencil mustache wasn't historically accurate for his 1939 Civil War–era film *Gone With the Wind,* but the phenomenally popular movie influenced the public mindset—a thin, closely trimmed, carefully maintained mustache came to indicate a sophisticated, debonair gentleman.

Fail Hitler

Concurrent with the pencil mustache, the other dominant facial hair style of the first few decades of the 20th century is unlikely to ever make a comeback because it was a signature physical feature of one of the worst villains in human history. Introduced in 1908, the toothbrush mustache was basically a small square of hair worn just under the nose. Popular media figures of the day grew them, including Walt Disney and silent film mega-star Charlie Chaplin. But so did genocidal German dictator Adolf Hitler. By the time World War II began, the toothbrush mustache—forever unofficially rebranded the "Hitler mustache"—had disappeared from everywhere except Germany.

Hello, Hipsters

The definitive American cultural norm of the 1950s: be upright, be upstanding, and be clean-cut. Amidst the anti-Communist "Red Scare," only political dissidents and creative types wore facial hair, doing so as an intentional small indicator of rebellion and a refusal to go along with the cookie-cutter, postwar suburban ideal. The facial hair trends of the 1950s all came from small but impactful subcultures, particularly the artsy, urban beatniks and those in the musical scene beatniks adored: jazz musicians. A goatee—a mustache connected to a small chin beard via thin trails of hair running down the face to create a circle of hair around the mouth—signified membership in one of those communities. Other hipsters brought back the Vandyke, a style briefly popular in the 1600s and named for Flemish painter Anthony van Dyck. It paired a mustache of some kind with just a small tuft of hair atop the chin.

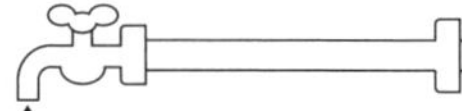

Most critically hated movie franchise:
***Police Academy*, with four 0 percent scores on Rotten Tomatoes.**

That '70s Look

While Westerns fell off TV and in movie theaters after decades of dominance, cowboy-adjacent trends proliferated in fashion in the 1970s. Along with plaid Western shirts and tight rancher-style blue jeans, men adopted the horseshoe, or cowboy mustache, as cowboys were held up as bastions of manliness. Other macho archetypes that were the center of fascination in the 1970s perpetuated the horseshoe, too, like wrestlers, bikers, and adult film stars. Now strongly associated with 1980s wrestling star Hulk Hogan, this facial hair style consisted of a bushy mustache with two straight-down lines flanking the mouth—like a thicker goatee, but without the element of hair on the chin.

Welcome to the 1980s

Hearing the words "1980s mustache" probably conjures up an image of Tom Selleck (*Magnum, P.I.*) or Burt Reynolds (*Stroker Ace*), the biggest TV and movie stars of the early part of the decade. American men, seeking to capture some of the sex appeal radiated by those guys, adopted their mustache style, which is what's known as a chevron. It's full, thick, and dips over the lip ever so slightly. It's not a rectangle, but a trapezoid in that it gets wider as it grows out from under the nose to over the lip. This medium-length, medium-thickness mustache became the standard of middle-aged male facial hair for the decade and is carried on to this day by another public figure who originated in the 1980s: Ned Flanders of *The Simpsons*.

Vice Is Nice

In 1984, *Miami Vice* debuted and inspired a litany of male trends. Seeking to look like the cool detectives played by Don Johnson and Philip Michael Thomas, men started wearing pastel shirts under light-colored blazers, boat shoes with no socks, and stubble. After decades of beards and mustaches dominating facial hair fads, Johnson demonstrated a third way—permanent five-o'clock shadow, which made a man look a little bit like he needed to shave. Men began to shave every few days or so, many aided by purpose-marketed trimmers like Wahl's stubble-preserving "Miami DeVice" electric razor.

What's Old Is New Again

No one style defines 21st-century facial hair. Hipsters in big cities were as likely to rock *Miami Vice*–style stubble as they were to wear ironically old-fashioned handlebar mustaches. Full beards made a comeback, too. Labeled "lumberjack style" and worn by what fashion magazines called "lumbersexuals," celebrities such as Prince Harry and *Thor* star Chris Hemsworth grew big bushy beards but kept them manicured, expertly styled, and precisely trimmed; a cottage industry of targeted beard-care products was worth about $20 billion by 2022.

Ancient Rome had female gladiators.

THE ONLY STATE WITHOUT...

No two states are created equal. Every state is the best at something or has the most of something. Each one also lacks or is free of something found in the 49 other states.

...termites: Alaska.

...ragweed: Alaska.

...a national park or national monument: Delaware.

...rabies: Hawaii. (The island state has strict animal quarantine laws.)

...squirrels: Hawaii.

...an official state welcome sign: Hawaii.

...workers' compensation insurance requirement: Texas.

...a natural lake: Maryland. (It has some manmade ones, though.)

...voter registration: North Dakota.

...a law requiring car insurance: New Hampshire.

...a McDonald's in its state capital: Vermont. Not only are there no Big Macs in Montpelier, but there's also no Dairy Queen statewide.

...tall buildings: There's nothing in Vermont taller than 124 feet.

...a law criminalizing strangulation: Ohio.

...a rectangular state flag: Ohio

...impeachment: Oregon. Elected state officials can't be impeached.

...a woman on its state Supreme Court: South Carolina.

...an official state song: New Jersey.

...a no-texting-while-driving law: Montana.

...a refugee resettlement program: Wyoming.

...salaried lawmakers: New Mexico. The state legislature is all-volunteer (they earn a per diem).

...an Amtrak station: South Dakota.

...an incorporated city: Hawaii.

...a straight line in its border: Hawaii.

...common law: Louisiana (it utilizes a civil law system).

...fewer than two syllables in its name: Maine.

...independent county governments: Connecticut.

...a state seal designed by a man: Idaho (it was designed by Emma Edwards Green in 1891).

...topography less flat than a pancake: Kansas. (Geographers proved it with a 2003 study.)

...a population of at least 600,000: Wyoming.

"BIGGER LUKE" AND OTHER FREAKY FAN THEORIES

A "fan theory" is just what it sounds like: fans of movies, shows, and books formulate theories based on supposedly hidden meanings or connections and then share them online. Is there anything to these theories? Usually not. But they make for some interesting bathroom reading.

THERE ARE TWO LUKE SKYWALKERS OF DIFFERENT HEIGHTS

Fan Theory: Two Luke Skywalkers exist in the original Star Wars trilogy, one taller than the other. This theory originated with a 2005 web comic that pointed out how short and scrawny Luke looks in *Star Wars: A New Hope* (1977), compared to how tall and buff he looks in *The Empire Strikes Back* (1980). As the theory gained traction over the years, numerous websites and articles expanded it to the point where there are now two competing theories. The "Canon Luke Hypothesis" posits that within the Star Wars universe, there exist two Luke Skywalkers: "Luke Prime" and "Bigger Luke." The "Hamill Hypothesis" posits that a slightly taller Mark Hamill lookalike was used simply to make the hero *appear* bigger in certain scenes in the movies.

The Clues: Side-by-side comparisons of Luke standing next to Han Solo seem to show the height discrepancies. Naysayers point out that this is due to lighting, camera angles, and where the characters are in relation to each other.

Then there's Princess Leia's line in *A New Hope* when Luke—in disguise as a stormtrooper—rescues her from a detention cell: "Aren't you a little short for a stormtrooper?" As the Wiki page "Bigger Luke" explains it, this line is...

> a thinly veiled acknowledgement of the existence of a size discrepancy between different versions of Luke Skywalker. Because this is an in-universe acknowledgment, it is generally deemed evidence in favor of the Canon-Luke Hypothesis, as opposed to the Hamill Hypothesis, as it seems very unlikely that a Star Wars character would acknowledge the existence of different actors.

The Truth? There's not a shred of evidence to prove any of this, but in 2021, Mark Hamill himself did address the theory on Instagram: "Luking for a really fun conspiracy? Luke no further. It's hard to believe how long we were able to fool everyone, but to be fair: the only time both of us appeared together at the same time was with Kermit on *The Muppet Show*." Hamill is referring to a comedy bit from a 1980 episode of *The Muppet Show* that features Luke Skywalker and his "cousin Mark" together on screen, achieved through camera trickery. (Or *was* it?)

...They were trying to rip off *Pong* and make it a one-player game.

THE *JURASSIC PARK* DINOSAURS AREN'T DINOSAURS

Fan Theory: The "prehistoric" creatures in *Jurassic Park* (1993) are not cloned dinosaurs, but rather genetically engineered beings created by scientists from reptilian and amphibian DNA to look like dinosaurs. This theory popped up on Reddit in the early 2020s, and while it seems silly—especially because Michael Crichton didn't mention this (directly) in the 1990 novel that launched the franchise—there are some compelling arguments that this is indeed the case. Plus, it fixes one of the movie's most glaring plot holes: the dinosaurs are all significantly inaccurate.

The Clues: Real velociraptors were the size of turkeys, and real T. rexes had feathers. In fact, *none* of the dinosaur species depicted in the first movie are accurate. But how could they be, considering they are all supposedly cloned from DNA extracted from a single mosquito preserved in amber? One of the scientists says they also used frog DNA to fill in the gaps. It begs the question: what else did they dabble with? Crichton's book does divulge that the dinosaurs can be engineered to be aggressive or docile, which wouldn't be the case if they were cloned. And in the following films, we do see "designer dinosaurs."

The Truth? As of this writing, there's yet another *Jurassic* movie in the works. Will it verify this theory? Or finally drive it to extinction?

BREAKING BAD IS A PREQUEL TO *THE WALKING DEAD*

Fan Theory: In the AMC TV show *Breaking Bad* (2008–13), a cancer-stricken chemistry teacher named Walter White—under the pseudonym Heisenberg—invents a potent strain of blue meth with the help of a former student, Jesse Pinkman. Somehow, these events are connected to—or perhaps even directly lead to—*The Walking Dead* (2010–22, also on AMC), which follows the survivors of an unexplained plague that turns the dead into mindless zombies.

The theory was born out of an "Easter egg" in an episode of the latter's spin-off show, *Fear the Walking Dead*, that featured the song "Negro y Azul: The Ballad of Heisenberg." That song had been written specifically for the episode of *Breaking Bad* that tells the story (in Spanish) of Heisenberg's rise.

The Clues: In a season-two episode of *The Walking Dead*, character Daryl Dixon raids his dead brother's drug stash, and there are mysterious—and quite familiar—blue meth crystals. (Blue meth doesn't exist in real life.) Daryl later describes his brother's drug dealer as a "janky little white guy" who called everybody "b****." That's a spot-on description of *Breaking Bad*'s Jesse. Also, the same red sports car appears in both shows: in *Breaking Bad*, Walter returns it to an unseen car salesman named Glenn; in *The Walking Dead*, a character named Glenn drives the same make and model. And an elaborate, unique coffee machine that was invented by a *Breaking Bad* character later shows up in the office of a *Walking Dead* character.

The last year that rock was the most listened-to music in the U.S.: 2016. Since then, it's been hip-hop.

The most compelling part of this theory is that *Breaking Bad*'s bad guy—mild-mannered drug kingpin Gus Fring—is *The Walking Dead*'s patient zero. Spoiler alert: when an explosion destroys half of Fring's face, he takes a few step before falling down and dying. Fring might have taken an unstable form of Heisenberg's meth (though no mention is ever made of him using), and not only did it keep him from dying right away, but it actually created the virus that nearly wipes out humanity in *The Walking Dead*.

The Truth? Robert Kirkman, *The Walking Dead* showrunner, laughs off the notion, as does *Breaking Bad* creator Vince Gilligan, who said, "I love that theory," during a question-and-answer session at the 2018 San Diego Comic-Con. (The key word being *theory*.) Walter White actor Bryan Cranston added, "Walt is dead, so he could be a zombie right now. Heisenberg zombie! My agents are out here, we should talk."

HOMER SIMPSON IS IN A COMA

Fan Theory: *The Simpsons* was a typical family comedy from its start in 1989 until a 1993 episode called "So It's Come to This: A Simpsons Clip Show," wherein a falling vending machine sends dopey dad Homer into a coma. He wakes up at the end of the episode, but the theory states he doesn't *really* wake up. Ever since, the show has basically been Homer's coma dream.

The Clues: For one, the family hasn't aged in decades. Sure, they're cartoons, but it's still odd. Before that 1993 episode, *The Simpsons* was more of a typical sitcom—with plots revolving around Homer trying to break into his boss's office to retrieve a nasty letter, or Homer stealing cable TV and creating a moral conundrum for Lisa. But after that season-four clip episode, Homer and his family start having much more fantastical adventures. They meet celebrities like Ron Howard and Mr. Spock (who beams away), and Homer gets all sorts of crazy jobs like astronaut, food critic, bass player, Springfield mayor, Springfield chief of police, Olympic curler, and more.

The oddest clue can be found in one of the few surreal episodes ("Homer the Heretic") that aired six months *before* the infamous vending machine episode; in it, Homer meets God (who has five fingers, compared to the Simpsons' four, the ramifications of which we don't dare tackle here), and He refuses to tell Homer the meaning of life, saying, "You'll find out when you die."

"I can't wait that long!" whines Homer.

"You can't wait six months?"

Seems oddly specific, doesn't it?

The Truth: A Redditor who goes by the name "Hardtopickaname" came up with the Coma Theory in 2015, noting the abrupt shift in the show's tone as the main clue. When asked about it, former *Simpsons* executive producer Al Jean called it "intriguing

Traditional food in Greenland: kiviak. It's an Inuit dish made of up to 500 small seabirds stuffed into a disemboweled seal and fermented for six months.

but false," pointing out, "It would mean back in 1993 we would presume the show was going on for years and years more and right before we left, threw this hidden monkey wrench in for all our successors."

The surreal 2022 episode "Lisa the Boy Scout," in which two hackers hijack a typically plotted show (Bart and Lisa become rivals at camp!) and threaten to reveal the show's unreleased storylines (including that Marge's sister Selma is actually her mother, and school nerd Martin is an adult undercover cop), the writers poke fun at the Coma Theory by depicting that Homer has indeed been in a coma, but it happened much earlier, in season two, when he unsuccessfully tries to jump over Springfield Gorge. D'oh!

FERRIS BUELLER DOESN'T EXIST

Fan Theory: *Ferris Bueller's Day Off* (1986) is a fever dream imagined by a bedridden Cameron.

The Clues: Writer-director John Hughes was known in the 1980s for making relatable movies about teens, including *The Breakfast Club* and *Sixteen Candles*. Those movies have some zany scenes, but they don't stretch reality the way *Ferris Bueller's Day Off* does.

If you're unfamiliar, the movie begins with teenager Ferris Bueller waking up and deciding that it's too nice of a day for school, so he fools his parents into believing he's sick, then calls his best friend, Cameron, and tries to persuade him to drive them to Chicago. But Cameron really is sick in bed and tells Ferris no and hangs up. "He'll call back," Cameron says to himself. "He'll keep calling." Therefore, Cameron reluctantly agrees to Ferris's scheme.

As the movie progresses, we see that Ferris is everything that the dour Cameron isn't: Ferris is charming and handsome, and he has a beautiful girlfriend, loving parents, and the adoration of the entire community. Even the school secretary says, "He's a righteous dude." When word gets around that Ferris is sick, someone paints "save Ferris" in huge letters on the water tower. Those words appear a few more times throughout the movie.

Cameron would never dream of taking his oppressive father's beloved red 1961 Ferrari 250 GT California Spyder. But Ferris talks him into it. And Cameron could never date a girl like Sloane, or jump up on a parade float and lead a rousing rendition of the Beatles' "Twist and Shout." Ferris can. In fact, there's no feasible way that Ferris, Cameron, and Sloane could have driven into Chicago from the suburbs, had a nice lunch, visited a museum, attended a Cubs game, spent time on the lakefront, gone to a parade, and made it back to the suburbs in time for dinner.

That's because it all happened inside Cameron's head. All those "save Ferris" signs? They were really Cameron trying to save himself.

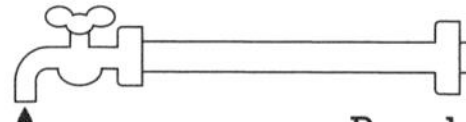

Popular toy: the teddy bear, inspired by Teddy Roosevelt. Unpopular toy: the William Taft–inspired billy possum.

The Truth? Hughes died in 2009 before the theory gained popularity, but it's likely he was merely taking liberties with reality in order to create a fun romp. However, if it *is* true that Cameron created a more confident version of himself in an imaginary Ferris, that's basically the plot of *Fight Club* (minus the fights).

TARZAN IS ANNA AND ELSA'S BROTHER

Fan Theory: Continuing Disney's relentless quest to kill the parents of its protagonists, in 2013's *Frozen*, princesses Anna and Elsa learn that their parents, the king and queen, were lost at sea in a shipwreck. In *Tarzan* (1999), an unnamed married couple are shipwrecked in Africa. They're later killed by a leopard, and their baby gets adopted by gorillas and grows up to be Tarzan. Could they be the same parents? It seems unlikely, as *Frozen* is set in a fantasy world with magic, whereas Tarzan is set on Earth at the turn of the 20th century (though both films have talking animals).

The Clues: The theory came about after a 2014 Reddit "Ask Me Anything" session with *Frozen* codirectors Chris Buck and Jennifer Lee. Responding to a question about what happened to the king and queen, Lee wrote, "According to Chris, they didn't die on the boat. They got washed up on a shore in a jungle island. The queen gave birth to a baby boy. They build a treehouse. They get eaten by a leopard..." Hmm. Fans have observed that Tarzan's parents look like Anna and Elsa's would after they aged a few more years. And their names, Sir John Clayton and Lady Alice Clayton, are pseudonyms to hide their royalty.

The Truth? Buck confirmed the theory in an interview...kind of: "In my little head, Anna and Elsa's brother is Tarzan. That's my fun little world." (Buck also codirected *Tarzan*.) Perhaps the king and queen were on their way to Rapunzel's wedding in *Tangled*, and maybe it was their ship that Ariel searches in *The Little Mermaid*. Buck tells fans, like Uncle Walt himself might have, "If you want to tie them all together, then do it. That's the spirit of Disney!"

But Wait! The fan theory was sunk by the plot of *Frozen 2*—also directed by Buck—which reveals that Anna's and Elsa's parents actually did perish in the Dark Sea.

* * *

"I realized that to make any kind of statement from music or anything else, you really have to simplify it, really bring it down to the LCD, the 'lowest common denominator,' so that people out there that don't play instruments can appreciate what you are doing, that they don't have to sit there and go to school to realize that what we've done is good."

—Gene Simmons

Ireland's population was 6.5 million before the 1851 potato famine. As of 2022, the population is still short of that number, at 5.1 million.

LUCKY FINDS

Ever stumble upon something valuable? It's an incredible feeling. Here's the latest installment of one of the BRI's regular features.

Diamond in the Rough

The Find: A large diamond

Where It Was Found: In the mud

The Story: There are people who spend years and years searching, without success, for a life-changing find at Arkansas's Crater of Diamonds State Park. Then there's Julien Navas, a Frenchman who visited the park "on a whim" while on vacation in January 2024. He paid the $13 digging fee and got started with the provided kit, but it was "back-breaking work"—and it was wet and muddy—so after a few hours with no luck, Navas decided to walk around and see if anything was on the ground's surface. And there it was: a brown diamond about the size of a pea (that Navas amazingly saw in the mud). Weighing 7.46 carats, it was the largest find at Crater of Diamonds in two years, and in the top 10 of all diamonds found there since the park opened in 1972. Estimated worth of the "Carine Diamond" (named for Navas's fiancée): between $40,000 and $130,000. "This is a magical place!" beamed Navas.

Medal Detector

The Find: An Olympic gold medal

Where It Was Found: In a trash bag

The Story: In 2021, Jordyn Poulter, a member of the U.S. women's Olympic volleyball team, brought home a gold medal from the Tokyo Games. In 2022, Maria Carrillo, owner of a barber shop in Anaheim, California, found that gold medal: it was in a plastic bag in the shop's parking lot. At first, she thought the medal was "some kind of toy or imitation," but her husband thought it might be authentic. They did some internet sleuthing and learned that a gold medal had been reported stolen. They took the medal to the police, who confirmed it was indeed real and that it belonged to Poulter. How'd Poulter lose it? "I just really forgot that it was in my car," she said. She also forgot to lock the car. A man (later arrested) stole the medal and, for some reason, threw it away. "As silly as that sounds," said Poulter, "it is the reality of the situation." But thanks to Carrillo, she got it back. "I was very emotional," said Carrillo, "because I knew I had in my hand something that took somebody a lot of work to earn."

What's the difference between reindeer and caribou?
Hardly anything.

A Fragment of Prehistory

The Find: A prehistoric skull

Where It Was Found: Along the Minnesota River in Renville County, Minnesota

The Story: After years of drought, by September 2021, the Minnesota River was much lower than normal. But it was still navigable, so two kayakers (unnamed in press reports) took to the water. While paddling near the exposed riverbank, they noticed something out of place: a brown piece of bone. Upon further inspection, they deduced that it could be the upper portion of a human skull. Was it a missing person or the victim of foul play?

They turned the bone over to police, who then sent it to the FBI, where a forensic anthropologist quickly realized that it was much too old to show up in any cold cases. Exactly how much older would require carbon dating.

Eight months after the bone was pulled from the riverbank, authorities announced that it was the skull of a young man who lived in the area 8,000 years ago. Although it was just a portion of the skull, it provided a wealth of information about Minnesota's Archaic period. The young man had eaten a diet primarily of fish, and, at some point in his life, he had suffered blunt force trauma to the head, but the wound healed.

Had the local authorities realized the bone fragment was that old, it would have been turned over to local Native Americans (it's the law). Once the findings were made public, the bone was sent to Upper Sioux Community tribal officials.

Pretty Goodwill

The Find: A rare Italian vase

Where It Was Found: At a Goodwill thrift store outside of Richmond, Virginia

The Story: In 2023, a horse trainer named Jessica Vincent was looking for knickknacks to display in her farmhouse when she came across a vase that stood out. Made of clear glass, it was decorated with delicate burgundy and green stripes. Vincent, 43, paid $3.99. Later, she looked at the bottom of the vase and noticed the words "Murano" and "Italia." Vincent posted a photo of her vase in a pair of Facebook groups, and one of the comments froze her in her tracks: "Those are very rare. Every collector would love to have that. But most people cannot afford them."

Vincent contacted an auction house and found out that the vase was designed by celebrated Italian artist Carlo Scarpa (1906–78) for Venini glass company on Venice's island of Murano, famous since the 13th century for its exquisite glasswork. "I always felt like I had a good eye," said Vincent. "But I'm really surprised that nobody picked it up before I did." Her lucky find was sold to an anonymous European collector for $107,100.

OWL FACTS

So who even gives a hoot? We owl do.

- Owls' ears aren't directly opposite each other. One is slightly higher up than the other, which makes the animal better able to determine the exact location of distant prey.
- Their eyes aren't balls—they're tubes. Those tubes don't move within the skull and they act like binoculars and offer incredible depth perception.
- An owl's eye can admit about three times as much light as a human's, and can focus 10 times faster. And the owl eye is covered with a nictitating membrane, an extra, transparent membrane that protects the eye while the bird is hunting.
- In part to compensate for not being able to move their eyes, owls can rotate their necks in a 270-degree rotation. Being fully rotated can cut off circulation to the brain, which is where their blood vessels with reservoirs take over.
- A group of owls is called a parliament. (C. S. Lewis's *The Chronicles of Narnia* features a group of owls in a parliament-like setting, which was the inspiration for this grouping name.)
- Tiniest owl: the elf owl, which is no taller than six inches and weighs a little over an ounce. They live in the American Southwest.
- Barn owls swallow their prey all at once. They eat about three mice a day and process the indigestible parts in an owl pellet.
- Not all owls hoot. Most do, but the barn owl screams or hisses, the eastern screech-owl whinnies, and the saw-whet owl sounds like a saw getting sharpened.
- Two of the toes on an owl's foot point forward, and the other two point backward.
- Owls don't make detectable sound during flight. Their feathers work to break the motion into smaller currents of air, which makes for almost no noise, aided also by the absorbent down of their feathers.
- The reason the western screech-owl population is in decline: they're the number one prey for the barred owl, who themselves are hunted by great horned owls.
- Two owls are official provincial birds in Canada: the great horned owl in Alberta, and the great gray owl in Manitoba.
- Across species, female owls are 40 percent heavier than male owls.
- Owls can't use their beaks to chew, so they instead use the appendage to rip the flesh of their prey.
- Most birds are equipped with a throat sac called a crop, which stores food for later consumption. Owls don't have a crop, so all food goes straight to the stomach, where a gizzard filters out that which can't be digested.

What's underneath the Washington Monument?
A zinc box stuffed with mementos, including coins.

THE NOT SO MERRY WIVES OF HENRY VIII

Like a modern-day Hollywood celebrity, the right and noble King Henry VIII was married six times. "Divorced, beheaded, died, divorced, beheaded, survived"...he just couldn't find a lady with whom he was compatible or who would live to tell about it. Here's a look back to the 16th century and the six wives of Henry VIII.

ONE: CATHERINE OF ARAGON (DIVORCED)

Catherine was born in 1485 to the ruling monarchs of Spain, Isabella I of Castile and Ferdinand II of Aragon, and was married by arrangement to Henry VII's eldest, Arthur, in 1501. (She'd been betrothed at the age of three.) Arthur died five months later, and Catherine became betrothed to the new heir, Henry VIII. Thanks to a long fight over the dowry from her first marriage, which had been half paid, it took seven years for the wedding to occur; it finally happened in 1509, after Henry VIII ascended to the English throne. He was 18; she was 23. Catherine ruled England in Henry's absence while he was leading troops into battle in France. They had six children together, but only one, Mary Tudor, lived past infancy. Henry grew frustrated with the lack of a male heir, and blamed Catherine. In 1527, Henry persuaded Pope Clement VII to grant him an annulment. The grounds: she had been married to his brother, so their subsequent marriage was unholy to God and must be abolished. Catherine claimed her first marriage hadn't been consummated, and the pope denied the request (because he didn't want to upset Catherine's nephew, Charles V, the Holy Roman Emperor). Because Henry's church wouldn't grant his request, Henry left the church—and took the rest of England with him. He ordered the creation of the Church of England, which was like the Catholic church but with one major rule change: divorce was allowed...at least for him. In 1534, the Church was created, the marriage was annulled, and Catherine was demoted to dowager princess, barred from court, and denied custody of or visitation with her daughter. She died in exile in 1536 at age 50.

TWO: ANNE BOLEYN (BEHEADED)

All that rigamarole was so that Henry VIII could marry again, to a woman he thought could produce a boy. That woman was Anne Boleyn, who had served as a lady-in-waiting to Catherine of Aragon. Anne had likely been born in 1501; her father, Thomas, was an earl and a knight in Henry's court, and her mother, Elizabeth

Howard, had also been one of the previous queen's ladies-in-waiting. Educated in Belgium and France, Anne returned to England in 1522 to find her sister, Mary, had become Henry VIII's mistress. Anne, trained in the ways of the French court and skilled in dancing, struck Henry's fancy instead. Their courting began in 1526, when he was still married to Catherine; the pair secretly married in 1533 before Henry and Catherine's marriage was annulled. A week after the annulment in 1533, Anne was crowned queen (while five months pregnant). She soon gave birth to a daughter, the future queen Elizabeth I. Anne became pregnant twice more, in 1534 and 1536, but the first pregnancy ended with a miscarriage and the second, a stillbirth. Desperate for an heir and looking for a way to cleanly dump his wife, Henry charged his advisor Thomas Cromwell with convicting Anne of adultery. In May 1536, Anne was found guilty of adultery, treason, and incest (false charges of an affair with her brother helped pit public sentiment against her); Henry annulled their marriage and had Anne beheaded.

THREE: JANE SEYMOUR (DIED)

Henry VIII mourned the death of wife number two by quickly hooking up with would-be wife number three: a day after Anne Boleyn's execution, he proposed to her and Catherine of Aragon's lady-in-waiting Jane Seymour (whom he'd been courting since before legal proceedings against Anne Boleyn began). They were married 10 days later. Religiously devout, steadfastly moral, and devoted to the king, Jane Seymour even persuaded him to welcome estranged daughter Mary Tudor back into the court. Jane promised to give Henry his longed-for male heir, and she did—future king Edward VI was born in October 1537. Jane Seymour is believed to be Henry's favorite wife, and not just because of the living son, but unfortunately for Henry (and for Jane), she shortly died from complications related to Edward's birth.

FOUR: ANNE OF CLEVES (DIVORCED)

Having finally secured a male heir, the once-again-single Henry VIII could marry for political reasons. Paranoid that the Holy Roman Empire—along with England's long-standing enemy, the Catholic nation of France—had designs on England, Henry sought a wife who could create a strategic alliance and turn down the heat. Advisor Thomas Cromwell played matchmaker and selected Anne of Cleves, a member of the ruling House of Cleves of Germany, a fellow Protestant nation. The two met in January 1540, when Anne was 24 and Henry was twice her age. He had been pleased with Anne's portrait, which had been sent to Henry ahead of time, but when the pair met in person, he found he didn't much like her; the marriage was reportedly never consummated. When the threat of France and Roman invasion passed, Henry

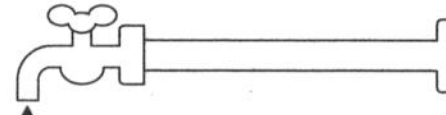

abandoned the political tool that had helped that threat subside: he annulled his marriage to Anne of Cleves in July 1540, just six months after it took place. She received a generous settlement: an annual salary, two homes in England, and various income-earning rental properties. She was able to maintain a place in Henry's court as the "king's sister" until she died in 1557 at age 41, and is the only wife of Henry VIII buried in the hallowed grounds of Westminster Abbey (she also outlived not just Henry, but all his other wives).

FIVE: CATHERINE HOWARD (BEHEADED)

Less than three weeks after being granted an annulment from his own Church of England to split with Anne of Cleves, Henry VIII married wife number five. He met her where he met other women: Catherine worked for one of his previous wives. Catherine Howard, the teenaged niece of the influential Duke of Norfolk and cousin of the executed Anne Boleyn, was a lady-in-waiting for Anne of Cleves. Her status as King Henry VIII's wife, and her very life, were probably doomed from the start. The head of the Church of England at the time, the Archbishop of Canterbury Thomas Cranmer, loathed Catherine and her family because they were Catholic. Cranmer also heard rumors that she'd been sexually abused as a preteen and had carried on two affairs—one with a royal courtier that continued after her marriage—meaning she hadn't been a virgin when she entered into her union with Henry. Those were offenses worthy of execution. In October 1541, Catherine confessed her so-called sins, and in February 1542, she was separated from her head at the Tower of London.

SIX: CATHERINE PARR (SURVIVED)

Henry VIII first showed interest in Catherin Parr in 1542; by that time, Catherine—the daughter of Henry's advisor Sir Thomas Parr and one of Catherine of Aragon's ladies-in-waiting (she had been named after that queen)—had been twice widowed, was working as a servant for Mary Tudor, and was engaged to Thomas Seymour, brother of Henry's deceased wife Jane Seymour. But Henry VIII laid claim, and Catherine consented because it made good financial sense for her and her family. Henry VIII left her alone during their marriage, and she actively helped raise Edward and Elizabeth. In 1545, her Protestant book of prayers, *Prayers or Meditations*, was the first book in English credited to a female author. Catherine Parr was such a radical Protestant and adherent to the Church of England that a contingent of anti-Protestant leaders tried to get her executed for being a heretic; Henry made the warrant go away. Four years into their marriage, in 1547, Henry VIII died, leaving Catherine free to finally marry Thomas Seymour. She died in August 1548 after contracting puerperal fever a week after giving birth.

Number of unsolved murders in the U.S. since 1965: 345,000.

UNCLE JOHN'S STALL OF FAME

Uncle John is continuously amazed—and pleased—by the unusual ways people get involved with bathrooms, toilets, and so on. That's why he created the "Stall of Fame."

Honoree: Noel Black and K. L. Goff, of the Blackwell Chamber of Commerce in Blackwell, Oklahoma

Notable Achievement: Littering toilets on neighbors' lawns to "wipe out" hunger

True Story: In 2024, Black and Goff of Leadership Blackwell announced—in a three-minute video with more bathroom puns than this Bathroom Reader—the Chamber's "Take the Plunge to Wipe Out Hunger" campaign. "This is not a crapshoot," assures Goff. The initiative works like this: if you wake up and find a white toilet covered with stickers in your front yard, that means "You've been dumped on!" Next to the toilet will be a sign with instructions and a number to call after you've made an important choice: pay $25 (or make an in-kind donation) to get the toilet taken away, or pay $50 to have the city remove it "and take a dump on someone else's yard of your choosing," says Black. Pay an extra $200, and they'll never ever put a toilet on your lawn again. The money supports the local food bank. However, if you pay nothing, the toilet will stay put for three to five days, and all your neighbors will know you didn't want to pitch in a few bucks to help out. At the end of the video, Black and Goff sing (not quite in unison or in tune), "We're toilet-ly committed...to you!" (Editor's note: it's adorable.)

Honoree: Radiant Plumbing & Air Conditioning, which serves Austin and San Antonio in Texas

Notable Achievement: Producing a bathroom-themed commercial worthy of an Oscar

True Story: Local commercials have always had a certain folksy charm, compared to slickly produced big-budget national commercials. And since the early 2000s, Radiant has been locally famous for its 30-second TV spots that riff off famous movies like *Dune*, *The Avengers*, and *The Terminator* ("Come with me...if you want to flush").

In 2023, Radiant's ads caught the eye of John Oliver, host of HBO's *Last Week Tonight* news/comedy show. Oliver issued the plumbing company a challenge: create a commercial based on a movie of Oliver's choosing, and if Radiant could pull it off, Oliver would donate $10,000 to the Central Texas Food Bank.

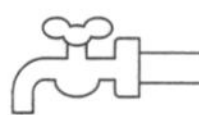

First celebrity to have a conspiracy theory about their death being fake: Roman emperor Nero (AD 68).

The only snag: the movie that Oliver chose was Paul Thomas Anderson's sprawling epic, *Magnolia*. The surreal drama weaves a dozen disparate—and depressing—storylines together over its three-hour run time, culminating with a truly bizarre ending. Could Radiant do it justice?

The result was *Magtoiletolia*. At nearly four minutes long, the "plumbing commercial to end all plumbing commercials" hits on all 12 storylines and ends with toilets raining from the sky, which, if you've seen the movie, will make you smile.

Duly impressed, Oliver aired the epic ad on an episode of *Last Week Tonight* and made good on his promise. Radiant matched the donation, and two Texas food banks received $10,000 each. You can watch *Magtoiletolia* online. (Though it will be funnier if you watch *Magnolia* first.)

Honoree: Alana Martin, an organizer with the American Cancer Society, Relay for Life of the Kenai Peninsula in Alaska
Notable Achievement: Coming up with a "race for the rest of us"
True Story: The Relay for Life is great and all, but it's five kilometers. If you'd like to raise money for cancer research without breaking a sweat, consider heading to Alaska in August for the Brewery to Bathroom .5K. You read that right: half a K. Entrants of all ages meet at the Kanai River Brewing Company for an 11:00 a.m. start time (late enough they can sleep in). Then everyone casually saunters off for the .5K, which is really only .31K (about a thousand feet). Along the course are randomly placed "demotivators," including a comfy couch (that you have to pay extra to rest in), a snack station with "doughnut holes, cookies, strudels, and Peeps," and signs making fun of people who exercise.

The turnaround point is the restroom at Soldotna Creek Park. (A pit stop is not mandatory, but why pass up the chance?) The winner isn't whoever crosses the finish line first, but whoever best embodies the "laid-back spirit" of the race. The silly event, which raises thousands of dollars annually for cancer research, is the brainchild of a former Relay for Life "runner" Alana Martin, who wants you to know: "If you are a marathon runner and you love to sweat and you are on the keto diet, we love you. We are super proud of you. We just aren't really going to show it."

* * *

"There's two kinds of people in prison. There's predators and there's prey and you have to decide which you're gonna be every morning. And you might decide you're going to be a predator, but someone else has decided you're going to be prey. It's probably the most tense place you'll ever be."

—Danny Trejo

IT'S RAINING CHAIR LEGS

From the "we're all different but the same" file, here are some English idioms and proverbs, along with their equivalents in other languages.

Once upon a time...

Somali: Story, story, a story of silk...

Kurdish: Once there was and there was not, there was...

Latvian: Once long ago in times long gone...

Korean: Back when tigers used to smoke tobacco...

Polish: Beyond seven mountains, beyond seven rivers...

And they lived happily ever after.

Afrikaans: Whistle, whistle, the story is done.

Norwegian: Snip, snap, snout, then this adventure is finished.

Greek: And they lived well, and we lived better.

German: And if they haven't died, they still live today.

Slovak: And they lived together happily, until they died.

To have your cake and eat it, too.

Italian: You can't have the barrel full and the wife drunk.

Polish: The wolf is full and the lamb whole.

French: To want the butter and the money from the butter.

Danish: You can't blow and have flour in your mouth.

German: You can't dance at two weddings at the same time.

The squeaky wheel gets the grease.

Chinese: The crying baby gets the milk.

Japanese: The nail that stands out gets pounded down.

Korean: The pointy stone meets the chisel.

Dutch: Tall trees catch loads of wind.

Portuguese: He who does not cry does not get breastfed.

Mind your beeswax!

French: Take care of your own onions!

Swedish: Take care of yourself!

Japanese: That's an unnecessary help!

Catalan: You have to do nothing of it!

Spanish: Don't stick your nose where it's not called!

It's raining cats and dogs.

Welsh: It's raining old ladies and sticks.

Serbian: Axes are falling.

Japanese: Earth and sand descending.

Greek: It's raining chair legs.

Spanish (Argentina): Pointing down turds are falling.

It's better to be safe than sorry.

French: Prevention is better than cure.

Italian: Better an egg today than a chicken tomorrow.

Japanese: Later worry less, start from safety is better.

Chinese: Being careful can help one sail a ship for ten thousand years.

Russian: God protects the safe.

Of the first 40 pilots hired by the U.S. Postal Service for airmail deliveries, 31 died in accidents.

THEY GOT THE BAND BACK TOGETHER

But in the wake of these disastrous reunions, maybe they shouldn't have.

LED ZEPPELIN

In 1980, Led Zeppelin split up almost immediately after drummer John Bonham drank himself to death at the age of 32. But just five years later, the surviving members of the most dominant hard rock band of the 1970s decided to get back together to meet fan demand and to help raise money to fight the African famine: Led Zeppelin took the stage at the Live Aid charity relief concert in July 1985 at Wembley Stadium in London. Bonham's drumming had been so forceful that the band needed two musicians to replace him on stage—Tony Thompson (of Chic) and Phil Collins. The live set was less than triumphant and barely even happened, as the group was onstage for just 20 minutes and played only three songs: "Rock and Roll," "Whole Lotta Love," and "Stairway to Heaven." The band was rusty. Singer Robert Plant had performed three solo shows in the week before Live Aid, and he'd almost entirely lost his voice, which he did after a brief pre-show rehearsal. Guitarist Jimmy Page's instrument didn't get tuned before the set, and nobody's stage monitors were operational. Still, despite the lackluster performance, Plant, Page, and bassist John Paul Jones secretly got together later in 1985 to rehearse as a group with an eye toward restarting Led Zeppelin. But the musicians found they no longer had any chemistry, and they called the whole thing off.

THE SUPREMES

At the end of the 1960s, the Supremes were the most successful vocal pop group ever to that point, hitting #1 a dozen times with Motown-released hits like "Baby Love" and "Stop! In the Name of Love." Lead singer Diana Ross became so much more famous than her golden-era bandmates, Florence Ballard and Mary Wilson, that after a few years of Motown marketing them as "Diana Ross and the Supremes," she exited the band in 1970 for a monumentally successful solo career. In 2000, the Supremes announced their intent to get back together for a nostalgic concert tour. But this wasn't the *real* Supremes; Ballard had been dead since 1976, and Wilson wouldn't come back because she was offered just $3 million for the endeavor, pennies

The original names of the hippos in the Hungry, Hungry Hippos game: Lizzie, Henry, Harry, and Homer.

compared to the $20 million the promoters promised Ross. The Supremes tour then consisted of Ross with Lynda Laurence and Scherrie Payne, who were members of the Supremes only after Ross's 1970 departure. Promoters still charged "real" Supremes prices, and there wasn't much demand for $250 concert tickets for this lineup. After an early tour stop in Columbus, Ohio, saw the Supremes playing to a half-empty arena that seated 20,000, the rest of the tour was canceled.

THE CARS

One of the biggest bands of the guitars-and-keyboards New Wave era, and the early MTV era, was the Cars. After scoring numerous catchy hits like "Just What I Needed," "Magic," and "You Might Think," the band broke up in 1988 over creative differences and so frontman Ric Ocasek could go solo and become a rock producer. After the 2000 death of bassist and co–lead singer Benjamin Orr, a full reunion was outside the realm of possibility, but in 2005, three of the other Cars—Greg Hawkes, David Robinson, and Elliot Easton—proposed the idea to Ocasek anyway. Ocasek was so opposed to the idea that he threatened to sue his former bandmates. Legally unable to use the name "The Cars," Hawkes and Easton (but not Robinson) launched the New Cars, filling out the lineup with singer-songwriter Todd Rundgren and Tubes drummer Prairie Prince. The group played a few sparsely attended concerts before calling it off when a tour bus accident left Easton with a broken collarbone. The band produced one album, *It's Alive!*, a critically lambasted and poor-selling mishmash of tracks hastily recorded at some of the New Cars' few concerts. *It's Alive!* mostly featured the New Cars covering old Cars songs, live versions of the New Cars performing Rundgren's 1970s hits (including "I Saw the Light"), and the only three new songs the band could finish writing and recording in time.

THE VELVET UNDERGROUND

The Velvet Underground never sold many copies of their dark, eerie art rock in the late 1960s and early 1970s, but they influenced countless musicians in their wake. Two big musical egos—Lou Reed and John Cale—dictated the direction of the band, and they fought over creative issues so much that Cale split in 1968. By 1973, Reed and every other original member was gone, too. Reed went on to a big solo career and enjoyed his status as a forefather of the punk rock movement. It would take the death of the Velvet Underground's mentor, Andy Warhol, to get them back together. The legendary pop artist managed the group in its early days and gave them exposure and a coolness seal of approval by making them the house band at his studio club,

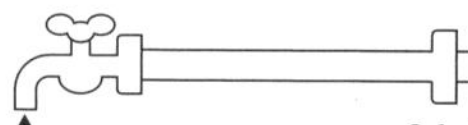

Of the 41 Broadway-designated theaters, only three actually sit on the street called Broadway.

the Factory. When Warhol died in 1987, Reed and Cole made a tribute album, *Songs for Drella*, and in 1990, they performed it in its entirety with fellow Velvets Maureen Tucker and Sterling Morrison. The old magic was there, and in 1993 the Velvet Underground embarked on a reunion tour, headlining in European clubs and opening for U2 in some cities. Plans were in place for a taping of *MTV Unplugged*, a new studio album, and a stadium tour of the U.S.—all of which Cale and Reed fought about. It was just like old times, so much so that the tour fell apart and the band split up again...this time permanently.

JEFFERSON AIRPLANE

As its sound and membership changed with the times, so did the name of the band originally known as Jefferson Airplane. The gritty psychedelic band of the late 1960s who gave the world "White Rabbit" and "Volunteers" gave way to Jefferson Starship, responsible for space-rocking 1970s hits like "Miracles" and "Jane." In the mid-1980s, Jefferson Starship became Starship, a soft-rock pop group that topped the charts with "We Built This City" and "Nothing's Gonna Stop Us Now." Confusingly, during the Starship era, Jefferson Airplane reunited. Throughout the band's history, some members had played in a side project called Hot Tuna, which in 1988 invited Jefferson Airplane members Paul Kantner and Grace Slick—with whom they were engaged in a lawsuit—up on stage during a San Francisco concert. That led to a 1989 reunion of nearly the entire late 1960s Jefferson Airplane lineup (they were short drummer Spencer Dryden). While other 1960s acts were enjoying comebacks at the time—The Who, Paul McCartney, George Harrison, Santana—audiences didn't want the new old Jefferson Airplane. The band's reunion record, *Jefferson Airplane*, peaked at #84 on the chart.

* * *

HOME, DEADLY HOME

According to the Consumer Product Safety Commission, in 2022, 10 million Americans went to the emergency room due to a household accident. Here's what hurt them the most.

1. **Flooring:** 2.135 million hospital visits
2. **Stairs or steps:** 1.027 million
3. **Beds or bed frames:** 912,875
4. **Bathtubs or showers:** 431,658
5. **Tables:** 327,363
6. **Chairs:** 319,276
7. **Ceilings and walls:** 293,762
8. **Couches:** 211,422
9. **Rugs or carpets:** 206,534
10. **Toilets:** 204,734

The *-bel* in the sound unit name *decibel* represents telephone inventor Alexander Graham Bell.

THE OBITS

These real death notices weren't written by journalists, but by the witty families of the dearly departed–or by the dearly departed themselves (before they were departed, of course).

Holly Blair exploded into glitter and bats on August 17, 2020. She is survived by four spoiled cats, two stinky dogs, three bad birds, a turtle and an utterly useless frog named Fred as well as three children and a husband of little to no importance. Her remains will be interred under a tree with the ridiculous multitude of animals she rescued both wild and domestic. Her future plans include drinking beer with Terry Pratchett and flying across the moon on her broomstick on Halloween. She has also promised to communicate with us from the beyond via the cockatiel psyche. We ask that everyone carve extra jack-o'-lanterns on Halloween this year in her honor. All hail the wicked witch of Juniper road!

–Wood River Chapel

Stocks, Mary Patricia (née Morris)–Pat Stocks, 94, passed away peacefully at her home in bed July 1, 2015...She left behind a hell of a lot of stuff to her daughter and sons who have no idea what to do with it. So if you're looking for 2 extremely large TVs from the '90s, a large ceramic stork (we think) umbrella/cane stand, a toaster oven (slightly used), or even a 2001 Oldsmobile with a spoiler...and 1,000 tools that we aren't sure what they're used for. You should wait the appropriate amount of time and get in touch. Tomorrow would be fine.

—Toronto Star

Walter George Bruhl Jr. of Newark and Dewey Beach is a dead person; he is no more; he is bereft of life; he is deceased; he has wrung down the curtain and gone to join the choir invisible; he has expired and gone to meet his maker. He drifted off this mortal coil on March 9, 2014, in Punta Gorda, Fla. His spirit was released from his worn-out shell of a body and is now exploring the universe. He was surrounded by his loving wife of 57 years, Helene Sellers Bruhl, who will now be able to purchase the mink coat which he had always refused her because he believed only minks should wear mink... Walt was preceded in death by his tonsils and adenoids in 1935; a spinal disc in 1974; a large piece of his thyroid gland in 1988; and his prostate on March 27, 2000.

—Cape Gazette

Terrance W. "Terry" Siebert died peacefully at his home, surrounded by his family on Monday, July 21, 2014, in his 58th year...Friends may visit with the family at the

Church of Jesus Christ of Latter-day Saints, Hamilton, on Thursday. It was Terry's last wish that his pallbearers be the Toronto Maple Leafs so they could let him down one last time.

—Franklin Funeral Home

Hicks, Sybil Marie (née Lyons). It hurts me to admit it... but I, Mrs. Ron Hicks from Baysville, have passed away. I passed peacefully with my eldest daughter, Brenda, by my side February 2, 2019 at 8:20 a.m. I leave behind my loving husband, Ron Hicks, whom I often affectionately referred to as a "Horse's Ass." I also left behind my children whom I tolerated over the years; Bob (with Carol) my oldest son and also my favourite. Brian (with Ginette) who was the Oreo cookie favourite, Brenda AKA "Hazel" who would run to clean the bathrooms when she heard company was coming. Barbara (with Gordon) the ever Miss Perfect and finally Baby Bruce who wouldn't eat homemade turkey soup because he didn't want to be alert looking for bones while he ate. I finally have the smoking hot body I have always wanted...having been cremated.

—*The Hamilton Spectator*

Renay Mandel Corren. A plus-sized Jewish lady redneck died in El Paso on Saturday. Of itself hardly news, or good news if you're the type that subscribes to the notion that anybody not named you dying in El Paso, Texas is good news. In which case have I got news for you: the bawdy, fertile, redheaded matriarch of a sprawling Jewish-Mexican-Redneck American family has kicked it. This was not good news to Renay Mandel Corren's many surviving children, grandchildren and great-grandchildren, many of whom she even knew and, in her own way, loved. There will be much mourning in the many glamorous locales she went bankrupt in: McKeesport, PA, Renay's birthplace and where she first fell in love with ham, and atheism; Fayetteville and Kill Devil Hills, NC, where Renay's dreams, credit rating and marriage are all buried; and of course Miami, FL, where Renay's parents, uncles, aunts, and eternal hopes of all Miami Dolphins fans everywhere, are all buried pretty deep. Renay was preceded in death by Don Shula.

—*The Fayetteville Observer*

Emily DeBrayda Phillips. It pains me to admit it, but apparently, I have passed away. Everyone told me it would happen one day but that's simply not something I wanted to hear, much less experience. Once again I didn't get things my way!...I've been a devoted daughter, an energetic teenager, a WCU graduate (summa cum laude), a loving wife, a comforting mother, a dedicated teacher, a true and loyal friend, and a spoiling grandmother. And if you don't believe it, just ask me. Oh wait, I'm afraid it's too late for questions. Sorry.

—*The Florida Times-Union*

In 1919, New York Yankees center fielder Ping Bodie competed against an ostrich in a spaghetti-eating contest—and won.

ALL ABOUT PEZ

To enjoy these facts, just tilt the book back and push each of them out, one by one.

- Among the flavors of PEZ over the years that flopped: cola, licorice, coffee, chocolate, and chlorophyll.
- PEZ is vegan. It's made without animal products and consists primarily of sugar with natural coloring and flavoring agents added.
- The original and only PEZ flavor for nearly 30 years: peppermint. Inventor Eduard Haas III formulated the candy in 1927 as a powerful mint intended to help people quit smoking.
- Haas later brought in Oscar Uxa as a business partner, who convinced Haas to sell PEZ in metal tins and then—to drive home the point of the candy as a smoking cessation aid—in a dispenser shaped like a cigarette lighter.
- The first PEZ dispenser, in the lighter style, debuted at the Vienna Trade Fair in 1949. It held 12 PEZ candy bricks, same as the head-topped dispensers that would arrive later.
- "PEZ" is an abbreviation of the German word for peppermint, *pfefferminz*. Haas took the first, middle, and last letters of the word to make PEZ.
- Today, the world's PEZ supply all originates at a single factory in Orange, Connecticut. The factory goes through more than 12,000 pounds of sugar each day to make 12 million individual candy pieces.
- How PEZ is made: 3,000 pounds of pressure are applied to the sugar mix inside of molds, which solidifies it into hardened candy bricks.
- PEZ debuted in the United States in 1952. The peppermint candy dispensed from nondescript containers flopped, so the company decided to market the products as candy and toys for kids instead of a stop-smoking tool for adults. In addition to new fruit flavors, the dispensers came topped with a playful head. The first ever kids' PEZ dispenser: Halloween Witch, launched in 1957.
- Preceding the Halloween Witch was a novelty toy: the PEZ Space Gun, which fired PEZ candies into the mouth as projectiles. It was quickly discontinued for safety reasons.
- The first licensed character to top a PEZ dispenser: Popeye, in 1958.
- PEZ terminology: The small tabs at the bottom of the dispenser to make it securely stand up straight are called feet. The part that pushes the piece of candy out when the head is tilted is a kicker.
- Bestselling PEZ dispenser of all time: Santa Claus.
- The rarest PEZ dispenser was one with an astronaut helmet as its topper. Prepared for the 1982 World's Fair in Knoxville, Tennessee, only two were ever made: a blue one and a white one. One sold for $32,000 on eBay.
- The other rarest PEZ dispensers: A set of two depicting Prince William and Kate Middleton to commemorate their 2011 wedding was built. The only ones were sold for $13,360, with the proceeds going to charity.

Arlington, Texas (population: 395,000), is the largest American city without any form of public transit.

A SOMEWHAT LENGTHY HISTORY OF MEASUREMENT

An inch is an inch, and an ounce is an ounce, but have you ever wondered why those things are what they are? Here's how the history of measuring things measures up.

EGYPT AND THE CUBIT

The oldest codified measurement system for which clear rules were written down and preserved was the cubit. Developed in ancient Egypt around the year 3000 BC, it spread around the world by way of the Egyptian empire's domination of northern Africa and the Middle East. The cubit is a measurement equivalent to about 18 modern inches, or 457 millimeters, and was derived from the average length of an adult male's lower arm, stretching from the elbow down to the tip of the middle finger.

The cubit was broken down into other subunits, including the digit, or the breadth of one finger; 28 of these was equal to one cubit. Four digits equaled a palm, five digits equaled a hand, 12 equaled a small span, 14 equaled a large span, and 16 equaled a t'ser. These units were convertible; for instance, seven palms equaled one cubit. It was a complicated system but one effectively used throughout Egypt: the cubit and all of its sub-measurements were used to design and build many of the most iconic structures of the Egyptian empire, notably the Great Pyramid of Giza.

The Egyptian Empire gave way to the Roman Empire, and Egypt came under Roman rule after a conquest in about 30 BC. The cubit system was already falling out of favor because it didn't really translate to all the other areas where Egyptian law was in effect—people from different parts of the world have different arm and finger measurements from one another, and so a cubit (and span, t'ser, palm, and digit) couldn't be universal. So when the Romans conquered Egypt, and, later, the British Isles, they brought with them and instituted their own tried-and-true (but imperfect) measurement methods.

THE ANCIENT GREEKS

After the Egyptian empire, but before the Roman empire, the Greeks held sway as the most influential culture in the ancient world. The Greece of antiquity had its own measurements, too, updated and tweaked from the Egyptian cubit system and still using rough estimates of the length of body parts.

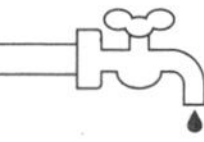

A daktylos was thought to be the average size of a segment of a Greek man's finger—and *daktylos* translates to "finger." One daktylos works out to about three-quarters of an inch. Four daktylos equaled a *palaiste* ("palm"), and four palaistes made a *pous* ("foot"). The Greeks also had their own cubit, or *pechos*, which is the same length as about 1.5 feet. They also introduced a measure of depth, the fathom. That's still used today, and it's still pretty much what the ancient Greeks said it ought to be: a fathom back then was the equivalent of about 6.1 feet, and a modern-day fathom is exactly six feet.

The Greeks measured distances with the *stadion*, or *stadium*, equal to 600 Greek feet. The problem was that the length of a foot varied across different parts of ancient Greece, resulting in confusion about the length of a stadion. In Athens, it measured 600 Greek feet, and the Romans would later adopt this as its own measurement for the stadion—it works out to 185 meters. (This is still in use today in sailing as a "cable," or 1/10 of a nautical mile.)

THE ROMAN WAY

During the dominant era of the Roman Empire—about 750 BC to AD 476—the emperor-run city-state had a global network of conquered lands. Its measurement system became the official rule of law, and elements of it are still used around the world today, particularly in the United States. The basic unit in the Roman system was the *uncia*, a unit of measure used for length as well as weight and volume. Also called a Roman inch (a word derived from *uncia*), its length was locked in at 0.97 a contemporary inch by Emperor Marcus Agrippa, who reigned from 63 to 12 BC.

Roman weights and measures revolved primarily around magnitudes of 12. In length, 12 uncia (which literally means "a twelfth") equaled one *pes*, or a Roman foot. The uncia was traced backward from the *pes*, literally "foot," based on the average length of an actual foot of Roman centurion soldiers. A Roman ounce, also called an uncia, constituted 1/12 of a Roman pound.

Our modern mile comes from ancient Rome, too. Called a *mille*, it was the equivalent distance of 5,000 Roman feet, or 2,000 steps, or 1,000 paces, or eight Roman stadia. (In contemporary measures, that works out to 1,480 meters, or 4,855 feet.) One measurement that didn't really stand the test of time was the *iugerium*: it represented the area that two oxen could reasonably plow in one day, determined to be a field of about 2,520 square meters.

A NEW METRIC

The metric system is a near-universal system of weighing and measuring the physical world. It's used in at least some official capacities in all but three countries: Liberia,

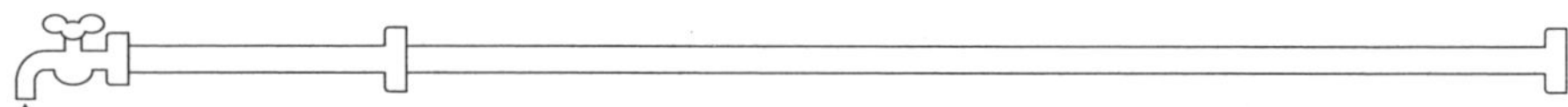

Word origin: in 1613, an academic who computed calculations was called a *computer*.

Myanmar, and the United States. Using a base-10 system, it's probably the most sensible and understandable measurement system possible, but it still needed a few people to invent and develop it, and it took more than 100 years before anyone seriously thought about implementing it. English clergyman John Wilkins (brother-in-law to Oliver Cromwell, Lord Protector of England during a brief period in the 17th century when the monarchy was abolished) wrote about it in 1668, calling it the "standard." It didn't catch on at the time, and two years later, French theologian and mathematician Gabriel Mouton independently came up with a similar idea of arranging weights and measures in increments of 10. The French scientific community took up Mouton's idea, as a theory, writing studies on it for decades.

In 1790, the French Revolution was over and the nation looked into the future, toward establishing itself as a first-world republic. To compete with other world economies, it needed a standard system of measurement—at the time, more than 300 different land-measurement unit systems were used across the country. France's national assembly asked for a universal standard for measurements that was based on increasingly smaller fractions of the circumference of the Earth. Like Wilkins's and Mouton's plans, it was decimal-oriented, with each unit moving up and down by magnitudes of 10. Officially implemented by French law in 1795, the system was called *metrics*, based on the Greek word *metron,* or "a measure."

The French Academy picked that name, and was also tasked with coming up with the titles and lengths of metric-system measurements. The standard unit, known as the meter, was calculated as being 1/10,000,000 the distance from the North Pole to the equator. Other measurements came from multiplying or dividing the meter by 10:

kilometer=1,000 meters

hectometer=100 meters

decameter=10 meters

decimeter=1/10 meter

centimeter=1/100 meter

millimeter=1/1,000 meter

Just four years after the metric system was instituted in France, conquering emperor Napoleon banned it. After the fall of Napoleon and his predecessors, the system was reinstituted in 1840, by which time it had spread and been eagerly adopted throughout the developed world, particularly by the scientific community because it was so logical and so easy to learn. In 1866, the U.S. Congress passed laws recommending that metrics be the official system used for American commerce. Adoption was voluntary, so it didn't stick, with a mishmash of Imperial and other

Only land mammal native to New Zealand: bats.

measurements preferred. The federal government tried to institute metrics again throughout the 1970s, and that movement similarly failed to gain a toehold. Even after Congress passed the Omnibus Trade and Competitiveness Act in 1988, which required federal agencies to get on board with metrics by 1992, it didn't take. That's all with the exception of the U.S. Army and U.S. Marine Corps, both of which have followed the metric system since 1957 for their equipment and weapons.

IMPERIAL SYSTEM

The ancient Romans invaded, occupied, and further settled Great Britain from AD 43 onward, and they brought their measurements with them. But they weren't the only outsiders to take over the area. Celtic and Anglo-Saxon measurement traditions were retained after the Norman conquest of 1066; and as the culture and nation of England evolved over the centuries, it adapted and modified measurements still in use today. This collection would eventually be codified as the Imperial System and include more universal lengths, like the inch, foot, yard, and furlong. Following the Norman invasion, other newly introduced measuring standards were mixed with some of the old ones. Land would be measured by the gyrd or rod, a unit of 5.5 feet. Forty rods equaled a furlong, which was the length of a furrow, or depression, that an ox could plough in a day.

But because England was ruled by monarchs, kings and queens took great privilege and pleasure in changing measurements as it suited them. By decree of Norman king Henry I around the year 1100, a yard would be the distance stretching from the tip of his nose to the end of his thumb on his stretched out arm. That was almost three feet, so it became three feet, otherwise known as a yard. In the late 16th century, Queen Elizabeth I changed the distance of a mile: rejecting the Roman length of 5,000 feet, the Queen said a mile was henceforth the seemingly obtuse 5,280 feet. That would make a mile the equivalent of exactly eight furlongs, making for a more practical conversion. (Of course, this was necessitated by Elizabeth's Tudor forebears establishing that a furlong is 220 yards.)

The Imperial System took off far and wide, but old habits die hard. In Ireland, for example, residents were way to replace a local agrarian-oriented system, and it took until the 19th century to fully get rid of "cow's grass" as a roughly defined unit of measuring out parcels of land. Most farmers had their own ever-changing, non-specific idea about how much land that was, and it was seen as equal to the amount of land where one could grow enough grass to keep one cow alive. Even in England, the old ways stuck around. There was a measurement dating back at least to the year 1000 called the barleycorn—that was the average length of a grain of barley, and it was adopted into the Imperial System as a length 1/3 of an inch, or 8.5 millimeters. Old

Salmon sushi was invented in Norway, then introduced to Japan.

and seemingly obscure though it is, it's still commonly used in the U.S. and the U.K.: it's the basis for measuring shoe sizes. What's the length difference between a size 7 and a size 8? One barleycorn. How long is today's inch? Three barleycorns.

As the British later colonized the world and established territories on nearly every corner of the Earth, they instituted this evolved Imperial System. It would eventually die out; England has used the metric system legally since 1965, although it still employs some other rules, such as for liquids. No Brit would order a metric half-liter of beer in a pub—they ask for a pint, or 16 ounces, based on an ancient Roman liquid measurement still seen in the modern American system. (The gallon, today a liquid quantity, began in the 1300s as the dry gallon, or the equivalent of eight pounds of wheat.)

THE AMERICAN WAY

The U.S. never adopted the metric system, and that might have been fated. The colonial period lasted for hundreds of years, with so many European nations establishing settlements in North America, that they all regionally entrenched their own measurement systems. Until the American Revolution, and the establishment of an autonomous government, colonists might encounter different systems relating to the English, Dutch, French, and Spanish methods of the era, or just regional variances. For example, the bushel, a volume measurement used by farmers to track grain, was widely used throughout the New World, introduced by British settlers. But a Connecticut bushel weighed 28 pounds, and a New Jersey bushel weighed 32 pounds.

To bring about much-needed uniformity, the U.S. Customary System was adopted in 1832, then edited throughout the 19th century. This became the new American standard, although it was largely based on parts of the British system, many of them affirmed by Queen Elizabeth I in the 16th century. Liquid measures begin with a cup, which historically is twice a gill (which was about 32 mouthfuls). A pint was then double a cup, and a quart was double the pint. Four quarts (short for quarter) went into a gallon. The United States retains its unique system to this day, without any signs of switching.

* * *

YOU'RE MY INSPIRATION: GANDALF

According to director Peter Jackson, he and Ian McKellen listened to interviews of *The Lord of the Rings* author J. R. R. Tolkien reading book excerpts to get an idea of how the beloved wizard is supposed to talk. And they got it, but it wasn't Tolkien's readings as Gandalf. Instead, "Ian based his performance on an impersonation of Tolkien himself," said Jackson. "He sounds the same, he uses the speech patterns, and his mannerisms are born out of the same roughness from the footage of Tolkien. So, Tolkien would recognize himself in Ian's performance."

If all 64 million YouTube creators comprised a country, it would be the 25th most populous nation on Earth.

CASSEROLE ORIGINS

It's been what's for dinner, or on the side, for generations of Americans growing up. Here's how these casseroles got to the table.

JOHN WAYNE CASSEROLE

Following the deaths of multiple relatives to cancer in the 1970s, 10-year-old Cara Connery organized a fundraiser for the American Cancer Society. With the help of her mother, in 1978 she began compiling the contents of what would later become *Cooking with Love from Cara and Her Friends*, a compilation of recipes sent to Cara by celebrities she approached. While he was dying of cancer, legendary movie tough guy John Wayne sent in a recipe for a breakfast casserole. In the book, it was called "John Wayne Casserole," and it was made of eggs, jack and cheddar cheeses, green chiles, heavy cream, tomatoes, and cayenne pepper. The book sold well, and in the early 1980s, the University of Mississippi Medical Center cafeteria in Jackson started serving a variation of the John Wayne Casserole. Listed on the menu under the same name, and still available every other Thursday, it swapped out the eggs for ground beef, and added Bisquick (for a crust), pickled jalapeño peppers, bell peppers, sour cream, and mayonnaise. That's now the more commonly known and prepared John Wayne Casserole.

KING RANCH CASSEROLE

King Ranch is the biggest ranch in Texas, but it doesn't produce chicken, the main protein in King Ranch Casserole—it's a cattle ranch. The dish was not first produced at King Ranch, or made by anyone associated with King Ranch. In a 1972 recipe contest for a Texas newspaper, "King Ranch Casserole" placed first and its popularity spread from there, although it wasn't widely known or prepared outside of Texas until the 1990s. What is it? It's a Tex-Mex dish, likely inspired by the Mexican dish chilaquiles, which uses most of the same ingredients; King Ranch Casserole, however, swaps out fresh foods for canned whenever possible, using foods more conveniently available to American home cooks in the mid-20th century. It's made by layering corn tortillas (or tortilla chips) with tomatoes, onions, bell peppers, cheese, chicken, chiles, and a sauce made from canned cream of chicken and cream of mushroom soups combined with chicken broth.

GREEN BEAN CASSEROLE

Campbell's Soup Company unveiled its cream of mushroom variety in 1934, and it became a common ingredient in casseroles, many of which originated on the labels of

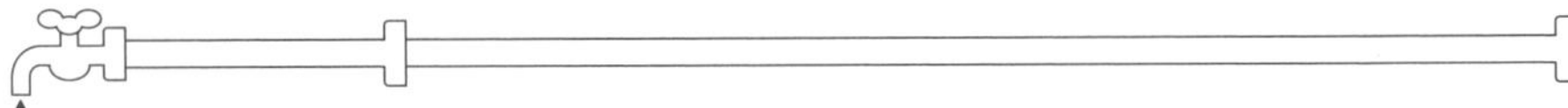

Flash floods kill more people in the desert than dehydration does.

Campbell's soup cans. Green Bean Casserole, now a standard Thanksgiving side dish, began as one of those recipes. In 1955, Campbell's Soup test kitchen worker Dorcas Reilly was tasked with creating a new casserole recipe to be printed on cream of mushroom soup cans. Noting its use as a binder in many other casseroles, both those created by Campbell's and those not, she thought the soup might taste good with another inexpensive and commonly available canned food: green beans. The final product tasted good, but it felt too soggy, gloopy, and colorless to Reilly. So she added one final ingredient as a topping: canned crispy fried onions.

CHICKEN TETRAZZINI

Chicken Tetrazzini is more or less spaghetti with diced chicken in a cream sauce, all mixed up together and baked in a pan in an oven. Multiple high-end restaurants claim to have invented it, but food historians say the most likely creator was Ernest Arbogast, head chef of San Francisco's Palace Hotel, who created the dish in honor of famed opera singer Luisa Tetrazzini performing for the first time in the U.S. in 1905. The popular New York restaurant Sardi's added it to its menu in the 1950s, and that recipe appeared in horror star and foodie Vincent Price's cookbook *A Treasury of Great Recipes*. By the 1960s, most frozen dinner companies offered heat-and-serve Chicken Tetrazzini, and a variation of the recipe was found in most major cookbooks, including *Betty Crocker's Hostess Cookbook*. By the 1990s, and after many appearances in many cookbooks, Chicken Tetrazzini was more commonly known as "chicken spaghetti."

CHILI MAC

Cincinnati is the origin point of Cincinnati-style chili. Not seen much outside of the Ohio city, Cincinnati chili is a sauce poured on top of spaghetti and topped with cheese and onions. Greek immigrants in the area had long made a version of the beef-and-tomato dish that was thin and boasted a Mediterranean flavor profile, including a prominent cinnamon taste. That likely inspired another dish that started not far away, in Columbus, Ohio. Marzetti's restaurant offered a cheap, filling meal that became a favorite among local Ohio State University students: a baked pasta made with elbow macaroni, tomato sauce, ground beef, and cheese. Restaurant owner and head cook Teresa Marzetti named the dish after her brother-in-law, Johnny. Johnny Marzetti (the food) spread throughout Ohio and the Midwest and was so popular that Chef Boyardee, Hamburger Helper, and other packaged food brands used it as the inspiration for many of their products. Since they couldn't use the name associated with trademarked Marzetti, they went with generic names like Chili Mac. That name stuck for the dish, regardless of its method of preparation.

Playing video games improves your eyesight's "spatial resolution," which distinguishes between shades of a color.

STATE YOUR HEALTH PROBLEM

In these times of high medical costs, more and more Americans are turning to the Internet for help. To that end, in the winter of early 2024, Soliant Health, a health care staffing company, "analyzed Google search data to identify the health queries that each state searches more frequently than any other." These are some of the results we think are most eye-opening and head-scratching.

ALABAMA
- How do you get monkeypox?
- Why do I sweat in my sleep?
- How to get rid of allergies?

ARIZONA
- How may hours of sleep do you need?
- How to relieve bloating?
- How long do allergies last?
- Can allergies cause a cough?

CALIFORNIA
- How many hours of sleep should you get?
- What is a juice cleanse?
- Can you live without a kidney?
- Why do I keep yawning?
- How to stop vertigo?
- How to stop night sweats?
- Why do I pee when I sneeze?
- Is swallowing gum bad for you?
- How to remove an ingrown toenail?
- Is it bad to sleep with your bra on?

DELAWARE
- How to get rid of hiccups?
- How much water should I drink a day?
- How many bones are in the human body?
- What is anemia?

FLORIDA
- What happens when you eat mold?
- How to relieve tension headache?
- How to relieve sinus headache?
- How to prevent arthritis?
- How do I know if I have pneumonia?
- How much melatonin is too much?

GEORGIA
- Why do I cough at night?
- How to treat ingrown toenail?
- How to stop acid reflux?
- How to stop tinnitus?
- How to relieve sciatica pain?

IDAHO
- Is melatonin safe?
- What causes low blood pressure?
- How do you get pink eye?
- How to pop your ears?
- How much caffeine is too much?

ILLINOIS
- Can you live without a spleen?
- Why do I drool when I sleep?
- What causes restless legs?
- What kills toenail fungus?
- How to prevent heart disease?

INDIANA
- What is a normal blood pressure?
- What is a bunion?
- Why am I always hungry?
- How to relieve gas pain?
- How to get rid of a cold sore in 24 hours?

KENTUCKY
- Why does coffee make you poop?
- Can you live without a spine?
- Is poison ivy contagious?
- How to prevent diabetes?
- How to prevent blood clots?
- What causes allergies?

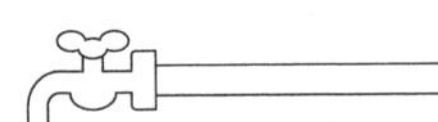

MARYLAND

- What happens when you swallow gum?
- What causes skin tags?
- What causes sleep paralysis?
- Why are my eyes red?
- Can allergies cause headaches?

MISSOURI

- How long can you go without sleep?
- Can you live without a liver?
- How to get rid of bloating?
- Why does my stomach hurt after I eat?
- What causes muscle spasms?
- What does a tick bite look like?
- How to relieve ear pressure?

NEW JERSEY

- Is diabetes genetic?
- What kills stomach virus?
- How to prevent dementia?

NEW YORK

- Why are my hands so dry?
- How to treat food poisoning?
- Why are my gums swollen?
- Are allergies genetic?
- Can you get allergies in the winter?

OHIO

- Can you die from a broken heart?
- How to stop a panic attack?
- How to prevent kidney stones?
- Can allergies cause swollen lymph nodes?

PENNSYLVANIA

- Is breast cancer genetic?
- How often should I workout?
- Why do I always feel tired?
- Is rainwater safe to drink?
- How to relieve period cramps?
- What kills toenail fungus instantly?

SOUTH CAROLINA

- Why do I bruise so easily?

SOUTH DAKOTA

- What is lupus?
- How long does food poisoning last?
- What side is your appendix on?
- What is vertigo?
- Why does my stomach hurt?

TENNESSEE

- What causes tonsil stones?
- Why does my throat hurt when I swallow?
- How to treat strep throat?
- Why are my ankles swollen?

TEXAS

- Why do I pee when I cough?
- What do blood clots look like?
- Why do I keep getting hiccups?
- How to relieve neck pain?
- Why do I keep sneezing?
- Why do I hear ringing in my ear?
- How long should you shower for?

UTAH

- How to get rid of dandruff?
- Why do I sweat so much?
- How to treat a burn?

WEST VIRGINIA

- How to stop snoring?
- How to get rid of a headache?
- What is a hernia?
- How is monkeypox transmitted?
- What causes dizziness?
- What is sleep apnea?
- What do bed bugs look like?

WISCONSIN

- Why is my eye twitching?
- How to get rid of nausea?
- Can allergies cause a fever?
- How to remove ear wax?

WYOMING

- What is Ozempic?
- What happens if you eat mold?
- What temperature is a fever?
- How long is flu contagious?

IT'S AN...EXPLOSION!

In some cases, the weirdest thing about a gender reveal party is that the guest of honor hasn't even been born yet. In other cases, that's the least weird thing going on.

It's a...Fad!

You can thank a blogger from Chicago named Jenna Karvunidis for the gender reveal party. And it's all because she loves cake, so much so that in 2008, she held a special cake-themed party to celebrate her pregnancy. When the first piece was cut, the icing inside was pink, revealing that Karvunidis was going to have a girl! Had it been a boy, the icing would have been blue. (The "blue for boys/pink for girls" classification goes back to the early 20th century but didn't become entrenched until the 1980s, when U.S. retailers integrated these color schemes into their stores.) Karvunidis posted the gender reveal on her blog. It went viral. Then it got picked up by a news outlet, then another, and another, and a fad was born.

At first, these cake-themed gender-reveal parties were mostly harmless—just a delicious way to celebrate the growing of a family. But the reveling revealers didn't stop with cakes. One Florida couple hired two boxers to fight each other in "giant baby costumes" (the baby boy knocked out the baby girl). Another Florida couple, to celebrate the birth of their tenth child, "bopped" an alligator with a balloon, coaxing the animal to bite it, thus scattering pink powder all over the place.

As odd as they can get, most gender reveal parties don't end up in the news. Here are some that did...for all the wrong reasons.

It's a...Puncture Wound!

For their gender reveal in 2018, one couple in Houston, Texas, decided to forego the traditional cake and do "something cool." They filled a balloon with confetti and gave the expectant mom a regulation dart—as in, the game of darts—as the mom's sister, Veronica Fernandez, recorded the reveal on her phone. To get the best vantage point, Fernandez set up a few feet beyond the balloon. Mom-to-be threw the dart, and the balloon popped. Confetti shot all over the place, but where was the dart? "I look down," said Fernandez, "because I feel a pinch and there it is sticking out of my foot." Never in her "wildest dreams" did she think the dart would get past the balloon. Afraid she might "bleed out" (a notion she said she'd gotten from watching *Grey's Anatomy*), Fernandez wouldn't let anyone touch the dart. Firefighters

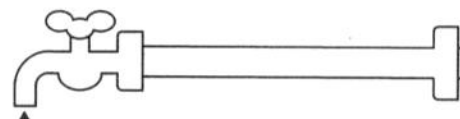

Sesame Street's Oscar the Grouch was originally magenta, but that color wouldn't look good on early color TV...

arrived, and they didn't touch it, either. The dart was removed at the hospital (and Fernandez didn't bleed out).

It's an...Explosion!

"We are very thankful no one was injured during the gender reveal incident," said the Kingston (New Hampshire) Police Department, "and sympathetic to the fact it startled the community." Boy, did it ever. The 2021 celebration was held at a quarry near town. Anthony Spinelli explained to police that he held the reveal at the quarry so the 80 pounds of Tannerite (an explosive substance used as a rifle target) wouldn't cause much damage. The massive blast was heard in two states, and it shook the walls of nearby homes. A judge fined Spinelli $620.

It's a...Castration!

A search for "gender reveal groin" delivered these two viral videos. Both feature the parents-to-be holding air cannons. They count down, press the release button, and out shoots a pink or blue blast of high-powered dust. Having never used these novelty devices before, none of the parents look like they know how to hold them. In one video, Dad hits the release button, and the powder shoots out of the top—as it should—but the plug backfires and hits Dad in the groin at point blank range, sending him down in agony. The same thing happens in the other video, except Mom and Dad are both holding their cannons upside down, and the powder shoots back at them, hitting Dad in the groin. (At least the second couple didn't hit their young daughter, who was standing right between them.) All three were blue, though it's unknown whether the dads noticed while they were writhing in pain.

It's a...Car Fire!

In 2019, expectant parents on Australia's Gold Coast revealed their baby's gender via a fad called a "burnout": a car drives past partygoers as a huge cloud of either pink or blue smoke billows out of its exhaust. At this party, the blue smoke shot out as planned—but then the car erupted in flames, which was not planned. Thankfully, it had already come to a stop in the middle of the road, so nothing else caught on fire. A 29-year-old man was convicted of dangerous operation of a motor vehicle. In 2022, police arrested a "serial burnout" suspect—who charged gender reveal party hosts for his services. He got four years in prison and his car was destroyed (for training purposes). "If you tear up the road," warned a police spokesman, "we'll tear up your car—it's that simple." Police also issued a stern warning that a burnout is an illegal "life-endangering offense."

...so Jim Henson made him orange (and then green).

It's a...Wildfire!

- In April 2017, an off-duty U.S. Border Control agent named Dennis Dickey was hosting a gender reveal party in Arizona's Coronado National Forest. As the guests watched in anticipation, Dickey aimed his rifle toward a straw target that Dickey had stuffed with colored Tannerite. The ensuing explosion released a cloud of blue smoke, indicating a boy. When the smoke cleared, the partiers saw flames in the grass that were spreading *fast*! The resulting Sawmill Fire lasted a week and burned more than 45,000 acres. Dickey was charged with a misdemeanor and ordered pay restitution for the cost of battling the blaze... which topped $8 million.

- In April 2020, a gender reveal party in Brevard County, Florida, went up in flames via, according to police, "Tannerite and a weapon." The fire burned 10 acres of grassland before firefighters were able to contain it. "Something as seemingly innocent as a gender reveal can turn into a large-scale disaster where homes are threatened," said the fire chief.

- In September—the time of year that western U.S. states are at their hottest and driest—of 2020, Refugio Manuel Jimenez Jr. and Angelina Jimenez held their gender reveal party at El Dorado Ranch Park in San Bernardino County, California. According to police, a "smoke-generating pyrotechnic device" started a grass fire. The family's attempts to extinguish it with their water bottles failed, and the El Dorado fire burned for more than two months and destroyed 22,000 acres. A firefighter was killed, which upped the couple's charges to involuntary manslaughter. Dad got a year in prison; Mom got a year's probation. And they were ordered to pay $1,789,972 in restitution.

It's an...Environmental Crime!

Cachoeira Queima-Pé is a 59-foot waterfall that feeds into the Queima-Pé River, which provides drinking water to Tangará da Serra in the drought-stricken state of Mato Grosso, Brazil. The river is as picturesque as it is vital. That's why locals turned red when the falls turned blue in 2022. The proud family posted a video of their gender reveal on Instagram...and promptly deleted it when the backlash hit. "What were they thinking?" was the common sentiment. An investigation revealed that a relative of the expectant parents (without the parents' knowledge) launched "Blue Lake," which is used to dye swimming pools and other bodies of water, into the waterfall. The man was fined 10,000 Brazilian reals (nearly $2,000) for throwing "solid, liquid, or gaseous waste or debris, oils, or oily substances" into the river.

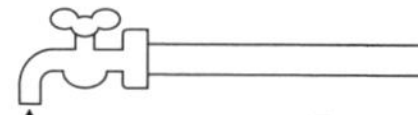

Rapper Pusha T wrote both the McDonald's "I'm Lovin' It" and the music for Arby's "We Have the Meats" jingles.

It's a...Pipe Bomb!

"On Saturday afternoon," said a statement from the Marion County (Iowa) Sheriff's office in October 2019, "five family members and the expectant mother gathered and placed gunpowder in the bottom of a homemade stand that was welded to a metal base plate." In other words, a pipe bomb. The family didn't realize how powerful the blast was going to be, especially after putting tape over the top of the pipe. A piece of shrapnel struck the head of 56-year-old grandmother Pamela Kreimeyer. She was killed instantly.

It's...Enough Already?

The California firefighter and the Iowa grandma aren't the only gender reveal–related deaths. In New York in 2021, a dad-to-be was killed while making a pipe bomb for his own child's gender reveal. And there have been at least two plane crashes during gender reveals that resulted in fatalities.

As for Jenna Karvunidis, created with inventing the gender reveal party in 2008, she thinks the fad has run its course. "Stop having these stupid parties," she wrote on Facebook in 2019. "For the love of God, stop burning things down...Nobody cares but you." Other critics have noted changing attitudes among many parents toward sex and gender in the ensuing years. Why even have them at all, asks Karvunidis, who brings it all back to her love of cake. "We don't need to get our joy by giving others pain. I think there's a new way to have these parties...Celebrate the baby...Let's just have a cake."

* * *

FOUR THOUGHTS ABOUT FARTS

"A happy fart never comes from a miserable ass."

—Martin Luther

"I burp, I fart. I'm a real woman."

—Kate Winslet

"Once you're in the sled, you have to sit still. If one of the guys farts, you just want to get to the finish and everyone is yelling and wants to get out of the sled."

—Helvis Lusis, Olympic four-man bobsledder

"If you let go of fart jokes, you've let go of a piece of humanity."

—Andy Samberg

Temperature in Loma, Montana, on January 14, 1972: -54°F.
Temperature on January 15, 1972: 49°F, a record swing of 103°.

BAD MOMENTS IN BATHROOM HISTORY

Here at the Bathroom Readers' Institute, we cover so much news, information, and technology surrounding the toilet culture of today that we thought we should dig deeper into history with these fascinating and downright horrifying stories about bathrooms and bodily functions of yore.

THE ERFURT DISASTER

In the late 12th century, the German city of Erfurt existed under the tenuous rule of the Holy Roman Empire. Local noblemen and city officials frequently argued with the Catholic Church over who controlled what, and one such dispute between Conrad of Wittelsbach, Archbishop of Mainz, and Ludwig III, the Landgrave of Thuringia, led King Heinrich VI to schedule a summit and mediation at Erfurt's St. Peter's Church. A large group of the empire's elite met in one of the church's buildings in July 1184. Just before the meeting was to begin, the church's floor, hundreds of years old, collapsed under the weight of so many people. It gave way, and everyone was violently dispatched into the space below—the latrine. Nearly everyone present died. Among the few survivors: Conrad, Ludwig, and King Heinrich—they'd been in an anteroom before the summit and were able to hold on for dear life to some iron bars on a window. Between 60 and 100 noblemen died, some from the fall itself but most from drowning in the vat of festering human waste into which they were plunged.

THE SINKING OF THE PRINCESS ALICE

On September 3, 1878, the SS *Princess Alice* steamship navigated the Thames River as it entered London to drop off the passengers of a daylong pleasure cruise to Kent and back. Around 7:30 p.m., a much larger ship, the SS *Bywell Castle*, attempted to pass *Princess Alice*, but the captain misjudged the distance and crashed into the smaller boat with great force. Panic ensued as the *Princess Alice* quickly sank just a few feet from the spot on the Thames where the city's sewage pumps twice daily dumped 90 million gallons of waste. About 130 people were rescued, but 16 of them died within two weeks; those passengers not immediately taken out of the water died within 10 minutes from exposure to toxic sewage. Their recovered bodies were covered in slime and reportedly decomposed at such an advanced rate that by the time they were salvaged, many were unidentifiable; they were buried in a mass grave.

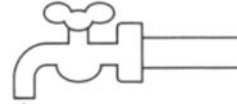

National sport of Argentian: *pato*, a combination of polo and basketball.

THE EVERLASTING PILL

Antimony is a shiny, shimmery metal, listed on the periodic table of the elements as Sb with an atomic number of 51. Ground into a powder and used for medicinal purposes (though with no real scientific merit) for thousands of years, it became a standard treatment for stomach pain in Europe during the Middle Ages. If fashioned into a pill, a chunk of antimony was swallowed, then it made its way through the digestive tract to allegedly work its magic. The swallower would poop it out, their ailments maybe cured, maybe not. At any rate, these pills were so expensive that the treatment became known as the Everlasting Pill, because once passed, one could be washed off and used over and over again. It wasn't uncommon for families to pass down their Everlasting Pill through multiple generations.

THE BATTLE OF AGINCOURT

The English army somehow won the Battle of Agincourt, a pivotal 1415 fight in the Hundred Years' War, despite a heavy mismatch. The French sent well-trained, heavily armed, and protected knights; the English put up a battalion of archers. The English side was also beset by a dysentery outbreak. A considerable swath of troops were too sick to fight, while those that could still stand slung their arrows at the French. And they all fought without pants. They were so affected by such frequent and severe diarrhea that to remove their pants each time wouldn't have been feasible. So they all simply set their trousers aside and let the poop come as it may while they fought.

THE DEATH OF THE DUKE OF BOHEMIA

Upon the death of Boleslav II, the Duke of Bohemia, in 999, his eldest son, Boleslaus III, became the duke. Believing his brothers wanted to kill him and usurp his power, Boleslaus ordered their murders. Oldřich, the youngest, fled to exile, while Jaromír, the middle brother, survived but was castrated. Jaromír eventually became duke. He sought assistance from the Roman Emperor when Oldřich tried to overthrow him; instead of providing help, the emperor imprisoned Jaromír for 21 years. After his release, he was able to reclaim the dukedom temporarily, but Oldřich again threw him into prison, and also blinded him. In 1035, the blind, castrated Jaromír was sitting on the toilet when he was impaled with a spear by an assassin from the rival Vršovci clan.

* * *

"The irony is of course that my career has lasted a whole lot longer than some of the people I've parodied over the years."

—"Weird Al" Yankovic

Taylor Swift's first job was removing praying mantis growth pods off the trees at her parents' Christmas tree farm.

CELEBRITIES BEHAVING NICELY

We hear lots of stories of famous folks behaving poorly. By contrast, these celebrities give famous people a good name.

RON PEARLMAN

It took three hours for a team of makeup artists to transform Ron Pearlman into the character Hellboy for the 2004 and 2009 comic book movies. In 2012, Pearlman sat in the chair once again to turn into the horned red half-demon...but not for a sequel. He was granting a surprise wish to a six-year-old leukemia patient named Zachary, who'd watched *Hellboy* more than 100 times in the hospital during treatment. The Make-A-Wish people said it wouldn't be possible to meet Hellboy, but they could take him on a tour of Spectral Motion, the effects company that created the character.

So imagine Zachary's surprise when he walked into a room, and there was Hellboy himself sitting on the couch! The two of them spent the day together, and later on, the effects team turned Zachary into a mini Hellboy from makeup pieces that were made on child-size molds. "The best part for all of us," said Spectral Motion cofounder Mike Elizalde, "is to see the look on their faces when Zachary was sitting next to Hellboy on the couch. Every time I look at that picture, I get a little emotional because of his body language. Everything about that says, 'I'm loving this. This is my wish fulfilled.'"

JOHN CENA

No celebrity has made more wishes come true than wrestler-turned-actor John Cena. In 2022, Guinness World Records recognized this feat after Cena granted his 650th Make-A-Wish (the next closest was under 200). Cena granted his first wish in 2002, which averages out to 32.5 wishes granted per year! (How does he find the time?)

"I can't say enough how cool it is to see the kids so happy," he said. "I truly want to show them that it's their day." And they're not all sick kids. His 650th Make-A-Wish was granted to Misha, a nonverbal teenager with Down syndrome who had to flee Ukraine after his family's house was destroyed by Russian forces. According to a WWE spokesperson, "To motivate Misha on their journey to safety, his mother told him they were on their way to find Cena." And when Cena received the request, he treated it like every other one: "I just drop everything. I don't care what I'm doing."

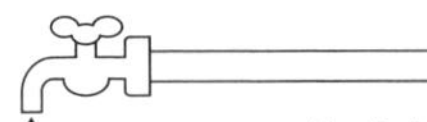

Let's bring it back: the only word for "the day after tomorrow" is the archaic *overmorrow.*

ZENDAYA

Gen-Z celeb Zendaya has proven that you can make it to the top and still be grounded. The superstar pop singer, former Disney child actress, and big-screen leading lady was one of the youngest people on *TIME* magazine's 100 most influential people of 2022. To paraphrase the movies she's best known for—the Tom Holland *Spider-Man* movies, in which she plays Mary Jane—she understands that with great power comes great responsibility. "I am really proud of the fact that I'm able to use people knowing my name and knowing who I am for good things."

And though it might not be as impactful as her work for more than a dozen charities—including the American Heart Association, Communities in Schools, Convoy of Hope, PETA, and UNICEF—Zendaya showed her *Spider-Man* costar how to be nicer. "I used to come across sometimes as a bit of a d*** to fans, mainly as I was always so surprised that they'd want a picture with me or signature or whatever." He says it's a "British thing." But Zendaya—who's become a close friend—"spotted this and quickly told me that this sort of reaction was going to be more aggro than just smiling and taking the picture. She totally changed the way I am able to be more comfortable in public."

LEBRON JAMES

Lots of celebrities pitched in after the 2019 Getty Fire, but only one brought a taco truck, and that was NBA superstar LeBron James. The wildfire burned 745 acres of the Brentwood neighborhood of Los Angeles, forcing thousands to flee their homes—including all those celebrities. And while they fled, over 1,000 firefighters rushed in and battled what turned out to be an incredibly difficult conflagration: driven by steady Santa Ana winds, with terrain between the luxury homes that was steep and inhospitable. Their tireless efforts saved LeBron James's home along with hundreds of others (though 10 were lost). While they were hard at work, James, whose favorite day is famously "Taco Tuesday," sent out a fully stocked taco truck for hungry first responders.

PATRICIA HEATON

There's talking the talk, there's walking the walk, and then there's going to Uganda to cook meals for 600 hungry children. That's what Patricia Heaton, known for her comedic chops on *Everybody Loves Raymond* and *The Middle*, did in 2018 with the nonprofit group World Vision, an international Christian organization whose mission is to help the "poor and oppressed." And these kids were heaps of both. Chased

What do Arkansas, Idaho, Illinois, Kentucky, Missouri, Tennessee, and Texas have in common? They all have a city called Paris.

out of their homes in war-torn South Sudan, the famished families were placed in a refugee settlement. "This first hot meal is a massive undertaking!" said Heaton. "The team there prepares food for hundreds—some days, thousands—of refugees. On the day I visited, there were about 600 people coming through, getting registered, and being served a meal. And so my friend and costar, Jen Ray, and I helped cook for 600 people. People who for the first time had just become refugees, many traveling for days on foot, and arrived with next to nothing at a place they would call home for who knew how long." She added that it was "like no cooking I've ever done before," and she wished she could do more, but, "every little bit we can provide means so much to them."

JAMES DOOHAN

During James Doohan's 85 years (1920–2005) on earth, he was a World War II hero shot six times while leading his troops to safety on D-Day, he had seven children, and he played the *Enterprise*'s beloved Chief Engineer Montgomery "Scotty" Scott on *Star Trek*, which has inspired thousands of people to study engineering. But it was Doohan's relationship with a troubled fan that he called "the best thing I ever did in my life." The young woman sent a letter to Doohan and told him she felt suicidal. His response:

> I called her and I said, "Hey, this is Jimmy Doohan. Scotty of *Star Trek*. I'm doing a convention in Indianapolis, and I want to see you there"... Boy, I'm telling you—I couldn't believe what I saw. It was definitely suicide. Somebody had to help her, somehow. And, obviously, she wasn't going to the right people, you know. Anyhow, I said to her, "I'm doing a convention two weeks from now in St. Louis, and two weeks from then." She also came to New York...That went on for two or three years, maybe 18 times. And all I did was talk positive things to her. And then all of a sudden—nothing. I didn't hear anything, and I had no idea what was happening to her because I never really saved her address. Eight years later, I get a letter saying, "I do want to thank you so much for what you did for me, because I just got my master's degree in electronic engineering."

* * *

"Don't knock rationalization; where would we be without it? I don't know anyone who could get through the day without two or three juicy rationalizations. They're more important than sex."

—Jeff Goldblum

Who is Eithne Pádraigín Ní Bhraonáin better known as?
Irish singer and composer Enya.

CANT SPEAK

"Thieves' cant" is an elaborate system of coded slang used by criminals in England in the 1600s and 1700s. It was a vernacular for a subculture that helped them communicate, but also helped them avoid detection while they did their criminal things.

Nim: to steal, rob, or swipe.
Bite: to steal.
Varlets: rogues.
Canters: thieves.
Dimber damber: head of a canters gang.
Black art: picking locks.
Bleating rig: stealing sheep.
Amuse: to throw dust or dirt into the eyes of a robbery victim to distract and disarm them.
Visiting the neighbors: burglary.
Whip jacks: thieves who pose as sailors to gain unfettered access to ships (so they can rob them).
Abram man: a thief who feigns insanity to get away with it.
Purse collector: a pickpocket.
Rank rider: a highwayman.
Aunt: a prostitute.
Shadow dance: to hide.
Crash: to kill another.
Rhino: cash, particularly stolen cash.
Blunt: cash, particularly stolen cash.
Tin: silver.
Booze: jewels.
Jem: a gold ring.
Whack: an individual's share of the loot after a group heist.
Star the glaze: break into a jeweler's shop and rob the place.
Tuck in bed: to render another person unconscious.
Bandog: a policeman.
Affidavit man: a criminal who will provide favorable testimony in court on behalf of other criminals, for a steep fee.
Resurrection men: thieves who steal bodies out of graveyards when paid by scientists and doctors to do so.
Boarding school: prison.
Going legit: death.

BEHOLD THE TURTLE, PART II

On page 33, we took a deep dive into the evolution of turtles and how their unique physiology allows them to live so long, but there's more to it than that. Now it's time to travel inside the Testudinidae mind.

SMARTER THAN THE AVERAGE REPTILE

"Generally people see reptiles as inert, stupid, and unresponsive," says animal cognition expert Anna Wilkinson of University of Lincoln, England. "I would like people to see that there is something much more complex going on." She points to a study of red-footed tortoises (known to pet owners as one of the more inquisitive species) that were taught to use a touch screen to get food. First, the tortoises were placed in front of a screen and, through trial and error, learned to bonk their beak on the correct circle to make a virtual strawberry (a red triangle) appear. Then they went after the virtual strawberry...which isn't *that* smart, but bear with us.

The tortoises were then placed in a real-world setting, where they quickly realized that bonking the correct circle will make a real strawberry appear. This ability to learn, solve problems to gain rewards, and transfer learning from one setting to another, says Wilkinson, puts tortoises at about the same intelligence level as pigeons and rats, adding, "I've trained dogs to use a touch screen and I'd say the tortoises are faster."

Turtles also have good memories; they can keep track of food sources, and even recognize people. Because moms don't stick around to raise their young, newly hatched turtles must be able to survive on their own from the get-go. And that requires making good decisions. They also happen to be expert navigators. But wait a minute: turtles don't have an especially large brain, or loads of neurons, so is there something else at play?

THE SIXTH SENSE

An interesting thing happened to Tilly the green sea turtle on her swim across the South Pacific Ocean in January 2022: she was heading on a clear course away from the eastern coast of Australia but abruptly turned around. Two days later, the volcano on Tonga erupted. A month and a half earlier, Tilly had been released from the Cairns Turtle Rehabilitation Centre in Queensland (after getting injured in a fishing

net), and had swum 1,160 miles in 47 days. "She was heading towards Vanuatu or the Solomon Islands in a straight line virtually and then...she did a complete U-turn," said Jennie Gilbert, a representative of the center, who tracked Tilly via a transmitter. "She was obviously feeling something, there must have been vibrations."

Whatever caused Tilly to turn around likely saved her life. And it's not surprising, as sea turtles have some uncanny abilities. Through *natal homing*, females can find their way to their nesting beach from halfway across the planet. Exactly *how* they can do this still eludes modern science. We do know they can navigate via the Earth's magnetic field via a symbiotic relationship with *magnetotactic bacteria*, whose movement is influenced by the magnetic field. They point the turtles in the right direction. Sea turtles also have an internal clock that tells them when to migrate to breeding grounds or feeding areas.

Again, is all this due to intelligence or instinct? Judging by another study of sea turtle navigation, instinct only gets them so far...and then they have to use their brains. In another study, 33 female green sea turtles were tracked via GPS as they tried to find their way from their nesting areas back to their feeding areas. Many of the turtles overshot their mark, and after realizing it, turned around and started a search pattern until they found undersea landmarks that led them to their destination. "We were impressed that they are able to find small islands," said researcher Nicole Esteban of Swansea University in the U.K. "But their navigation is crude."

WHAT ABOUT THAT BEAK?

If turtles weren't the only reptiles with a shell, they'd be known for being the only ones with a beak, anatomically described as "a corneous lamina covering the maxillar and mandibular (jaw) bones." The word *corneous* means "horny structure" (as in, horns), and turtles utilize their formidable beaks to grab, tear, cut, and shear food, and they even defend themselves by snapping. (The common snapping turtle can cut through bone.)

How they got their beaks is still unknown. Turtles developed through what's called *mosaic evolution*. Different features adapted independently from one another and at different times (which is how we got the duck-billed platypus, a rare beaked mammal). When prototurtles started to become their own order after the fusing of the ribs, not all species developed shells—resulting in strange creatures shaped like turtles but covered in scales. Then came *Eorhynchochelys sinensis*, "dawn-beak turtle," which was a six-foot-long turtle with no shell, but it did have the first known reptilian beak.

In lieu of teeth, the beaks had serrated edges that performed like teeth. Scientists don't yet know what led to this adaptation, but it caught on, and now all modern

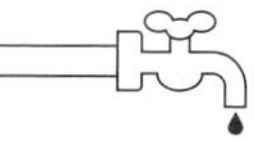

"Cloud suck" is paraglider slang for an updraft that pulls you up into a cumulus cloud, sometimes as high as a jetliner.

turtles have beaks, just as they do shells. Both traits developed separately but came together in one common ancestor that also has yet to be discovered.

The prevailing theory: because some turtles' front feet were adapting into flippers, that made it harder to catch and manipulate prey, so the species that adapted beaks had an extra hand, so to speak. Now, all turtles have beaks. (Over time, sea turtles have become quite skilled with their flippers: they use them to karate-chop jellyfish and roll oysters along the sea floor.)

BUM BREATHERS

Longtime Bathroom Reader fans know that some turtles can breathe through their rear ends. (We make sure to reiterate this fact every few years.) Here's the science behind it. Called *cloacal respiration*—or, as the Aussies call it, "bum breathin'"—this adaptation allows several species of freshwater turtles to survive through the coldest winter months. Being exothermic (cold-blooded), the turtle's internal body temperature matches its surroundings. That's why they need to bask in the sun: so they can warm up and breathe and digest their food.

As the days shorten and temperatures start nearing the freezing mark, turtles eat as much as they can and then find a place to *brumate*. Some, like box turtles, find a secluded spot in the woods and burrow in soft soil. Their metabolisms slow down to next to nothing, and they enter a state of *torpor*. When the weather warms up, they come to and find a sunny spot in which to thaw.

Turtles that spend most of their lives in or near water use a different tactic. They submerge themselves in nearly freezing water, beneath a layer of ice, for months at a time. But turtles have lungs, not gills, so how can this be? The colder they get, the slower their metabolism; the slower their metabolism, the less oxygen they require. And there is a minimal amount of oxygen in water, a.k.a. H_2O. The cloaca (bum hole) sucks water in and whooshes it around, extracting just enough oxygen to keep the animal alive.

BONE APPÉTIT

Another key to turtles' long lifespans: they're open to trying new things. For example, giant tortoises have long been thought to live solely off plants and grasses—although there have been accounts of these "herbivores" eating crab shells, possibly for the calcium. Then, in 2020, on Frégate Island in the Seychelles archipelago, a researcher filmed a female giant tortoise (slowly) chasing a flightless tern chick around on the forest floor. After a few failed attempts, the tortoise finally got her beak around the chick's head...and gobbled it down. Calling the seven-minute hunt "horrifying and amazing," lead researcher Justin Gerlach of the University of Cambridge said, "This is completely unexpected behavior and has never been seen before in wild tortoises."

First city where at least 50 percent of new vehicle registrations were for electric cars: San Francisco, in 2023.

Then there's the amazing story of Manuela, a pet tortoise who was thought to have escaped her family's yard in Brazil. Thirty years later, the family found Manuela upstairs in a crowded attic, with only a tiny space between boxes and very little food or light. The pet was thought to have survived on various insects and termite grubs (and was reportedly "happy" to have human contact again).

ENDANGERED SPECIES

Stories like these have shown over and over that tortoises and turtles are problem solvers, they can improvise, they can show affection, they can recognize and befriend people, and they have an understanding of the world that we've yet to comprehend. But after surviving every major extinction of the past 250 million years, today, more than half—187 of the 360 known turtle species—are threatened.

The rapid decline in turtle populations began, not surprisingly, with the Industrial Revolution. They're highly valued for their eggs, shells, skin, and meat. The other major factor is habitat loss. As humanity expands, turtles tend to decline. The pet trade also plays a major part.

Among the most critically endangered is the ploughshare tortoise, which sells for $50,000 each on the black market. The few remaining ploughshares are being kept in a compound on Madagascar, protected by armed guards and razor wire.

Sea turtles are the most threatened. Not only are their prehistoric feeding grounds teeming with fishing nets and boat propellers, but their nesting beaches are in constant danger of encroachment. Even in ideal conditions, very few hatchlings survive to adulthood. Many beaches are protected from people, but not from light and sound pollution. Hatchlings navigate by the full moon and are drawn toward the surf—artificial light and traffic noise can lead them astray. Result: all seven species of sea turtles are on the endangered list, three of them critical.

TURTLE CROSSING

Steps are being taken by scientists, activists, and charities to slow this decline, and if you want to help, just search for "save the turtles" and go from there. In the meantime, some tips:

- Be aware of, and respect, turtle habitats in your area. Many of these are designated with signs; most are not. Keep unleashed dogs out of these areas, as they can unintentionally dig up burrows, or flush small turtles out of their safe spots into the danger zone.
- If you see a turtle in the road, and you can *safely* remove it without getting flattened yourself, move it to the side of the road (in the same direction it was traveling). Their ancestral travel routes predate our roadways.

- Don't try to "relocate" a turtle. Species like box turtles don't ever travel very far from their small patch of woods, and if you find one and let it go somewhere else, it will try to find home. The greater the distance it's moved, the lower the animal's chance for survival.

- Buy pet turtles only from official breeders, and never buy an endangered species. Taking one female out of the wild can cause immeasurable damage to the population.

- Give sea turtles a wide berth—in the water and on their nesting beaches. Only ever drive on beaches that allow it.

ADIEU

So, after everything that herpetologists have learned about them, can we know what turtles are thinking about? Not yet, or perhaps ever. But there's a lot going on in those scaly heads. Ponder for a moment the sea turtle that enjoys a symbiotic relationship with her coral reef. Every day, she "mows" the fast-growing grasses and algae that would otherwise take over the reef. She eats the sponges that compete with the corals for space on the reef. She even "gardens" by dispersing seeds within her nutrient-rich waste. And in return, the reef provides her with food and shelter, just as it did when she first sought protection in the crevasses as a hatchling. It's hard to imagine, then, when this sea turtle's internal clock tells her it's time to head off to her breeding grounds, that she doesn't turn around as she's leaving, admire her handiwork, and give a nod goodbye.

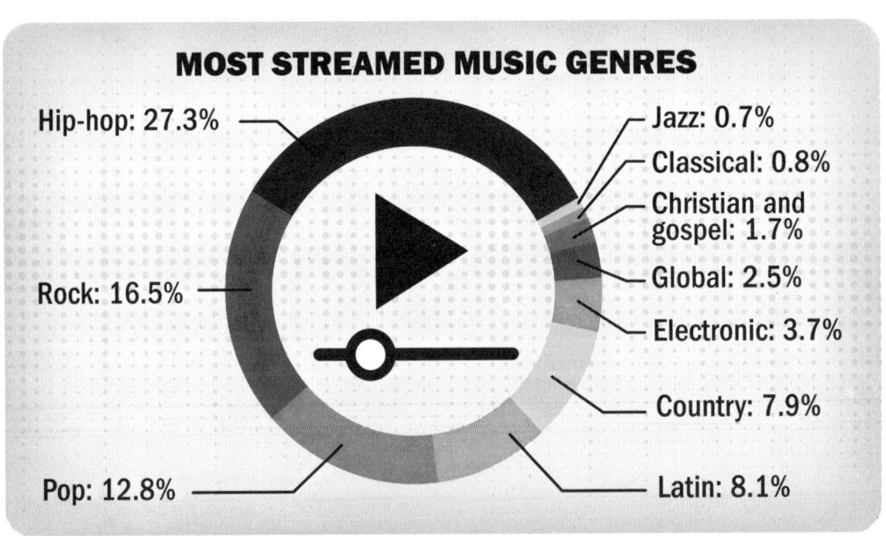

CAMP IN THE WOODS, NOT THE LEFT LANE

Digital safety signs have dotted America's highways for years now. They're supposed to warn of construction, delays, closures, and dangers sedately and clearly, but many operators couldn't resist making the signs funny—with mixed reviews. The U.S. Federal Highway Administration will outlaw the wit by 2026, so here are some of the greatest hits of what's going to be a dying fad.

**WHO HATES SPEEDING TICKETS?
RAISE YOUR RIGHT FOOT**

**VISITING IN-LAWS?
SLOW DOWN
GET THERE LATE**

**BUCKLE UP
#YOLO**

DON'T HIT THE CAR IN FRONT OF YOU

**100 IS THE TEMPERATURE
NOT THE SPEED LIMIT**

**BUCKLE UP
WINDSHIELDS HURT**

**CAMP IN THE WOODS
NOT THE LEFT LANE**

**HOCUS POCUS
DRIVE WITH FOCUS**

**TRUST THE FORCE
BUT ALWAYS BUCKLE UP**

**NO OSCAR FOR BEST LEADFOOT
SLOW DOWN**

**ONLY RUDOLPH SHOULD BE LIT
DRIVE HIGH GET DUI**

**YOU'LL NEVER GET TO WORK ON TIME
HAHA!!**

**TEXTING WHILE DRIVING?
OH CELL NO**

**AGGRESSIVE DRIVING IS THE PATH
TO THE DARK SIDE**

TEAMWORK MAKES THE MERGE WORK

**DRIVE HAMMERED
GET NAILED**

**FOUR I'S IN MISSISSIPPI
TWO EYES ON THE ROAD**

**DOES YOUR BLINKER NOT WORK
OR WHAT?**

**DON'T BE A STINKER
USE YOUR BLINKER**

DID IT COME WITH A TURN SIGNAL?

**ARRIVE ALIVE TO YOUR SWEETHEART
SLOW DOWN**

**IS THIS HEAVEN?
NOW, IT'S IOWA. TRAVEL SAFELY.**

**WE'LL BE BLUNT
DON'T DRIVE HIGH**

**DON'T MAKE A POUR DECISION
DRIVE SOBER**

**TO: DRIVER
FROM: SEATBELT
"I THINK WE CLICK"**

**SANTA SEES YOU WHEN YOU'RE
SPEEDING**

**HEY BOBBLEHEAD
STOP LOOKING AT YOUR PHONE**

**GET YOUR HEAD OUT OF YOUR APPS
DRIVE SAFELY**

**TURN SIGNALS,
THE ORIGINAL INSTANT MESSAGE**

In the three days after its 2013 release, *Grand Theft Auto V* made $1 billion.

INEXPLICABLE CANCELLATIONS

TV shows come and go all the time. Most of them get pulled off the air if not enough people tune in. Others get canceled for the most bizarre and surprising reasons.

SHOW: *Bridget Loves Bernie*

DETAILS: The fifth-most-watched show in the 1972–73 TV season was a brand-new comedy: *Bridget Loves Bernie*, a gentle romance about a pair of newlyweds navigating married life. Real-life couple Meredith Baxter and David Birney portrayed Bridget and Bernie, respectively. While the CBS show attracted millions of viewers each week, it also received a large number of complaints over its then-controversial premise—Bridget is a Catholic, and Bernie is Jewish. Objecting to its portrayal of the ups and downs of an interfaith relationship, Rabbinical Assembly of America executive vice president Rabbi Wolfe Kelman called *Bridget Loves Bernie* "an insult to some of the most sacred values of both the Jewish and Catholic religions." By February 1973, three major Jewish organizations called for a boycott of the show and urged members to file complaints with CBS.

CANCELED: Hating the bad press, CBS decided to end the controversy by canceling *Bridget Loves Bernie*. It ran for one season and remains the most-watched first-season show to ever be canceled by a major broadcast network.

SHOW: *Longmire*

DETAILS: The A&E cable network debuted *Longmire* in 2012. A throwback to the TV Westerns of the 1950s and 1960s, the show starred Robert Taylor as a taciturn sheriff meting out justice in contemporary Wyoming. The only Western on American television at the time, *Longmire* found an audience, and a big one: every week, about five million people tuned in to watch Sheriff Longmire bust bad guys. In 2013, A&E renewed *Longmire* for a third season, announcing at the time that the show was its most-watched drama series of all time.

CANCELED: Ratings for *Longmire*'s third season stayed at that consistently high level of five million regular viewers, but A&E canceled it in 2013. The reason: the vast majority of *Longmire* viewers were over the age of 50. Companies that buy commercial space on TV prefer to reach a younger demographic of viewers aged 18 to 49, as that group is believed to have more disposable income and not yet be settled into lifelong brand loyalties, making them more willing to buy new products they see in TV ads. Viewers

In Japan, Studio Ghibli employees are given time off every spring to watch the cherry blossoms bloom, a practice known as *hanami*.

over 50 are considered set in their ways and not as affected by advertising. So even if a show has a large overall audience, as *Longmire* did, it may be the wrong kind of audience, like *Longmire* had. (Happy ending: Netflix revived *Longmire* for its streaming service, which doesn't feature advertising, and the viewers got to enjoy another three seasons.)

SHOW: *The Life of Riley*

DETAILS: The hit radio show on ABC and then NBC that ran from 1944 to 1951 starred William Bendix as factory worker Chester A. Riley, a know-it-all who frequently got himself unnecessarily and hopelessly involved in the personal problems of others. In one of his first major projects, Jackie Gleason played Riley in the 1949–50 TV version; Bendix couldn't get out of his movie contract at the time. Though the show would later win the first-ever Emmy Award for narrative programming, NBC was forced to cancel *The Life of Riley* in the middle of the TV season.

CANCELED: At the time, individual sponsors paid for the product of a show, in exchange for controlling all of the ad time. Pabst Brewing Company sponsored *The Life of Riley*, but initially agreed to pay for only 26 episodes, wishing to renegotiate footing the bill for the 13 additional episodes that comprised a standard season of TV in the 1950s. Pabst ultimately decided it didn't want to be in the TV business, and so *The Life of Riley* went off the air abruptly. (The series was later revived with Bendix starring as Riley, and it enjoyed better success.)

SHOW: *Chicken Soup*

DETAILS: In 1988, ABC successfully converted comedian Roseanne Barr's stand-up act into the hit sitcom *Roseanne*. A year later, *Roseanne* served as the lead-in to another sitcom based on a well-known comedian with a strong persona. *Chicken Soup*—a comedy about the romance between a middle-aged Jewish man and a middle-aged Catholic woman—starred Jackie Mason, a regular on talk and variety shows since the 1950s. *Chicken Soup* benefitted from airing right after *Roseanne*. It ranked as the #10 show on TV for the 1989–90 season, pulling in an average of 18.2 million viewers per episode. That wasn't quite enough for ABC, however.

CANCELED: That year, *Roseanne* was the most-watched show on television, with 23.4 million viewers. *Chicken Soup* lost 20 percent of *Roseanne* viewers, so ABC yanked it off the air after broadcasting just eight episodes. (Though ABC denied it, there was also speculation that the network wanted to distance itself from Mason: during promotion for *Chicken Soup* concurrent with the run-up to the New York City mayoral election, Mason made disparaging, racially charged remarks about candidate, and eventual winner, David Dinkins.)

Olympic gold medals are made of silver with gold plating. (They haven't been made of solid gold since 1912.)

OOPS: STRANGE LAWSUITS EDITION

Some things just go better together...like peanut butter and chocolate, or our "Oops!" and "Strange Lawsuits" features.

BEEP! BEEP! BEEP! BEEP! BEEP! BEEP! BEEP! BEE—

The Oops: Late one night in September 2020, a janitor named Joseph Harrington was cleaning a laboratory at Rensselaer Polytechnic Institute, a private research university in Troy, New York. But, as he later described it, "annoying alarms" were making a ruckus. The culprit: a freezer full of cell cultures that had to be kept within three degrees of −80 degrees Celsius. The alarms were triggered because the temperature had risen two degrees, but the cell cultures weren't yet in any danger. Staffers at the lab had placed a repair call, and they installed a lockbox over the electrical outlet so no one could unplug the freezer. They even posted a sign *on* the freezer:

> THIS FREEZER IS BEEPING AS IT IS UNDER REPAIR. PLEASE DO NOT MOVE OR UNPLUG IT. NO CLEANING REQUIRED IN THIS AREA. YOU CAN PRESS THE ALARM/TEST MUTE BUTTON FOR 5–10 SECONDS IF YOU WOULD LIKE TO MUTE THE SOUND.

Harrington decided to flip the circuit breaker, thinking he was turning off the alarm, but he didn't understand the settings...and turned off the freezer.

The next morning, the researchers discovered that most of the cell cultures had perished, and, with them, 20 years of irreplaceable research—including a few experiments they said "had the potential to be groundbreaking."

The Lawsuit: The university sued the cleaning company for whom Harrington worked for $1 million, the estimated cost of the mishap, for failing to properly train Harrington. As their lawyer told CNN, "A cleaner should be trained to not attempt to remedy an electrical issue." Harrington maintains he was just trying to help.

THE WRONG GUY

The Oops: One morning in 2006, Guy Goma, a computer tech from the Republic of the Congo, showed up at BBC headquarters in London to interview for a job in the network's IT department. A few minutes later, Guy Kewney, a British tech expert, showed up for a live interview on BBC News. Both men checked in and were told to wait in different waiting rooms.

A few minutes later, a producer entered Goma's waiting room and asked, "Are you Guy?" He said yes and was swiftly escorted to another part of the building, where he was applied with makeup, despite his insistence that, "I'm just here for a job interview." Then Goma was escorted to a TV studio and fitted with a microphone. He thought it was all part of the interview process.

The lights came on and BBC News business journalist Karen Bowerman introduced Goma as "Guy Kewney, editor of the technology website *News Wireless*," and bid him, "Good morning."

After a look of utter shock, Goma replied, "Good morning," and then Bowerman jumped right into the interview, asking him if he was surprised by a recent verdict in a big tech case involving Apple. "I am *very* surprised," Goma stated. Realizing he was on live television, Goma politely finished the interview, despite not knowing anything about the case (although he correctly predicted that more people would start getting their music from the internet).

Afterward, when producers realized their goof, they retaped the interview with the right Guy (which never even aired); Goma didn't get the IT job.

The Lawsuit: The accidental interview went viral, making Goma an early internet star. And the BBC, he claims in a lawsuit filed 17 years later in 2023, "made millions" off the video but never paid him "a penny" in royalties.

In the meantime, Goma had used his 15 minutes of fame to land a few more TV spots—including a tongue-in-cheek interview on BBC News a week later where he apologized to Kewney for "taking your spot." But in the end, Goma says he became a punchline and was subsequently unhirable, so he's suing for lost wages. "When I see that they are paying people millions here and there, that clip made them richer." Without any further news reports, it's likely the lawsuit, which he announced on a podcast while promoting his guest-hosting stint on a talk show, fizzled.

THAT HURTS A LOT

The Oops: In 2023, a construction crew on Hawaii's Big Island built a three-bedroom home on a lush one-acre plot of land near the ocean. As there weren't yet any houses in this area that had been zoned for development, the crew allegedly counted the number of telephone poles to find the correct lot—parcel 115—instead of hiring a surveyor.

After the house was built, the developer—Keaau Development Partnership (which had hired construction the company)—sold the home to a buyer for $499,000. But then, just before the closing documents were signed, the title company discovered a problem: the house had been built on the wrong lot: parcel 114.

That particular acre had been purchased five years earlier for $22,500 by a California "relationship coach and energy healer" named Anne Reynolds, on the

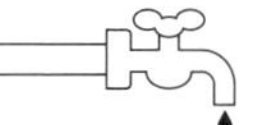

advice of her daughter, who lived in Hawaii. Reynolds had planned to build a healing retreat on the land, until the COVID-19 pandemic put everything on hold. Meanwhile, Reynolds received numerous offers from a developer to purchase the lot, but she said no each time.

She didn't even find out about the goof until June 2023 when a Hawaii real estate agent called her in California to inform her there was a house on her land—that they'd already sold. "It's terrible," Reynolds complained to SFGATE.com. "I felt like I wanted to cry."

Meanwhile, because the developer didn't actually own that lot, the sale fell through. And because Reynolds's lot now had a house on it, her property taxes doubled. Adding insult to injury, squatters had moved in and trashed the empty home. "There was poop in the toilet," she said. "Not only inside the toilet, but on the toilet seat."

The Lawsuit: Keaau Development Partnership sued Reynolds. The developer not only sued Reynolds (whom they claim benefited monetarily from the goof), but also, per SFGATE.com, "the construction company, the architect, the county, and even the previous owner of the land Reynolds bought."

The construction company's lawyers, in a letter to Reynolds, assured her that "best efforts were made to ensure that the home was built on the correct property," and that Keaau had "not maliciously built on parcel 114."

Keaau's lawyers maintain that Reynolds was "unjustly enriched" because the construction had increased the value of her property without her having to invest in the building, and that, by rejecting Keaau's offer to exchange any other identical plot on the street for hers, Reynolds was being "unreasonable." (Her reason for rejecting the offer? They don't "align with her zodiac sign.") "Keaau Development Partnership is the only entity that has suffered hundreds of thousands of dollars' worth of losses," the company claims. Reynolds's lawyer accused Keaau of "pure bullying"; Keaau's lawyers countered by saying they were "not bullying."

"I know that for Hawaiians the land is sacred," Reynolds told *Business Insider*. "There's a sanctity to the land, and it must be revered and respected." As of last report, there's still an empty house on one parcel of that land.

* * *

A HIGHER THREAT

Maybe it's because their height makes them a taller target, but giraffes are more likely to be killed by a lightning strike than humans are. Between 1996 and 2010, there were five documented instances of lightning fatally striking a giraffe. That works out to a rate of .003 lightning deaths per 1,000 giraffes, 30 times the fatality rate for humans.

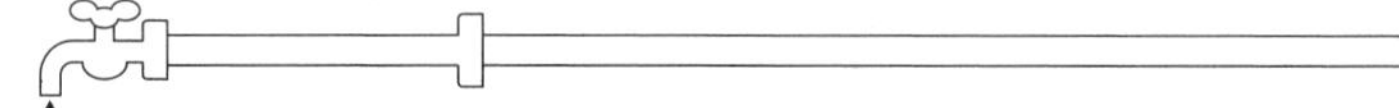

What's a *confetto*? A single piece of confetti.

THE JAPANESE ART OF...

On a recent trip to Japan, Uncle John noticed that part of the country's culture involves making parts of one's regular life into art–if not just making traditional art, too. Many of these practices are heralded specifically as a "Japanese art." Can you match the Japanese art form or cultural value to its English description? Answers are on page 341.

1. Mokuhanga
2. Wabi-sabi
3. Momijigari
4. Kisetsukan
5. Dorodango
6. Kokedama
7. Mottainai
8. Sumi-e
9. Ikebana
10. Takeami
11. Chanoyu
12. Shikake
13. Kyudo
14. Kintsukuroi
15. Shinrin-yoku
16. Kiyomeru
17. Kakeibo
18. Suminagashi
19. Kaizen
20. Suiseki
21. Tsundoku
22. Rakugo
23. Ikigai
24. Ogata

a) Flower arranging
b) Thriftiness
c) Repairing pottery with gold
d) Book collecting
e) Marble art
f) Woodblock printing
g) Ink painting
h) Living
i) Making moss balls
j) Making mud balls
k) Gradual, conscious improvement
l) Bamboo weaving
m) Living without waste
n) Archery
o) Cleaning
p) Forest bathing
q) Storytelling
r) Living with purpose
s) Appreciating rocks
t) Prescriptive interior design
u) Leaf hunting
v) Seasonal living
w) Preparing and serving tea
x) Finding beauty in imperfections

WHERE ARE ALL THE KILLER BEES?

No matter now tranquil things may appear to be, there's always something out there that someone tells us we're supposed to be afraid of, some nightmarish threat that hasn't hit yet...but will soon. And then it passes, and everything is fine, until the next panic arrives. This kind of thing has happened a lot over the last 40 years or so.

Threat: Y2K

What Was Supposed to Happen: In the early days of computer programming, expensive data memory space was saved by abbreviating year dates to two digits—"79" instead of "1979," for example. As more and more systems and vital parts of the global infrastructure adopted such methods of operation, a fear developed that when the year 2000 came around, computerized power grids, banks, air traffic control networks, and other vital systems would interpret the year "00" as 1900, and would thus stop working or get confused and erase data because it would think it hadn't come into existence yet. The feared result: everything would fail, and society would be plunged into darkness, chaos, and apocalypse.

What Actually Happened: By 1998, the "Y2K bug," as the calendar issue came to be known, had terrified the masses, and private businesses spent $100 billion to recode vital computerized systems to stave off the threat of disastrous shutdowns. While a constant stream of "what if?" scenarios fueled TV news reports and alarmist bestsellers, tech workers labored quietly to ensure that none of the dreaded scenarios would happen. They'd been aware of the issue since the late 1980s and had been planning accordingly. Only the true doomsayers anticipated planes falling from the sky and bank accounts being erased when the world celebrated the new millennium on the evening of December 31, 1999. When the clock struck midnight, everything progressed as usual and the Y2K bug didn't cause any damage.

Threat: Murder hornets

What Was Supposed to Happen: The two-inch-long Vespa mandarinia, or Asian giant hornet, is the largest hornet in the world. Native to east Asia, these insects painfully sting humans and also kill honeybees by the hive, running through an entire bee community to feed its own colonies. This could prove threatening to the world's food supply if they succeed in killing off nature's most efficient crop pollinators. The

If you start with the French word *oui*, which means "yes," and move each letter ten spaces forward in the alphabet, you get the English word *yes*.

Asian giant hornet isn't much of a problem in east Asia, but they'd be considered an invasive species if spotted anywhere else; in 2019, the first of them were spotted in North America, in both Washington state and the bordering Canadian province of British Columbia. They were so big and threatening, the media nicknamed them "murder hornets."

What Actually Happened: For more than a year, a nation lay in wait for the arrival and spread of the murder hornets. But they never moved out of the Pacific Northwest. In October 2020, authorities tracked the spotted hornets and found a nest in Nanaimo, British Columbia, and destroyed it. Later that same month, the Washington State Department of Agriculture found another murder hornet nest in the border town of Blaine, Washington. That one was destroyed, too. That pretty much ended the threat of the Asian giant hornet outside of Asia.

Threat: Acid rain

What Was Supposed to Happen: Massive industrial production in the Midwest pushed so much pollution into the atmosphere in the first few decades of the 20th century that by the 1980s, it was linked to overall higher global temperatures as well as something called "acid rain." Toxic, acidic substances like sulfur and nitrogen oxides were so prominent in the emissions from thousands of smokestacks that they were carried away by the air and dumped into lakes. That water evaporated, and the resulting rain poured down poison on the ground from above. The rain falling out of the sky in some places was literally acid, and if something didn't change, it was going to poison us all (or melt our skin).

What Actually Happened: In 1953, ecologist Gene Likens set up the Hubbard Brook Experimental Forest in New Hampshire's White Mountains to study forest and river patterns. A decade into the project, Likens's team discovered that the rain samples they collected were 100 times more acidic than they should have naturally been. After conducting more research and consulting with other scientists from around the world, Likens published the 1974 study *Acid Rain: A Serious Environmental Problem*. He provided proof that lakes in the Northeast were beset with pollutants—sulfur and nitrous oxide specifically—chugged out by coal-burning factory smokestacks in the Midwest. Some rain samples were discovered to be as acidic as grapefruit juice. The rain, and water, were poison; huge numbers of fish populations were depleted. By 1980, mainstream news outlets were talking about acid rain, but nothing much was done about it because the Reagan administration rolled back so many environmental regulations, and industrial-backed scientists dismissed acid rain as an empty, isolated threat. It wasn't until the environmental movement of the late 1980s and early 1990s, triggered by congressional hearings about global warming caused by factory pollutants,

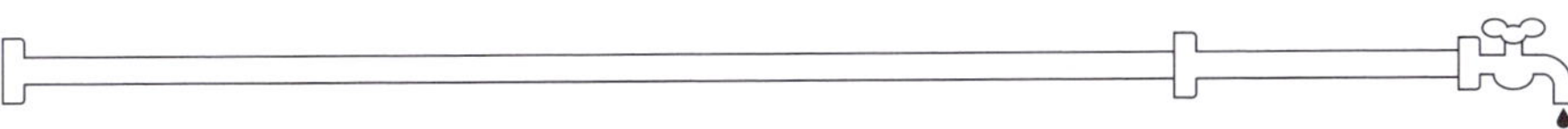

that the government acted. President George W. Bush helped create a program where American factories had to pay for the right to pollute, thus limiting the supply of pollution. It worked. Within 10 years, the lakes in the Northeast tested by Likens were 80 percent less acidic, and the acid rain has disappeared around the U.S., too.

Threat: Killer bees

What Was Supposed to Happen: In 1956, bee breeders in Brazil attempted to jumpstart the local honey industry but weren't getting far with low-production native species of honeybees. The solution: crossbreed them with imported African honeybees to create a new bee that could thrive (and produce) in a hot tropical climate. The result: the Africanized honeybee, a vicious, venomous insect that produced honey inconsistently and in not great quantities. Even worse: in 1957, 26 queens and many swarms of worker bees escaped their apiary outside São Paolo, Brazil, and headed north, breeding with more common honeybee species, both wild and commercial, along the way. By 1989, they'd moved up to the U.S.-Mexico border, and their arrival in Texas was imminent. They were labeled "killer bees" for good reason—they'd killed 1,000 humans since their escape, stinging 10 times more than other bees and giving chase for a quarter of a mile. Entry into the U.S. was also potentially economically problematic. Their tendency to crossbreed with and attack other bees threatened the U.S. bee industry, the honey industry, and the fate of billions of dollars' worth of bee-pollinated crops.

What Actually Happened: While the killer bees moved quickly through South and Central America, their travel around the U.S. was at a much slower pace. They moved into Texas in 1990, Arizona in 1993, California in 1995, and Oklahoma, Nevada, and Florida by the early 2000s. The pace was so relatively glacial that it gave authorities enough of a jump to track and destroy their hives and swarms. The bees never much threatened any American industry, and the last major sighting occurred in Colorado in 2014—after which authorities eradicated them.

*　*　*

WINKING AROUND THE WORLD

U.S.: Depending on the context, a wink can signal that you share a secret bond, that you are romantically attracted, or that you're lying.

Latin America: Winking signals an attraction...and nothing else. So only use it if you mean it.

Australia: Signals an attraction, but it's considered rude and disrespectful.

West Africa: Signals to a child to stay out of the room while company is over.

Asia: Considered a vulgar gesture to be avoided.

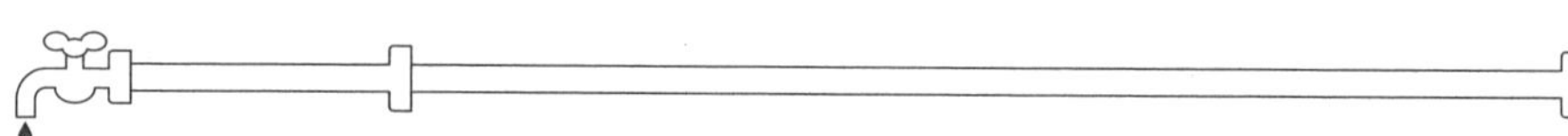

If you're average, you'll move house 11.7 times in your life.

WILLIS VS. TETRIS

Here's the story of how a kid beat Tetris*—a seemingly unbeatable video game—brick by brick by brick by brick by...*

READY PLAYER ONE

Remember completing a video game, and the immense satisfaction you felt? Or—for you slightly older readers—remember getting to plug in your initials on an arcade game when you racked up the all-time high score? Willis Gibson knows what that feels like, and maybe a little something more: he beat a game that nobody else had beaten in nearly 40 years' time, and a game presumed to actually be unbeatable.

Tetris is one of the most famous and popular video games ever, known even to people who don't play video games. It was invented by a Communism-era Soviet Union software engineer named Alexey Pajitnov in 1985 and released to the world by Nintendo in 1989. Included with every Game Boy handheld game console sold from 1989 onward, more than 200 versions of *Tetris* have appeared on more than 70 different video game systems. With more than 520 million copies sold, it ranks as one of the top two best-selling games ever; even the cell phone version, available since 2006, has sold 100 million copies, making that the third best-selling game ever on its own.

GAME ON

The premise and rules of *Tetris* are simple. Different permutations of four-unit block modules fall from the top of the screen one at a time. The player has to rotate and place the blocks together *just so* in order to form complete lines and clear the board. If any holes are left in the lines, the lines won't clear, and the bricks just keep stacking up; if bricks reach the top, it's game over. All the while, computerized versions of Russian folk music play, which, along with the gameplay itself, induces a trancelike state.

Each level, reached after a certain number of lines are cleared, gets a little bit harder because the bricks descend at a continuously faster speed. After just a few levels, they're falling down so quickly it takes a master to manipulate and place them in the fraction of a second provided for each.

It just so happens that Willis Gibson is such a *Tetris* master. He made the game into a hobby (bordering on a part-time job) in 2021, shortly after he turned 11 years old. Within a few months, and keeping up a daily, three-to-five-hour practice schedule, he'd gotten such a handle on *Tetris* that he started entering and winning *Tetris* tournaments, competing against gamers more than twice his age. In October 2023, competing under the pseudonym of "Blue Scuti," Gibson qualified for the biggest contest of its kind, the Classic *Tetris* World Championships. He finished in third place—and at age 13, was the youngest contestant in tournament history.

KILL SCREEN ENGAGE

In older video games, particularly puzzle-based ones like *Tetris*, there is no "end" to the game per se. Each progressive level is essentially the same; it just gets harder and harder because of speed. Programmers have to write code for every level, however. So, on most classic games, they'd just stop creating and making the code at a level they figured no one would ever reach because it was so high. If a player *does* make it that far, they're met with what's known in the video game world as a "kill screen": at that point, the game crashes and freezes, and nothing can be played anymore. It's "game over" in the purest sense—but it's also the undeniable finish line of titles like *Tetris*.

Tetris has been played since 1985, and available worldwide since 1989, yet nobody had ever made it to a kill screen in that time—if it even had one, that is. Until 2011, more than two decades into its existence, none of the hundreds of millions of *Tetris* players had gotten past level 29; the pieces fall too fast at that point, and that level was commonly accepted to be the end of the game. Then the network of *Tetris* experts around the world figured out special gaming techniques, controller tricks, and other strategies to advance farther and farther. That information fed into an artificial intelligence program designed to be extremely good at *Tetris*. The AI made to level 236 in 2021, but that's only because it manipulated and rewrote the *Tetris* code (because AI can do that).

A CHRISTMAS MIRACLE

Four days before Christmas in 2023, Gibson, a few weeks shy of his 14th birthday, sat down at his video game setup in his bedroom in Stillwater, Oklahoma. He fixed a camera on himself and hooked it up to feed to the internet. His intent was to complete the job he'd been training for: Gibson was going to beat *Tetris*, and he was going to have video proof of it.

Over the course of just 38 minutes, Gibson breezed through the entirety of *Tetris*. At one point near the end, he couldn't even believe his own skills. "I'm going to pass out," he muttered. At another time, he almost buckled under the weight of self-imposed pressure, seemingly invoking the game to "please crash." But then, after whipping across level 157 of *Tetris*... everything stopped. The game indeed crashed and then froze. Gibson erupted into happy screams and interjections. He'd done it—the 13-year-old had achieved the supposedly unachievable and completed the rarest task in video game history.

BLOCKED OUT

Gibson's history-making *Tetris*-beating video quickly went viral, and it got the attention of the video game media and of video game professionals, who hailed him as a hero. Maya Rogers, the CEO of *Tetris* publisher Tetris Inc., released a statement calling Gibson's run "a feat that defies all preconceived limits of this legendary game."

Gibson probably would also hold the record for the highest score in *Tetris*, but the game's scoring mechanism was programmed to display only six digits. His "999,999" score is inaccurate—the player himself calculates that he ran up around 6.8 million points.

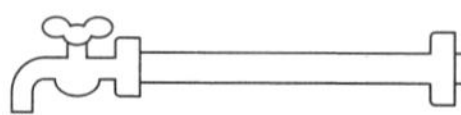

More than 80 Russian soldiers can fit in the MI-26, or *Halo*, the world's largest helicopter.

NACHO WI-FI

Who says neighbors don't communicate anymore? What they choose for a Wi-Fi name can say a lot about them.

Never Gonna Give You Wifi

Get Off My LAN

GetYourOwn DamnRouter

Close Your Bathroom Curtains

Thou Shalt Not Covet Thy Neighbors Wifi

Wifi Art Thou Romeo

FBI Surveillance Van

No More Mr. Wi-Fi

Wi Believe I Can Fi

Drop It Like It's Hotspot

One if by LAN

No_Signal

Connecting...

Try The Other Neighbor

Trust in God but Protect Your WiFi

Silence of the LANs

Bill Clinternet

John Wilkes Bluetooth

Vladimir Routin

Winona Router

Luke Skyrouter

LAN Solo

Jar Jar Links

Lord of the Pings

The Password is...

Bandwidth Together

Girls Gone Wireless

WiFi Fo Fum

Who What When Where WiFi

New England Clam Router

Password is gullible

404 Network Unavailable

Nacho Wi-Fi

It Hurts When IP

WhyYouOnlyCallMe WhenUrFi

Take My WiFi Please

ItsMineNotYours

I can see you from my window

Virus Detected! Do Not Connect!

This LAN Is My LAN

Tell My Wifi Love Her

Pretty Fly for a Wifi

The Promised LAN

Wi Oh Wi

We've Been Trying to Reach You About Your Car's Extended Warranty

Bill Wi the Science Fi

Mom Use This One

Keep it on the Download

Extremely Slow Wifi You Don't Want to Use

Every Day I'm Buffering

No Wi-Fi for You!

Hide Yo Kids, Hide Yo Wi-Fi

Panic at the Cisco

Router? I Hardly Know Her!

Router Limits

Wi-Fight Club

Chance the Router

Wu Tang LAN

Life in The Fast LAN

Alice in WonderLAN

I Now Pronounce You Man and Wi-Fi

IP Frequently

Friendly Neighborhood Spider-LAN

Rebellious Amish Family

Click Here for Viruses

Not The Wifi You're Looking For

Funny Wifi Name

Because-Fi

Inigo the Modem

YOU STOLE *WHAT?*

You may be able to steal a base, or a glance, or someone's heart, but can you steal a driveway? Yes, you can...along with plenty of other strange things.

GREA$E

It takes an entrepreneurial mind to look at those big drums of used grease and old cooking oil stored behind fast food restaurants and see dollar signs. Apparently, once that sludge is refined, it can sell for $4 to $5 per gallon as biodiesel. In 2024, two men from Monticello, New York—Gary Rivera and Jonatan Soriano, both in their 20s—procured a pump, six large tanks, and a rented moving truck to pull off their heist. They would have gotten away with it, too, if they hadn't been so brazen. During a theft at Taco Bell, an employee named Khalio White spotted River and Soriano in the act as they syphoned the drum behind his restaurant, and then moved on to do the same thing at a Popeye's across the street. White gave the police the license plate number of the truck and the two grease thieves were apprehended while, ironically, filling up at a nearby gas station.

I SCREAM, YOU SCREAM...

This guy must really like ice cream. Or he likes stealing trucks. News reports did not specify. Travis Jones, 35, stole an idling delivery truck from the parking lot of a West Haven, Connecticut, business in January 2024 while the driver was inside the store. State police put out an APB for a truck hauling $30,000 worth of ice cream. They caught Jones driving south on I-95.

FAST GETAWAY

For 10 years, the Mason County (Washington) Sheriff's Office had been using their radar trailer to keep drivers from speeding. It would seem that one driver didn't like the digital reading telling him how fast he was going. Result: "Our beloved RADAR trailer decided to take an unscheduled road trip," the police said, "courtesy of a white male in his 30s, cruising in a black '90s Ford short box truck." As of last report, the "speed-defying hero" (the trailer, not the thief) hadn't been located. "Let's reunite this trailer with its true calling, keeping our streets safe and sound!"

REST IN PIECES

If you plan to donate your body to science, there are few places more prestigious for it to end up than Harvard Medical School. This was not the case, however, from 2018 to 2023, when Cedric Lodge was in charge of the institution's morgue. He was also

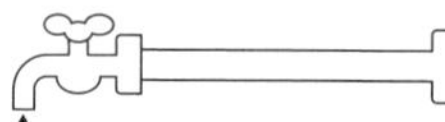

Some deaf people use sign language while they're dreaming.

in charge of a crime ring that sold body parts over the Internet. Lodge's wife, Denise, processed the transactions via a PayPal account for items such as "head number 7" and "braiiiiiins." According to prosecutors, the crime ring (which also involved a mortuary in Arkansas) made off with "two dozen hands, two feet, nine spines, portions of skulls, five dissected human faces, and two dissected heads." As of last report, Denise had pled guilty, and Cedric, not guilty. But Denise's defense—that it was basically a victimless crime, or "more of a moral and ethical dilemma"—probably won't help either of their cases.

THE DRIVEWAY THAT DROVE AWAY

In December 2023, Amanda Brochu began receiving calls from people telling her they were "sent by a landlord to replace the driveway" of her Orlando-area home. A number of different contractors—five in all, according to counts by Brochu's son—showed up over the course of just a few days to take measurements. When she confronted one of them, he told her that her landlord, a Tampa man named "Andre," had reached out to him for a quote for replacing the driveway. But Brochu didn't have a landlord; she owned the home and had just put it on the market.

Later, when Brochu was away from home, she looked at her Ring camera app and saw that the workers had returned, and they were digging up her driveway with a bulldozer! She called the cops, who arrived to find "only dirt" where the driveway had been. And no workers. The only lead they had was a number that a contractor had given to Brochu. When a detective called the number, the person hung up, and then texted that it was a "mistake," and then gave them a fake number for the contractor. The trail went cold. It appears that Brochu was the victim of a scam—but exactly what the thieves did with her driveway is unknown.

END OF BROADCAST

Brett Elmore of Jasper, Alabama, received some odd news one morning in February 2023. "They called me and said the tower was gone. And I said, 'What do you mean, the tower is gone?'" What they meant was that the 200-foot-tall radio tower that WJLX, the AM radio station for which Elmore serves as general manager, used for its broadcast had been stolen. Police had no leads. Elmore suspects that the thieves were able to dismantle and haul away the tower because construction at the nearby poultry plant may have allowed them to blend right in. Scrap metal sells pretty fast, so it's unlikely Elmore will ever see his tower again; a new one would cost at least $100,000. According to press reports, the thieves have yet to be caught, and the station was still off the air. "People have reached out and asked how they can help," said Elmore, "but I don't know how you can help unless you have a 200-foot tower and an AM transmitter."

BASEBALL BIZARRE

Hey, batter, batter! Buy me some peanuts and Cracker Jack at the odd ball game!

 I CAN SEE YOUR UNDERWEAR

During the dog days of summer, when afternoon games are played in the scorching sun, players can get very uncomfortable wearing cotton uniforms that must be made strong enough to withstand sliding in the dirt and grass at full speed. So, for Spring Training 2024, Nike and Major League Baseball unveiled the next step in uniform evolution: Nike Vapor Premier. The new jerseys and pants were lighter for improved performance, stronger for improved durability, and designed to keep players cooler. Problem was, the fabric was so sheer that fans could see the players' tucked-in shirts... and even the tags on their underthings.

Fans had fun with it, with one tweeting, "Kinda crazy the MLB has been around for like 120 years and they messed up...pants." But not all players were amused. "It looks like a knockoff jersey from T.J. Maxx," said one anonymous Baltimore Orioles player. MLB officials promised to "look into it."

 GETTING TO FIRST BASE

You don't have to be a baseball expert to know that when you hit the ball, you run to first base. But only those with a keen insight of the game, like Chicago Cubs shortstop Javier Baez—a.k.a. "El Mago," a.k.a. "The Magician"—knows that you don't have to *keep* running toward first as long as you stay inside the baseline. Baez was at bat in a May 2021 game against the Pittsburgh Pirates, with a runner on second and two outs. What happened next for the Pirates has been called the strangest baseball play of the century...and also the dumbest.

Baez hit a grounder to Pirates third baseman Erik Gonzalez, who swooped it up and threw it toward first in what should have been a routine play to end the inning. But the throw drew first baseman Will Craig off the base toward home. Craig caught the ball, but instead of going back and stepping on first base (which would have made Baez out, and made it impossible for the runner to score), he decided to tag Baez out instead. So Baez stopped running, turned around, and started heading back toward home plate. Craig gave chase with the gloved ball stretched as far ahead of him as he could, but Baez stayed one step ahead. By the time they were both only a few feet from home plate, Craig saw that the runner that had been on second, Wilson Contreras, was sprinting home! Craig awkwardly tossed the ball to the catcher, who had to reach up for it, and wasn't fast enough to tag Contreras out. Contreras scored, but the run

Most expensive private plane: a Boeing Airbus A380 that seats 535 people, bought by a Saudi prince for half a billion dollars. He calls it the "Flying Palace."

wouldn't count unless Baez made it to first base safely. Still standing next to Craig, he excitedly crossed his arms in a "safe" sign and then high-tailed it toward first base... which nobody was covering. The catcher threw the ball to the second baseman who was running toward first base, but it went behind him into the outfield, so after Baez safely slid into first base, he jumped back to his feet and headed to second. "The calliope has crashed to the ground," pontificated the commentator, "in a comedy of errors by the Pittsburgh Pirates." And some brilliant base-running by El Mago.

 TRADING PLACES

It might seem impressive to play two positions in one game, but that wasn't the case for New York Mets catcher Travis d'Arnaud one night in 2017. A number of the Mets' infielders were injured, so d'Arnaud was told to trade his catcher's glove for a fielder's glove and go play third base—a position he'd never played. Showing how little confidence the coaches had in their new third baseman, they made d'Arnaud switch to second base whenever a right-handed batter was up (righties are most likely to hit toward third base). That happened more than 20 times throughout the game, and each time it did, d'Arnaud and second baseman Asdrubal Cabrera swapped positions. It made for an odd-looking scorecard, which would usually look like: "d'Arnaud, C" (where C is for catcher). But the scorecard for that game looked like this: "d'Arnaud, 2B-3B-2B-3B-2B-3B-2B-3B-2B-3B-2B-3B-2B-3B-2B-3B-2B-3B-2B-3B-2B." The strategy worked: the only ball hit toward the displaced catcher was a pop fly to second. He caught it, and the crowd went wild.

 SWEPT AWAY

Over the course of a 162-game season, each team plays a total of 52 "series" that comprise three or four games against the same team before the next team comes to town or the host team travels to another town as the visitor. If one team wins every game of a series, it's labeled a "sweep." The last team to avoid being "swept" by any other team in the regular season was the St. Louis Cardinals in 1943, and that was the only time that it happened in the modern era until 2023. By the time the Baltimore Orioles finished the 2023 season with a 101–61 record, they'd played an unbelievable 91 series, going back to the previous year, without another team achieving a sweep against them. (Then came the postseason: the Orioles were swept by the Texas Rangers in three games in the American League Division Series.)

* * *

"If you let your head get too big, it'll break your neck."

—Elvis Presley

The red throne rooms in China's Forbidden City were painted with a mixture of tung oil, clay, hemp, and pig's blood.

LOUIE MATTAR'S PERPETUAL MOTION MOBILE

From the dustbin of history, here's the story of one man and his two friends who took a coast-to-coast road trip in a ridiculously souped-up, convenience-laden Cadillac...and never once stopped.

AUTOMOTIVE MATTARS

Louie Mattar had cars in his blood. He was born and raised in Detroit, the once-booming headquarters of the American automotive industry and the birthplace of mid-20th-century car culture. Mattar must have absorbed some of that ingenuity and engineering excellence because he went on to be an engineer, inventor, and product designer, creating safety devices for the auto industry and the U.S. military. During World War II, the U.S. Navy made frequent use of a minesweeper by Mattar that saved untold lives of servicemen.

But what he really liked was cars, and modifying them to serve his own ends. In the late 1940s and early 1950s, the American auto industry was entering a creative and economic peak, and Mattar envisioned a world where cars could be used for almost anything, vehicles in which one could comfortably live for an indefinite period of time.

INTO THE WOODS

In 1946, Mattar purchased a brand-new 1947 Cadillac Fleetwood and set out to turn it into an RV suitable for long-term camping trips. He and his wife liked to head deep into the wilderness for a week or two at a time, and that informed the modifications that would make self-sustained car-based living not just a possibility but a reality for Mattar.

His vehicle had all the amenities of a modern RV, ingeniously crammed into the limited space of a four-seater Cadillac.

Mattar ran an auto repair shop in San Diego, which became the home base for transforming his Cadillac Fleetwood into a vehicle loaded with all of the necessities and creature comforts he required. He spent about seven years and $35,000 (the equivalent of more than $400,000 today) of his own money to do it.

ROOM FOR IMPROVEMENT

Mattar adopted many ambitious additions and amenities for his already luxurious vehicle, including:

Elephants can communicate by making low-frequency rumbles that send vibrations through the ground.

- He installed a chemical toilet in one of the rear seats, ensuring he'd always have a place to go.
- He also put in a kitchen sink and, on the outside, a shower and a drinking fountain (concealed inside of a taillight). They connected to a 50-gallon water tank embedded within the car.
- The water helped to operate a hookah-style Turkish water pipe installed in the dashboard and came out of a tap in "Louie's Bar," installed inside the glove box. The bar also contained spigots that dispensed soda water and whiskey and included room to hang glasses.
- Decades before mobile phone technology was practical, Mattar's car had a fully operational telephone that could communicate with any landline across the country, if the car were near enough to a base station to relay the call.
- Because Mattar didn't just want to survive while camping, but to live in style while doing it, he included a refrigerator and a television set—rare for even homes to have in the early 1950s.

GETTING ON BOARD

Mattar wanted to have a way to launder and iron his clothing in his car, as two weeks away from home, in the woods, was a long time to go without freshly cleaned shirts. So he installed a rudimentary clothes washer along with an ironing board and iron (in an apparatus that folded down over the back seat), despite protests from his wife. She didn't think it was necessary to do laundry if she and her husband would be away from home only for a week or two—nor did she want to have to toil with that chore while on a little vacation. Mattar agreed, but he thought that washing and ironing clothes would be necessary for longer trips. And that got the inventor thinking about taking his Cadillac Fleetwood out for excursions longer than two weeks, and onto the open road instead of the deep woods. In 1952, Mattar began planning to take a cross-country jaunt in his car, to prove it was roadworthy and test out all of its features under real-world conditions. To prove he'd made something truly special, and perhaps to attract media attention, Mattar figured he could take his car all the way from California to the East Coast and back...without stopping.

ON THE ROAD

Because Mattar was mapping out his trip across the United States before the nation's interstate freeway system was in existence, he discovered that the most practical route stretched from Los Angeles to New York and back. Total distance: 6,320 miles. To propel "Louie Mattar's Fabulous Car"—or the "Fabulous $75,000 Cadillac" as he and reporters

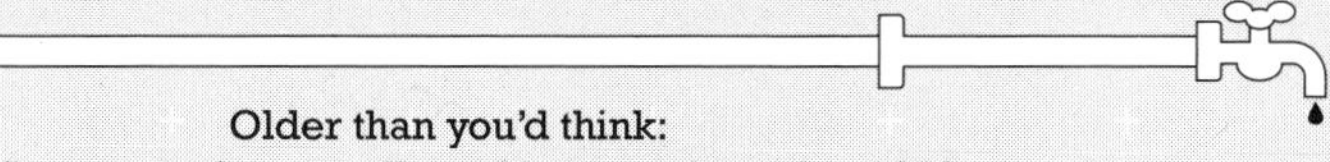

**Older than you'd think:
the first patent for a cardboard box was issued in 1856.**

touted it—without stopping for gas or maintenance (the on-board toilet eliminated the need for pit stops), the engineer would need to build up the car even more.

First, Mattar recruited two friends to take the journey with him, and the three men woud take turns driving and performing repairs as needed. Then he built retractable standing platforms—work surfaces—on all sides of the car. Two men could work while one drove, and they could even tinker with the engine while it was in motion, thanks to Mattar's idea of adding windows to the hood.

A towable trailer solved a lot of problems. Not only did it offer a patio-like sitting area for visiting reporters (with an intercom that relayed voices to and from the driver's seat), but it also carried spare tires and parts, a secondary 30-gallon water drum, 15 gallons of motor oil, and 230 gallons of gas. That stock was used to fuel up the vehicle while in motion, but Mattar also prearranged exactly three fueling stops at airfields outside of Omaha, Kansas City, and Camden, Illinois.

AUTOMATIC TRANSMISSION

Some elements of the drive would be uncomfortable, and there were no solutions for such issues. For example, switching out drivers would mean all three guys would have to climb all over each other to change seats while someone kept their foot on the gas so that Mattar could stick to his promise of a nonstop drive. Other car maintenance issues were taken care of by Mattar's inventing-and-engineering know-how. In the 1950s, every 2,000 miles was the recommended interval for an oil change, so a 6,300-mile trip would require multiple new oil infusions. Mattar built and installed a device that changed the car's oil, while the engine was running, exactly every 1,000 miles. He also developed a radiator-monitoring system that determined when fluids seemed low and would automatically top them off.

Flat tires would be frequent and inevitable on the less-than-smooth system of back roads and two-lane highways that Mattar's team would navigate. To account for that, Mattar included in the Cadillac's wheels a hydraulic jack with a wheel on the shaft, which raised the flat tire up while in motion. From the nearby platform, a passenger could lift the tire off the hub, hand it off to his cohort, and bring in a new tire. Once installed, the tire was automatically inflated by an engine-triggered compressor hidden in the wheel's axle.

FLEETWOOD PACKED

In September 1952, with much fanfare provided by the Los Angeles media, Mattar and his two assistants turned on the ignition of the 8,500-pound Cadillac and headed east. Arrangements had been made with every town along the way—police provided escorts to guide the Cadillac through traffic lights so Mattar wouldn't have to stop at

Largest commercial air fleet in the world: American Airlines, with 980 aircraft.

red lights or slow down (or cause any accidents). This perpetual motion machine—not in the scientific definition, but in practice—successfully completed its mission. Mattar's Cadillac barreled back into Los Angeles exactly seven days after the voyage began, having never stopped along the way.

Mattar and his "Fabulous $75,000 Cadillac" became minor celebrities for a couple of years, inspiring more wanderlust in its inventor. In August 1954, Mattar's team headed out on the road again, with an even longer trip: this time, they crossed North America the other way, from north to south, traveling from Anchorage to Mexico City—a distance of 7,482 miles. Encompassing multiple international crossings, Mattar's crew managed to conduct border and customs inspections without having to stop the car.

BETTER PULL OVER

Mattar would eventually return to his San Diego auto body shop, where he worked for decades. He died in 1999 at the age of 89, having never parted with or mass-produced his Fabulous Cadillac, which he occasionally took out for trips both short and long—his original intention. He seemed to harbor no regrets about keeping for himself the priceless vehicle, which his grandson has loaned to the San Diego Automotive Museum. "If I sold that car and had all the money in the bank, I wouldn't meet the important people I do," Mattar told reporters in the 1990s. "That's worth all the money in the world."

* * *

NINE RULES FOR COYOTE AND ROAD-RUNNER CARTOONS

As written by Looney Tunes animator extraordinaire, Chuck Jones.

1. The Road-Runner cannot harm the Coyote except by going "beep-beep!"
2. No outside force can harm the Coyote—only his own ineptitude or the failure of Acme products.
3. The Coyote could stop anytime—if he were not a fanatic. (Repeat: "A fanatic is one who redoubles his effort when he has forgotten his aim." —George Santayana)
4. No dialogue ever, except "beep-beep!"
5. The Road-Runner must stay on the road—otherwise, logically, he would not be called Road-Runner.
6. All action must be confined to the natural environment of the two characters—the Southwest American desert.
7. All materials, tools, weapons, or mechanical conveniences must be obtained from the Acme Corporation.
8. Whenever possible, make gravity the Coyote's greatest enemy.
9. The Coyote is always more humiliated than harmed by his failures.

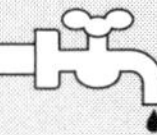

Every day, the U.S. Postal Service processes an average of 23.5 million packages.

INTERNET MUSIC FIRSTS

The transition from listening to music on records, tapes, and CDs to consuming it online–from iPods to iPhones to Spotify and Apple Music–happened so fast we need to rewind and better understand how it happened. Here are some monumental moments in the history of online music.

First MP3. German electrical engineer Karlheinz Brandenburg developed the MP3, the digital file format that made possible transmitting and downloading music files online. The first song he converted into digital format, in 1991, was Suzanne Vega's 1987 hit "Tom's Diner."

First concert broadcast online. Mbone (shorthand for Multicast Backbone) was a service used by techies in Silicon Valley to broadcast academic conferences over the Internet. On June 24, 1993, Severe Tire Damage, a band consisting of Silicon Valley software company employees, played a concert at Xerox Palo Alto Research Center and broadcast it on Mbone.

First online album leak. In 1993, being online meant using services like Prodigy, America Online, and CompuServe. Fans of anything could discuss their obsessions on message boards. Depeche Mode fans gathered in a chat room on CompuServe, where they shared an advance copy of the band's 1993 album *Songs of Faith and Devotion* in clunky digital audio files that took hours to download via dial-up modems' slow Internet connections.

First streaming radio station. On November 7, 1994, the University of North Carolina at Chapel Hill's college radio station, WXYC, became the first radio station in the world to simulcast its over-the-air broadcast with a live online stream. Listeners tuned in from as far away as Mexico and Poland.

First single released exclusively online. As a publicity stunt on June 27, 1994, CompuServe teamed up with hugely popular rock band Aerosmith to offer the first-ever downloadable song by a major-label artist. The song "Head First," recorded for but not used on the 1993 album *Get a Grip*, was free to CompuServe subscribers. (It took an hour, at minimum, to download.)

First single sold online. Three years after Aerosmith made a song available on the Internet for free, fellow classic rock act Duran Duran began selling their music over the Internet. In 1997, fans could buy the radio version of "Electric Barbarella" for 99 cents and a longer "Internet Only" mix for $1 from the website of Duran Duran's label, Capitol Records. It wasn't released to record stores until two weeks after its digital debut.

The U.S. presidential limo is always stocked with a few pints of the president's blood type...just in case.

First album available to download online for a fee. Two weeks before his 1999 album *Hours* hit stores in physical formats, David Bowie placed the record on his website for downloading. Cost: $18.

First online music service. Streaming music services like Spotify, legal download haunts like the iTunes Music Store, and user-upload-powered sites like Soundcloud all appeared in the wake of services that allowed subscribers to download copyrighted music for free. The first of those, Napster, launched in 1999 and led to a global decline in record sales; labels got the site shut down by 2001, citing rampant copyright infringement and theft.

First downloads on the iTunes Music Store. Apple made a big dent in online piracy by opening the iTunes Music Store on April 28, 2003, with 200,000 songs available. Intended to help customers fill their iPods with $9.99 albums and 99-cent singles, the company has never revealed what the first downloads were. But on launch day, the most downloaded album was Beck's 2002 *Sea Change*; the most downloaded song was U2's 2002 single "Stuck in a Moment You Can't Get Out Of."

First music video on YouTube. Adam Quick's "Vernal Lullaby," a video collage of a soundscape consisting of noise samples and a bit of the Queens of the Stone Age song "This Lullaby," was the seventh video ever added to YouTube. Appearing on May 7, 2005, it's the first music video (of billions) to ever appear on the video site.

First song with a million downloads. The first time a song went platinum based solely on paid, legal downloads from services like iTunes, and not from the sales of CDs or tapes, was Gwen Stefani's #1 hit "Hollaback Girl" in October 2005.

First digital-only #1 hit. Gnarls Barkley, an electro-funk supergroup consisting of singer CeeLo Green and DJ Danger Mouse, released the ballad "Crazy" in 2006. It reached #2 on the pop chart, but #1 on other American genre charts and in a dozen countries and territories around the world. Releasing right when downloading was supplanting sales of CDs, "Crazy" is the first single to go all the way to #1 without being available in a physical media format.

First surprise album. Just 10 days before it became available in 2007, Radiohead announced that it had recorded the album *In Rainbows*. Fans couldn't buy it in physical form; they could only download it from a special website that allowed them to pay whatever they wanted for it, including paying nothing. (Reports vary, but the average price paid was between $2 and $6).

The Swahili word *kujenga* ("to build or construct") inspired the name of the game Jenga.

STRANGE CELEBRITY LAWSUITS

We're back with one of our regular features: unusual legal battles involving famous people.

The Plaintiff: Donnie Yen, one of China's highest paid martial-arts action stars who has appeared in such American movies as *Shanghai Knights*, *Rogue One: A Star Wars Story*, *Mulan*, and *John Wick: Chapter 4*

The Defendant: The promotional partners—named in press reports as Beijing Qi Tai Cultural Development Group—for *Iceman: The Time Traveler* (2018), a Chinese-language action-comedy sequel starring Yen as a Ming Dynasty warrior who travels through time and gets in fights

The Lawsuit: *Iceman* was reviled by critics and fans alike. It took a huge loss in theaters and became a disaster for the production company. Why? Because the first movie, *Iceman*, had also bombed—and it's risky to make a sequel to a bomb. That's why the producers hired two of China's most celebrated filmmakers for said sequel: scriptwriter Manfred Wong and director Raymond Yip Wai-man.

On November 3, 2018, while *Iceman* was tanking in theaters, the backers issued an "official blog post" on Weibo apologizing to Wong and Wai-man, saying that the movie's poor performance wasn't their fault. "From filming to post-production and completion," they wrote, "*Iceman: The Time Traveler* is through-and-through Donnie Yen's work." They accused Yen of changing the script to "modernize" it, of refusing to wear a wig, and of making the editors cut scenes that undermined his lead status. The result was an "87-minute scattershot plot." Then they accused Yen of refusing to promote the movie.

The scathing blog post was online only for four hours before it was deleted, but that was long enough for screenshots to show up in press reports around the world. Yen sued for defamation. His lawyers wrote that the post "severely harmed Donnie Yen's reputation, and has caused much distress for Yen, his family, working partners, and fans." They also pointed out that absolutely no one working on *Iceman*, or on any of Yen's earlier movies, had ever accused the beloved Chinese action star of behaving like this. He was suing for an undisclosed amount, which he said he would donate to charity.

The Verdict: There were no further press reports, which usually means an "undisclosed settlement." In a lengthy post of his own, Yen categorically refuted all 20 accusations and lashed out at the "immoral" backers: "If they said an actor had such god-like superpower of...changing the script, controlling the shooting,

editing, promotion, wouldn't he also have the power to stop a film's release?" He also questioned the timing of the blog post: "How can you believe that by maliciously dissing an actor, you can bring a higher rating for the film and consequently better box office results?" Whatever those backers were up to, their plan failed. And Yen's star has only grown brighter.

The Plaintiff: Fred Rogers, host of the PBS kids' show *Mister Rogers' Neighborhood*, and his company Family Communications Inc.

The Defendants: Adam Troy Mercer, M. B. Madison, and Edward E. Stephens of the Missouri Knights of the Ku Klux Klan

The Lawsuit: In 1990, a phone number associated with the Klan was circulated among elementary and middle schools in Independence, Missouri. When the children called the number, they heard on the other end of the line—with the show's gentle music playing in the background—a recording of an impressionist who sounded just like Mister Rogers making racist threats and saying things like "AIDS was divine retribution."

When local civil rights groups and religious institutions learned about the messages, they alerted the children's show icon, who sued the Klan for defamation and copyright infringement, calling the phone message "racism, white supremacy and bigotry—the antithesis of everything Rogers and Family Communications Inc. stand for."

The Verdict: A federal judge ordered the three men to turn all their tapes over to the police, and issued a restraining order barring the KKK from ever impersonating Mister Rogers again.

The Plaintiff: Seven deputies with the Adams County Sheriff's Office (ACSO) in Ohio

The Defendant: Afroman (real name: Joseph Foreman), a rapper known for the early 2000s hits "Crazy Rap (Colt 45 & 2 Zig-Zags)" and "Because I Got High"

The Lawsuit: In August 2022, ACSO received an anonymous tip that Afroman, 48, was a marijuana trafficker and a kidnapper who kept victims in his "basement dungeon." A task force showed up with a search warrant and, after a few hours, found no basement dungeon (or even a basement) or any evidence of drug trafficking (just "the ends of a few blunts" from personal use).

It's unclear who provided the tip, or why, but Afroman later accused the police of damaging his gate and front door, and of disconnecting his security system, all of which cost $20,000 to fix. He also said they confiscated $5,000—which were his tour earnings—and later returned the cash, minus $400 (which the department blamed on an intial "miscount"). He also complained that the heavily armed tactical unit scared his ex-wife and kids, who live nearby. "I asked myself, as a Black man in America, what can I do to these cops?" His solution: "Make a funny rap song about them and make some money, use the money to pay for the damages they did and move on."

Afroman wrote two songs about the raid and used his security footage in their videos. In "Mama's Lemon Pound Cake," he raps, "It tastes so nice / it made the sheriff want to put down his gun / and cut him a slice." (The other song is called "Will You Help Me Repair My Door?") He then sold merchandise with images from the raid, and compared one deputy (the one that eyed the pound cake) to the portly Peter Griffin from *Family Guy*.

The following March, four deputies, two sergeants, and one detective from ASCO sued Afroman and his distribution company for invasion of privacy and defamation—claiming they've suffered "humiliation, ridicule, mental distress, embarrassment, and loss of reputation." They even received death threats. The cops were suing for all the profits from the songs, videos, and merchandise that they appeared in without their consent, and for all of that music and merchandise to be deleted and destroyed.

Afroman said he will countersue "for making me suffer financially in my industry because just that accusation [of kidnapping] makes people raise an eyebrow about you."

The Verdict: Pending. At last report, a judge had partially denied Afroman's request for dismissal; he threw out the cops' privacy claim but allowed the "false light, unreasonable publicity of private lives, and defamation" claims to proceed.

That's because Afroman didn't stop with the songs and merchandise; he posted still images from the raid along with alarming accusations on all of his social media pages—including that the police "tried to kill me" (even though he wasn't home when the raid occurred), that they stole his money, that one officer is a lesbian, and another is a pedophile. Most of those posts were deleted, but Afroman still maintains he has the right to defame the "criminal" and "racist" cops just like they defamed him. However it ends up, he thanked the police for making him a "bigger star." "I don't want to pay these guys nothing, but worst case scenario, if I had to pay them, off the publicity and fame they gave me, it might be fair just to shuffle them a few coins."

The Plaintiffs: Ray M. Dolby and Dolby Laboratories, Inc., a British American corporation known for its surround-sound systems in movie theaters, which launched in the 1960s with the Dolby Noise Reduction System that reduces background hissing noises on cassette recordings

The Defendant: Thomas Morgan Robertson, who goes by the stage name Thomas

It's estimated that 6,400 fatal traffic accidents occur in the U.S. each year due to "drowsy driving."

Dolby, an English singer and composer known for the 1982 new wave hit "She Blinded Me with Science"

The Lawsuit: As a teen in the early 1970s, Thomas Robertson was never far from a keyboard or a cassette tape recorder, which earned him the nickname "Dolby"—after the sound company. By the late 1970s, when Robertson was a budding pop star, he adopted the stage name Thomas Dolby to avoid being confused with popular singer Thomas Robinson. He contacted company founder Ray Dolby, just to make sure it was okay to use the surname.

It was, with some conditions: "We reached an agreement that it was OK for me to use the name as long as it didn't bring the company name any ill repute. I think at first they thought I was some sort of punk rocker who might cause problems."

The first problem came when "She Blinded Me with Science" made Thomas Dolby a star; Dolby Labs demanded that his record company change his name. Demand denied.

Then, when Dolby decided to expand into film music and compose the score for 1986's *Gothic*, that led to even more problems. "They filed legal proceedings against me, despite the fact that I made several compromising gestures aimed at satisfying them, such as not endorsing any stereo equipment." The tech company was primarily concerned that, on *Gothic*'s movie poster, the "Music by Thomas Dolby" credit and the "Dolby Stereo" logo would be only a few inches apart, thus fooling people into thinking that Thomas Dolby was in charge of Dolby Labs. Claiming their "trademark will be irreparably harmed if defendant continues to use the name 'Thomas Dolby,'" the lawsuit demanded that Dolby change his name. Demand denied. Dolby countersued. Then it got ugly.

The Verdict: The singer won. He was allowed to keep his stage name, "Thomas Dolby," but he can't use the name "Dolby" by itself, or ever print "Dolby" larger than "Thomas." Nor can he "do anything to intimate that he is responsible for the quality of the sound reproduction." So basically, Dolby the singer can never get into the audio business. The judge ordered Dolby Labs to pay $50,000 in the countersuit; they offered Dolby $500,000 to pick a new name. Offer denied.

When the singer later broke his silence about the whole affair, he accused the corporation of bullying him—even going so far as to hire a private detective to go to his house and pretend to be a journalist requesting an interview. Request denied. "They tried to use their corporate might to crush me."

* * *

"When I'm in a slump, I comfort myself by saying if I believe in dinosaurs, then somewhere, they must be believing in me. And if they believe in me, then I can believe in me. Then I bust out."

—Mookie Wilson, MLB player

THIS PAGE IS THE GOAT

Initialisms are abbreviated words or names in which all of the letters are pronounced—like AT&T or CBS. Acronyms are made up of the first letters of multiple words that form a word themselves. Here are the origins of some well-known acronyms so entrenched in our language that you may not have known they are acronyms.

ACRONYM: GOAT
MEANING: "Greatest of all time"
ORIGIN: Most commonly used to refer to stellar athletes, GOAT entered the lexicon in 2000 when LL Cool J—one of the greatest of all time at rapping—released an album with the explanatory title (and his real name) *G.O.A.T. featuring James T. Smith: The Greatest of All Time*. The rapper was inspired by boxer Muhammad Ali, who frequently referred to himself as the greatest of all time, and legendary New York street basketball player Earl Manigault, who was nicknamed the GOAT. "So I just decided that I was going to take 'GOAT' and greatest of all time and make an acronym," LL Cool J said.

ACRONYM: YOLO
MEANING: "You only live once"
ORIGIN: It exploded as a youthful slang term in the 2010s, uttered by people to encourage others—or themselves—to take risks or to shore up confidence, but its history predates the millennium. It first entered occasional usage in the 1940s, and "you only live once" was a well-known phrase dating to the 19th century. In 1993, the first trademark was filed for "YOLO" by a clothing company, and it took off as a slang term among the jet-ski community in the late 1990s.

ACRONYM: Fubar
MEANING: "F***ed up beyond all recognition"
ORIGIN: If a snafu leads to disastrous and deadly consequences, particularly in combat, things may be described as totally fubar. Like *snafu*, *fubar* (or FUBAR) got its start as military slang among American GIs during World War II, who used the term to describe a hopeless situation or to graphically write something off as tragically unfixable. The phrase was likely derived from a term that soldiers fighting the Nazis may have heard—the German word *furchtbar* translates to "terrible" but its connotation is "hopeless."

ACRONYM: SWAT

MEANING: "Special weapons and tactics"

ORIGIN: Any fan of police procedurals is familiar with this elite law enforcement team specially trained and equipped to handle active shooters, terrorists, riots, and hostage-rescue situations. Its predecessor was created by the Philadelphia Police Department in 1964 to stop a bank-robbery ring; that police team was called the Special Weapons Attack Team. Two years later, the Los Angeles Police Department formed Special Weapons and Tactics. The LAPD group was more of a riot squad, created to assist what was perceived as an under-equipped regular police department during the 1965 civil rights riots in Watts.

ACRONYM: EGOT

MEANING: Emmy, Grammy, Oscar, Tony

ORIGIN: The hottest new drama of the 1984–85 TV season, and the most stylish and hip, was the NBC detective show *Miami Vice*. Philip Michael Thomas was thrust to fame for his role as Det. Ricardo Tubbs, and in an interview with the Associated Press, he excitedly laid out his ambitious plan to "EGOT." "That stands for Emmy, Grammy, Oscar, and Tony," he said. "Hopefully in the next five years I will win all those awards." Thomas didn't accomplish an EGOT within five years, or ever—he was never nominated for any of those individual awards. Regardless, Thomas wore an "EGOT" necklace for a while, similar to the one that inspires character Tracy Jordan (Tracy Morgan) to successfully aim to win all four awards in a 2009 story arc on the hit sitcom *30 Rock*, which popularized the phrase.

ACRONYM: CARE

MEANING: Cooperative for American Remittances to Europe

ORIGIN: A box of goodies and comfort items sent to a loved one who's deployed or off at college is called a "care package," and that phrase gets its name from an acronym. As part of the rebuilding and humanitarian efforts after World War II, a new organization formed in the U.S. called the Cooperative for American Remittances to Europe. The organization collected and sent food to devastated and impoverished communities throughout Europe; it was so successful, it was later renamed the Cooperative for Assistance and Relief Everywhere and the program was expanded worldwide. Bundles came to be known as "CARE packages" and then just care packages.

There are 5.17 billion people on social media—nearly 64 percent of the global population.

HOTEL ROOM HACKS

Whenever Uncle John stays at a hotel, he brings all his rubber duckies so he can play with them in the tub. That has nothing to do with this article. We just thought you should know.

- When you check in, ask for a free upgrade like a bigger room or one with a better view (if there's a vacancy). Hotels want return business, so this might be easier than you'd expect. Be nice to the clerk, and mention if it's a special occasion like an anniversary. Hotels also reward loyalty with perks, so ask if they have a free loyalty program.
- For more peace and quiet, request a room away from the noisy ice machines and elevators, and on the top floor so you won't be bothered by footsteps through the ceiling. Stuff a rolled-up towel under the door to keep the room even darker and quieter.
- No microwave? No problem. You can use hot water from the coffee maker to heat up oatmeal or ramen noodles. No use traveling hungry!
- When you're packing prior to the trip, toss in a few extra hangers. Some hotels don't provide that many, and they're often secured to the dowel in the closet, so you can't take one out and use it to hold the blinds shut to keep that pesky streetlight—or morning sun—from keeping you awake.
- Other items that can come in handy: earplugs and a sleeping mask, electrical tape to cover up bothersome LED displays, a mini power strip to make sure there are enough convenient outlets, and a dirty clothes bag. (And a Bathroom Reader.)
- If your room doesn't include enough horizontal surfaces to keep your stuff on, or even to work on, utilize the ironing board in the closet.
- Most hotel rooms have only a stirring spoon, so bring your own cutlery (and even a plate) so you can eat your leftovers without your hands.
- Concerned about germs? Bring some disinfectant and wipe down all the surfaces, light switches, and doorknobs. You can keep the "germiest" item, the TV remote, in a slider storage bag or, in a pinch, the provided plastic shower cap.
- Some hotel rooms have an...odor. Either because the maids used too much cleaning product or too little. Or they're just musty. Place a car air freshener over the air conditioning/heating vent, and set it to full blast.
- If your room has a slot next to the door to store your key card while you're inside, leave a second key card—or any same-sized plastic card—in there while you're gone. That way, the air conditioner and/or heat will stay on while you're gone, keeping the room a pleasant temperature to return to.

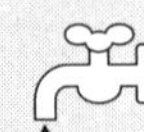

In 2023, Merriam-Webster added 690 new words to its online dictionary, among them *mid*, *simp*, *padawan*, *generative AI*, and *ngl* ("not gonna lie").

ELVIS PRESLEY, 1935 TO 1977 TO...?

He'd be 89 now, and with his well-documented affinities for narcotics and fried peanut-butter-and-bacon sandwiches, the odds that the King hasn't left the building yet are slim. But if he did, in fact, fake his 1977 death like so many fans and supermarket tabloids have claimed over the years, he was successful in leaving fame behind. Here's a history of the origins, development, and impact of the notion that Elvis is alive.

THE AIRPORT THEORY

Elvis Presley died in the bathroom of his Graceland estate in Memphis, Tennessee, on August 16, 1977, at age 42. As the world mourned, numerous news outlets ran a story about an individual matching Elvis's description and distinctive appearance being spotted at Memphis International Airport hours after the King's reported death. The individual bought a ticket to Buenos Aires, Argentina, under the name Jon Burrows—the same name Elvis had used as a fake name when checking into hotels and lying low. The story was unsourced, with no witnesses named, so it was impossible to substantiate. It's probably not true, for those reasons and because Memphis didn't offer international flights in 1977.

THE FAKE DEAD BODY THEORY

Hundreds of mourners gathered in Memphis for Elvis's funeral on August 18, 1977. Photos of videos secretly captured of the event depict some pallbearers having a hard time lifting the King's casket, made of solid copper and weighing a reported 900 pounds. There's no way that Elvis, even at his heaviest, would make for a coffin that unwieldy, leading to the theory that the body inside—visible from the waist up for the open-casket funeral—was a highly detailed wax dummy kept from melting in the Memphis summer heat by a heavy cooling system within the casket. Elvis's cousin Gene Smith would later tell reporters that Elvis didn't look like himself: his nose, sideburns, hands, and hairline seemed artificial.

THE POOL HOUSE THEORY

Elvis's Graceland home became a major tourist attraction after the singer's death, and on December 31, 1977, a fan named Mike Joseph visited and snapped a lot of photos. Several years later, when he was looking at one photo very carefully, he noticed a man looming in the doorway of the pool house. Elvis's close friend Joe Esposito identified the figure as another pal and Graceland regular, Al Strada. But tabloids insisted the figure was Elvis himself.

THE MICHIGAN THEORY

It became a joke and a cliché for comedians, movies, and TV shows to mention Elvis sightings, and to observe that they always occurred at some remote grocery store or fast-food restaurant. That all started with a real (alleged) Elvis sighting in 1988: Louise Welling of Vicksburg, Michigan, told the *Vicksburg Journal* that she saw a man wearing a trademark Elvis-style spangled jumpsuit in line at a Kalamazoo supermarket, Felpausch, buying an electrical fuse. Later that day, Welling's own daughter saw the same Elvis-like character eating several Whoppers at a nearby Burger King—Elvis's favorite fast-food place.

Residents and reporters in the Kalamazoo area kept their eyes peeled for Elvis sightings after those two related incidents, and stories of anything or anyone that *could* be Elvis were disseminated by the media. He was usually spotted at grocery stores and gas stations. The true identity of this "Elvis" was never determined.

THE WITNESS PROTECTION THEORY

Around the same time that Elvis was allegedly hanging around Kalamazoo, Gail Brewer-Giorgio published the book *Is Elvis Alive?* Convinced that Elvis hadn't died, Brewer-Giorgio sifted through thousands of publicly available FBI documents about the King and pieced together an argument that points to the singer's involvement with an FBI takedown of "the Fraternity," an organized crime syndicate. Elvis, a well-known admirer of police (he collected badges, and went out on nightly patrols as a self-appointed officer of the law in Memphis in the 1970s), agreed to help out the FBI after they alerted him to the existence of the organization after he sold an airplane to one of its members. When the Fraternity learned that Elvis was working for the feds, he had to fake his own death and go into hiding or he would have been killed.

THE SECRET COMEBACK THEORY

Elvis Presley's singing style was so distinctive, and his drawl so pronounced, that it's easy to turn out a moderately successful imitation. But a *really* good one? That can and did fool some people. In 1988, the small country music label LS Records claimed that a limousine pulled up to the office one day and a man who wished to remain anonymous dropped off a recording of a song called "Spelling on the Stone." Label head Lee Stoller listened to the song and thought it sounded like Elvis, and the content of the song supported that theory—"Spelling on the Stone" refers to the King's misspelled middle name ("Aaron" instead of "Aron") on his tombstone, which Elvis-is-alivers had frequently claimed was a hint that the singer wasn't really dead and buried. LS Records released "Spelling on the Stone" to country stations without a credited singer but with plenty of press materials that suggested the performer was an undead Elvis. The song was a minor hit (it reached #82 on the country chart), and wherever it got significant radio airplay, Elvis sightings curiously increased. Music

writers later identified the true performer of "Spelling on the Stone" as Dan Willis, an LS Records musician.

THE *HOME ALONE* THEORY

For whatever important reason Elvis may have pretended to be dead or had gone off the grid—to escape fame or criminals, or some other motivation—he'd probably steer clear of exposing himself on screen in a major Hollywood movie. But in 1991, shortly after the blockbuster Christmas comedy *Home Alone* debuted on home video, a rumor circulated that Elvis appeared in the movie as a featured extra for several minutes. The scene in question: Kate McAllister (Catherine O'Hara) pleads with an airport ticket agent to let her on a plane to get back to her young son, left home by himself. Throughout the scene, a tall man who sort of looks like Elvis stands behind O'Hara, silently waiting for his turn at the desk. In 2015, director Chris Columbus told *USA Today*, "If Elvis was on the set, I would have known," while in 2018 paranormal investigator Kenny Biddle ID'd the extra as Gary Richard Grott, who worked on dozens of movies, and died in 2016—and wasn't Elvis.

THE LEGOLAND THEORY

Even in hiding, Elvis needs to get out and have some fun once in a while. Or at least that's what people were thinking in 1999. Several sightings of Elvis were registered at the Legoland amusement park in Southern California—a man matching the description of a 60-something King of Rock 'n' Roll was seen at the attraction's opening. An investigation by park management quickly unlocked the mystery: it had hired Elvis impersonators for the grand opening, and they'd been walking around the park out of costume.

THE ELVIS IS ALIVE (BUT HE JUST DIED) THEORY

In January 2015, an obscure website called Empire News reported that the body of a white-bearded 80-year-old man was discovered under a bridge in San Diego. He seemed to be homeless and had no identification, but people who knew him called him Jessie, and authorities ran a DNA test to determine his identity. They got a match: it was Elvis Presley. The news story was picked up by other, bigger news outlets and briefly went viral on social media, particularly when the picture of the deceased man was included—he looked just like Elvis would look had he lived into old age. (And the name Jessie? That was obviously picked by Elvis in tribute to his stillborn twin, Jesse.) Just as quickly as the story spread and got people's hopes up (and then made them sad), the whole thing was debunked. Empire News is a satire news site, and it bears the disclaimer "intended for entertainment purposes only."

THE NEVER-LEFT-HOME THEORY

What if Elvis didn't die, and didn't even leave his home? That's the idea behind

What do elephants have in common with humans? Most of their bodies are covered with hair that's thickest on top of the head.

a theory floated in 2016. An Elvis fan visited the King's home-turned-museum, Graceland, that summer and captured video of an estate groundskeeper going about his job. The groundskeeper sort of looked like Elvis, if Elvis were older, and the video garnered millions of views on YouTube, with some people thinking that this quiet, hardworking gardener was actually Elvis. Another Graceland visitor ended the speculation with her own YouTube video: in it, the man identifies himself as Bill Barmer, who doesn't speak with an Elvis-like Southern accent, and who isn't remotely close to Elvis's age.

THE GUEST OF HONOR THEORY

Elvis's palatial Memphis home, Graceland, hosts an annual birthday celebration each January 8. In 2017, fans gathered to commemorate Elvis's 82nd birthday, and the festivities were broadcast over the internet via livestream. Someone watching noticed a figure who stood just behind the stage, staring down the camera the whole time. A man with identity-obscuring white beard, sunglasses, hat, and prominent jaw could be—as some followers of the website Elvis is Alive pointed out—Elvis himself. The man even came with a security detail of several bodyguards. This means that either Elvis attended his own birthday party...or some other old man did.

* * *

FAN THEORY: THE SIMPSONS ARE ALL GENIUSES

While it may seem like middle-child Lisa is the only smart Simpson, sharp-eyed viewers point to several episodes that suggest the entire family has superior intelligence.

GRANDPA: In flashbacks, it's revealed he was a quick-witted World War II pilot and later a successful pianist.

HOMER: In a season 12 episode, Homer learns he's had a crayon stuck up his nose since childhood; after it's removed, he regains his brainpower. But after "smart Homer" is rejected by his friends, he sticks the crayon back in and reverts to his stupid self.

MARGE: The former-straight-A-student-turned-homemaker excels at challenging professions (real-estate agent, gym owner, author). But seeing how troubled Lisa is, Marge keeps her smarts to herself.

BART: Flashbacks reveal Bart was once a bright student, but he also notices Lisa's unhappiness—along with how happy Homer seems to be. So, Bart too plays dumb (but secretly uses his smarts to concoct elaborate schemes).

MAGGIE: We find out in season 15 that the Simpsons' baby girl has an IQ of 167. That's not surprising, considering Maggie once orchestrated and perfectly executed a *Mission Impossible*–style plan to rescue other babies—and her pacifier—from a mean teacher.

Your car will spend about 95 percent of its lifetime parked.

CARE FOR SOME RING OF FIRE?

There are thousands of hot sauces out there. They all seem to taste pretty much the same, but the manufacturers are in competition with one another to: 1) make them as hot as possible, and; 2) give them the most ridiculous punny names, often about their heat and their negative effects on your digestive system. These are all real sauces.

Strained Brain

Dr. Chilemeister's PhD of Pain

Crazy Jerry's Mustard Gas

Curry On

PuckerButt's Voodoo Prince Death Mamba

Hemorrhoid Helper

Ring of Fire

Professor Payne Indeass's Anal Angst

Sir Fartalot's Hot Sauce

Tom's Roid-Rippin' Hot Sauce

Ghost in the Darkness

Don't Be a Chicken S***

Satan's Blood

Pure Evil

Cat in Heat

I Am Sofa King Stew Ped

Harry Pooter: A Magically Explosive Potion

Fire Ant Juice

Weed Killer

Queen of Farts

A Little Nukey

Area 51: The Hot Sauce That Doesn't Exist

Sphincter Shrinker XXX

Wet Fart XX Hot with Pooh

Yippie Cayenne Mother Pepper

Chili the Kid

Chairman Meow's Revenge

First Responder's EMS

Nuckin' Futs

I Like Pig Butts

Spontaneous Combustion

Lethal Ingestion

Widow, No Survivors

Vicious Viper

Fire & Spice

Santa's Smokin' Chimney

Fire in the Hole

Magma, an Eruption of Disastrous Proportions

Total Insanity

Krakatoa!

Gator Swamp Gas

Toxic Waste

Pain Is Good

Vampfire

Colon Blow

Red Rectum Revenge

Crapper Jon's

Liquid Stoopid

Backfire

Scorned Woman

Jamaica Hell Fire

Firearrhea

Sudden Death Sauce

The End: Flatline

Keef Cowboy's claim to fame: in 1975, the rapper from Grandmaster Flash & the Furious Five coined the term "hip-hop."

A RARE CONDITION

What all diseases have in common: they're unpleasant at best and tragic at worst. A few are just so interesting and fascinating–and, fortunately, exceedingly rare–that Dr. Uncle John insisted we tell you about them.

Idiopathic Hypersomnia. Clinically serious, medical-grade sleepiness. It's diagnosed when an individual routinely sleeps for nine solid hours or more each night and wakes up still feeling fatigued and their condition doesn't improve throughout the day.

Kleine-Levin Syndrome. Overwhelmingly affecting teenage boys, who sleep a lot anyway, this "Sleeping Beauty syndrome" causes patients to submit to sleep for as long as 20 hours at a time, waking up only to eat and use the bathroom before going right back down. And while excessive fatigue is a symptom of clinical depression, clinical depression is an after-effect of Kleine-Levin Syndrome.

Hyperekplexia. Also named Jumping Frenchmen of Maine Disease after it was first identified in French Canadian lumberjacks in the late 19th century, it makes the body have extreme overreactions to stimuli like sudden noises or surprises. A stricken individual will involuntarily jump high, flail, scream, fall down, or hit others.

Morgellons. Sometimes incorrectly diagnosed with a mental-health problem, a patient with Morgellons looks like they're frantically scratching at bugs they believe are crawling under their skin but aren't really there. That's because the disease causes the skin to have a painful itching, biting, or stinging feeling, along with the development of lesions that never heal or fibers that emerge from under the skin. Once considered a delusional mental-health disorder, it's now believed to be caused by tick bite.

Jerusalem Syndrome. After visiting the Holy Land, a patient (of any religious background) may manifest this psychological disorder. The sufferer can turn toward fundamental religious views and delusions that he or she is the Messiah. It lasts about five to seven days and goes away on its own (often after some embarrassment).

Geographic Tongue. So named because it makes the tongue look like a map of geographic features, with red and white swirly patches resembling depictions of mountains and hills. It's unknown what causes these potentially painful tongue lesions to develop, but they can be exacerbated by stress, allergies, and spicy food.

Maple Syrup Urine Disease. In this inherited condition, the body can't process amino acid strings that form proteins, leading to a build-up of substances in the urine

Only lake that was around when the dinosaurs lived:
Lake Zaysan in eastern Kazakhstan, which formed 70 million years ago.

(and neurological damage). When they're eliminated through the urine, it gives the pee a sweet, distinctive smell very similar to that of maple syrup.

Porphyria. Patients with this condition cannot produce heme, a protein that facilitates cells' ability to hold oxygen. This causes a substance called porphyrins to build up in the liver, which it pushes into the urine for release out of the body. Not only does the toxic presence of porphyrins cause violent mood swings, but when they are excreted, they turn urine and feces purple.

Congenital Insensitivity to Pain. Feeling pain keeps a person safe—sharp and hot things can hurt the body. People with this condition, caused by a double gene mutation, cannot differentiate between sharp and dull, or sense cold or hot things, so they may touch a hot stove and feel nothing as it blisters and burns their hand. It also curiously leads to a loss of the ability to smell and an inability to sweat.

Birdshot Chorioretinopathy. So named because the most distinctive characteristic of the disease is the appearance of orange spots in the eye that resemble bird eggs, in addition to general inflammation. Not only are the spots visible from the outside, but they float around and lead to blurry vision, poor night vision, glare, and, sometimes, complete blindness.

Fibrodysplasia Ossificans Progressiva. In this frightening condition, the skeleton slowly encroaches into the rest of the body and overtakes it. Connective tissue—muscles, tendons, and ligaments—is all eventually taken over by newly formed bones. "Stone Man syndrome" eventually leads to an inability to fully move.

Sjogren's Syndrome. This autoimmune condition tricks the body into attacking itself. Specifically, the body shuts down the glands used to produce and distribute moisture. This makes various ducts and glands dry and inflamed, and it hinders the body's ability to produce important liquids like tears and saliva.

Pachyonychia Congenita. This disorder encompasses an odd suite of skin conditions. Patients may find themselves with extremely thick or weirdly shaped toenails and fingernails, as well as painful blisters and raw calluses on their feet and palms, white patches on the tongue, and bumps on the elbows and knees.

Marie Antoinette Syndrome. According to lore, former queen of France Marie Antoinette witnessed her hair turn completely white the night before her death by guillotine because she was so stressed and frightened. That's a real medical condition, also called *canities subita*. The hair loses all pigment in a very short time as a reaction to extreme distress.

Finger-licking good: it's illegal to eat chicken with a fork and knife in Gainesville, Georgia.

MOUTHING OFF

ON WRITING

Some thoughts from those folks who arrange words for a living.

"I apologize for such a long letter—I didn't have time to write a short one."

—Mark Twain

"Writing is not necessarily something to be ashamed of, but do it in private and wash your hands afterwards."

—Robert A. Heinlein

"A writer is a person who cares what words mean, what they say, how they say it. Writers know words are their way towards truth and freedom, and so they use them with care, with thought, with fear, with delight. By using words well, they strengthen their souls."

—Ursula K. Le Guin

"The best time to plan a book is while you're doing the dishes."

—Agatha Christie

"Easy reading is damn hard writing."

—Nathaniel Hawthorne

"Writing is a solitary endeavor, but not a lonely one."

—Danielle Steel

"I have to write because if I don't get something down then after a while I feel it's going to bang the side of my head off."

—Terry Pratchett

"Either write something worth reading or do something worth writing."

—Benjamin Franklin

"As a writer, a failure is just information."

—Toni Morrison

"THE ROAD TO HELL IS PAVED WITH ADVERBS."

—Stephen King

"DON'T TELL ME THE MOON IS SHINING; SHOW ME THE GLINT OF LIGHT ON BROKEN GLASS."

—Anton Chekhov

RANDOM ORIGINS

Once again, the BRI asks–and answers–the question: where does all this stuff come from?

BINGO

Before above-board state-run lotteries were commonplace, games involving the matching of randomly drawn numbers called out by an authority figure to numbers printed on a card and assigned to a player were a popular attraction at traveling carnivals. In 1929, one such game, called Beano, was a hit at carnivals around the U.S. Players would pay a few cents to buy a card printed with a grid of numbers. Then a carnival worker would pull discs with numbers written on them out of a cigar box, and if players had that number on their cards, they'd mark it with a dried bean. The first player to complete a full line of five beans vertically, horizontally, or diagonally would yell out "beano!" and win a few bucks. Toy designer Edwin S. Lowe, of the E.S. Lowe Company, played some Beano at a carnival and tweaked the game slightly into something unique that he could patent and sell. In 1930, Lowe launched a board game version of the game that he called Bingo. The rules were the same, but players could mark their cards with whatever they wanted, not just beans, and had to call out "bingo!" to announce a completed line.

CHATEAUBRIAND

That word refers to a particular fancy steak house presentation of a beef roast and also to its preparation method and namesake. After the coveted filet mignon and other precious cuts are removed from the tenderloin, butchers and cooks are left with a cut of beef that weighs about two pounds, stands about four inches thick, and is long, oblong, and greatly varied in thickness. That makes it tough to cook on its own–if the center finishes at medium rare, the sides have burnt to a crisp. In 1822, a man known only as Monsieur Montmireil, who served as the personal chef to French writer and aristocrat Vicomte de Chateaubriand, came up with a way to prepare the roast so that it all came out with the same level of doneness. Montmireil stuffed the cut with seasoned beef marrow, then wrapped the whole thing inside two low-grade beef cuts (which he discarded after cooking). The extra meat absorbed heat, protecting the exterior, while the stuffing provided moisture. The result: an evenly cooked *Chateaubriand,* named after his boss. Both then and now, the dish is served to parties of two or more at traditional steak houses, alongside roast potatoes and a veal-stock-and-tarragon sauce.

THE GATORADE SHOWER

In the closing moments of an important football game when the outcome has just been decided, or just after the game clock expires, the winning coach might find himself doused in a ritualistic, celebratory shower of Gatorade. Players will sneak up and dump the team's communal jug of sports drink over the top of the coach's head, ice and all. The very first soaking happened to Chicago Bears' coach Mike Ditka, courtesy of players Steve McMichael and Mike Singletary, after the team's 1984 win over Minnesota. But it's a very TV-friendly moment, made famous when the New York Giants embraced the act during the 1985 and 1986 seasons. In the 1985 season, the struggling team's coach, Bill Parcells, took out his frustrations on defensive tackle Jim Burt. After an unexpected decisive win over Washington, Burt got his revenge by dumping a Gatorade cooler onto Parcells. The next season, Giants linebacker Harry Carson picked up the Gatorade shower as a tradition and good luck charm. Every time the Giants won a game that year, up to and including the Super Bowl, Carson doused Parcells with Gatorade. It became a cultural touchstone, so much so that when the Giants were invited to the White House in early 1987, they dumped a Gatorade cooler (filled with popcorn) over President Ronald Reagan.

SPIKING A FOOTBALL

In 1965, NFL commissioner Pete Rozelle helped pass a rule banning giving game balls to spectators—being forced to replace the football multiple times per game was too expensive for the league at the time, in its pre–big money days. New York Giants wide receiver Homer Jones liked to celebrate significant scores by tossing the ball into the crowd after crossing the goal line, and he was about to do just that after he caught an 89-yard touchdown pass during a home game in 1965. Then he remembered Rozelle's ban on throwing the ball into the stands and, really not wanting to be fined or otherwise punished, Jones invented a new celebratory tactic: instead of tossing the ball into the stands, he threw it forcefully into the ground. The crowd cheered, and when he was later asked what he called the act that other players around the league quickly adopted, Jones called it a "spike."

LOL

The use of slang and abbreviations to form a unique shorthand is a big part of communicating online, in the social media networks and phone-texting conversations of the 21st century, and in the computer networks, chat rooms, and online bulletin boards of the 1980s from which the Internet would eventually take shape. Sometime

In 2023, Seiji Suwa of Japan threw a peanut 156.7 feet, setting a world record.

in the early 1980s, a Calgary, Alberta, teenager and computer hobbyist named Wayne Pearson was talking to friends in a chat room on a text-only service called Bulletin Board System. One of Pearson's friends landed a joke, and it made Pearson laugh out loud, though he was alone at his computer monitor. "It wasn't just enough to type 'hahaha' into the chat to let him know I thought that was funny," Pearson later told reporters. "So, I basically instead of trying to type out really quickly 'That made me laugh out loud,' I just sort of typed 'LOL.'" Using that abbreviation to remotely inform others that they were "laughing out loud" caught on with users of Bulletin Board System, and when the Internet spread around the globe, LOL spread with it.

E-BOOKS

In the 2000s, hardback and paperback books were joined by the first major new way to publish and enjoy the written word in a century: electronic books, or e-books. Devices like Amazon's Kindle and Barnes & Noble's Nook could hold thousands of books, downloadable instantly and sold at a lower price point than print books, and readable in whatever type size was comfortable, on an innovative "e-paper" screen that didn't induce eyestrain. The commercial arrival of e-books came about 30 years after the technology to distribute books digitally was created. In 1971, the University of Illinois was one of the few American colleges with a powerful and sophisticated mainframe computer, and students could sign up to use it. Michael Hart used that computer to type in by hand the entire Declaration of Independence, then put it up on a network so other early home and institutional computer users could download it. Six people read the document that way, the first ever e-book created and distributed. Hart would later start Project Gutenberg, a service to archive and distribute historically important and public domain books via the Internet, free of charge; he typed in the first 100 books himself.

ALBUM COVERS

Recorded music went mainstream in the 1910s, with companies selling music on the 78-rpm format. Those records held about three minutes of music, and in the 1920s and 1930s, "albums" of multiple 78s were packaged and sold together. Whether sold individually or together, all those vinyl records were housed in plain white or brown sleeves or envelopes. Then in 1939, 23-year-old Alex Steinweiss took a job as Columbia Records' first art director. Seeking to differentiate itself from the competition with visual advertising, Columbia wanted Steinweiss to produce magazine ads and promotional displays for department stores' record departments. But Steinweiss came up with the

The winner of the World Monopoly Championship is awarded $20,580—the same amount of "Monopoly money" included in each board game.

idea for the most important graphical element the record industry would ever get, and another form of product touting. He hired a photographer and ventured to the Imperial Theatre in New York City; there, he asked the management to temporarily remove whatever was on the marquee and replace it with the name of an album Columbia wanted him to promote: "Smash Song Hits by Rodgers & Hart." The photographer took a picture of the marquee, and that image became the basis for the first album cover (of *Smash Song Hits by Rodgers and Hart*). Instantly, the cover became a physical manifestation of the music inside the sleeve, as well as a powerful promotional tool.

CIGARETTES

Tobacco is native to the Americas, and it famously provides a stimulant effect when it is burned and its smoke inhaled. The Aztecs, and other Indigenous groups in what's now Mexico and Central America, consumed tobacco by rolling crushed leaves inside discarded maize husks. That evolved into the cigar (shredded tobacco wrapped in whole tobacco leaves), which Spanish colonists and conquistadors brought back to Europe, where they became a luxury product. In the Spanish city of Seville, cigar smokers would drop their butts onto the streets, where beggars and street vendors would collect them and roll whatever tobacco remained from them inside scraps of paper. They smoked these themselves or sold them, calling them *cigarillos*, Spanish for "little cigars." By the 18th century, these cheaper cigar alternatives were being professionally manufactured from imported tobacco elsewhere in Spain, as well as in Portugal, Italy, England, and France, where they acquired the name *cigarette*, French for "little cigars."

* * *

DELAWARE ISN'T BORING!

- Because of a lack of business taxes, there are more companies officially incorporated in Delaware than there are people who live in Delaware.
- Jamaican reggae icon Bob Marley lived in Delaware for a few years in the 1960s and worked at a Chrysler plant.
- The first female serial killer in American history, Patty Cannon, lived (and killed) in Delaware.
- A small unattached portion of Delaware sits inside of New Jersey.
- According to comics lore, Superman's city of Metropolis is in Delaware.
- The first iteration of the American flag was flown for the first time in the Battle of Cooch's Bridge in 1777, the only Revolutionary War battle in Delaware.

A premature baby will sleep for up to 22 hours a day.

WHEN WORLDS COLLIDE

Humans and animals, occupying the same space at the same time—with memorable results.

Seal of Disapproval

In 2018, a group of friends were kayaking off the coast of New Zealand's South Island when a fur seal popped its head out of the water and smacked Kyle Mulinder in the face...with an octopus. The culprit could instead have been a sea lion, not a seal; the experts whom NPR contacted for their report disagreed. The takeaway, however, is that the marine mammal smacked the human with a cephalopod. "Whoa!" shouted Mulinder as he tried to figure out what just happened. Then he looked down and saw the dead octopus floating next to his kayak. He shooed it away with his paddle. "I'm not sure who got more of a surprise: the seal, the octopus, or me," he wrote on social media along with a video of the slap, which went viral.

What's going on here? "The idea of a sea lion hitting a person aggressively with an object," said animal behaviorist Peter Cook of the New College of Florida, "I've never heard of that happening. I'd be very surprised." More likely, the kayakers had unknowingly wandered into the sea lion/fur seal's feeding area. And both of those species are known to play with their food—or, at least, to smack it against the water to break it up. It would seem that Mulinder's face was simply in the wrong place at the wrong time.

Eye of the Bee Holder

In 2019, a Taiwanese woman, identified in press reports as He, visited a family member's grave when she unwittingly picked up a few miniscule hitchhikers: not long after, her left eye started hurting and swelling up. "It was very painful. Tears wouldn't stop coming out of my eye. I was scared to death." She ended up at Fooyin University Hospital, under the care of the head of ophthalmology, Dr. Hung Chi-ting. "I saw something that looked like insect legs," he said at a news conference, "so I pulled them out...one at a time without damaging things inside." By the time Dr. Hung was finished, he'd removed four tiny "sweat bees" from beneath He's eyelid. And it's a good thing he got to them before they got any bigger. Otherwise, her eyeball might have needed removal.

In case you're wondering, tiny sweat bees (Halictidae) can be found on every continent except Antarctica. And, as their name implies, they're attracted to perspiration because of the salt in it. "They nest near graves and in fallen trees," said Dr. Hung, "so it's easy to come across them while hiking in the mountains."

After *The Queen's Gambit* premiered on Netflix in 2020, sales of chess sets rose by 87 percent in the U.S.

What Stings in Vegas

The Venetian Resort is among the most luxurious hotel-casinos in Las Vegas, a city that lies within a vast desert where scorpions roam. Michael Farchi, a 61-year-old contractor from Agoura Hills, California, learned all about Nevada's scorpions during a Venetian vacation in December 2023. At around 8:00 a.m., he was jolted out of his sleep by searing pain in his groin. He darted to the bathroom and discovered an orange scorpion clinging to his underwear. "It felt like a sharp glass or a knife… stabbing me in my private area." According to *The Daily Beast*, a "traumatized" Farchi still had symptoms two months later and is "lawyering up."

Big Birds

"I let the dogs out of the cage. Next minute, turn around. There's an emu." And it wasn't alone. Ruby Buchanan of Broken Hill, New South Wales, and a friend were walking her kelpies (Holla and Smiley) on a "bush track"—what the Aussies call a trail in the outback. The only reason they were on that particular trail was because a friend had recommended it. But that friend neglected to warn them about the emus that reside there, and that it was their nesting season, which makes them extra aggressive… especially toward dogs.

All of a sudden, nearly a dozen of the six-foot-tall flightless beasts had Buchanan, her friend, and her dogs surrounded. The birds charged. The two women ran back to their ute (a small SUV), while Holla and Smiley ran off into the brush. Buchanan was having trouble finding her keys, so the women ran around the ute a few times, until Buchanan's friend managed to climb up on top of another nearby car, just out of the angry birds' reach, while Buchanan herself evaded the birds by playing "hide and seek" with them on the ground. Then the emus went after the dogs, which gave Buchanan enough time to find her keys. All four of them made it into the safety of the ute without a moment to spare. Good thing, too: "An emu can pursue a dog and kick it and potentially kill it," warned National Parks Western Area manager Jaymie Norris. "It was so terrifying," said Buchanan, "because I was looking at the dogs hoping that they weren't going to get attacked, but it was also very funny."

Saving Rocket

One night in 2024, three Burton, Michigan, friends enjoying their weekly cookout were visited by a raccoon. "He was very reluctant and skittish at first," John Ptaszenski told *USA Today*, "but when he realized we weren't a threat, he got closer to us and eventually let us even pet him." They named the animal Rocket, and it wandered off back into the shadows. About 20 minutes later, Rocket returned, making a "weird

Italian explorer Christopher Columbus was a year older than Italian painter Leonardo da Vinci.

gesture," waving its little hands and making "odd noises." That's when the men realized the raccoon was choking. "We all thought it was gonna die," Bill Messenger told CBS News, but they weren't going to let that happen. "[Rocket] was one of us at that point."

Messenger darted over and started smacking the raccoon on the back. "A little lower," said the other friend, Tyler Walen, while Ptaszenski's son recorded it all on his phone. Finally, after a few more smacks on Rocket's back, something launched out of the animal's mouth. Crisis averted. That something: a slice of American cheese, still in the plastic. "If we didn't catch that on camera," said Ptaszenski, "no one would have ever believed it."

Sorry, Not Sorry

Imagine you're on a boat, or a small yacht, blissfully floating on the open ocean, when, *SLAM!* Your vessel lurches sideways and you're almost knocked off your feet. "What was that?" *SLAM!* Now you do fall down. As the slams continue, you radio for help: "The orcas are here!" As of 2024, this nightmare scenario has happened at least five times in four years—mostly in the Strait of Gibraltar, which separates Europe and Africa. In all, more than 500 sailboats, fishing boats, rigid inflatables, and motorboats have reported incidents there. On October 31, 2023, the yacht *Grazie Mamma*, owned by a Polish cruise company, was sailing past Portugal when an "unknown number" of orcas spent 45 minutes "causing major damage and leakage" until the vessel sank. On May 12, 2024, a pod of orcas sank a 49-foot yacht with a couple on board.

So far, no one has been seriously injured, as the "killer whales" (actually the largest members of the dolphin family) seem most interested in the boats themselves. The animals even carry parts of the boats away. The spree began in 2021 with a pregnant female known as White Gladis, whom press reports said "may have been traumatized by a past boat collision." Once she started slamming boats in the Strait of Gibraltar, the behavior spread—via teaching—to other pods.

Marine biologists are flummoxed. Could this just be a "fad" among these highly intelligent apex predators—especially the juveniles, who are obsessed with the vessels' rudders? (Another documented orca fad: carrying dead salmon on their heads.) Are they playing? Or is there some darker reason? "I definitely think," said Monika Wieland Shields, director of the Orca Behavior Institute, "orcas are capable of complex emotions like revenge." But in an open letter to frightened seafarers, some of whom have resorted to throwing firecrackers at the orcas, 30 scientists wrote that the behavior is "more likely related to play/socializing than aggression" and urged "the media and the public to avoid projecting narratives on to these animals." As of this writing, there hasn't been one documented incident of a wild orca killing a human.

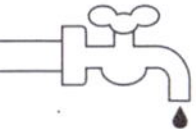

PLEASE SLOW DRIVELY

That title is a real sign posted outside of a California preschool—and it's intentionally incorrect, to get drivers to slow down. We don't know what excuse these other signs and labels have.

At a market:
Please Satanise Your Hands Here

At a bus stop:
Failure to be at the bus stop at the scheduled time will result in missing the bus

On a nutrition website:
Download advice on feeding newborns to teens

On a jar of honey:
Help save bees by the mouthful

At a grocery store:
Shelf-checkout Lanes

On a package of meat:
BONELESS STUFFED BUTT WHOLE

On a package of cold cuts:
WILD SMOKED CANADIAN

On a restaurant menu:
Seizure Salad

Outside of a restaurant:
DO NOT SECURE BIKES TO FECES

In a hotel lobby:
FREE WIFE

In a laundromat:
Washing machine is not sorry for inconvenience

A sign in a parking lot:
DO NOT READ UNDER PENALTY OF LAW

A neighborhood road sign:
DO NOT EXCEDE 20 CHILDREN

Below a traffic sign with a right arrow:
KEEP LEFT

An electric freeway sign:
LIZZARD WARNING

On a carton of eggs:
This product may contain eggs.

In an instruction manual for an iron:
Do not iron clothes on body.

Welcome sign at the Texas State Fair:
HOWDY FOLKS! We're glad your here!

At a grocery store:
Please remember you're shopping bags

On the label of a letter opener:
Safety goggles recommended

On a package of meat:
Assorted Scrotums: Buy 4 get the 5th FREE

At a rec center:
NO SWIMMING IF YOU CAN'T SWIM

At a resort:
The swimming pool is temporarily closed due to the David-19 situation.

In a public restroom:
PLEASE PAY YOUR PARKING FEE BEFORE EXISTING

Most valuable LEGO Minifigure: the "San Diego Comic-Con 2013 Exclusive Spider-Man" with red lower legs. He's worth around $5,500.

AMAZING COINCIDENCES

Mystery writer Agatha Christie once wrote, "Any coincidence...is always worth noticing. You can throw it away later if it is only a coincidence." Or you could put it in a Bathroom Reader.

MEET CUTE

His name was Randy Lee Cooper, and one night in July 2020, Cooper, 27, stole a Toyota Land Cruiser and led police on a chase through Newberg, Oregon. Her name was Kristin Nicole Begue, and the 25-year-old was driving through Newberg that same night in a stolen Buick Regal. Begue had just driven through an intersection when she collided with Cooper in his stolen car. If you're keeping count, that's two grand theft auto cases solved with one accident. And judging by the suspects' mug shots—printed side-by-side in news reports—Cooper and Begue look like they'd make a cute couple. (No word if they ever got together.)

FUNERAL FOR TWO

A 67-year-old Brazilian woman named Marciana Silva Barcelos was riding in the hearse carrying her husband's casket on the way to the man's funeral when the driver made an abrupt stop. The hearse was hit from behind by another vehicle. The impact jolted the husband's coffin forward; it slammed into Barcelos and killed her.

WAY TOO SOON

The Oakland, California, hip-hop band The Coup stirred up controversy in September 2001 when their fourth album, *Party Music*, was scheduled for release. The record label had to delay it at the last minute due to the cover image: members Boots Riley and Pam the Funkstress are holding a detonator; rising behind them are the Twin Towers in New York City on a sunny day. And the top portions of both buildings are exploding. (The image was intended to represent "music destroying capitalism.") The cover was slated to start printing on September 11, the same sunny day on which terrorists blew up the Twin Towers. Despite Riley's insistence on keeping the cover, the album was delayed until November and released with a different image. "This was done long ago," explained a label spokesperson about the cover, "and never meant to be any literal interpretation of an event."

ONE TO NOTHING

Brooks "the Human Vacuum Cleaner" Robinson, a Baltimore Orioles baseball legend, is widely regarded as the best defensive third baseman of all time, but this

In 2020, Al Blaschke became the oldest skydiver at 103. In 2021, 104-year-old Dorothy Hoffner broke his record. In 2024, at 106, Blaschke reclaimed it.

coincidence stems from his obscure offensive record. Robinson, who played from 1955 to 1977, had the odd distinction of batting in the only run when his team won 1–0. He did that a whopping 10 times, which was still a Major League record when Robinson died on September 26, 2023. That night, the Orioles beat the Washington Nationals by a score of (you guessed it) 1–0.

THE SMARTEST DAY

Every math nerd knows that March 14, also styled 3/14, is "Pi Day" (because 3.14 is the beginning of pi, a famous irrational number representing the ratio of a circle's circumference to its diameter). Coincidentally, on Pi Day in 2018, the famed British physicist Stephen Hawking died. March 14 also happens to be the birthday of Albert Einstein, born on Pi Day in 1879.

Bonus Coincidence: Hawking was born on January 8, 1942, exactly three centuries to the day after the death of famed Italian astronomer and mathemetician Galileo Galilei.

WHATWASTHATAGAIN?

Speaking of Galileo, in 1610, the Italian astronomer pointed his state-of-the-art (at the time) telescope at Saturn, but didn't know what to make of the blurry, yellowish blob around it. His first thought: "It has ears." Galileo sent the news to some contemporaries in a coded letter:

SMAISMRMILMEPOETALEUMIBUNENUGTTAUIRAS

Galileo had intended for the unscrambled anagram to read "*Altissimum planetam tergeminum observavi*," which means "I have observed that the highest planet is threefold." But that's not what German astronomer Johannes Kepler took from it. When he unscrambled the letters, he came up with "*salve, umbistineum geminatum Martia proles*," which means "Be greeted, double-knob, children of Mars." Kepler assumed that Galileo had discovered two moons orbiting Mars, when Galileo had actually discovered Saturn's rings. So what's the coincidence? Mars does have two moons, but they wouldn't be discovered for another two and a half centuries.

A LIFE CUT SHORT

Back when there were things called newspapers, the thin columns of left-aligned type caused a lot of words to get hyphenated—which led to this odd coincidence. A 1945 edition of the *Guardian* included the obituary of a British fighter pilot named Sir Douglas Bader, who'd lost both legs in World War II; the article described him as "a leg-end in his own lifetime."

Before switching to acting, Samuel L. Jackson was studying to become a marine biologist.

FITTING TRIBUTE

After Silver Screen legend Marlene Dietrich died in her Paris, France, apartment on May 6, 1992, following a career of nearly 70 years, her photos were plastered all over the nearby city of Cannes—for an unrelated reason. Months earlier, the Cannes Film Festival organizers had chosen a classic photograph of Dietrich to grace the posters of that year's festival...without any way of knowing she'd die *during* the festival.

CASTAWAYS

The Federated States of Micronesia comprises more than 600 islands that are spread over 1.5 million square miles of the Pacific Ocean. One of the most remote of those islands is Pikelot, a 31-acre dot in the sea, covered with palm trees and a white sand beach. In August 2020, three fishermen got stranded on Pikelot after their 23-foot-long boat ran out of fuel. After three days of surviving on coconuts and water from a shallow well that had been dug long ago, they were rescued after a U.S. Air Force tanker pilot out of Guam spotted them—thanks to the huge "SOS" sign the castaways had made on the beach using palm fronds.

Four years later, three brothers on a 20-foot skiff got shipwrecked on that very same island after swells pushed them off course and their motor stopped working. The brothers also made a message in the sand—this one said "HELP." After a week, the pilot of a U.S. Navy reconnaissance jet spotted the message, and the brothers were saved.

Bonus Coincidence: One of the U.S. Coast Guard rescuers, Petty Officer 2nd Class Eugene Halishlius, was Micronesian. "I could see on their faces, 'Whoa! Who's this guy pulling up that can speak our language?'" Only later did Halishlius and the three castaways find out that they are third cousins. "It's a crazy world," Halishlius said.

END OF THE ROAD

One of the biggest U.S. news events of the 1990s was the "low speed chase" in which double-homicide suspect—and football and Hollywood legend—O. J. Simpson led police down a Los Angeles freeway while riding in a white Ford Bronco, a vehicle that became indelibly linked to the events of that day. It's fitting, then, that on the day of Simpson's death in 2024, General Motors announced a major recall (due to cracked fuel injectors) of 22,270 Ford Broncos.

* * *

ACTUAL NEWSPAPER CORRECTION

In a recipe for salsa published recently, one of the ingredients was misstated, due to an error. The correct ingredient is "2 tsp. of cilantro" instead of "2 tsp. of cement."

THE REAL AND FAKE WORKS OF NORVAL MORRISSEAU, PART II

Here's the conclusion of the saga of one of Canada's most acclaimed artists, and how imitations of his works led to the largest art fraud the world has ever seen. *(Part I is on page 93.)*

WHEN DRUGS FAIL, TRY ART

While the high-end art galleries and art dealers who bought likely fraudulent Morrisseaus were upset enough to sue in order to stifle the news and thus protect their (sketchy-in-retrospect) investments, private art collectors who'd spent a fortune on what they realized to be unequivocally phony Morrisseau paintings were also angry over their own unwitting investments in deception.

One of those victims was John McDermott, Canada's most renowned operatic tenor. He'd purchased a Morrisseau painting from a gallery years before, and in the wake of the exposure of the fraud, he conducted his own research about the origins of his artwork. In doing so, he realized that the chain of command came to a halt with Thunder Bay, Ontario, thugs Gary Lamont and David Voss. They'd moved into art trading after building up criminal records largely related to Thunder Bay's illegal drug trade.

AND NOW, A BARENAKED LADY

McDermott reported all of his findings to authorities, along with a potential smoking gun: Voss had been the supplier of Morrisseau paintings to the same gallery that Morrisseu first accused of fraud back in 2001. Another upset buyer looking to investigate Morrisseau's claims and expose the people responsible was, oddly enough, another well-known Canadian musician. The suburban Toronto–based pop-rock band Barenaked Ladies sold millions of records in the 1990s and 2000s and had a string of hits, including the #1 "One Week." Kevin Hearn plays keyboards and guitar for the band, and its success enabled the musician to follow his passion of art collecting, particularly art made by Indigenous Canadians.

In 2005, Hearn paid $20,000 (Canadian) to acquire Morrisseau's *Spirit Energy of Mother Earth* from the questionable Toronto gallery that Morrisseau had warned in 2003 was in possession of a slew of fakes. Even before he could ask, gallery officials told Hearn not to worry about the news going around of all those phony Morrisseaus, to which their institution had been connected—this painting was the real deal, they assured the musician. Confident that he had an authentic piece, Hearn lent the

What do California, Pennsylvania, Tennessee, and West Virginia have in common? They all have a city called Peanut.

canvas to the Art Gallery of Ontario for an Indigenous artists show in 2010. After a few days, the gallery took *Spirt Energy of Mother Earth* down, believing it to be a fake. Upset over being cheated as well as over the ongoing exploitation of Morrisseau, Hearn sued the gallery that sold him his painting.

SEARCH PARTY

Meanwhile, and unhappy with the investigation (or lack thereof) by official government channels, Hearn took it upon himself to use his wealth to assemble a team of private investigators to expose the Morrisseau fraud ring. With a team of lawyers in tow, Hearn and his team interviewed more than 200 people in and around Thunder Bay, along with known associates of Voss and Lamont, collectors who had purchased paintings purportedly created by Morrisseau, and the artist's surviving relatives.

Conversation after conversation revealed the same story. Lamont and Voss claimed to be legitimate dealers of legitimate works, and also claimed they had a personal connection to Morrisseau, who approved their business; Lamont said that Morrisseau was a friend of his family. None of that was true, of course, but Hearn and his team discovered that Lamont ran a home for Indigenous youth, which he used as a fake factory. By force or by threat of violence, dozens of Indigenous children were made to make Morrisseau-style paintings. Lamont and Voss then put the paintings up for sale on eBay or sold them to auctioneers and art dealers who didn't ask any questions about their authenticity. At least 400 bogus works were produced in that manner, according to Hearn's investigation.

SEE YOU IN COURT

Much of this information was divulged during the legal proceedings over Hearn's lawsuit against the Toronto gallery. Countering expert testimony declaring *Spirit Energy of Mother Earth* to be fake, the defense called in a handwriting expert, who said that Morrisseau's signature on the reverse of the canvas seemed authentic, casting doubt on Hearn's claims. In Canadian law, the burden of proof falls on the plaintiff to prove the art is fake, and Hearn couldn't do that. The judge ruled that although Hearn failed to prove that his painting was a fake, he believed that a fraud ring generating who knows how many fakes did exist. Legally, that was a tie, and the decision went to the defendants.

Smarting from the loss (he'd later appeal and win $41,000) and undeterred from uncovering the truth and bringing Lamont and Voss to justice, Hearn teamed up with filmmaker Jamie Kastner to make a documentary called *There Are No Fakes*. A recounting of the Morrisseau fakes saga up to that point, the 2019 film received little attention, but a Thunder Bay homicide detective named Jason Rybak sought it out on the advice of the mother of a murder victim.

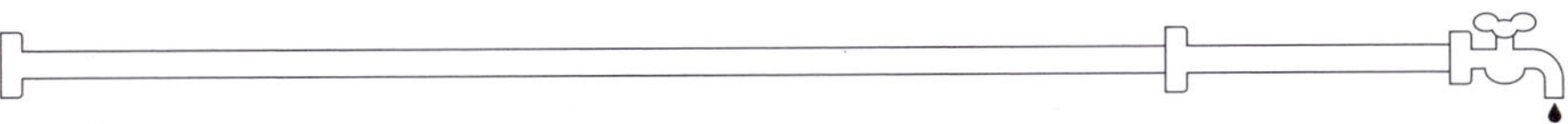

Lauryn Hill has won eight Grammy Awards, the most of any female rapper.

FROM MURDER TO DEATH

The slain body of Thunder Bay teenager Scott Dove had been discovered in December 1984. The prime suspect at the time: future underworld drug dealer and possible counterfeit art ring mastermind Gary Lamont. He was never charged due to a lack of conclusive evidence. The case had haunted Rybak, and he remained in touch with Dove's mother. She caught *There Are No Fakes* and told Rybak about it because it spoke at length about Lamont's involvement in the Morrisseau matter. Via the Thunder Bay Police Department, Rybak opened an investigation into the art business because he hoped it might lead to new evidence in the cold case of Scott Dove.

While Rybak didn't get any new answers about the murder, or a conviction, he wound up deeply invested in the fraud investigation. He brought in the American FBI's Art Crime Team to teach local police officers sophisticated techniques for identifying fraudulent art. A lot of old-fashioned police work was involved too, and, along with focusing on the whereabouts and activities of Lamont and Voss, Rybak built his case mainly by proving that it was more or less impossible for Morrisseau to have legitimately made as much art as all those galleries, auction houses, and collectors claimed that he had: the vast majority of the contested pieces were purportedly painted in the 1970s and 1980s, a time when Morrisseau wasn't painting much—and when he was, he was trying out other styles. A few additional suspect pieces carried a signature and a copyright date from 2008 and later—especially odd, considering Morrisseau died in 2007.

RING, RING

Rybak and the FBI determined what no other previous investigation had uncovered. The Morrisseau ring had been operational for more than 20 years and largely gotten away with it. In 1996, Rybak found, Voss started a small-scale forgery ring. With a knack for imitation—and finding Morrisseau's simple, colorful style easy to re-create for non-discerning buyers who just wanted to buy *something* by the artist to brag that they could—Voss made the fake paintings himself, by himself. He sold so many that within a few years, he'd set up teams of forgers in Ontario and Alberta, whom he instructed in the ways of making Morrisseau-esque paintings.

By 2002, Lamont stole the idea from his old friend and crime-world crony and started a forgery ring that also specialized in imitating Morrisseau. The market for the artist's work was so substantial that it could sustain, and even lavishly support, two groups churning out a regular supply of paintings. Lamont's sweatshop-like art factory was headed up by Benji Morrisseau—nephew of the artist everyone was paid to forge. There was even a third group associated with the fix, led by Jeffrey Cowan, whose job it was to come up with fake origin stories and falsified chains of ownership for all the bogus paintings generated by the Voss and Lamont crews.

The only Southeast Asian country never to have been colonized by a European nation: Thailand.

A REALLY BIG FRAUD

By Rybak's estimates, a volume of phony Morrisseaus somewhere in the tens of thousands flooded the art-trading world. Auction houses, galleries, and dealers all made substantial profits on the paintings that were easily identifiable fakes, seemingly without really caring about passing on fraudulent merchandise. The fake Morrisseau industry was altogether worth about $100 million—of which the artist and his estate got nothing.

It's impossible to track down or even count all the fake paintings, but Rybak went looking. He served warrants on homes registered to Lamont and Voss in Thunder Bay and found hundreds of pieces that hadn't been sold yet. Then he found 300 more being stored at a private home in Calgary. All three homes had indications that they weren't just storage facilities for the art, but the places where the forgeries occurred. Following the money, and cross-referencing with collectors and institutions that touted their ownership of a Morrisseau, Rybak found even more phony pieces. Of note, the painting hanging in the Canadian Senate building was fake, and so was one in the collection of the Smithsonian in Washington, D.C.

NO ART IN PRISON

A two-and-a-half-year investigation involved the work of 100 law-enforcement officials, including 270 interviews, and that led to everything Rybak needed to make arrests and press charges. In March 2023, eight people connected to the forgery rings were arrested, including Lamont, Voss, and Cowan. They were charged on a total of 40 counts of forgery, fraud, and possession of stolen property with the intent to sell. While somewhere in the neighborhood of 1,000 pieces of phony art were seized and linked to Lamont and Voss, that number represents only a fraction of what was produced and sold. Officials estimate that there are between 3,000 and 10,000 fake Morrisseaus in circulation. Still, even with the amount authorities located, it's the biggest art fraud by volume ever uncovered.

Lamont received a prison sentence of five years. At press time, Voss and Cowan were awaiting their sentencing hearings.

* * *

WHY ARE PIZZA AND ICE CREAM PLACES THE ONLY RESTAURANTS CALLED "PARLORS"?

In 1888, a lunch spot in San Francisco billed itself as "quiet" and "home-like," starting a trend of restaurants adopting décor that evoked the feeling of a private home. At the time, a home's main room for hosting guests was called a parlor, so restaurants with that homey feel called themselves "parlors." A major ice cream craze developed in the 1890s, and operators utilized the "parlor" name and it stuck; the same was true for the pizza places that opened in large numbers in the 1950s.

Highest point in South America: Aconcagua Mountain (22,837 ft.). The lowest: Laguna del Carbón (344 ft. below sea level). Both are in Argentina.

COINED ON SCREEN, PART I

Sometimes, a screenwriter knows the perfect word to use in a certain scene. Other times, the perfect word needs to be invented. Here are some of our favorite terms popularized by or created for well-known films and TV shows.

SPAM

The canned meat (most likely short for "SPiced hAM") had been around for 40 years by the time the absurdist British comedy troupe Monty Python had fun with the name in a 1970 *Flying Circus* sketch about a restaurant that includes Spam in every dish, while Vikings in the corner sing, "Spam, Spam, Spam, Spam, Spam, Spam, Spam, Spam, lovely Spam! Wonderful spam!" It turned out that Usenet posters in the early 1990s loved quoting Monty Python, so it makes sense that one of those posters (whose name is lost to history) referred to an unsolicited mass email, or "something that keeps repeating to mass annoyance," as *spam*.

NIMROD

Bugs Bunny really took this word down a few notches. Nimrod of the Bible was a "mighty hunter before the Lord" and the great-grandson of Noah. But in a 1932 *Looney Tunes* cartoon, Bugs refers to hapless "wabbit hunter" Elmer Fudd as "such a nimrod!" Now it means "idiot."

GODFATHER

Mario Puzo's 1969 novel and its 1972 movie adaptation taught the viewing public that the head of a mafia organization is called the *godfather*. According to Puzo, "The term didn't exist before I used it." It did, in fact, since at least 1963 when it was recorded in a government hearing. But until Francis Ford Coppola's masterpiece of filmmaking came out, most people thought of a godfather as only a man who sponsors a child at baptism or pledges to take over for absent parents.

DEAL-BREAKER

Just like the proverbial "red flag," a *deal-breaker*, in dating terms, is when you ponder parting with a potential partner over a problematic personality peculiarity (like if they unnecessarily use alliteration). The phrase originated in the late 1970s and wasn't heard much outside of business or political circles until Liz Lemon made it go mainstream on the sitcom *30 Rock* (2006–16): "If your boyfriend is over thirty and wears a name tag to work, that's a deal-breaker."

Ultimate Frisbee is officially known as Ultimate because *Frisbee* is trademarked.

REGIFT

Hello...*Newman*! *Seinfeld* gave us this useful word that means to pass along a gift you don't like to someone else (which will inevitably lead to laughs). The 1990s sitcom also gave us the terms "close talker," "low talker," "double dip," "sponge-worthy," "shrinkage," and "yada yada yada."

FRIEND ZONE

Poor Ross. In the 1994 *Friends* episode "The One with the Blackout," even Joey could tell that his unlucky-in-love friend didn't ask out Rachel in time, and now it's too late, because Ross has become "the mayor of the friend zone." If you've ever developed romantic feelings for a friend who just wanted to stay friends, then you were the mayor of your own friend zone.

CATFISH

Nev Schulman's 2010 documentary, *Catfish*, about a woman who makes a false online profile just to harass someone, got its name from this story, shared by the woman's husband:

> They used to tank cod from Alaska all the way to China. They'd keep them in vats in the ship. By the time the codfish reached China, the flesh was mush and tasteless. So this guy came up with the idea that if you put these cods in these big vats, put some catfish in with them and the catfish will keep the cod agile. And there are those people who are catfish in life. And they keep you on your toes. They keep you guessing, they keep you thinking, they keep you fresh. And I thank God for the catfish because we would be droll, boring, and dull if we didn't have somebody nipping at our fin.

Schulman turned his documentary into the hit MTV show *Catfish*, and in 2014, the new definition of the word was added to the online version of the *Oxford English Dictionary*, much to the chagrin of word purists. Oxford editor Katherine Martin assuaged their fears: "These are words that are common enough that you are likely to encounter them, and may have to look up their meanings. Many may not make it into the more traditional *Oxford English Dictionary*. For some of these, we will say, 'What was that?' in a decade; others may become the next *selfie*. The English-speaking public will choose." (It's been a decade since that article was written, and we're still saying *catfish* to refer to something other than seafood.)

Turn to page 332 for more words and phrases we learned from TV and movies.

BEHIND THE OLD HITS

It feels like some songs have just been around forever—like these. Here are the stories behind the creation of some of the tunes that have become part of the fabric of the world.

"OH, MY DARLING CLEMENTINE"

When Spanish conquistadors explored and colonized southwestern portions of North America, they brought with them the melody of an old Spanish folk song used with many different lyric sets. That song made its way into the Indigenous cultures of the area in the form of the 1800s tragic love ballad "Romance del Conde Olinos o Niño." Mexican participants in the California Gold Rush of the 1840s and 1850s often sang it during their workday, and English-speaking workers got the melody from them. In 1863, songwriter H. S. Thompson lifted the melody and added new lyrics to create "Down by the River Liv'd a Maiden," a tongue-in-cheek, faux-tragic love song about a dead romantic partner. By the end of the 19th century, that tune had given way to a Western-tinged ditty about another interesting but doomed woman, credited alternately to Barker Bradford or Percy Montrose and performed on the early vaudeville circuit: "Oh, My Darling Clementine."

"HERE WE GO ROUND THE MULBERRY BUSH"

Today, His Majesty's Prison Wakefield is a high-security prison housing some of the U.K.'s most egregious criminal offenders, but it opened in 1594 and at one point housed female prisoners. Sometime in the 1800s, a cutting from a mulberry tree was taken from a nearby golf course and left to grow at HMP Wakefield, which it quickly did. The tree became a centerpiece of the prison yard, and female inmates would do their daily guided evening exercises around the tree. That inspired the repetitive lyrics (including "here we go round the mulberry bush" and "this is the way we wash our face"). As inmates were released and resettled elsewhere, they took the song with them, and it was first published in 1840.

"SHE'LL BE COMIN' 'ROUND THE MOUNTAIN"

First appearing in print in Carl Sandburg's *The American Songbag* in 1927, it was sung to the same melody as the Black American slavery spiritual "When the Chariot Comes," and was reinvented as a work song by railroad builders in the Midwest in the 1890s. That first appeared in *Old Plantation Hymns* in 1899, and referred to the second coming of Christ and the world-ending events, with "she" being a supernatural chariot. Labor groups co-opted it for use as a song about Mother Jones, a labor rights rabble-rouser who would travel wherever she was needed. The railroad version evolved into a children's song.

"ENTRANCE OF THE GLADIATORS"

That's the actual name of the song we generally know as generic circus music, or the fanfare we associate with the entry into the big tent of all the animals, clowns, and performers. It was written in the late 1800s, just before the rise in popularity of the circus but in honor of a different and also bygone form of public entertainment: gladiator fights in ancient Rome. In 1897, Prague-born Austro-Hungarian army band member Julius Fucik was promoted to bandmaster. That same year, he wrote what would become the most famous of his more than 400 works, a mid-tempo march called "Grande Marche Chromatique." But Fucik was also in the midst of an interest in the Roman Empire, so he quickly renamed the song "Einzug der Gladiatoren," or "Entrance of the Gladiators," imagining that it could have been used for such a purpose centuries earlier. "Entrance of the Gladiators" was considered cutting-edge at the time, in terms of its use of chromatic scales and of bold sounds made by newly developed brass instruments. Fucik's version was kind of slow; the arrangement we're most familiar with today was put together in 1910 by Canadian composer Louis-Phillipe Laurendeau, who made it faster, set it in a brighter key, and adapted it for a smaller band—after which it started getting used by circuses in North America.

"MY OLD KENTUCKY HOME"

Before 1852, popular American songwriter Stephen Foster primarily wrote songs ("Oh! Susanna," "Camptown Races") for the lucrative minstrel-show market. Singers would wear blackface, adopt broad and offensive Black stereotypes, and deliver songs denigrating Black people. But then Foster read the antislavery novel *Uncle Tom's Cabin* by Harriet Beecher Stowe, inspired by the abolition movement, and he was a changed man. He wrote a sad ballad called "Poor Old Uncle Tom, Good-Night," but then decided to take out the book references to make for a more relatable song about the loss of one's childhood home, with subtle allusions to the horrors of slavery remaining. Because *Uncle Tom's Cabin* was set in Kentucky, the song became "My Old Kentucky Home, Good-Night!" Almost immediately, in an unfortunate ironic twist, Foster's song was presented and received as a wistful tune glorifying plantation life. Foster sold the song to sheet music publisher Firth & Pond, who marketed it to minstrel shows, which then popularized it as a blackface number. When the Civil War broke out, "My Old Kentucky Home, Good-Night!" gained popularity among soldiers injured and lonely on the battlefield, far from their homes. By the early 20th century, when it became a tradition for the crowd to sing the tune en masse before the running of the Kentucky Derby horse race, the last two words had been dropped. After a century of countless sing-alongs and band performances at sporting events around Kentucky, it became the state's official song in 1986.

The world's longest table—which fed 7,000 people in Cairo, Egypt, in 2019—was almost two miles long.

TERRRIBLE TYPOS

Typos are a dish best served clod.

MIND YOUR BISINESS

In 2014, a large-scale road project disrupted several businesses along Shepherd Drive in Houston, Texas, and their customers didn't realize they were open during construction. The storefronts *were* open, and they were losing sales. So the business owners collectively requested that the city put up signs that said "Business Access." A few days later, workers put up six blue road signs that said..."Bisiness Access." Despite angry calls from those "bisinesses," it took a news report from a local station to get the signs removed. City officials pledged to resolve the matter immediately and blamed the goof on an "outside contractor." "It is a big deal," complained a medical staffer at one of the affected businesses. "Our patients came in and said, 'What is *that*?' So, yeah, it was a big deal."

ADDING INSULT TO INJURY

After enduring the tragic loss her son and brother in separate incidents of gun violence in 2023, Somona Sharp of Wimauma, Florida, had to deal with a joint headstone riddled with typos—a headstone that had cost her $7,500. They got her son's birthdate wrong, and his picture was missing; they also misspelled her brother's name and added the wrong Bible verse. After getting nowhere with the headstone maker, Monalisa Monuments, Sharp contacted a local news station that dispatched a reporter to the company, where the owner explained that Sharp had signed off on the proof (which Sharp denies). "To come out here and have to see this," she said at the gravesite, pointing at the typos, "it just makes me angry."

IT'S OFFCIAL!

Imagine receiving a scholarship acceptance letter in the mail, but on the very first line—printed in large letters across the top—there's a glaring typo. In 2022, Florida State University's football program sent such a letter to 18-year-old defensive end Lamont Green Jr., and it began with "OFFCIAL OFFER." Oops. Green's father (a former FSU and NFL player) posted a photo of the typo online...and then quickly deleted it. But not before the sporting press could pile on: "This is a truly brutal look for Florida State," wrote BroBible. "This is something that would have happened during the Willie Taggert era, but the Mike Norvell era is supposed to be different and less embarrassing. This does not help to progress that narrative." In the end, the typo didn't keep Green from accepting the offer.

FLIGHTS OF FANCY

For about five hours on April 5, 2006, a first class ticket on an Alitalia Airlines flight from Toronto, Canada, to Lanarca, Cyprus—which would normally cost $3,900—was only $39. Apparently, an employee at the now-defunct Italian flagship carrier made a goof while updating the fares in the computer that morning. News of the ridiculously low fare was posted on a website called FlyerTalk, and by the time Alitalia corrected it, nearly 2,000 people had taken advantage of the "sale." At first, an airline official said the lower fares wouldn't be honored because they were caused by a "technical error." But after taking a drubbing online and in the press, all of the tickets were honored. The typo reportedly cost Alitalia $7.2 million.

CHISELED IN SOTNE

In July 2022, construction was nearing completion on Apex Friendship Elementary School in rural North Carolina when the school's large concrete sign was installed out front. A couple of hours later, the sign was hastily uninstalled. But it was too late: at least two people had already posted embarrassing photos on social media. The sign read "APEX FIRENDSHIP." Lisa Luten, communications director for Wake County Public School System, blamed the mistake on a subcontractor. "We're a school system," she insisted. "We take spelling seriously."

FAT FINGER ERROR IN YOUR FAVOR

In May 2022, Citigroup, the parent company of Citibank, was involved in one of the "biggest blunders in banking history." The culprit: a typo—or a "fat finger error." Citibank was supposed to wire $8 million in interest payments to lenders of cosmetic company Revlon, but instead accidentally wired the lenders $900 million. In most cases, funds received by mistake must be given back, but in New York, a legal exception lets you keep it if you are legally entitled to it and honestly thought it was sent on purpose. Though a few of the lenders did send the money back, many assumed it was early repayment of their loans. Citigroup sued to get it all back, but a judge sided with the lenders—even in light of a chat conversation between two employees at one of the lenders that had been admitted into evidence: "I feel really bad for the person that fat fingered a $900mm erroneous payment. Not a great career move," one wrote; the other replied, "How was work today honey? It was ok, except I accidentally sent $900mm out to people who weren't supposed to have it." Citibank ended up losing half a billion dollars.

SO SAYETTH THE LORD

This terrible typo appeared on the cover of an Ash Wednesday church bulletin that made the rounds on the internet in 2018. Beneath a graphic of an ashen cross is a paraphrasing of Genesis 3:19. *"Remember that you are butt dust and into dust you shall return."*

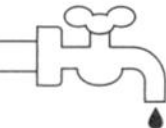

The fastest land vehicle—ThrustSCC, at 763 mph—is more than twice as fast as the fastest helicopter—the Eurocopter X3, at 293 mph.

MOUTHING OFF

MANLY WORDS

"Man up!" "Be a man!" "Act like a man!" What does it all mean, though? It's complicated.

"Waste no more time arguing what a good man should be. Be one."

—Marcus Aurelius

"Being a male is a matter of birth. Being a man is a matter of choice."

—Edwin Louis Cole

"MAN IS NEVER SO MANLY AS WHEN HE FEELS DEEPLY, ACTS BOLDLY, AND EXPRESSES HIMSELF WITH FRANKNESS AND WITH FERVOR."

—Benjamin Disraeli

"A man may conquer a million men in battle but one who conquers himself is, indeed, the greatest of conquerors."

—The Buddha

"The ultimate measure of a man is not where he stands in moments of comfort and convenience, but where he stands at times of challenge and controversy."

—Martin Luther King Jr.

"It takes more courage to reveal insecurities than to hide them, more strength to relate to people than to dominate them, more 'manhood' to abide by thought-out principles rather than blind reflex.

—Alex Karras

"The real man smiles in trouble, gathers strength from distress, and grows brave by reflection."

—Thomas Paine

"If boys don't learn, men won't know."

—Douglas Wilson

"Try not to become a man of success, but rather try to become a man of value."

—Albert Einstein

"THE TRUE MEASURE OF A MAN IS HOW HE TREATS SOMEONE WHO CAN DO HIM ABSOLUTELY NO GOOD."

—Samuel Johnson

A CARNIVAL OF CARNIVAL GAMES

Step right up, don't be shy, pay a dollar and win a prize! (The prize? These stories about the origins of those arcade and carnival midway games that entertain—and frustrate—us.)

Whac-A-Mole

Before video games took over arcades in the late 1970s, gaming halls in Japan were dominated by mechanical games, many of them made by the company TOGO. In 1974, TOGO engineer Kazuo Yamada created a game called *Mogura Taiji,* or "Mole Buster." Consisting of a box outfitted with a series of holes and some mechanical moles, the moles popped up through the holes at random, imploring the player to bop each one on the head with a soft mallet. The game proved phenomenally popular in Japan: it was the second-highest-grossing arcade title overall in 1976 and 1977, and sold well as a home toy, too. TOGO demonstrated Mole Buster at the trade show International Association of Amusement Parks and Attractions for North America in 1976, and carnival game dealers Gerald Denton and Donny Anderson took notice. Completely stealing the idea from TOGO, they thought the arcade game would work better in the U.S. as a carnival game. Denton and Anderson hired engineer Aaron Fechter—who created the animatronic robots behind ShowBiz Pizza and Chuck E. Cheese—to create a new attraction, to be housed in a trailer. Adding in compressed air to push up the moles, Fechter's game was called Whac-A-Mole and was licensed to carnival entertainment maker Bob's Space Racers, which instituted the game in fairs and midways in 1978. That company still makes the original Whac-A-Mole, and the game is its biggest moneymaker ever—the company headquarters sit on Whac-A-Mole Way in Holly Hill, Florida.

Pop-A-Shot

It took nearly a century after the invention of basketball—by Springfield College teacher and coach James Naismith in 1891—for someone to turn the game into a single-player sport, and it would be another college coach who did it. In 1981, longtime Marymount College basketball coach Ken Cochran was forced to retire at age 48 after a heart attack and a long recuperation. He desperately missed basketball, and, seeking ways to stay involved in the sport in a way that wouldn't stress his heart, Cochran attempted to invent a basketball version of baseball's pitch-back net, which could return the ball instantly to a practicing shooter. Inspired by a garbage can–style basketball hoop and mini foam ball, he created the Triple Shot, a series of three small rims and

backboards placed side by side atop a ramp. He hired a machinist and cabinetmaker to construct his prototype, which he installed at a Kansas sports camp as an arcade game. (Cost: $1.00 for 10 shots, and a free T-shirt for anyone who made at least seven shots.) The game was so popular that Cochran entertained offers to bring it to other camps and sports bars. But the Triple Shot was too unwieldy to move, so he made it a single-hoop contraption, changed the name to Mini Basketball, and changed the pricing mechanism to $1 for a minute of unlimited shooting. After adding in an electronic scoring component, he changed the name to Pop-A-Shot and started a company to manufacture them; the game soon populated bars, arcades, and carnival midways.

Dunk Tank

Today, it's popularly known as the "dunk tank." An individual sits on a little stool and antagonizes and insults passersby so that those passersby will pay to throw a series of balls against a target. If the ball hits the bull's-eye, it triggers a mechanism on the stool to release, sending the sitter plunging into a tank of cold water below in an act of satisfying humiliation. All of this is an evolution from an extremely racist (and dangerous) game played throughout carnivals and fairs beginning in the 1880s. The absolute origin is lost to history, but the game was colloquially known as African Dodger. There was no stool, target, or water tank used; instead, fair organizers paid a Black man to stand behind a backdrop that covered his whole body except for his head. Attendees would then pay a certain amount of money to throw objects—usually baseballs, raw eggs, or rocks—at the man's head. It wasn't unheard of for people to bring in their own objects to throw, nor was it uncommon for the subject of African Dodger to suffer injuries (some potentially life-threatening). By the 1910s, African Dodger fell out of favor for its brutality, and midway operators subbed in African Dip, a game involving suspending a Black man over a tank of water, with balls thrown at a target instead of his head. (That said, some African Dodger games could still be found into the 1950s.)

Skee-Ball

Joseph Fourestier Simpson was always trying to get rich, and he wanted to get a patent on something that would pay dividends forever. After coming up with improvements on an egg crate and the clasp of a trunk, he devised a miniature variation of bowling for use in arcades, fairs, and amusement parks: roll a wooden ball so it would get enough momentum to leap into an area with different cups assigned higher point values depending on their size (and difficulty). He called it Skee-Ball because the angled ramp reminded him of a ski jump course. Simpson got his patent in 1908 and the game became a huge hit in various sites along the Atlantic City boardwalk.

Property taxes have been around for at least 7,000 years.

NEPO BABY BOOM

There's been a lot of talk in the media the last couple of years about "nepo babies"—famous people who maybe enjoyed some extra advantages or a head start because they had successful parents in the business. Here are some little-known second-generation stars.

Celebrity: Actor Zoey Deutch
Lineage: Daughter of director Howard Deutch and actor Lea Thompson, who met while making *Some Kind of Wonderful.*

Celebrity: Actor Riley Keough
Lineage: Daughter of musicians Danny Keough and Lisa Marie Presley (the daughter of Elvis Presley).

Celebrity: Musician Norah Jones
Lineage: Daughter of sitar player Ravi Shankar, who recorded with the Beatles.

Celebrity: Actor Sigourney Weaver
Lineage: Her father, Sylvester "Pat" Weaver, was president of NBC and created *Today* and *The Tonight Show.*

Celebrity: DJ Steve Aoki and actor Devon Aoki
Lineage: Their father, Rocky Aoki, started restaurant chain Benihana.

Celebrity: Actor Paul Giamatti
Lineage: His father, A. Bartlett Giamatti, was president of Yale and commissioner of Major League Baseball.

Celebrity: Singer Adam Levine of the rock band Maroon 5
Lineage: His father, Fredric Levine, started the department store chain M. Fredric.

Celebrity: Dwayne "The Rock" Johnson
Lineage: The former wrestler's father and grandfather were also pro wrestlers.

Celebrity: Actor Lily Collins
Lineage: Her father is pop star and Genesis singer Phil Collins.

Celebrity: The Beastie Boys' Adam Horovitz, aka Ad-Rock
Lineage: His father was acclaimed playwright Israel Horovitz.

Celebrity: Actor John David Washington
Lineage: His father is Denzel Washington.

Celebrity: Actor O'Shea Jackson
Lineage: His breakthrough role came in *Straight Outta Compton* where he played his father, rapper-actor O'Shea Jackson Sr. (better known as Ice Cube).

Celebrity: Steven Spielberg
Lineage: His father, Arnold Spielberg, built one of the first mainframe computers and invented the computerized point-of-sale cash register.

Celebrity: Singer-songwriter Carly Simon
Lineage: Richard L. Simon, her father, is the "Simon" in book publisher Simon & Schuster.

Celebrity: Actor Margaret Qualley
Lineage: Her mother is actor Andie MacDowell.

Celebrity: Singer Whitney Houston
Lineage: Her mother was gospel star Cissy Houston; her cousin is singer Dionne Warwick.

Celebrity: Actor and comedian Hannah Einbinder
Lineage: Her mother, Larraine Newman, was an original cast member on *Saturday Night Live*.

Celebrity: Actor Daniel Day-Lewis
Lineage: His father, Cecil Day-Lewis, was the poet laureate of the United Kingdom from 1968 to 1972, and also wrote popular mystery novels under the name Nicholas Blake.

Celebrity: News anchor Anderson Cooper
Lineage: His mother, fashion designer Gloria Vanderbilt, started the designer jeans craze, and is a descendant of railroad tycoon Cornelius Vanderbilt.

Celebrity: Actor George Clooney
Lineage: His father is TV personality Nick Clooney, whose sister was actor and singer Rosemary Clooney.

Celebrity: Actor Tony Goldwyn
Lineage: The *Scandal* star's father was movie producer Samuel Goldwyn Jr., the son of movie studio founder Samuel Goldwyn (the G in MGM).

Celebrity: Actor and comic Maya Rudolph
Lineage: Her mother was 1970s soul singer Minnie Riperton, who sang the #1 hit "Lovin' You."

Celebrity: Actor Mariska Hargitay
Lineage: Her parents were bombshell actor Jayne Mansfield and boxer Mickey Hargitay.

Celebrity: Actor Rashida Jones
Lineage: Her mother was *The Mod Squad* actor Peggy Lipton and her father is music industry giant Quincy Jones.

Celebrity: Fashion designer Stella McCartney
Lineage: Her father is musician Paul McCartney.

Celebrity: Actor Maude Apatow
Lineage: She got her start at a young age in movies with her mother, actor Leslie Mann, made by her father, director and producer Judd Apatow.

Celebrity: Actor Alexander Skarsgård
Lineage: His father, Stellan Skarsgård, is one of Sweden's most respected actors.

Celebrity: Model Kaia Gerber
Lineage: Her mother is supermodel Cindy Crawford.

* * *

"When the going gets tough, the tough reinvent." —**RuPaul**

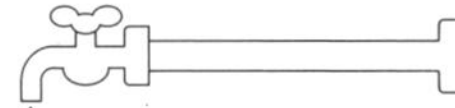

Only U.S. city without a consonant: Aiea, Hawaii.

METAPHORICALLY SPEAKING

Uncle John loves similes, metaphors, and analogies like a plumber loves a...whatever it is that plumbers really love. (Wow, coming up with one of these is harder than you'd think!)

Shall I Compare Thee...?

We use similes and metaphors all the time, but what exactly are they? A *simile* is a way to describe something by saying it is "like" or "as" something else, as in, "I feel like crap." Because *crap* is widely viewed as bad, people will understand that you feel bad. And bees are busy, so "busy as a bee" is another simile. Technically, a simile is a type of *metaphor*, which is basically the same thing, but without the "like" or "as"—for example, "She's an open book." An open book is easy to read, and so is she. These days, these comparisons even take the form of memes and gifs. Instead of commenting, "I don't want to participate in this discussion anymore," you post a gif of Homer Simpson slowly backing off into the hedges.

An *analogy* uses a metaphor to illustrate a larger point, as seen here in this Bible verse from Proverbs: "As cold waters to a thirsty soul, so is good news from a far country." Since time immemorial, writers have relied on these literary devices to add depth and texture to their works, like a seamstress might use a...crochet hook...to...? We give up. Read these instead.

Great Metaphors in Classic Literature

"My love for Linton is like the foliage in the woods. Time will change it, I'm well aware, as winter changes the trees—my love for Heathcliff resembles the eternal rocks beneath—a source of little visible delight, but necessary."

—Emily Brontë, *Wuthering Heights*

"His face is all bubukles and whelks and knobs and flames o' fire; and his lips blows at his nose, and it is like a coal of fire, sometimes plue [sic], and sometimes red; but his nose is executed, and his fire's out."

—William Shakespeare, *Henry V*

"Even on Central Avenue, not the quietest dressed street in the world, he looked about as inconspicuous as a tarantula on a slice of angel food."

—Raymond Chandler, *Farewell, My Lovely*

"She tried to get rid of the kitten which had scrambled up her back and stuck like a burr just out of reach."

—Louisa May Alcott, *Little Women*

Of the four states that begin with the letter *a*, the only one that doesn't also end with an *a* is Arkansas.

"Everybody loved to have him around, too; he was sunshine most always—I mean he made it seem like good weather. When he turned into a cloudbank it was awful dark for half a minute, and that was enough; there wouldn't nothing go wrong again for a week."

—Mark Twain, *The Adventures of Huckleberry Finn*

"In the wavering firelight Gandalf seemed suddenly to grow; he rose up, a great menacing shape like the monument of some ancient king of stone set upon a hill."

—J. R. R. Tolkien, *The Fellowship of the Ring*

"She entered with ungainly struggle like some huge awkward chicken, torn, squawking, out of its coop."

—Sir Arthur Conan Doyle, *The Adventure of the Three Gables*

"Impressions poured in upon her of those two men, and to follow her thought was like following a voice which speaks too quickly to be taken down by one's pencil."

—Virginia Woolf, *To the Lighthouse*

Great Metaphors in Modern Literature

"Outside her breath rises in a fine mist and the snow keeps falling, like a ceaseless repetition of the same infinitesimally small mistake."

—Sally Rooney, *Normal People*

"The pain just increases like a violinist going up the E string. You think it can't get any higher and it does—the pain's like that, it rises and rises."

—John LeCarre, *The Spy Who Came In from the Cold*

"The waves rolled in like blue metal tubes carrying an egg white of foam on their peaks, then broke in a thousand glittering splinters and came up to the street with an oh of wonder and fear from those watching."

—Elena Ferrante, *My Brilliant Friend*

"What are the stars but points in the body of God where we insert the healing needles of our terror and longing?"

—Thomas Pynchon, *Gravity's Rainbow*

"Every now and then a perverse downdraft would make the smoke whirl and puff toward him and he breathed some of it in. It built dreams in the same way that a small irritant may build a pearl in an oyster."

—Stephen King, *The Gunslinger*

"He looked like a great clay voodoo doll made animate."

—Cormac McCarthy, *Blood Meridian*

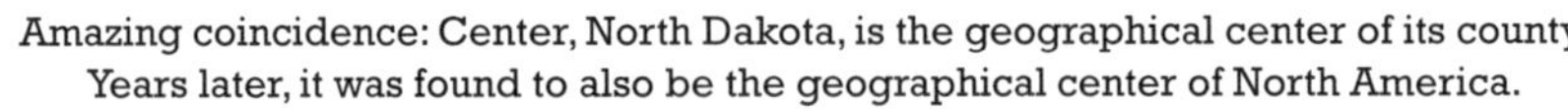

Amazing coincidence: Center, North Dakota, is the geographical center of its county. Years later, it was found to also be the geographical center of North America.

"Over her shoulder she spit out words to us like rotten pieces of apple."

—Toni Morrison, ***The Bluest Eye***

Metaphors That Are Funny on Purpose

"The ships hung in the sky in much the same way that bricks don't."

—Douglas Adams, ***The Hitchhiker's Guide to the Galaxy***

"The Right Hon. was a tubby little chap who looked as if he had been poured into his clothes and had forgotten to say 'When!'"

—P. G. Wodehouse, ***Very Good, Jeeves***

"He stared at Miss Flitworth's frozen, worried, pleading smile like a baboon looking for meaning in the Rosetta stone."

—Terry Pratchett, ***Reaper Man***

"Lucy...was doing a charcoal sketch of Barbra Streisand. From memory this time. It was a full-faced rendering, with teeth like baseballs and eyes like jellied fire."

—Hunter S. Thompson, ***Fear and Loathing in Las Vegas***

"I believe it was Shakespeare, or possibly Howard Cosell, who first observed that marriage is very much like a birthday candle, in that 'the flames of passion burn brightest when the wick of intimacy is first ignited by the disposable butane lighter of physical attraction, but sooner or later the heat of familiarity causes the wax of boredom to drip all over the vanilla frosting of novelty and the shredded coconut of romance.' I could not have phrased it better myself."

—Dave Barry

Metaphors That Are Funny...But Not on Purpose

"The pain hit him like a waterfall of icy water."

—Terry Goodkind, ***Wizard's First Rule***

"For a long while, conversation was impossible, because I was bouncing up and down on the seat like a jackhammer."

—Stephenie Meyer, ***Twilight***

"Overhanging her precarious body was a jaundiced face whose skin resembled a sheet of parchment paper punctured by two emotionless eyes."

—Dan Brown, ***Deception Point***

"His voice is warm and husky like dark melted chocolate fudge caramel...or something."

—E. L. James, ***50 Shades of Grey***

Muhammad Ali's funeral processional was 23 miles long.

WEIRD CANADA

Canada—the land of Mounted Police, poutine, Wayne Gretzky, Celine Dion...and some really strange news stories.

 Undead in Montreal

In 2022, police in Montreal issued Nick Fatouros a parking ticket. He contested the citation, then left Canada to travel through Central and South America for the next two years. When he returned home, he received a 14-page letter from Quebec's provincial Ministry of Justice seeking payment of the still outstanding parking ticket from out of his estate—because the government believed he was dead. "I was laughing. I said, 'Wow, that's news to me,'" Fatouros, not dead, told reporters. He tried to clear things up and retain his "alive" status but had difficulties. "It's very hard to get through, very hard to get through," he said. The Ministry of Justice later apologized to Fatouros, attributing the mistake to a clerical error. "The Collector of Fines mistakenly used a letter template used to correspond with an estate rather than the one normally used to communicate with a defendant. We apologize for the situation," the office said in an email to a local news station.

 Milk Was a Bad Choice

Real estate agent Mike Rose was showing a home in Kamloops, British Columbia, one afternoon in July 2022. While waiting for a potential buyer to show up for a viewing, Rose found himself very thirsty, or "unusually dehydrated" as he'd later tell a court, owing to a new medication, stress, and the summer weather. Rose looked in the refrigerator of the for-sale-but-still-occupied home for some water to drink, but instead found a jug of milk. He then drank directly from the container, then placed the jug back in the fridge. Home seller Lyska Fullerton saw what Rose did on surveillance footage and confronted the real estate agent, who was replaced as the broker on the property. "When you have professionals in your home, you feel like you can trust them," Fullerton told reporters. "And I learned quite a lesson in this." So did Rose: he had to pay a $20,000 fine.

 Your Kid Could Paint That (and Did)

Mario Perron worked as an art teacher at Westwood Junior High School in Montreal. He lost that job in February 2024 after some of his students found his personal website and they and their parents were offended by what they discovered there: Perron had taken his students' artwork and was selling it on mugs, clothing, phone

cases, and more. Even worse: the pieces Perron was selling were stylized portraits of his students with their names attached. He charged as much as $94 for works titled "Charlotte's Creepy Portrait" or "Julia's Creepy Portrait." "Imagine your 13-year-old son coming home from school today with a story that his art teacher is selling students' artwork online," parent Joel DeBellefeuille said. "That is completely insane." Not only did Perron lose his job, but he and the Lester B. Pearson School District faced a $1.5 million copyright infringement lawsuit.

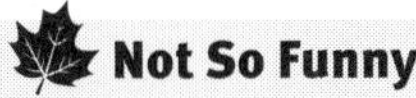

Not So Funny

Two Montreal-based comics, Emma Achour and Coralie LaPerrière, formed an Instagram account called "No Girls in the Lineup." The goal: to call out sexist comedy club bookers who never put female comedians on the bill. Over the first few months that the account was operational, "No Girls in the Lineup" often highlighted Le Troquet, a club in Gatineau, Quebec. Then, in June 2023, a new face began to appear in ads for the venue's Thursday night comedy show: Sonia Bélanger. Her slots were so frequent that Achour and LaPerrière really thought they'd gotten through to Le Troquet and affected change for the positive by getting some stage time for a fellow female comic. They were wrong: Bélanger isn't a real person. Nobody by that name ever performed at Le Troquet, nor did any woman—Sonia Bélanger's photo was A.I.-generated and appeared only in ads. "It's crazy how much effort goes into just not booking a female comedian," read a subsequent posting on "No Girls in the Lineup."

Dogged Determination

Toronto-based company DNA My Dog is a major animal genetic testing firm. Customers from Canada and the United States send in a cotton swab rubbed against the inside of their dog's cheek; for $200, the company tests it for genetic indicators of allergies and health problems and also a full breakdown on the dog's breed. A news team at WBZ in Boston were skeptical of DNA My Dog and its "highly accurate" guarantee, so reporter Christina Hager took a swab of her own cheek, paid the testing fee, and sent it to three Canadian animal genetic testing firms. Two rejected the sample; DNA My Dog's analysis determined that the swab belonged to a dog that was 40 percent Alaskan malamute, 35 percent shar-pei, and 25 percent Labrador. (We can assure you that Hager is descended from none of these breeds.)

* * *

"The only things that smell good are fat and sugar. Tofu being boiled doesn't smell good. Anything that smells good is fattening."

—John Madden

Is it your birthday? Then you have a 6.7 percent chance of dying, higher than on any other day. Happy birthday!

BAD BUSINE$$

Whether a giant tech company or a tiny fish market, the drive for profits can involve some bizarre tactics.

SOUL CRUSHING

A March 2024 commercial called "Crush" for Apple's new iPad Pro drew ire online, and from at least two celebrities. The 60-second ad features a large hydraulic press slowly crushing an arrangement of items while the Sonny & Cher song "All I Ever Need Is You" plays in the background. In stunning high definition, the cameras capture the cacophonous destruction of numerous physical objects the device is designed to digitally replace: a trumpet, a classical guitar, a piano, a turntable, a typewriter, a globe, a stone bust, a full-size arcade game, an alarm clock, a chess set, a sewing mannequin, lamps, books, cameras, two computer monitors, and about a dozen cans of paint...which oozes out in a technicolor rainbow between the two metal slabs. Then, after the press rises and the smoke clears, lo and behold, there's the new iPad Pro. A voiceover proclaims, "The most powerful iPad ever is also the thinnest."

Apple was trying to make the point that people can use the new device as a replacement for all those physical objects—"Just imagine all the things it'll be used to create," CEO Tim Cook posted on X. But many people, particularly those in creative fields, felt the ad represented crushing human creativity and culture itself. "The destruction of the human experience," posted Hugh Grant, "courtesy of Silicon Valley." Justine Bateman, in a reply to Cook's post about the new product, asked, "Truly, what is wrong with you?"

Cook didn't respond, but the company later issued an apology admitting that, "We missed the mark."

"HILARIOUS"

In late March 2016, Google announced that it was introducing the "Gmail Mic Drop" button. When you hit send, "everyone will get your message, but that's the last you'll ever hear about it," wrote the company in an announcement. "Yes, even if folks try to respond, you won't see it." Not only that, but the email you send will be enhanced by a gif of a cartoon Minion, dressed as the queen of England, dropping a microphone.

Everyone assumed, given the time of year, that Gmail Mic Drop was simply an April Fool's Day joke. Google wouldn't actually enable that button, would they? They did. Right next to the regular "Send" button. What could go wrong? This: "Thanks to

Mic Drop I just lost my job," wrote someone anonymously on the Gmail help forum:

> I am a writer and had a deadline to meet. I sent my articles to my boss and never heard back from her. I inadvertently sent the email using the "Mic Drop" send button. There were corrections that needed to be made on my articles and I never received her replies. My boss took offence to the Mic Drop animation and assumed that I didn't reply to her because I thought her input was petty (hence the Mic Drop). I just woke up to a very angry voicemail from her which is how I found out about this "hilarious" prank.

Several others on the forum reported similar stories of inadvertently hitting the Mic Drop feature button, and they pleaded with Google to remove it. Being an April Fool's Day prank, it was only up for a day, anyway. The company later said they didn't *mean* to add the button. "It looks like we pranked ourselves this year. Due to a bug, the Mic Drop feature inadvertently caused more headaches than laughs. We're truly sorry."

HONESTY MAY VARY

Taco Bell came under fire after a penny-pinching New Jersey couple sued the fast food giant's parent company, Yum! Brands, for false advertising. In May 2018, Nelson Estrella-Rojas and Joann Estrella saw a TV commercial for a $5 Chalupa Craving Box deal, so they got in their car, drove to the restaurant, purchased two of the box deals... and noticed that the receipt was for $12.18, before taxes. After store management stated they weren't beholden to the price shown in the TV spot because of the ad's fine print, the couple filed a lawsuit for the "time wasted driving to the subject Taco Bell, the gasoline expended to drive their vehicle to the subject Taco Bell, and in the amount of $2.18."

Taco Bell defended its practices by claiming there was a "prices may vary" and "at participating locations" disclaimer at the end of the ad. But the lawsuit claimed the disclaimer was too quick to decipher, and accused Taco Bell of intentionally misleading consumers because of "a desire to secure increase[d] profits."

Yum!'s corporate leadership countered, "Our advertisements are truthful and accurate, and we will defend this case vigorously."

IT SAYS SO RIGHT IN THE NAME!

What would you expect from a product called Tito's Handmade Vodka? That it's made by Tito, it's handmade, and it's vodka. Well, two out of three of those being true *is* bad, according to vodka fan Trevor Singleton, who filed a class action lawsuit against the

Texas-based company for implying that their vodka is "handmade" in an "old-fashioned pot still," and that it costs more because of the "better quality associated with handmade products." After looking at the lawsuit's allegations, a more apt name for the spirit might be "Tito's Made in Fully Automated Buildings with Floor-to-Ceiling Stills and Almost Zero Human Involvement Vodka." The distillery reportedly bottles "500 cases an hour" and sells "15 million bottles annually." That would require some very fast hands.

The lawsuit was filed in 2016, and Tito's asked for a dismissal, which was denied. Then came reports of an "undisclosed settlement." There have been at least eight other class action suits filed against the distillery. But they still call it Tito's Handmade Vodka, and their home page still includes the copy: "[W]e still make it in batches, use old-fashioned pot stills, and taste-test every batch to make sure you get only the best."

WHAT ARE YOU LOOKIN' AT?

In September 2018, workers at a Kuwaiti fish market tried to "liven up" their product by sticking plastic googly eyes on the fish to make them look fresher than they were. Flummoxed shoppers posted the abominations online, including one unappetizing fish whose googly eye had slipped to reveal a very real—and very yellow—eye underneath. The photos went viral, prompting the Kuwaiti Ministry of Commerce to shut down the shop. (Meanwhile, a rival fishmonger began to advertise their "Fish Without Cosmetics!")

UPON FURTHER REVIEW

If we can't trust businesses to play it straight, at least we can trust our fellow consumers when it comes to online reviews, right? "Don't trust online reviews," warns Kay Dean, a former federal criminal investigator who founded Fake Review Watch (FRW). She's identified "thousands of fake reviews across Google, Yelp, Facebook, and other platforms, and has compiled evidence of review fraud conducted by thousands of businesses."

FRW's "Busted!" page hosts a rogue's gallery of overly self-congratulatory business owners, such as Mark Mohrmann, a New York City–based orthopedic surgeon who, along with his wife, garnered fake positive reviews from friends and family and hired contractors to post fake positive reviews on websites such as "ZocDoc, Google, Yelp, Healthgrades, Vitals, md.com, ratemds.com, and the Better Business Bureau." They also suppressed negative reviews, which is really scary when it's a surgeon. Dr. Mohrmann was fined $100,000.

Then there's the case of the ironically named Integrity Chiropractic. Dean's investigation discovered more than 100 fake five-star reviews, which were removed by Google. "The magnitude of the fraud is alarming," she says.

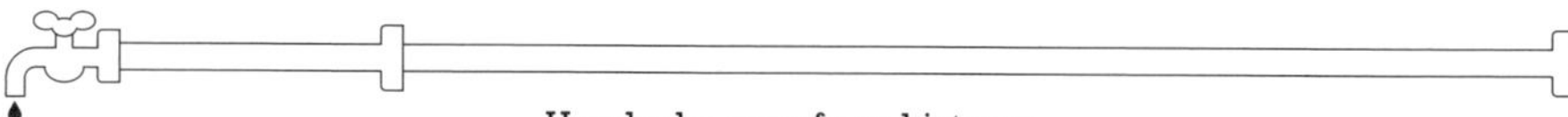

Headache cure from history:
drinking tea brewed from a powdered human skull.

THAT'S WHAT SEA SAID

Uncle John told us he really wants a boat—not to take it out on the water, just so he can come with a punny name for it. Sorry, Uncle John, but these are already taken.

Nauti by Nature
Knotty Buoy
Yachty or Nice?
The Wet Dream
Pharm A Sea
Eggs-Ta-Sea
Seasquatch
Unsinkable II
Sand Witch
Gone Fission
Fish & Chicks
Fishful Thinkin'
Fishizzle
Tuna Colada
Sushi Hunter
Aft R All
Never Land
Hypnautic
401K
Kids' Inheritance
Aquaholic
Liquid Asset
Wine Down

5 O'Clock Somewhere
Cirrhosis of the River
Midlife Crisis
She Got the House
Usele$$
Debt Finder
Future Poor Person
Empty Pockets
Wasted Seamen
Favorite Mistake
Watts Knot 2 Luv?
That's What Sea Said
Chum Dumpster
Weather or Not
Aboat Time
Anchor Management
Angler Mgmt
Knot for Sail
The Filthy Oar
One Moor Time
The Codfather
Sea-Batical
Deez Knotz

Joan's Ark
Fin & Tonic
Breaking Bass
Ship for Brains
Bull Ship
The Sturgeon General
Net Fish and Chill
In a Meeting
Some Assembly Required
Knotical Nonsense
The Grateful Dad
A Wave from It All
Therapy
Changes in L'Attitudes
da Boat
Break Wind
Ship-faced
B-Yacht'ch
Zombies Can't Swim
Bow Movement
Floater
Seaulator
Yachta Yachta Yachta

According to the U.S. Bureau of Labor, 90 percent of millennials move out of the house by age 27. Of those, 50 percent move back in at some point.

THE DEMISE OF THE MANUAL TRANSMISSION

When we first started publishing the Bathroom Reader nearly 40 years ago, manual cars were ubiquitous. Now, they're going the way of so much other 20th-century technology considered primitive by today's standards. (Though there are still some BRI staffers who refuse to give up their stick shifts.)

BACKGROUND

Learning to drive a stick shift requires hand-eye-foot coordination, and a lot of patience and attention until it becomes second nature. But if you think that sounds hard, try driving one of the original early 20th-century automobiles: they had to be crank-started, and driving required pushing and pulling buttons and levers, all while steering, shifting, and braking. As car manufacturers found new ways to automate mechanical functions and move them under the hood, the only holdovers were the clutch pedal and the stick shift. That's because it took decades to perfect the automatic transmission, which changes gears automatically so the driver needs only to brake and steer. But perfect it they did, and today, 95 percent of passenger cars have automatic transmissions.

Manual transmission is commonly referred to as a "manual," "clutch," "stick shift," or "stick." If you've never seen one, or aren't familiar with the concept, know that there are three floor pedals—a gas pedal and a brake pedal, along with another pedal on the left called a clutch—and a handle to the driver's right that's the stick shift. The gear knob atop the stick typically has a diagram indicating the car's shift pattern, or what position the stick needs to be in for each gear.

SMOOTH OPERATOR

How to drive a manual? The lower the car's speed, the lower the gear it needs to be in, so you start out in first gear; then, when you reach between 10 and 30 mph (depending on the car), you engage the clutch by stepping on it with your left foot, then quickly move the stick shift into the position for second gear, and then release the clutch as you resume accelerating with your right foot on the gas. If you've performed this task correctly, your gears didn't grind loud enough for the entire neighborhood to hear, your car didn't stall, you're not detecting the scent of a burnt clutch, and now you're in second gear. Congratulations. Repeat for third gear, fourth, and so on (older cars may stop at third gear, while others go up to sixth).

What's going on behind the scenes? Lots. Simply put, engines spin, and that

spinning spins the car's wheels. But even though a running engine spins constantly, the wheels don't. Depressing the clutch acts to put the car in neutral—that is, it decouples the drive shaft from the engine shaft—enabling a change to a different gear. What exactly are gears? Toothed wheels that, when synchronized, fit perfectly together when spinning. The gears control the power that the engine transfers to the wheels. Achieving that synchronization is why it took so long for car companies to perfect the automatic transmission. The first real attempt was the 1939 Oldsmobile Hydra-Matic; within 20 years, more than 85 percent of U.S. cars were automatics.

MANUAL VS. AUTOMATIC

But throughout the 20th century, automatics were more expensive and less fuel efficient than manuals. Manual clutches required fewer parts and were therefore easier to build and repair, which is why the baseline models of most cars were usually manuals. As the technology improved, though, automatic transmissions (and power steering) made for smoother rides.

But as this gradual takeover was occurring, it soon became a point of pride to drive a stick shift—especially a high-performance one. Car aficionados prefer the control over speed and maneuvering that a clutch allows. It really does create a different "driving experience": Your left foot is on the clutch, your right foot on the gas. Your left hand is on the wheel, your right hand gripping the stick. All four appendages work in unison with the engine to provide a ride that could never happen with the cruise control engaged, your pinky on the steering wheel, and the other hand holding your coffee.

STUCK IN NEUTRAL

Today's automatics shift seamlessly between up to nine gears, but that's just one reason why you don't see that many manuals left on the road.

- The first problem is evident in this headline: "How to drive a stick shift in 12 easy steps." Those 12 steps (via insurance broker The Zebra) require more than 3,000 words—and include this anecdote: "In 2017, it was reported that a man in Birmingham, Alabama, stole a flatbed delivery truck and was pursued by police—but in an extremely low-speed chase because he didn't know how to drive a stick shift!"
- It's true: many drivers of stick shifts will roll the car backward on a hill before starting forward again. It's disconcerting and dangerous.
- Carmakers are aiming for more automation, not less, creating vehicles that require little to no human involvement: driverless, or at least with a hands-free mode. Cars also come with cruise control and lane control. Most commuters prefer these amenities. If you deal with stop-and-go traffic for several hours a day, a manual can get old fast.

- Automatic transmissions can shift from gear to gear faster and more efficiently than a human driver—and they don't grind the gears while learning how—which brings up shelf life. Clutches wear out over time. They used to last only around 50,000 to 70,000 miles; today's high performance models typically make it about 80,000 miles before a costly replacement. An automatic transmission will last at least 200,000 miles.
- For most car companies, it's simply not profitable to produce cars with manual transmissions, especially as hybrids and electric cars become more prevalent. Electric cars have only one gear.

LIFE IS A HIGHWAY

"The forces at work against the manual transmission are insurmountable," writes Gearpatrol.com editor Tyler Duffy, "and even the #savethemanuals hashtag has profound 'old man shouting into the wind' energy." If you do want to purchase a new car with a manual transmission in the United States, time is running out: just under 4 percent of cars sold in the country are manual, and that number's declining as EV numbers grow. In Europe and Japan, manuals are still the norm, not the exception. That's because gas—or petrol—costs much more, so it makes sense for skilled manual drivers to take advantage of the slight advantage in fuel economy. In the U.S., gas prices are lower, so it's not as much of a concern.

Mercedes and Volvo are the two most recent big car companies that have completely ceased the production of manual transmission cars. But if you do have the need for some hands-on and feet-on speed, chances are there's a manual transmission driving club near you, or you can join the "Stick Shift Driver Pride" group or "The Manual Gearbox Preservation Society" on Facebook.

Manual transmission loyalists will be happy to know that the stick shift is still an option for some off-road 4X4s and pickups, along with certain models of more affordably priced cars like the Honda Civic and Ford Mustang. For those with extra cash lying around, a brand new 2024 7-speed Porsche 911 Carrera T starts at $124,900. When Porsche announced there'd be no 911 manual transmissions among their 2025 models, their concerned customers were crushed that yet another luxury carmaker was going to stop making stick shifts (a move Ferrari had made a few years earlier). Porsche reassured everyone that this was just a hiatus, and their most popular manual model will return. But who knows for how long? And to think, when the first luxury sports cars with automatic transmissions started hitting showrooms in the 1980s, serious drivers scoffed at them. (Many still do.)

* * *

"Always borrow money from a pessimist. He won't expect it back." **—Oscar Wilde**

Hot news: the decade from 2014–23 contained the ten warmest years since recordkeeping began in 1850.

MEDICAL LISTS

If your astonishment from reading this article lasts more than four hours, consult a health-care professional immediately.

9 Peculiar Prescription Drug Side Effects

1. Amnesia
2. Unusual impulsive behavior
3. Abnormal dreams
4. Toxic epidermal necrolysis (painful body rash)
5. Inability to stay still
6. Fingernails and toenails fall off
7. Fingerprints vanish
8. Sleep-living (eating, making love, or driving while in a dreamlike state)
9. Blue, green, purple, or black urine

First Responder Mnemonic Incident Report: M/ETHANE

1. *Major Incident?* Assess whether vast resources will be required.
2. *Exact Location:* Ensure that those resources will find their way there.
3. *Type of Incident:* Communicate the general nature of the incident.
4. *Hazards:* Describe any obstacles.
5. *Access:* Determine the most practical routes to enter and leave.
6. *Number of Casualties:* Provide a preliminary assessment of the dead and/or injured.
7. *Emergency Services:* How many required firetrucks, ambulances, personnel are needed?

8 Full Names of Medical Eponyms

1. Alois Alzheimer
2. Hans Asperger
3. Burrill Bernard Crohn
4. George Gilles de la Tourette
5. Robert J. Graves
6. Maurice Reynaud
7. George Huntington
8. James Parkinson

11 Names of Surgical instruments

1. Mayo scissors
2. Dunhill forceps
3. Babcock forceps
4. Lane tissue forceps
5. Spencer Wells forceps
6. Norfolk and Norwich retractor
7. Langenbeck retractor
8. Littlewood forceps
9. McIndoe scissors
10. Sawtell forceps
11. Gillies forceps

8 Nursing Slang Terms

1. *Frequent flyer:* A patient in the ER so often the nurses know them.
2. *Princess/Prince/Diva:* A patient who demands to be pampered.
3. *Walkie-talkie:* A patient who requires minimal care because they can walk and talk.
4. *Total:* A patient requiring total care (i.e., feeding tube, urinary catheter).
5. *Happy juice:* IV pain medication to keep the patient comfortable.
6. *Milk of amnesia:* Intravenous propofol to sedate the patient.
7. *Code brown:* The patient has s*** the bed.
8. *Celestial discharge:* The patient has died.

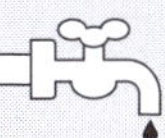

10 Annoying Things Patients Do, According to Doctors

1. Act mean to nurses.
2. Show up without a list of symptoms and medications.
3. Lie about medications or habits.
4. Ask too many impertinent questions.
5. Have bad breath.
6. Exaggerate symptoms.
7. Talk or text on the phone.
8. Badmouth other doctors.
9. Put too much faith in "Dr. Google."
10. Bother them in public.

8 Average Surgery Costs (U.S.)

1. Heart valve replacement: $170,000
2. Heart bypass: $123,000
3. Spinal fusion: $110,000
4. Hip replacement: $40,364
5. Knee replacement: $35,000
6. Angioplasty: $28,200
7. Hip resurfacing: $28,000
8. Gastric bypass: $25,000

9 Average Annual Salaries (U.S.)

1. Medical receptionist: $37,000
2. Phlebotomist: $43,000
3. Registered nurse: $94,480
4. Primary care physician: $197,400
5. Oncologist: $464,000
6. Urologist: $515,000
7. Cardiologist: $525,000
8. Plastic Surgeon: $536,000
9. Orthopedist: $558,000

13 Ailments with No Cure

1. Arthritis
2. Asthma
3. Cancer
4. Common cold
5. Celiac disease
6. Diabetes
7. Hepatitis B
8. HIV/AIDS
9. Irritable bowel syndrome
10. Multiple sclerosis
11. Muscular dystrophy
12. Psoriasis
13. Rabies

8 Kooky "Cures" from Yesteryear

1. Tobacco smoke enema to treat cholera.
2. Swishing urine to whiten teeth.
3. Dead mouse paste to ease a toothache.
4. Milk transfusion into the bloodstream to form white blood cells.
5. Lying inside a dead whale carcass to treat rheumatoid arthritis.
6. Goat testicles implanted into a man's scrotum to cure impotence.
7. Waterboarding to treat various forms of mental illness.
8. Snake oil. Yes, they actually used it to treat arthritis and bursitis.

8 Odd Modern Procedures

1. Rotationplasty: removal of the knee and reattaching the lower leg, rotated 180 degrees, so the ankle becomes the knee.
2. Osteo-odonto-keratoprosthesis: restoring sight with a tooth.
3. Hemispherectomy: removing half of the brain to treat seizures.
4. Dimpleplasty: drilling tiny holes in the face to create dimples.
5. Pokertox: botox that hides the "tells" of poker players.
6. Hi-def liposculpture: creating fake "six-pack" abs.
7. Palm line surgery: surgically extending the "life line" in palm reading.
8. Hemorrhoidectomy: sweet, sweet relief!

The equivalent of tongue twisters for American Sign Language speakers are called "finger fumblers."

WORD ORIGINS

Ever wonder where certain words came from? Here are the interesting stories behind some of them.

VESTAL

Meaning: Pure and chaste

Origin: "The maidens who served the Roman goddess 'Vesta' were required to be absolutely chaste and were therefore called 'vestal virgins.'" (From *Dictionary of Word Origins,* by Jordan Almond)

WINDFALL

Meaning: A sudden influx of money or assets

Origin: "This word was first applied to trees. On many of the old English estates, the timber might not be felled by the nobles, it belonged to the King; but trees blown down by storms were except from this royal holding; hence, an unexpected piece of good fortune was a *windfall.*" (From *Dictionary of Word Origins*, by Joseph T. Shipley)

BOOTLEG

Meaning: A fake or unauthorized copy surreptitiously sold

Origin: "The formation of this word is due to the smugglers' practice of concealing bottles inside the long leg part of their boots. The ultimate source of boot is not known." (From *Oxford Dictionary of Word Origins*, by Julia Cresswell)

SPUD

Meaning: Potato

Definition: "The colloquial American name 'spud' arises from the narrow, spade-like tool of that name used in digging potatoes." (From *2017 Curious Word Origins, Sayings & Expressions*, by Charles Earle Funk)

URCHIN

Meaning: An ill-behaving child

Origin: "Our word *urchin* used to be the word *hurcheon,* which came from the Old Northern French term *herichon,* which was itself derived from the Latin term *heroics*, all of which mean 'hedgehog.' The word *urchin* first appeared in the mid-1300s, and was soon used to describe all sorts of supposedly hedgehog-like folks, including hunchbacks, ugly people, and significantly for our purposes, elves and goblins, because the folklore of the day assumed that these beings would occasionally take the form of a hedgehog. Elves and goblins are mischievous, of course. The term *urchin* would also shift to mischievous children, which it did around the mid-16th century." (From *The Complete Idiot's Guide to Weird Word Origins*, by Paul McFedries)

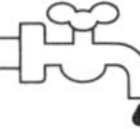

Ironic headline: "Cybertruck Catches Fire After Running into Fire Hydrant and Getting Wet."

PUMP

Meaning: A woman's shoe with a low heel

Origin: "The classic 'pump' shoe lacks straps or other fasteners, and the key to the shoe staying on one's foot is its snug fit, rather like the piston of a pump. In fact, back in the 16th century, such pistons in pumps were known as 'pump shoes' from their vaguely shoe-like shape. It's likely that the 'pump' shoe took its name, in a 16th-century pun, from these close-fitting 'pump shoe' pistons." (From *The Word Detective*, by Evan Morris)

JAYWALK

Meaning: To cross a street haphazardly without regard for safety or the law

Origin: "The *jay* part of the word comes from *jayhawk*, a nickname for a foolish peasant from the American South since Civil War days. Hence, to *jaywalk* is to walk in a street carelessly (and foolishly) without obeying traffic rules and signals." (From *Word Origins*, by Dhirendra Verma)

HOBNOB

Meaning: To aggressively socialize or engage in social climbing

Origin: "In its present form it has been in our language since Shakespeare's day. In fact, it is found in at least one of his plays. Originally, it appeared in Chaucer's time as *hobnob*, meaning literally 'to have and have not' or 'hit-or-miss.' In those days, and through the centuries since, the term was used to describe the social practice of alternating in the buying of drinks: one chap buys a round, then his friend buys the next. First he has, then he has not, the honor of treating. Gradually the term *hobnobbing* came to mean any form of social intercourse on easy, familiar terms." (From *Dictionary of Word and Phrase Origins*, by William and Mary Morris)

MANURE

Meaning: Animal dung used as fertilizer

Origin: "Originally a polite word related to *main-oeuvre*, 'manual labor,' this was degraded into a euphemism by those who did not like the word *dung*—and, as always happens, it has taken on the characteristic odor of the word for which it was substituted." (From *Phrase and Word Origins*, by Alfred H. Holt)

PECULIAR

Meaning: Strange, negatively unique

Origin: "The root of it is in the Latin word for 'cattle.' In ancient days property was largely in cattle—*pecus*—and such property belonging especially or exclusively to a person was called *peculium*. From this word comes 'peculiar,' and by extension of meaning anything specially belonging to or characterizing a person is said to be peculiar to him." (From *Word Ancestry*, by Willis Arnold Ellis)

WHEN YOU GOTTA GO

Spoiler alert: everybody dies. These people at least shuffled off this mortal coil in interesting ways.

DON'T HAVE A COW

Joao Maria de Souza was in bed with his wife, fast asleep, in their bedroom in Caratinga, Brazil, when something fell through the roof and right on top of him. As he woke up, he realized that it was a cow. It had escaped from a nearby farm and climbed onto the roof of de Souza's one-story house. The corrugated roof collapsed under the one-ton weight of the cow, and the animal fell directly onto the man, breaking his leg. Taken to a hospital while he was conscious and talking, de Souza died a few hours later from internal bleeding. Local authorities investigated the incident to determine whether the cow's owner could be charged with involuntary manslaughter. "I didn't bring my son up to be killed by a falling cow," de Souza's mother, Maria, told reporters.

A COLD WAY TO DIE

Nguyet Le, general manager of an Arby's outlet in Louisiana, was closing up the restaurant by herself one night in May 2023. She headed into the walk-in freezer and the door slammed shut behind her, and then, she couldn't get out. The mechanism designed to open the door from the inside malfunctioned, while an emergency button had been disconnected some time earlier. With no one else inside the restaurant to hear Le's calls for help or her pounding on the inside of the door, she was stuck in the freezer overnight in −20°F temperatures and was found six hours later, frozen to the ground and deceased. Such walk-in freezer incidents occur about 60 times each year in the United States.

DEATH BY CHOCOLATE

In 2016, 24-year-old Svetlana Roslina fell into a giant vat of melted chocolate in the Sergiev Posad candy factory in Fedortsovo, near Moscow. Reports vary on how the mishap occurred, with some sources saying she dropped her cell phone and was attempting to retrieve it, and others saying she was sucked in while emptying a sack of flour. Regardless of how she ended up in the vat, the incident ended in tragedy for the mother of two when she ended up getting minced by the mixing equipment, with only her legs remaining intact.

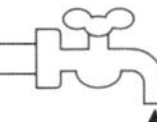

What are the D ring, C ring, B ring, Cassini Division, A ring, F ring, G ring, E ring, and the Phoebe ring? The rings of Saturn.

TAKEN OUT AT THE BALL GAME

In August 2018, hardcore Los Angeles Dodgers fan Linda Goldbloom celebrated her 79th birthday and 59th wedding anniversary by taking in a home game against the visiting San Diego Padres. Goldbloom and her husband, Erwin, had seats in the loge section, on the first base side behind home plate and just above the protective netting that shields spectators from errant foul balls. In the top of the ninth inning, a Padres batter hit one such ball out of play, and it sailed just above the netting and struck Goldbloom in the face. "It came so quick that we didn't have time to react. Nobody did in our area," Erwin Goldbloom told reporters. Taken to a nearby hospital, Linda Goldbloom died four days later from an acute intracranial hemorrhage caused by the baseball. This is only the third recorded time in history a baseball fan died after being struck by a ball leaving the field of play.

FOR WHOM THE BELL TOLLS

The Santa Magdalena *romería* is a traditional Catholic celebration that takes place two weeks after Easter in Spain. In 2024, a 30-year-old man was visiting the Sant Llorenç church in the Pinell de Brai region when the church's bells were rung to help announce the beginning of the festivities. While the bell rang, it struck the man on the head, and he died on the spot. The mayor of El Pinell de Brai declared three days of mourning and canceled the rest of the *romería*. "There has always been a tradition of ringing the bell for Santa Magdalena," mayor Laura Vallespi, said. "Unfortunately, this did not end well today."

A SHOCKING DEATH

While enjoying a day of recreation at Georgia's Lake Lanier in July 2023, 24-year-old Thomas Miner took a flying leap off of a dock, intending to swim for a while. Instead, he was immediately met with an electric shock so powerful that it rendered him unconscious. A friend tried to rescue Miner via a rowboat, and two others swam to reach him; both described a burning sensation and electrical charge in the water. After a nearby power box in no way connected to anything in the lake was shut off, Miner was rushed to a hospital, where he died from electrocution. It's not yet clear how he was electrically charged to death...by water.

* * *

CANINE TRIVIA

What do German shepherds, Dutch shepherds, bloodhounds, Belgian Malinois, Labrador retrievers, Doberman pinschers, beagles, and English springer spaniels have in common? They're all police K-9 dog breeds.

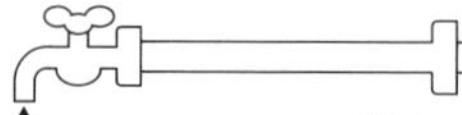

There have been 107 billion humans throughout history, about half of whom died in infancy.

COPS ON FACEBOOK

In the past few years, you may have noticed that local police departments have increased their presence on social media. Judging by these posts, they've been having a lot of fun with it.

BRAINTREE (MA) POLICE DEPARTMENT

We'd kindly ask that anyone thinking about criming today to please stay inside and not crime. It's too hot for you...it's too hot for us. Let's pick it back up in a few weeks when it's below 90.

TOPEKA POLICE

Congrats to whoever from Shawnee County won the $1 million prize in the lottery. All of our Officers showed up to work today, so we can rule them out.

SEATTLE POLICE DEPARTMENT

@JoshK: Hey @SeattlePD, I think the mounted patrol monitoring the Comicon line is a bit of overkill, no?

@SeattlePD: They're just there to keep an eye on things. But you can just pretend they're centaur cosplayers, if you'd prefer.

NSW (AUSTRALIA) POLICE FORCE

Have you received poor customer service from your local drug dealers?...We have people standing by at the phone ready to take you calls.

LAWRENCE (KS) POLICE

REMINDER: We realize politics can make emotions run high, but being mad at a presidential candidate in a debate is NOT a reason to call 911.

TASMANIA POLICE

This Is a Call for drivers attending tonight's Foo Fighters concert. Don't let the traffic get the *Best of You*, it is *Times Like These* drivers need to exercise patience, we don't want you to be *Dead on Arrival.*

DENVER POLICE DEPARTMENT

We see you rollin, but we ain't hatin' HAHA...Seriously though, #Denver, please remember to #ConsumeResponsibly this 4/20 weekend.

LEICESTER POLICE

Not a scam: If you've committed a burglary in the #Leicester area within the last week—come to our #police station & claim a FREE iPad.

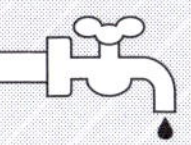

Top U.S. dog breeds: 5) poodle; 4) German shepherd; 3) golden retriever; 2) Labrador retriever; 1) French bulldog.

QUEENSLAND POLICE SERVICE

Don't drive through flooded roads because #YOLO. If you hold up your end of the bargain, we'll never, ever use #YOLO again. Deal? #bigwet

SEGUIN (TX) POLICE DEPARTMENT

@JGarcia: Can y'all write me a note for work?

@SeguinPD: Dear Justin's boss, The roads are bad and are going to get worse. Much worse. Please let him stay home...And, he needs a raise.

NSW POLICE FORCE

On a scale of one to people eating tuna at work, how annoying are drivers that don't keep left?

STIRLING (UK) POLICE

Just to be clear, "I was looking for a Pokestop" is not an acceptable reason for being on the roof of a shop with a crowbar at 2am!

ALLEN COUNTY (KS) SHERIFF'S DEPARTMENT

We will be blocking all Allen County access to Facebook, Twitter, Snapchat, Instagram, Tumblr, and YouTube between February 28 and March 1.

SOLIHULL (UK) POLICE

Arrested a 28yr old man today for stealing a Twilight Saga DVD box set, store owner suggested making him watch it as punishment.

LAWRENCE (KS) POLICE

@JimmyKegin: @LawrenceKS_PD National Donut Day and nothing but crickets from you? I'm a little disappointed.

@LawrenceKS_PD: Sorry, the wifi in the kitchen of @DunkinDonuts has been spotty today. We'll be out in 3 or 4 hours.

WYOMING (MN) POLICE

Do NOT drive drunk. I will find you. I will arrest you. I will make you listen to One Direction cover bands on the way to jail.

CANTERBURY (UK) POLICE

Male wanted for 9 months arrested in a dentist by #Canterbury CPT. He was down in the mouth and braced himself...no need for a cavity search.

NSW POLICE FORCE

Please watch out for de-brie as truckload of cheese has rolled and blocked the Hume Motorway near Goulburn. Please avoid the area unless you're bringing crackers...

At 9.7 million, Los Angeles County has a higher population than 28 European countries.

FAMOUS DAD JOKES

Not dad jokes that are famous, but dad jokes that are about famous folks.

Q: Why does Snoop Dogg carry an umbrella?
A: Fo' drizzle.

Q: What concert costs only 45 cents?
A: 50 Cent featuring Nickelback.

Q: Which rapper takes the longest naps?
A: Jay Zzzz.

Did you know that Jim Carrey once lost the use of his left arm? He was all righty then.

Q: How long does Lionel Richie sit on the toilet?
A: All night long.

Q: What's made of brass and sounds like Tom Jones?
A: Trombones.

"I have a crush on Beyoncé."
"Whatever floats your boat."
"That's 'buoyancy'."

Q: What is Robert Downey Jr.'s favorite metal?
A: Iron, man!

Q: What do celebrity horses eat?
A: Matthew McConaughay

My computer's got the Miley virus. It's stopped twerking.

Q: Why did Adele cross the road?
A: To say hello from the other side.

Q: Why didn't the vampire attack Taylor Swift?
A: She had bad blood.

Q: How do you make Lady Gaga angry?
A: Poke her face.

I lost my pizza slicer, so I used a Bryan Adams CD. It cuts like a knife.

Q: What do you call a playlist with all your favorite country songs?
A: Johnny Cache.

Q: Who is a penguin's favorite pop star?
A: Seal.

Q: How did Barack propose to Michelle?
A: He got down on one knee, showed her a ring, and said, "I don't want to be Obamaself."

Can you please tell me who the actor was that played Forrest Gump? T hanks.

Q: What's Beethoven's favorite fruit?
A: Ba-na-na-naaaaa!

This Just In: Boy George has been attacked by an irate lizard on the set of *I'm a Celebrity*! They should have hired a calmer chameleon.

Q: Why doesn't Mike Tyson have a PlayStation?
A: He's an Xboxer.

Q: What did Mr. T say when heard that Dave Grohl challenged him to a celebrity boxing match?
A: "I pity the Foo!"

Did you hear about Lionel Richie getting food poisoning? He was in the bathroom all night long.

LOST IN TRANSLATION

When signs in foreign countries are written in English, any combination of words is possible. Here are some real-life examples from people who at least gave it a good try.

On a printer: "Please wait patiently for the failure of the system."

At a park: "It is forbidden to dog."

At a beach: "Shartcuts sharten life. (Avoid swallowing.)"

On a urinal: "Please urinate with precision and elegance."

On a fitness gadget: "Lympatic massage which dangerously reduces belly while sleeping."

On a tip jar: "Don't eat invoices."

On a hand dryer: "Deep into your hands. Withdraw your hands slowly. Blow your fingers finally."

On a pet bowl: "The product is subject to the object."

On a public notice: "Today is under construction. Thank you for understanding."

On a urinal: "Tame the child."

On a doorway: "No authorized entry please."

At a hotel: "Welcom turist. We spik Inglish."

At a restaurant: "Please do not see it while drinking drink."

On a toy: "Children under the age of three should not be used alone. Keep away from fire."

At a park: "Give the grass a little love, the grass will reward you an extension of green."

At a swimming pool: "Use swimsuit, be careful, be camera."

In a condo complex: "No smoking any alcohol."

On a shower: "Two for a bathing suit."

On a piggy bank: "Break it. Cut your hand carefully."

On a light fixture: "It's bright when people come. People die when they leave."

On a traffic cone: "Leaky caution."

At a family-fun arcade: "Obliged use socks."

On an automatic door: "Windy, this door does not open, please access from both sides."

On a car jack: "Always confirm strangeness of vehicle while lift is operating."

On a plunger: "The toilet unclog went off with a bang."

In a subway: "Hello. Stand far-far can?"

On a pack of prank chewing gum: "Warning—don't joke to sickman and cowardiness. No entrance."

At a park: "Uncontrolled disease land life in troubles."

At a bank: "Please keep the money."

At a motel: "One bedroom is unusually valuable."

At an airport: "Forbidden to throw seagulls."

At a park: "Prohibit cringing pets into the park."

At a restaurant: "Dear international customers—sorry."

WHO WANTS TO GO TO THE HOSPITAL?

It took a long time for hospitals to become trusted, caring, scientific institutions. Here's a look into the history of the sick bay.

4,000 BC In ancient Egypt, religious temples across the empire in cities like Memphis, Thebes, and Dendera are built as grand complexes, including what would now be called medical schools and teaching hospitals. Temple priests who specialize in medicine—having studied Egyptian medical texts like the *Book of Hermes* and the *Ebers Papyrus*—look after the admitted sick. In the night, the priests take patients into the temple's innermost areas, seeking the advice of the gods to tell the patients in their dreams what is wrong with them, so the priest-doctors can develop the proper course of treatment. Sometimes patients get better, sometimes they don't; either way, they are expected to pay the volunteer priests a modest offering.

450 BC In ancient Greek mythology, Asclepius, the son of Apollo, is the god of medicine. In his honor, Greeks open temple-adjacent clinics where priests can cure patients of their ailments both physically and spiritually. Such temple-hospitals are built at Cos, Trikka, Rhodes, Peramum, and elsewhere.

431 BC Small clinics on the island of what is now Sri Lanka pop up. They adhere to exacting standards of cleanliness, nutrition, and gentle care provided by nurses.

400 BC The concept of public health is born in ancient Greece following a malaria epidemic in Athens. The sickness and death is so widespread and all-encompassing across class and status that physicians believe outside factors are to blame, not angry gods. The so-called father of medicine, Hippocrates, writes *Airs, Waters, and Places* at this time, citing environmental causes for diseases and establishing a precursor to the germ theory developed in the 19th century. The reason so many people need to check into Greek hospitals: they drank water that came from a stagnant, malaria-infected swamp.

230 BC Asoka—emperor of Hindustan, which stretches over the Indian subcontinent—creates a chain of 18 hospitals around the empire.

Inspired by the Sri Lankan hospitals of two centuries prior, the institutions are said to be rigorously maintained with attitudes that reflect science more than spirituality. (Asoka's hospital in Surat is still operational today.)

100 BC The needs of the vast, ever-invading Roman armies necessitate the birth of the military hospital. The Roman government builds *valetudinaria* specifically to treat ill and wounded soldiers. It is a public-relations move as much as a practical one—Emperor Hadrian wants to show off the might of Rome and also wants to prevent his soldier brigades being decimated by disease, injury, and death.

AD 331 In the early 300s, Christianity revolutionarily becomes the state religion of Rome, ushering in the era of the Holy Roman Empire. In 331, newly converted Emperor Constantine orders that all the "pagan" hospitals, built in the ancient Greco-Roman traditions, be closed, in favor of conscientious, Christian-oriented facilities. In the old hospitals, patients were typically isolated from the public and from one another. With Christianity serving as a guidepost, new hospitals are encouraged to take a more hands-on approach to the sick, inspired by Christian beliefs that patients should be connected to the community.

The first Christian hospitals, run by specific religious orders (still commonplace today), open in nine cities around the Holy Roman Empire. These particular institutions, *infirmitoria*, remain open for nine centuries, run by monks from nearby monasteries. Sworn to an oath of service to the sick, the monks also grow gardens full of medicinal plants and build pharmacies. Over time, the hospitals open to not just local patients but to sick and injured travelers and religious pilgrims.

370 St. Basil the Great, while serving as the bishop of Caesarea (now part of Israel), asks the Holy Roman Empire to build a hospital to treat a health crisis: leprosy. Requiring isolation because of the highly contagious (and incurable) nature of their disease, patients with leprosy are housed and treated at a hospital purpose-built for them, the first specialized-treatment medical facility in history.

500 At Montecassino, south of Rome, in the early sixth century, St. Benedict establishes the first hospital that operates under the

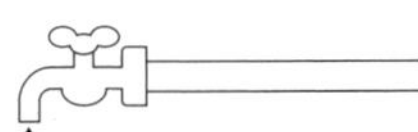

belief that caring for the sick is the primary duty of Christians. Monks who join the order take up such work as their calling. That passion and devotion includes not just a hospital but also one of the first medical schools in Europe. Infirmaries run by monks become the standard hospital procedure for the next 600 years or so.

542 The Hôtel-Dieu opens in Lyon. Similar to the Holy Roman Empire's medicine-first hospitals, but harkening back to the ancient spiritually focused hospitals of Egypt, this and other French institutions (such as Paris's first hospital, opened in 660) combine elements of both traditions. Built near monasteries and staffed by monks, these French hospitals have medicinal gardens and on-site pharmacies but also focus on trying to heal the soul, thought to be the source of medical maladies.

790 In the late eighth and early ninth centuries, head of the Abbasid Caliphate, Hārūn ar-Rashīd, orders a college to be built and operated alongside every mosque in his realm (which comprises most of today's Middle East), along with a hospital. In Baghdad, there is a specialized institution devoted to psychiatric care. Baghdad is also home to dozens of free infirmaries for the sick. This system lasts well into the Middle Ages.

1090s The Crusades begin at the end of the 11th century and lead to combat injuries that require medical attention. Venturing into foreign lands also exposes Crusaders to new diseases, viruses, and infections to which they have no immunity. The routes to and from the Middle East become dotted with the first military hospitals. The Roman Catholic monastic Knights Hospitallers of the Order of St. John build a 2,000-patient-capacity hospital in the Holy Land in 1099 that is especially devoted to diseases of the eye.

1140s The Crusades—and the medical fallout from them—normalize hospitals and the hospital experience for Europeans. The volume of hospitals explodes throughout Europe, with one exemplary institution being the Hospital of the Holy Ghost, opened in Montpellier, France, in 1145. It wll evolve into the most prestigious teaching hospital and medical school in Europe throughout the Middle Ages. Meanwhile, the Benedictine order of monks create more than 2,000 hospitals over the next 350 years.

What do the characters of Superman and Frankenstein have in common? Both were created by teenagers.

1500 Government-sponsored health care takes root in Europe. Most cities and medium-sized towns across the continent have some kind of hospital or medical facility overseen by the local government.

1524 The Hospital de Jesús Nazareno opens in what is now Mexico. It is built at the spot where Spanish conquistador Hernán Cortés met Aztec emperor Montezuma II. In the midst of eradicating the Aztecs and claiming vast areas of the Americas for the Spanish crown, Cortés built the first hospital in North America. It's still open today.

1540 King Henry VIII of England, denied a divorce from his wife from the Roman Catholic Church, calls for the establishment of the Church of England. Catholic institutions are summarily eradicated from England, thus completing what had already been a gradual transfer of authority over hospitals from monasteries to secular jurisdiction.

1639 French authorities occupying Quebec City open the Hôtel-Dieu du Précieux Sang, the first hospital in what will become Canada. Five years later, French noblewoman Jeanne Mance moves to Montreal specifically to team up with the religious order the Sisters of St. Joseph to build a hospital in the burgeoning colonial population center. That becomes the Hôtel-Dieu de St. Joseph. Both hospitals remain operational today; the Sisters of St. Joseph is the oldest nursing organization in North America.

1663 A hospital for soldiers opens on Manhattan Island. It's the first dedicated medical facility in what will eventually become the United States.

1710s With no hospitals built in England since the days of Catholic-run health care, the voluntary hospital movement springs up to address the need for more aid. Five major hospitals open in London, supported by charitable donations of largesse from the wealthy, where patients receive their care for free. Similar hospitals open up in other English-controlled areas of the time, including Ireland, Australia, and the American colonies. In the New World, these charity hospitals are affiliated with poorhouses, or almshouses, and the first is established by Pennsylvania founder William Penn in 1713.

1751 Pennsylvania Hospital begins seeing patients. With an official charter from the English crown, it's the first incorporated hospital in the New World.

The first recorded printings of the words *doorbell*, *dinner party*, and *sponge cake* were in Jane Austen novels.

1890s Following the discovery (and proof) that germs cause disease, and that antiseptics and antibiotics can treat them, the hospital experience radically changes. By the early 20th century, hospitals are modern, increasingly technologically advanced facilities devoted first and foremost to hygiene and stopping the spread of disease as well as treating it.

1929 Baylor Hospital in Waco, Texas, offers a pilot insurance plan, covering hospitalizations, to local schoolteachers. It is separate from regular health-insurance plans and, because it is offered at a group rate to create discounts, it's the predecessor to future collective insurance plans and health-maintenance organizations like Blue Cross/Blue Shield.

1946 Congress passes the Hospital Survey and Construction Act, which subsidizes the funding of hospitals and health-care facilities around the U.S., in part to stimulate post–World War II economic growth and in part to treat those wounded long-term. The bill includes pre–Civil Rights Movement language, banning discrimination from race, religion, and national origin in publicly funded hospitals, but also allowing for "separate but equal" facilities in racially segregated regions of the U.S.

1951 The Joint Commission on the Accreditation of Hospitals (JCAH) is formed. A voluntary hospital regulatory industry group, it allows facilities to submit themselves for accreditation, which increases their public stature and acts as a guarantee of quality care to the public.

1965 Under the banner of President Lyndon Johnson's "Great Society" social reforms, Congress signs Medicare and Medicaid into law. Providing free or reduced health-care costs to the elderly, infirm, and poor, the program covers hospital and physician costs as well as some in-home care.

1965 The federal Office on Economic Opportunity, another "Great Society" project, authorizes and opens neighborhood health centers. Bigger and more equipped than a standard doctor's office, but not as outfitted as a full hospital, they're full-service medical care clinics for low-income citizens and communities without ready access to hospitals. These are the precursors to both government-subsidized free clinics and for-profit urgent-care clinics.

WEIRD ANIMAL NEWS

Just some wild news from the wild kingdom.

BEE AWARE

Repeatedly, and over the span of many months, preschooler Saylor Class went to her parents with a common childhood complaint: there was a monster living in her bedroom wall. Her parents dutifully did what they could to assuage her fears, which they believed were related to anxiety over the arrival of a new baby sibling; they pretended to look for any monsters and even used water disguised as "monster spray" to deter them. But Saylor insisted she could hear something, so her mother, Ashley Class, called in pest control, who used a thermal camera to uncover the true source of the sounds. Behind the girl's bedroom wall was a 100-pound honeycomb, home to around 50,000 bees—whose collective humming sounded like a monster to the little girl. The bees were removed but had already caused tens of thousands of dollars' worth of damage.

STINKS SO GOOD

In the U.S., it's called Axe Body Spray; in the U.K., it's called Lynx. In both countries, it's heavily marketed to its target audience and biggest buyer—teenage boys—with ads that indicate women will respond favorably to the pheromones released by the application of the pungent, cologne-deodorant aerosol hybrid. A collective of sheep farmers in the U.K. discovered that the "Africa" scent of the spray has a profound effect on their herds. Sam Bryce learned from the Facebook group Ladies Who Lamb that the spray can be used to quell aggressive behavior in rams. Lynx covers up, and makes the rams nose-blind to, the pheromones released by one another that lead to fighting. "There's no argy-bargy, no rowing," she told reporters in 2024. Another British shepherd, Caitlin Jenkins, uses Lynx Africa to persuade mother sheep to accept abandoned and orphaned lambs as their own.

BIRD ISN'T THE WORD

Back in May 2023, police in the Indian city of Mumbai spotted a shady-looking character hanging out near the docks. That individual was a pigeon, and it was considered suspicious because it had two rings tied to its legs with notes that looked like they were written in a Chinese script. Police detectives quickly ascertained that this pigeon clearly was a spy working for the Chinese government. They captured the

Pete Rose was banned from baseball (for betting) by MLB commissioner A. Bartlett Giamatti, whose son is actor Paul Giamatti.

bird and sent it to the most logical bird prison available, the Bai Sakarbai Dinshaw Petit Hospital for Animals. Eight months later, investigations indicated that the pigeon was a bird trained to race over open water in Taiwan (which explained the rings and the notes), and that it had escaped and accidentally flown thousands of miles to India. The bird was released from captivity on its own recognizance.

STATUE OF LIMITATIONS

The Roman Catholic Church granted sainthood to Francis of Assisi shortly after his death in the early 13th century. Because he is the patron saint of animals and of treating wildlife with kindness, statues of Francis are frequently displayed in parks and preserves, and animal lovers also display them on their properties. In January 2024, an animal ironically got itself stuck in one of those tribute reproductions. The Humane Animal Welfare Society in Waukesha, Wisconsin, responded to a report from a homeowner who said a coyote had lodged its entire head inside the hollow at the bottom of their Saint Francis of Assisi statue. HAWS workers brought the hypothermic coyote to the Wildlife in Need Center, where she was given the nickname "Frannie" and treated for two weeks before being released back into the wild.

SEEMS FISHY

Mutekimaru Channel is a YouTube account based in Japan, popular because it offers content that nobody else does: its creator streams live video of his fish playing video games. The operator rigged a Nintendo Switch system controller so that when one of his fish swims over a particular area, it triggers an action in the game. A new fish gets to try to play every 12 hours. In 2023, Mutekimaru Channel was the victim of credit card fraud. When a fish was playing the game *Pokémon Scarlet and Violet*, the game crashed, bringing up the Nintendo Switch homepage; once that was up, the fish managed to access Mutekimaru's account, including stored credit card information. Not only did the fish move 500 yen to the game account, but it then used those Nintendo credits to buy accessories for golfing in *Nintendo Switch Sports*.

NEITHER DUNG NOR DUNG BEETLE

Insect researchers in Queensland, Australia, discovered in 2024 an entirely heretofore unseen species of longhorn beetle. Entomologist James Tweed came across the large beetle with shaggy white hair during a camping trip and first didn't even think it was a bug—when he saw the beetle on a leaf, he thought it was a splatter of bird poop. "It's very unique," Tweed told reporters about the white covering on the insect. "There are not many insects out there that have that trait."

Dolphins have been observed fending off attacking sharks from a whale while the whale is giving birth.

UGLY SHOE ORIGINS

Beauty is in the eye of the beholder, even when it comes to footwear. These popular, best-selling shoes may be trendy, and they're undoubtedly comfortable, but they're also almost universally known for being style failures. Here are the birth stories of some of those famously unattractive (but still successful) footwear styles.

Shoe: Uggs

Description: Clunky sheepskin boots

Story: In the late 1800s, shepherds and sheep-shearers in Australia made sheepskin foot coverings by using leather straps to wrap spare lengths of the material around their feet and ankles. The material was naturally resistant to the lanolin that came off sheep's wool, which quickly degraded boots made out of other materials. Then during World War I, British and Australian pilots laced sheepskin onto their feet to fend off frostbite during unpressurized—and thus brutally cold—combat flights. Those pilots were the first to nickname the boots "Uggs," shortened from "Flying Uggs," with "Ugg" itself being shorthand for "ugly." In 1933, the Blue Mountains Ugg Boot company formed in New South Wales, followed by Mortel's Sheepskin Company in the 1950s, but Australian sheepskin boots wouldn't go worldwide until the 1970s when competitive surfers touring the world utilized them to instantly warm their feet after a spell in the cold ocean. Australian surfer Brian Smith moved to California in the 1980s specifically to sell sheepskin boots, establishing UGG Imports. The footwear sold brisky, a beneficiary of the "Australian craze" of the 1980s spurred by *"Crocodile" Dundee* and bands like Men at Work. The shoes then came roaring back to popularity in the mid-2000s, seen on trendsetters like Paris Hilton and Lindsay Lohan.

Shoe: Crocs

Description: Plasticine clogs covered with holes

Story: Friends Scott Seamans, George Boedecker, and Lyndon Hansen took a boating trip to Mexico in 2002. Seamans was a businessman working with Canadian company Foam Creations on a version of a non-wooden clog with the style choice of cutouts (holes) all over the shoe. They weren't selling, but Seamans took the shoes on his trip thinking they'd be good boat shoes—which they were because they were odor-resistant, comfortable, didn't slip, and floated in water. He added a strap to the back to ensure they wouldn't fall off. The three friends started a company to sell the shoes they worried were too ugly, but sold out their stock at a Fort Lauderdale,

Actual headline: "Former *Eastenders* Actress Slams 'Pretentious' Restaurant After Husband Accidentally Eats Napkin."

Florida, boat show. They were embraced not just by boaters—nurses and restaurant servers liked them too, for the same reasons. By 2006, they were selling $200 million worth of shoes that they named Crocs because from the side, they sort of looked like crocodile snouts. (And they're not made from plastic or rubber but Croslite, a patented, proprietary blend of resin developed by Foam Creations.)

Shoe: Platform sneakers

Description: They look like running or basketball shoes, but then they're sitting on huge rubber platforms that give the wearer three or four more inches of height

Story: These regular-looking sneakers made absurdly tall with a thicker rubber sole unsurprisingly started as a joke. In Charles Ludlam's 1976 fashion-satire play *Caprice,* platform sneakers are among the creations of a designer gone mad. Platform boots were on their way out at the time, and Ludlam was playing on that. But the play was such a hit that platform sneakers entered the public consciousness, and in 1984 real-life fashion designer Norma Kamali—who helped popularize the very 1980s trend of shoulder-pad-embracing female clothing—created some. New York City nightclub scenesters adopted homemade platform sneakers into their elaborate party costumes in the late 1980s and early 1990s, while Converse and Chanel released commercial versions in 1993 and 1994. But the huge shoes got really big in the latter part of the 1990s, when pop group and fashion influencers the Spice Girls wore them frequently, pairing them with minidresses. The British quintet preferred the Buffalo London brand, but Steve Madden, No Name, Guess, and Superga all released commercially successful takes on the idea. Sales peaked in 1998, and the fad died out in 1999—right about the time when the Spice Girls craze did, too.

Shoe: Reebok Pump

Description: Athletic shoes that promise increased performance because of an air pump in the tongue

Story: In 1988, Nike dominated the athletic shoe market with the Air Jordan—expensive, Michael Jordan–endorsed, highly coveted footwear designed for basketball but also for fashion. Distant competitor Reebok sought to acquire customers by going after a different market segment—their shoes would offer the practical, if unsexy, attribute of superior ankle support. That idea came after the Reebok Advanced Concepts team couldn't figure out a way to make a shoe that increased vertical jump (and thus compete with Air Jordans), so it utilized inflatable-shoe-tongue technology lifted from ski boot maker Ellesse, which Reebok had just acquired. Essentially an air bladder built into the shoe, with a pump button on the outside, it allowed for a more stable and secure fit, particularly for the ankles. To make up for the lack of flash in

The power of this fact compels you! The country with the most exorcists is Italy, with 290. (The U.S. has about 150.)

the Reebok Pump, the company paid a fortune in endorsements from NBA stars Dee Brown and Dominique Wilkins, who wore the shoe in their respective Slam Dunk Contest victories in 1990 and 1991. Reebok cut into Nike's business, selling $500 million worth of its $170 shoes, but the fad was over by 1993. Pumps were 30 percent heavier and much boxier than Air Jordans, and basketball players, professional and amateur, re-embraced those.

Shoe: Heelys

Description: Sneakers rendered clunky and boxy because they have to hide the machinery that makes them instantly convertible into roller skates

Story: Roger Adams roller-skated from the time he was nine months old: his parents owned the Adams-Tacoma Roller Bowl outside Seattle, the largest roller rink in the Pacific Northwest. An amateur engineer and tinkerer, Adams hated his 1990s job as a mental-health hospital supervisor in Oregon. In 1998, he took a post-divorce vacation to Huntington Beach, California, and was enthralled with the beachside and boardwalk skate culture—crowds of people skateboarding and rollerblading all day long—and it reminded him of his childhood pastime and family business. He put his inventing skills to work, combining sneaker-style roller skates from the 1970s with the inline skate tech of the 1990s. He sliced open a pair of tennis shoes, installed skateboard wheels, and created what he called Heelys, which were everyday shoes with hidden, retractable wheels that turned them into roller skates. All the wearer had to do was shift their weight to their heels, and the wheel would click down or back up again. Adams opened the Heelys company in December 2000 and sold out every pair at a trade show. Within five years, he had 700 employees and $32 million in sales, with more than a million pairs sold. The trend wasn't without controversy, and the thing that made Heelys so attractive to kids and young adults is what led to their quick exit from the marketplace: Heelys (and knockoffs) caused an injury rate of 51 per 100,000, a third of those mishaps befalling kids using the shoe for the first time. The U.S. Product Safety Commission issued a warning on Heelys, and they were perceived as such a dangerous distraction that numerous schools and public gathering places in Europe and North America banned the shoes outright.

* * *

CASUAL FRIDAY, FOR HEALTH

A new reason for offices to relax business dress codes? Wearing a necktie can reduce blood flow to the brain by as much as 7.5 percent, and can also increase pressure in the eyes. (Not to mention that, because they're rarely cleaned, they're great at harboring germs.)

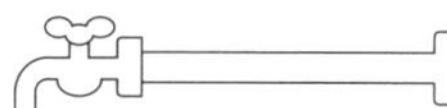

There were 108 male Supreme Court Justices before Sandra Day O'Connor joined the court in 1981.

MOUTHING OFF

INFAMOUS LAST WORDS

We look to our leaders and champions for a legacy of words, some wisdom uttered with their final breaths. But everybody dies—even very bad people—and some of them say some pretty startling things in their last moments.

"I don't care if I live or die. Go ahead and kill me."

—Jeffrey Dahmer, serial killer, before he was murdered

"Yeah, I think I'd rather be fishing."

—Jimmy Glass, murderer, before he was executed

"I have conquered for you a large empire. But my life was too short to take the whole world. That I leave to you."

—Genghis Khan

"Aim right at my heart."

—Benito Mussolini, Italian dictator, before he was executed by firing squad

"FOR THE COMING MAN."

—Adolf Hitler, before his suicide, to an underling, answering a question about who the Third Reich was fighting for

"Shame on you, you know no sin."

—Muammar Gaddafi, dictator, as he was attacked by a mob

"We didn't commit suicide, we committed an act of revolutionary suicide protesting the conditions of an inhumane world."

—Jim Jones, cult leader, before he led a mass suicide

"You can be a king or a street sweeper, but everyone dances with the Grim Reaper."

—Robert Alton Harris, murderer, before he was executed

"I'm the most famous human being not only that is alive but the most famous human being that has ever lived. And I'm not even dead yet."

—Charles Manson

"THEY WILL NOT DESTROY ME OR BREAK ME; I SHALL DEFEAT THEM ALL."

—Slobodan Milošević, in his prison cell to an associate while awaiting trial for war crimes

RENDER NONVIABLE

What is that vaguely innocuous title phrase describing? You might not want to know, but you'll have it figured out after reading these lists of professional doublespeak and jargon. Decoded.

The Military

Friendly fire: shooting and/or bombing your own troops.
Incontinent ordnance: friendly fire.
Accidental delivery of ordnance: friendly fire.
Rapid oxidation: fire (as in, flames).
Energetic disassembly: an explosion.
Air support: bombing raid.
Terrain alteration: a really big bombing raid.
Servicing the target: bombing the target.
Terminate with extreme prejudice: kill.
Arbitrarily deprive of life: kill.
Render nonviable: kill.

The Government

Upskilling: training.
Alternative facts: lies.
Value engineering: cutting costs.
Mistakes were made: we made mistakes.
Efficiency: fewer workers working longer hours.
Interruption of economic expansion: recession.
Meaningful statistical downturn: recession.
Negative economic growth: recession.

People and Professions

Vertical Transportation Engineer: elevator operator.
Domestic Engineer: homemaker.
Sanitation Engineer: trash collector.
Surface Engineer: painter.
Materials Spreader: painter.
Environmental Hygienist: janitor.
Vehicle Appearance Operative: car washer.
Optical Enhancement Agent: window washer.
Hospitality Coordinator: restaurant host.

The electric toothbrush was invented in Switzerland in 1939.

Director of First Impressions: receptionist.
Economically Marginalized: unemployed.
Involuntary Undomiciled: homeless.
Executive Producer: an actor with a good agent.

At the Office

Let's hit the ground running: We don't have the budget to train you.
We don't need to reinvent the wheel: Let's copy what someone else is doing.
Action item: This item will be lacking any of the fun definitions of "action."
Synergy: This is going to take more people than we originally thought.
Let's circle back on this: I don't want to think about this right now.
Your idea won't scale: Your idea sucks.
Feel free to ping me: Don't you dare ever ping me.
Gentle reminder: Make me remind you again and you'll be sorry.
I don't have the bandwidth: I'm already overworked and you're giving me more work.
To piggyback off that point...: You're done talking. Now it's my turn.
Off-topic: A topic that isn't boring.
Moving on: If we keep going off-topic, this meeting will never end.
Bottom line: I get to have the last word because I said, "Bottom line."
We have to feed the gorilla: Your position has been eliminated.
A refocusing of the company's skill set: You're fired.
At the end of the day: We still haven't retired this tired cliché?

Composing a Work Email

Dear ____: I've never sent a work email until now, and I think this is how you start it.
Hi ____: I begin this email informally (with my tail between my legs) because I need something.
____: Beginning an email with just the recipient's name says you really mean business!
Please confirm receipt: Or just tell me in three weeks that it went to your junk folder.
Let's continue this offline: My written words obviously aren't getting through to you, so let's see how my mouth words do.
Kind regards: I also don't know how to end a work email.
Best: This is the most neutral, least-offensive sign-off I can possibly think of.
All the best: Please don't fire me.
Sincerely: If you've been paying attention, you'll have noticed that I end most of my emails with "Best"—so the fact that I'm using "Sincerely" here means this email is actually important! Who am I kidding? Nobody reads to the end of an email, anyway.

MUD SPORTS

Get the hose ready. It's the dirtiest article in the book.

MUD WRESTLING

If all that comes to mind when you think of mud wrestling is scantily clad women rolling around a muddy ring while men hoot and holler—well, that is a big part of mud wrestling. But this sport is ancient, going back to the Greeks and Romans, and even earlier in India. In 2500 BC, the Greeks knew it as *pale*, and it is now known by the name *Kushti*, meaning "heroic sport," practiced in India, Pakistan, and Iran, where it's still popular—and taken very seriously. For the wrestlers, the sport is their life. They all live together in an *ahkara*, where the *pehlwans* (wrestlers) learn from the *ustads* (teachers) how to live a life of purity. No smoking or alcohol, no meat besides chicken, and no sex is allowed. Even the mud, made from special oil-soaked clay, is purifying. They cover themselves in it and wrestle one another.

As for the not-quite-as-pure sport of women's mud wrestling, that began in Akron, Ohio, in 1938, when two men, Michael Wittrock and Tyler Carroll, sponsored the first match, fought between Mildred "Cyclone" Burke and Leona "Babe" Gordon. (Cyclone won.)

In the decades since, women's mud wrestling has remained a popular but unofficial sport at bars, block parties, and other places of debauchery. It's mostly done for fun, but there are rules: to keep the women from slipping, they have to wrestle on their knees. And there's no kicking, punching, biting, or hair pulling. As with politics, however, mudslinging is allowed.

In 2003, a group of women mud wrestlers decided to take the sport back from the men who organize and (mostly) watch it, and the Chicago Mud Queens was born. This underground wrestling organization held events at bars all over the Windy City in the 2010s. Not only were the matches not faked, but these ladies were in it to win it. "We're breaking stereotypes," said Erica de Marco, who wrestled under the name "Ultimate Whorrior." "When you think of mud wrestling, you think of girls rolling around seductively, but we bring strength to it."

SUOPOTKUPALLO

That's Finnish for "swamp football," or "swamp soccer" in the U.S., and it's exactly what it sounds like: two teams consisting of five field players and a goalie compete on a field of deep mud. How deep? It's so deep that playing for more than a few minutes at a time is exhausting, even for those in peak physical condition (we get tired just

Striped mammals can't have a spotted tail, but spotted animals can have a striped tail.

watching it!). That's why there are no limits to the substitutions a team can make, but changing shoes is not allowed. The sport began in 1998, when its founder, Jyrki "The Swamp Baron" Väänänen, was inspired by the rigorous swamp strength-training exercises that the Finnish ski team had to endure.

The Suopotkupallo World Championship takes place in Vuorisuo, Finland, every year. The game has since spread around the world: Scotland is the headquarters of Swamp Soccer U.K., which has held World Cups from Turkey to India and China. Currently, there are about 300 swamp soccer teams consisting of men and women—there may even be one near you.

WATTOLÜMPIADE

That funny word is German for the "Mud Olympics." The *Watt* are mud flats that stretch for miles along the mouth of the Elbe River near Hamburg. Every August since 2004, for one weekend, thousands of spectators show up to cheer on hundreds of "mudletes," or *Wattlets*, as they go for the gold in events such as mud soccer, mud volleyball, mud handball, mud sledge racing, mud eel racing, a long-distance rubber boot toss, and whatever else the organizers can think of. There's also a contest for best team name and funniest costume. (This takes place prior to the events, because afterward, the costumes are too muddy.) The Mud Olympics—which benefit a local cancer charity—also feature a music festival called Mudstock (which is fitting, given that two of the three American Woodstock music festivals devolved into big mud pits).

MUD BOGGING

Whether you call it mudding, mud running, mud racing, mud hogging, or mug bogging—or, whether you're affiliated with the National Mud Racing Organization or the American Mud Racers Association—you can count on at least one vehicle ending up upside down. In the mud.

Mud bogging was born in the American South in the 1970s, the same time that 4x4 trucks became popular. Races of yesteryear took place in those modest trucks, but today's "mud racers" drive dragster-style designs with raised bodies, massive tires, and supercharged engines. And they're not just big 4x4s: there are trick cars, funny cars, even a VW Bus with a bright yellow floral pattern...that quickly becomes brown. The goal is not speed but power—to see who can drive their truck the farthest through a several-feet-deep bog, or who can prevail in a thunderous duel of muddy tug-of-war.

Since 2006, mud parks have popped up through the Deep South, where regular folks can take their "ATVs, UTVs, buggies, lifted Jeeps, and Mega Trucks" to get dirty. According to *Motor Trend*, the mud park culture has invented its own musical genre: "hick-hop, a collision of Southern rock, country, and rap. The lyrics are often

In July 1986, the #1 song was "Invisible Touch" by Genesis. The #2 song was "Sledgehammer" by Peter Gabriel, the former lead singer of Genesis.

about rolling coal, jacked-up trucks, moonshine, and big bonfires." Mud boggers have even been featured on a slew of basic-cable shows, most recently on Discovery's *Mud Madness*. "Between the custom builds, challenging mud courses, deep-rooted rivalries, intense action, and a wild social party scene, cameras capture all the elements of the sport."

And while mud bogging may be big business, as it is with most mudletes, these guys and gals don't take themselves too seriously. Just look at what they call their rigs: "Six Pack," "Lil Willys," "Nasty Habits," and "Unnamed & Untamed." Even the festivals have silly names: South Florida Slingin', Michigan Mud Jam, Vermonster 4x4, and Trucks Gone Wild.

TOUGH MUDDER

Tough Mudder cofounder Will Dean's favorite movie is *The Shawshank Redemption*—especially that classic line, narrated by Morgan Freeman: "Andy Dufresne—who crawled through a river of s*** and came out clean on the other side." That's the whole idea behind Tough Mudder, except they don't make you crawl through raw sewage. Not that what you do have endure is much better. We'll get to that in a sec.

Dean, a former counterterrorism officer for the British government, started Tough Mudder in New York in 2009 with his childhood friend Guy Livingstone. They based their company on an outdoor team-building regimen Dean had entered into a business-plan contest at Harvard Business School. The plan didn't win that contest, so Dean left Harvard and started the company anyway. The first Tough Mudder took place in May 2010 in Allentown, Pennsylvania. Today, there are events all over the world.

"At its core, Tough Mudder is simple," explains Dean. "It's a 10-mile obstacle course." The point is not to win the race, but for you and your team to work together to complete the course. The camaraderie is the point: "Whether you've done one in Germany or Australia, it's the same experience, which means that you share something with others who have been through a Tough Mudder. If I go running in my Tough Mudder T-shirt in the park in London, and see another Tough Mudder T-shirt coming my way, it's natural to high-five that person."

But be warned: these shared experiences are not for the faint of heart, or for anyone with a heart condition. Obstacles include "Electroshock Therapy," where you run through a muddy pool while ducking under a low electric fence ("All the muscles in the world won't soften the blow of 10,000 volts!"); "Cry Baby," where you crawl through a muddy tube full of tear gas; "Arctic Enema," where you submerge yourself in a dumpster full of ice-cold water; and "Cage Crawl," where you lie on your back in a shallow pool of mud, with your face just above the surface, a horizontal chain-link fence a few inches above you, and have to use your hands to pull your way to freedom before the mud overcomes you (just like Andy Dufresne).

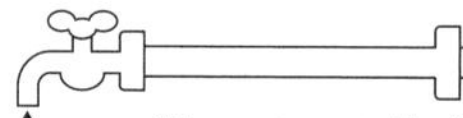

Almost cast: Emilio Estevez was considered for the role of Daniel in *The Karate Kid*. His brother, Charlie Sheen, was considered for the bully, Johnny.

HEAD-SCRATCHING HEADLINES

Some come from newspapers, some from the Internet; some are obvious, some are baffling.

Sleeping Pilots Are Rare, Says Airline

Boulder the Size of a Large Boulder Removed After Blocking Highway 21

Newest Residents from Elsewhere

STRAWBERRY TRUCK OVERTURNS ON SAN JOSE FREEWAY, CREATES JAM

Fire Crews Called After Smoke Seen in Sky Turned Out to Be a Cloud

Rooms with Broken Air Conditioners Are Hot

Cold Weather Causes Rise in Heating Bills

World Bank Says Poor Need More Money

NASA Sets its Sights on Probing Uranus

Biden at 81: Often Sharp and Focused but Sometimes Confused and Forgetful

OLD MAN HAD CAVITY IN ONE TOOTH BUT OTHER TWO ARE FINE

Report of Armed Man with Pan Making Threats at 2190 Bacon St

Police Arrest Everyone on February 22nd

Homeless Man Under House Arrest

Pub Food Handlers Told Not to "Scratch Backsides"

Weibo Cracks Down on Posts About Weibo Crackdowns

Cybertruck Catches Fire After Running into Fire Hydrant and Getting Wet

Search and Rescue Team Accidentally Finds Jay Leno While Looking for Missing Hiker

Japan's Likely New Prime Minister, Britney Spears Back in Court and More

Sports: Butt Ready for Some Action

Ranchers Struggle Against Giant Meatpackers

Tiny Dog Saves Medium Man from Large Moose

Kangaroo Injured in Low-Speed Chase Through Alps

TWO SLICED OVER SALAD, ONE TOSSED IN JAIL

Chainsaw-Wielding Mayor Enrages Museum Board

Sharp Decline in Knife Attacks

Australia has been inhabited for 50,000 years, but humans didn't make it to nearby New Zealand until about 800 years ago.

PAPERBACKS VS. THE AXIS POWERS

From the dustbin of history, here's the story of how one of the biggest coordinated literacy efforts ever undertaken helped countless American soldiers cope with the horrors of World War II.

ROUGH DRAFTS

When more than four million Americans were deployed between 1917 and 1918 to fight in Europe in the Great War, later known as World War I, much of the American production and industrial apparatus switched to supporting the war effort. The country's librarians, booksellers, and book publishers wanted to do their part, too, which inspired the American Library Association to start a nationwide drive soliciting book donations. Whatever they received through the mail and in drop-off bins around the country would be sent to troops stationed overseas to help them pass the time—and keep their minds off the terrors of combat, or the agony of recovering from injuries in military hospitals.

By the time the ALA's book drive got off the ground, however, the war was over. But when World War II broke out in Europe, and it started to look like the U.S. may join the Allied forces, the ALA revisited their books-for-troops idea, creating the Victory Book Campaign. After the United States officially entered the war following the Japanese bombing of Pearl Harbor in late 1941, the Victory Book Campaign's organizers ambitiously aimed to collect 10 million books in 1942. The group met its goal, but the excitement was tempered. The reason: most of the books they received were ones people would otherwise have just thrown away. If they weren't dirty or falling apart, they were hopelessly out-of-date (unappealing to troops in their late teens and twenties) or otherwise unreadable.

MAKING REVISIONS

At the beginning of 1943, the Victory Book Campaign once again solicited donations, gently prodding charitable Americans by asking for "good books," however they chose to define that. Meanwhile, the library-based organization connected with the Council on Books in Wartime, a group formed by representatives of the major publishing houses of the era. The latter operated with the same objective as the Victory Book

Only pair of sisters to both have #1 solo albums: Solange Knowles and her big sis, Beyoncé.

Campaign—get books into the hands of the soldiers who could use them—but they'd print up new, cheap copies of their own books (and charge the government for them).

To make sure they didn't print hundreds of thousands of useless or impractical books, the Council on Books in Wartime worked with U.S. Army librarian Ray Trautman. Together they designed a line of special paperback books printed on inexpensive stock with pocket-sized dimensions—small and slim by design, so they could easily fit in the breast pocket or pants pocket of a standard G.I.'s uniform. That innovative format became Armed Services Editions.

HOT OFF THE PRESSES

The first print runs of Armed Services Editions books arrived with soldiers stationed in both the European and Pacific theaters. The initial book off the presses: *The Education of Hyman Kaplan*, a collection of funny stories by Leonard Q. Ross (pen name of *The Joys of Yiddish* author Leo Rosten). The books cost publishers seven cents per copy, and they were distributed free of charge. Physical limitations capped each book's length at 512 pages, and if a work had been abridged to fit into that format, a note on the cover said so—publishers didn't want readers to ever think that any of the books had been censored for content. Soldiers were encouraged to pass the books along when they were done with them, until they were worn out.

The Council on Books in Wartime considered a lot of factors when deciding what books to include in this line. They wanted to entertain soldiers as well as educate them, and wanted to provide a wide array of titles so that the average shipment would have something for everyone in a squadron. Members of the Council on Books in Wartime undertook survey missions to military hospitals and safe zones to inquire about what kinds of books the men wished to see in the future. Armed Forces Editions would eventually comprise more than 1,300 titles, which included literary classics, new fiction, poetry, history, biography, humor, and even art—one of the more popular titles was an original, brand-new collection of paintings and sketches sent in by avid readers/enlisted soldiers.

THE BESTSELLER LIST

Within a year of implementation, Armed Services Editions were a massive hit. In 1944, the *New York Times* covered the efforts and called the books "as popular as pinup girls," noting they were shipped out at a rate of 100,000 copies per day. In some hard-to-reach spots, books were parachuted in with supplies and cargo. The military even arranged with enemy combatants, under the Geneva Convention, to send the books into prisoner-of-war camps in the Pacific Islands. The books were especially

Earwax is produced from specialized sweat glands.

popular among soldiers in traction in military hospitals, distracting from injury, fear, and homesickness.

Publishers who contracted with the Armed Services Editions line used the opportunity as a second chance to publicize books that had been forgotten or that hadn't been a hit with their commercial release. *Typee* by Herman Melville sold moderately well back upon its original publication in 1846, but the Armed Services Edition revived interest in the work, which is set in Polynesia. One soldier wrote in to the program saying he originally didn't want to read it, but he had been so bored in a foxhole that he had no choice but to pick it up. "Hot stuff," he wrote. "That guy wrote about three islands I'd been on!" *The Great Gatsby* is a school-assigned, universally acknowledged American classic today, but sold only 20,000 copies between its publication in 1925 and the death of author F. Scott Fitzgerald in 1940. Then more than 12,000 copies in the Armed Services Edition were gobbled up by soldiers, making *The Great Gatsby* a sleeper hit.

TORN-OUT PAGES

In survey after survey, soldiers said they preferred books with some kind of sexual content. Armed Services Editions obliged. One of the most popular titles in the line was Lillian Smith's *Strange Fruit*, a lurid and graphic tale of forbidden interracial romance. Readers also demanded new stories, so in 1943, just after it became a bestseller in its initial commercial run, Betty Smith's *A Tree Grows in Brooklyn* was picked up by Armed Services Editions—thanks to the 15,000 soldiers who requested it.

The program didn't publish just anything, even if it was popular, old and established, or requested. Organizers of the Armed Services Editions decided from the start that it wouldn't publish any titles that could be considered insulting to any of the United States' allies in the fights against Germany, Japan, and Italy, or that spoke negatively about a racial, ethnic, or religious group. That's why Zane Grey's 1912 western *Riders of the Purple Sage,* one of the most widely read books in American history, had its military print run canceled: it depicts the 19th-century Mormon settlers of Utah in a disparaging way. And after a Republican-controlled Congress passed a law to prevent Democrats from pursuing the military vote by banning the distribution to troops of written material that contained "political argument or political propaganda," a run of *Yankee from Olympus* was canceled (that's Supreme Court Justice Oliver Wendell Holmes's 1944 biography—it said nice things about democratic president Franklin Roosevelt). E. B. White's *One Man's Meat*, a low-key book about life on a Maine farm, was similarly deemed too controversial. In 1944, Congress amended the law, and both books were printed and released.

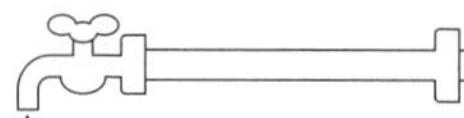

Poll results: 74 percent of U.S. adults spice up their meals with hot sauce.

CLOSING THE BOOK

World War II had ended in Europe and Japan by 1945, but Armed Services Editions fiction and nonfiction titles kept rolling off the presses until 1947. The need to distract from doom and death was over, but plenty of American personnel remained stationed in Europe and Asia as part of the postwar rebuilding efforts, and they had plenty of downtime to fill. The last book published in the line: *Home Country* by Ernie Pyle.

While the books steadfastly never promoted a particular political mindset, they did encourage American ideals, like a plurality of ideas and perspectives and freedom of speech. After frightening reports of rampant book burning in Nazi Germany making their way to the U.S. in the early years of World War II, President Roosevelt sent a memo to booksellers in 1942. It read, in part, "No man and no force can take from the world the books that embody man's eternal fight against tyranny." This was part of Roosevelt's Four Freedoms program, pillars of values that he consistently reminded soldiers and civilians were at stake in World War II, in contrast to the Nazi campaign of death, fear, and fascism.

BOOK REPORT

Clearly, the Four Freedoms influenced the Armed Services Editions. After the war, soldiers returned home spooked by the Nazis' attempts to eradicate not only large swaths of people but their culture, too. The cultural consensus in the 1940s among the youth was that censorship in all its forms was bad, personal expression was beautiful and necessary, and there should be no restrictions on either. A generation of well-read young men helped lead to literary movements like the Lost Generation and the Beat Generation.

Another cultural impact of the Armed Services Editions? Those titles popularized and legitimized the paperback. Before the war, the cheaper way of producing books was reserved solely for what were considered less-than-noble genres of fiction, like pulp, romance, horror, and other second-tier titles. The new paperback movement opened up the market for quality literature produced in an affordable way, and took paperback publishing into the mainstream.

* * *

THE TRISTATE SENATOR

James Shields is the only politician in American history to serve three different states in the U.S. Senate. He represented Illinois (1849–55), Minnesota (1858–59), and Missouri (1879).

NICE STORIES

Enjoy these stories with happy endings.

SO DAM CUTE

When you're a fish, and you reach a certain age, there's only one thing on your mind: swim upstream until you reach those calm, welcoming spawning grounds. But when there's a giant thing blocking your way, you just swim at it and swim at it until you die. If only there were someone there to open the door, so to speak.

In the city of Utrecht in the Netherlands, there is: *de visdeurbel*, which translates to "the fish doorbell." It was the brainchild of an ecologist named Mark van Heukelum in 2020, who noticed the backups of fish gathered at a canal boat lock that was closed to boat traffic in the spring, which happens to be spawning season. Other canals have fish ladders, but those are expensive. So Van Heukelum's idea was to install an underwater webcam, have local citizens monitor it, then let those viewers click a button to alert the city when there's a fishy traffic jam. At that point, a worker is dispatched to manually open the lock and let the fish through.

At first, the townsfolk thought Van Heukelum's plan was a joke. But after the webcam went live in March 2021, they took their duties seriously. And when word started spreading that Dutch fish were "ringing the doorbell" to be let through a lock, everyone wanted in on the action. Now, every spawning season, millions of people from all over the world check in on Utrecht's live stream, helping to keep thousands of fish alive...in the real stream.

I LOVE YOU TUTU

In 2003, Bob and Linda Carey moved from Arizona to Brooklyn. Bob, a professional photographer, was having trouble adapting to the big city. It got even worse after Linda was diagnosed with breast cancer. She had it treated early, so there was only a 30 percent chance of a recurrence...however, Linda learned just three years later that she had metastatic breast cancer. That diagnosis began an "emotional roller coaster" for both Linda and her husband. Bob helped where he could while Linda was undergoing chemotherapy, but it started to wear on him. "Caregivers aren't always well taken care of," she said. "I recognized that he needed to get out of the house and do something for himself. At one point I said, 'Why don't you take your tutu and go on a road trip for a couple of days?'"

Wait...his tutu? Bob—a big, burly man with a thick matte of chest hair—likes to wear a pink tutu (and nothing else) and photograph himself inserted into urban and natural landscapes. It's not as creepy as it sounds. The exquisite photos manage to be

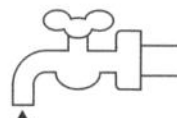

both goofy and serene. But the important thing is, they make Linda laugh.

Her fellow cancer patients also got a kick out of Bob's photos, so he kept at it. Fast-forward to the 2020s, and Bob and Linda (who's still in treatment) are running The Tutu Project, a foundation that helps metastatic breast cancer patients and their families pay for non-treatment expenses like groceries and utility bills. Want to help their cause, and get a laugh yourself? Buy Bob's books, *Ballerina* and *TUTU*, which feature fine art photos of the tutu-wearing man striking a pose everywhere from the rim of the Grand Canyon to an actual New York City Metropolitan Opera House stage performance of *Swan Lake*. "We are not the norm," says Linda.

MUSIC SOOTHES THE SAVAGE BEAST

Any given year, over 100,000 Americans are in need of a new kidney. In 2014, Don Herbert was one of them. He'd already spent 12 years on the waiting list for a new liver—that transplant went well, but in its aftermath, stage 4 kidney disease was now threatening to keep Don from growing old with his wife, Belinda. Don, a born-again gospel singer, leads a trio called the Parables of Christ, in Salisbury, North Carolina. One fateful Saturday in October 2014, Don and Belinda drove to a church craft sale in nearby Kannapolis. Don planned to stay in the car, but he noticed that loud gospel music was playing inside the church.

Don just had to go in and meet that someone: Pastor Tim, as the worshippers call him at Mercy Independent Baptist Church. But Tim B. Jones is more than a pastor. He moonlights as an operating room technician; it's his job to ensure a "safe and sterile environment" during surgery. The two men sparked an immediate friendship over their mutual love of gospel music, and Pastor Tim invited Don's trio to perform at Mercy's next revival.

Before that took place, Don received another medical blow: he had blockages in his heart, and the procedure to address that would destroy his already-failing kidneys and put him onto permanent dialysis. Belinda posted a passionate plea on Facebook, asking if anyone had it in their heart to donate a kidney. One person did: Pastor Tim.

Don said it's "mind-boggling to know that someone is willing to give a part of themselves. I don't even know how to respond to that." Tests confirmed that, despite great odds, Pastor Tim was a perfect match, and the transplant was a go.

Shockingly, while surgeons were removing Pastor Tim's kidney, they discovered an aneurism in an artery that hadn't been detected during the presurgical tests. If it hadn't been found during that surgery, it would have burst.

So, as it turned out, the pastor's lifesaving gift ended up saving his own life, too. "Right before Don showed up, I was ready to leave," said Pastor Tim of that first meeting at the church. "I would have missed him, but I believe in the will of God, and I believe God puts people in your path for a reason."

Depending on how it's grown, the *Brassica oleracea* plant can produce cabbage, broccoli, cauliflower, kale, collard greens, Brussels sprouts, or kohlrabi.

WHAT IS GRIMACE?

Admit it: you've always wondered. And we're happy to investigate, because here at Uncle John's, we don't believe there's such a thing as "useless information."

FROM FOE TO FRIEND

It's one of pop culture's biggest mysteries, right up there with, "What is Goofy?" (According to the Disney character's voice actor, he "seems to be in the canine family" but is not a dog. Or a cow. He's just Goofy.)

Grimace is a whole other matter.

When the purple blob made his McDonaldland debut in 1971, he was called "Evil Grimace." (McDonaldland is the name of the fictional fantasyland where Ronald McDonald and his fantastical friends live.) More creepy than evil, Grimace had four arms, was covered with scales, and was always trying to steal milkshakes from Ronald and Ronald's kid friends. A year later, a softer, gentler Grimace was reintroduced with a more reasonable number of arms (two). Now, he's Ronald's dopey friend, and he simply loves milkshakes.

But what *is* he? Or it?

As the 20th century wore on and Americans had more troubling matters to deal with (like wondering what Goofy is), Grimace faded into the background and disappeared from public view altogether in 2003 with the rest of McDonaldland. Now he's back, and more mysterious than ever.

AN ENIGMA WRAPPED IN A MILKSHAKE

Looking to the fast-food giant for answers only leads to more questions. A 1999 episode of *The Wacky Adventures of Ronald McDonald* animated series provides a backstory: Grimace hails from Grimace Island, where there are more...whatevers just like him. There's his brother, King Gonga; Grandma Winky; Aunts Milly and Tilly; and Uncle O'Grimacey (who just *loves* a green Shamrock Shake). But it's never mentioned what they all are.

In 2003, a McDonald's spokesperson referred to Grimace as a "giant taste bud." That was reiterated in a 2012 corporate tweet; then, in 2021, a Canadian McDonald's franchise manager's interview answer went viral: Grimace "is an enormous taste bud, but a taste bud nonetheless." That makes "taste bud" the leading theory, but hordes of Grimace fans didn't like that explanation, with one astutely commenting, "If Grimace is a taste bud meant to show how good the food is, why on earth would you name the damn thing after an expression of disgust?"

In 2023, McDonald's officially reintroduced Grimace for his 52nd birthday, but instead of putting an end to the mystery (which wouldn't be good for business), they

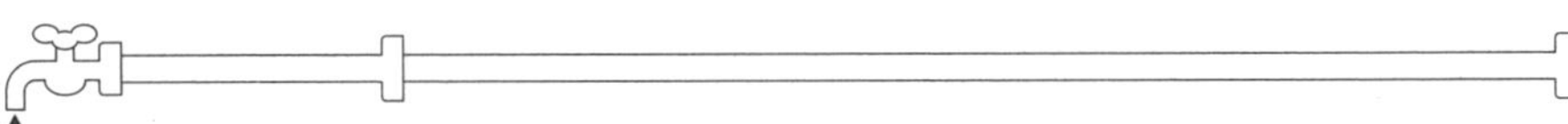

kept it alive: "Our timeless bestie has become a fan-favorite known for his signature fuzzy purple look, friendly and playful personality, love for shakes, and of course—ambiguous nature. What exactly is Grimace? Perhaps we'll never know."

THE HORROR!

For the 2023 birthday promo, McDonald's released the purple Grimace Shake... which received mixed to middling reviews. *People* magazine described it as "fruity and sugary." *Mashed* called it a "groan-worthy and troubling tribute to a garrulous grape-colored goofball who deserves so much better."

Then something happened that McDonald's did not expect. From the depths of TikTok emerged the disturbing "Grimace Shake" trend: users uploaded short horror movies detailing the purported effects of drinking the purple concoction. In one video, victims lay dying on a playground...drooling purple goo. In another, they're lying on a car hood...drooling purple goo. Or they're in their bed...drooling purple goo. The TikTokker behind the fad, @thefrazmaz, said he was inspired by a Burger King Halloween promotion featuring a Whopper with a frighteningly black bun. "It's just supposed to be a meme about, 'It's a really weird color, it's not good for you.' Grimace is collecting victims. It's just funny."

In response to the trend, the savvy McDonald's social media team tweeted a close-up of a frightened Grimace, with the caption, "Mee pretending i don't see the grimace shake trendd." Don't lie, Grimace. We know you're watching us...and we're watching you.

ACCORDING TO THE INTERNET, GRIMACE IS...

- "a monster from an island"
- "a milkshake out the cup"
- "a glob of fat"
- "a blob of jelly"
- "a giant gumdrop"
- "a large, purple gland"
- "a Lovecraftian monster from the same netherworld as the Stay-Puft Marshmallow Man"
- "a former human who drank so many milkshakes he turned into a monster"
- "the disturbing result of an unholy alliance between Barney the Dinosaur and a shmoo"
- "an out-of-its-crust Taro Pie" (a Hawaiian McDonald's menu item with lavender filling and chunks of purple taro fruit)
- "a space alien"
- "a large, mean, scary character in the shape and color of an eggplant [designed] to permanently frighten children away from vegetables (with the exception of french fries, of course)"
- "a horribly deformed genetic mutant"
- "an 'eating machine' that can consume copious amounts of McDonald's food at an alarming rate and thinks only of eating McDonald's food at all times"
- "Grimace represents whatever odd, mushy substance they really make their food from."
- "[There may be] dozens of separate, distinct, Grimace clones out there."

Why do dogs like playing with squeaky toys?
Because the squeaks sound like dying prey.

COINED ON SCREEN, PART II

More words and phrases originating from the business of show.
(Part I is on page 274.)

GASLIGHT

In 1938, British playwright Patrick Hamilton wrote a thriller play called *Gas Light*, about a husband in 1880s London who tries to drive his wife insane by insisting that the gas light in their apartment isn't getting dimmer when he's gone...when in fact it *is* getting dimmer, and he's responsible for it, but he can't let her know his dark secret. The hit play later ran on Broadway and has been adapted for the big and small screens, most famously the 1944 film *Gaslight* starring Charles Boyer and Ingrid Bergman. In the 1960s, writers began to "verb" the title into *gaslighting*, which means "manipulating someone to the point where they question their own reality."

PAPARAZZI

Tazio Secchiaroli was a famous Italian photojournalist known for doing whatever it took to get a photo. In 1958, when famous Italian director Federico Fellini was cowriting *La Dolce Vita* (*The Good Life*)—the classic 1961 film about Rome's nightlife—he saw one of Secchiaroli's photos of a striptease at a nightclub, and it was inspiration for the character Paparazzo, who, along with his fellow news photographers, stalks and swarms celebrities. The origin of the name is a matter of debate: it could have come from a George Gissing novel, or (our preferred origin), "It is indeed an Italian family name," wrote one Fellini scholar, "probably a corruption of the word *papataceo*, a large and bothersome mosquito."

YOU'RE TOAST

Until 1984, *toast* had two meanings: "cheers!" and "browned bread." But just before the squad in *Ghostbusters* face off against the ancient Sumerian god Gozer, who's taken the shape of a woman, Bill Murray announces, "This chick is toast!" Almost immediately, the adjective meaning "dead as a doornail" started appearing in print (usually in reference to a scandalous politician) and five years later in *Die Hard*, when one of the terrorists celebrates after destroying a SWAT armored vehicle with a missile: "Oh my God, the quarterback is toast!"

HIGH-MAINTENANCE

"The are two kinds of women," Harry tells Sally in 1989's *When Harry Met Sally*, "high-maintenance and low-maintenance." "Which kind am I?" asks Sally. "The worst kind: you're high-maintenance, but you think you're low-maintenance." Screenwriter Nora Ephron didn't pluck this expression out of thin air; the *Oxford English Dictionary* traces its usage back to the early 1980s. Along with "transitional relationship" and "I'll have what she's having," its inclusion in Rob Reiner's pop-culture-influencing rom-com made it a part of the lexicon...which doesn't sit well with some people, like *The Atlantic*'s Megan Garber, who writes: "An assessment that is also a rebuke, *high-maintenance* is one of those breezy truisms that is so common, it barely registers as an insult."

AS IF!

Amy Heckerling's *Clueless*—a 1995 comedy based on Jane Austen's 1815 novel, *Emma*—is yet another movie with multiple additions to the lexicon. Cher complains about her teacher, "He said my debates were unresearched, unstructured, and unconvincing. *As if!*" *Clueless* has also been credited with popularizing the informal apology "my bad"—which had actually been around for about a decade, mostly on basketball courts, then was *everywhere* after *Clueless*. And Cher and her friends didn't coin the sarcastic interjection "Whatever!" but they did popularize flashing a sarcastic *W* with your hands while you're saying it.

TEXAS

No, the name of the state wasn't coined in a movie. Its origins predate the European conquest, when Indigenous people used a similar-sounding word (that sounded like "tayshas") that meant "friends." But over in Norway, the lowercase word "texas" has become slang for a "wild, crazy situation"—as seen here in this November 2023 headline: *"Han har aldri solgt flere biler til utlandet: Helt texas, sier bransjesjef."* Translation: "He has never sold more cars abroad: 'Completely texas,' says the industry manager." And that usage *was* inspired by a movie—by several, actually: American Westerns. They've been wildly popular in the northern European country since the 1970s. At some point the Norwegians noticed that a lot of crazy stuff went down in the Lone Star State, hence their adoption of this term. To see what the Norwegians saw, check out these Texas-set Westerns: *Red River*, *The Searchers*, *Duel in the Sun*, *Rio Grande*, *The Outlaw Josey Wales*, and the film with the wildest, craziest ending that Uncle John *still* can't get over: *Old Yeller*.

LIKE A LIGHT BULB

Uncle John had the bright idea to save every funny light bulb joke he found until he had enough to make a Bathroom Reader page. It's taken 20 years.

Q: How many golfers does it take to change a light bulb?
A: FORE!

Q: How many choreographers does it take to change a light bulb?
A: Five!...Six!...Seven!... Eight!

A: One.
Q: How many time travelers does it take to change a light bulb?

Q: How many hipsters does it take to change a light bulb?
A: Oh, it's an obscure number. You've probably never heard of it.

Q: Why did the hipster burn his hand?
A: He changed the light bulb before it was cool.

Q: How many aerospace engineers does it take to change a light bulb?
A: Just one. It's not rocket science.

Q: How many South Americans does it take to change a light bulb?
A: A Brazilian.

Q: How many tech support reps does it take to change a light bulb?
A: "We are unable to duplicate your problem. All our bulbs are working fine."

Q: How many polite New Yorkers does it take to change a light bulb?
A: Both of them.

Q: How many skateboarders does it take to change a light bulb?
A: One, but it takes him about 50 tries.

Q: How many mimes does it take to change a light bulb?
A:

Q: How many surrealists does it take to change a light bulb?
A: To get to the other side.

Q: How many punk rockers does it take to change a light bulb?
A: Two—one to turn the bulb, and one to kick the ladder out from under him.

Q: How many ski instructors does it take to change a light bulb?
A: Two—one to screw it in, and one to say, "Nice turns, man!"

Q: How many Freudians does it take to change a light bulb?
A: Two—one to change the bulb, and one to hold my mommy...er, LADDER, I MEAN LADDER.

Q: How many cable repairmen does it take to change a light bulb?
A: One. He'll be there sometime between 8:00 a.m. and 5:00 p.m.

Q: How many Germans does it take to change a light bulb?
A: One, because Germans are efficient and not very funny.

Q: How many mystery writers does it take to change a light bulb?
A: Two—one to screw in the light bulb, and one to give it a surprising twist at the end.

AT 25: GENERATION X

When this book hits store shelves, people who were born in 2000 will be turning the pivotal age of 25, when adulthood really *begins. To put things in perspective for Gen Z, here's what some notable Gen-Xers (those born from 1965 to 1980) were up to in their 25th year.*

DAVE GROHL (JANUARY 14, 1969)

Claim to Fame: American rock singer and musician, best known as a member of Nirvana and the Foo Fighters

At 25: He went from drummer to frontman.

Story: In 1994, Grohl began the most intense year of his life on a European tour with Nirvana. He had became the Seattle trio's drummer four years earlier on *Nevermind*, the album that launched the 1990s grunge movement and made Nirvana's shy singer, Kurt Cobain, a superstar. But the tour was cut short in early March after Cobain—who was severely depressed, suffered from chronic stomach pain, and was addicted to heroin—came down with bronchitis and then overdosed (not accidentally) on champagne and Rohypnol in his Rome hotel room. "Things got weird towards the end," recalled Grohl. "There were drugs around...And I didn't do the drugs and so I was just out of that world, you know?" A few weeks later, Cobain committed suicide by shooting himself at his Seattle home.

"My soul went dead to music," Grohl said of Cobain's suicide. He spent his 25th summer wandering around the Irish countryside alone, contemplating quitting the business altogether. But then: "I was winding around these country roads—so beautiful...and I come upon this hitchhiker...that had a Kurt Cobain T-shirt. And to me that meant: 'You can't outrun this thing.'"

Not long after Grohl returned to the States, he was offered a coveted spot as the new drummer for Tom Petty and the Heartbreakers, and even joined them for a song on *Saturday Night Live*. His name also came up as a possible replacement drummer for Pearl Jam.

Grohl, however, wanted to form his own band, but not with the other surviving member of Nirvana, bassist Krist Novoselic. (It would be "uncomfortable" for the other members, Grohl said.) He'd already had something in mind. A year earlier, before Cobain finally showed up to what would become Nirvana's final recording session, Grohl had recorded a few solo songs he'd been working on, including "Exhausted," "Big Me," "February Stars," and "Butterflies."

Now he had the opportunity to get back in the studio. "I had recorded the first record by myself, playing all the instruments." And what about a name? "I wanted

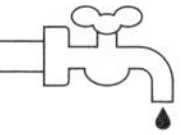

people to think that it was a group. I figured that Foo Fighters—a World War II term for UFOs—might lead people to believe that it was more than just one guy. Silly, huh?" He sure thinks so now: "Had I actually considered this to be a career, I probably would have called it something else, because it's the stupidest f***ing band name in the world."

MELANIA TRUMP (APRIL 26, 1970)

Claim to Fame: Slovenian American First Lady to U.S. President Donald Trump

At 25: She immigrated to the United States.

Story: The first—and as of this writing, only—Gen-Xer to be part of the First Family in the White House, Trump is also only the second foreign-born First Lady (Louisa Adams, wife of John Quincy Adams, was the first). When she was a little girl growing up in Yugoslavia (now Slovenia), Melanija Knav's dream was to become a fashion designer. But by age 16, her natural beauty landed her a gig as a fashion model, and she never looked back. (One of her modeling jobs, at 23, had her portraying the first female president of the United States.) By the time she was 25, she was newly spelling her name Melania Knauss and working as a model in Paris when she caught the eye of another 25-year-old, Italian modeling agent Paolo Zampolli. He had his eye on the New York real-estate market—with the idea of having beautiful models help sell his listings—and he sponsored Knauss's immigration to the United States.

She arrived in the Big Apple in 1996. Two years later, Zampolli introduced Knauss to 52-year-old real-estate mogul Donald Trump. "Well, he was very charming and we had the great sparkle," she told ABC News in 2018. "He came with a date. So he asked me for the number and I said, 'I will not give you my number. So if you give me your numbers, I will call you.' So I see what kind of numbers he will give me. Because I don't want to be one of the ladies. And he was known as kind of a lady's man."

The pair dated on an off for seven years before they were married in 2005.

MARIAH CAREY (MARCH 27, 1969)

Claim to Fame: American pop singer known for her incredible vocal range...and for *that* Christmas song

At 25: She recorded *that* song.

Story: As the only music artist whose first five singles hit #1 on the U.S. *Billboard* Hot 100, the "Songbird Supreme" was already a superstar by 25. Even still, making a Christmas album was a risk. "Back then, you didn't have a lot of artists with Christmas albums," said her collaborator, Walter Afanasieff. "It wasn't a known science...and there was nobody who did new, big Christmas songs."

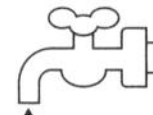

Her close friends and family know her as Robyn Fenty. The rest of us know her by her middle name: Rihanna.

Carey had loved Christmas carols since she was a little girl in New York, and she *really* wanted to do the album. So, in the summer of 1994 (after recording the duet "Endless Love" with Luther Vandross in the spring), she decorated her Miami home with Christmas decorations. Then, while Afanasieff played various melodies on the piano, Carey tried out lyrics. When he fell into a "boogie-woogie, kind of rock," Carey started singing, "I don't want a lot for Christmas"; then, recalled Afanasieff, "It was like a game of ping-pong. I'd hit the ball to her, she hits it back to me."

The result: "All I Want for Christmas Is You." Released that October, Carey spent the holidays watching the song top the holiday charts—which it has subsequently gone on to do *every* Christmas since. *Slate* called the Afanasieff-Carey collaboration "the only Christmas song written in the last half-century worthy of inclusion in the Great American Songbook."

The song has lost some of its cheer in recent years, after the collaborators had a falling out. In 2017, Carey told *Billboard* magazine, "I am proud of this song that I wrote basically as a kid on my little Casio keyboard." To which Afanasieff later relied, "She doesn't play anything, she doesn't play keyboard or piano. She doesn't understand music...[or] know a diminished chord from a minor seventh chord to a major seventh chord." He credits Carey and her vocals for making "All I Want for Christmas Is You" a hit, "but she definitely does not share credit where credit is due." (For what it's worth, Carey has earned $3 million in royalties every year from this song alone.)

In 2023, HappyOrNot, a customer feedback company, asked 215,000 retail workers to name their "most-hated Christmas song." The "winner" was...well, you know.

ELON MUSK (JUNE 28, 1971)

Claim to Fame: South African–Canadian businessman known for his involvement with SpaceX, Tesla, and X (formerly Twitter)

At 25: He lost a bid to become the CEO of his first tech company.

Story: In 1995, after attending the University of Pennsylvania (from which he would later be awarded two degrees), Musk was living in Palo Alto, California, in charge of his first tech company, Zip2, which was an early online directory that was intended to replace the yellow pages phone books. With a $28,000 investment from his father, Musk asked his brother to join him from Canada. (They'd moved there from South Africa to live with their mom when Elon was 18.) "Things were pretty tough in the early going," Musk told Stanford University students at a talk in 2013. "I didn't have any money. In fact, I had negative money. Huge student debt...So, I got a cheaper office than a place to stay, and I slept on the futon."

With its low overhead and lucrative contracts with the *New York Times* and the

In the time it takes you to read this fact, your body will shed about 60 dead skin cells.

Chicago Tribune, Zip2 was able to turn a profit from the outset, but in 1996, 25-year-old Musk was unsuccessful in his attempt to become CEO. The board members wanted someone with more experience. Despite his failure to take over leadership, Musk stayed with the company, which was bought by Compaq in 1999 for $300 million. Musk used his $22 million payout to start his next company, an online bank called X.com, which merged with another company a few years later and became PayPal.

RACHEL MADDOW (APRIL 1, 1973)

Claim to Fame: American cable news host and liberal commentator

At 25: She met the love of her life.

Story: As a 17-year-old Stanford University student, Rachel Maddow—a California-born athletic star with long blond hair—was "outed" in a school newspaper article called "Freshman lesbians face coming out with fear, release." By the time Maddow was 25, after becoming the first open lesbian to win a Rhodes Scholarship, she was living in western Massachusetts, doing odd jobs while working on her doctoral dissertation in politics about the AIDS epidemic. Maddow told the *New Yorker* in 2017, "I remember applying to a video store—this was when we still had video stores!—and not getting a job."

Then, one fateful day, the 25-year-old was hired to clean up the yard of Susan Mikula, a 40-year-old artist and photographer. "It was very *Desperate Housewives*," Maddow recalled. "I know that people don't believe in love at first sight; it was absolutely love at first sight. Bluebirds and comets and stars." The two women have been together ever since.

A year later, one of Maddow's odd jobs turned into an unexpected career: she earned minimum wage as a news reader for WRNX in Holyoke, Massachusetts, before landing a job at the progressive radio network, Air America. "I stumbled into that job, but it just really clicked," said Maddow. "I found I really liked explaining things." In 2024, MSNBC's weekly *The Rachel Maddow Show* was the network's highest-rated program, with average viewership of 2.5 million.

SHANIA TWAIN (AUGUST 28, 1965)

Claim to Fame: Canadian singer-songwriter, known for "Any Man of Mine" and "Man! I Feel Like a Woman!"

At 25: She changed her name to Shania and got her first recording contract.

Story: Eilleen Regina Edwards had a rough childhood. Living near the poverty line, she was raised by her mom and abusive stepdad in Timmins, Ontario. By the age of 10, Eilleen had found solace in songwriting; not long after that, she was singing her

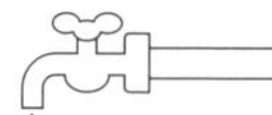

songs in front of people. "In terms of economic status, I couldn't afford to go to a performing arts school—my education was in a bar."

At 21, Eilleen left home to make it big in Toronto, only to return to Timmins just one year later to raise her three younger siblings after their parents were killed in a car accident. A few years later, Eilleen changed her name to Shania, rumored to be a loose translation of "on my way" in Ojibwa. By 25, Twain was honing her craft with a regular singing gig at a resort in Huntsville, Ontario. "My naivety was good, because I was just focusing on proving myself as an artist, not as a woman, and that's a very big difference." It was there, one fateful night in 1991, that a record producer named Norro Wilson saw Twain perform and invited her to Nashville, Tennessee, the "Country Music Capital of the World."

Her first album, *Shania Twain*, sold 100,000 copies. Not exactly superstar numbers, but it did catch the eye of renowned producer Robert "Mutt" Lange, whose résumé included AC/DC, Foreigner, Def Leppard, Bryan Adams, and Michael Bolton. Lange produced her second album, *The Woman in Me*. (He also became her husband, for a time.) The follow-up, *Come on Over*, spent 50 weeks at #1 on its way to selling 34 million copies, making it the best-selling female country album of all-time—and the top-selling country album by any member of Generation X.

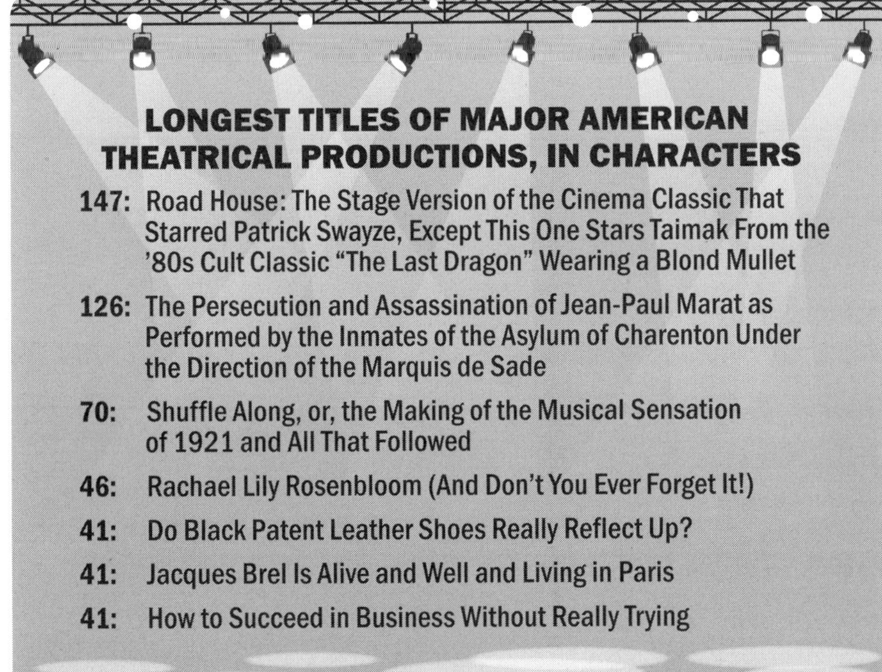

LONGEST TITLES OF MAJOR AMERICAN THEATRICAL PRODUCTIONS, IN CHARACTERS

147: Road House: The Stage Version of the Cinema Classic That Starred Patrick Swayze, Except This One Stars Taimak From the '80s Cult Classic "The Last Dragon" Wearing a Blond Mullet

126: The Persecution and Assassination of Jean-Paul Marat as Performed by the Inmates of the Asylum of Charenton Under the Direction of the Marquis de Sade

70: Shuffle Along, or, the Making of the Musical Sensation of 1921 and All That Followed

46: Rachael Lily Rosenbloom (And Don't You Ever Forget It!)

41: Do Black Patent Leather Shoes Really Reflect Up?

41: Jacques Brel Is Alive and Well and Living in Paris

41: How to Succeed in Business Without Really Trying

The dirtiest part of your body: your mouth. (Try washing it out with soap.)

WE'RE NUMBER ONE!

Almost every country in the world does something better or more than every other country. Here are the worldwide champions of some very specific categories.

Salt consumption: China—17.7 grams per person per day.

Cattle: India—more than 300,000,000, or 32.6 percent of the world's cow population.

Lamb consumption: Mongolia—145.5 pounds per person per year.

Patriotism: United States—41 percent of residents say they think it is the best country on earth.

High school graduates: South Korea—96.5 percent of students finish secondary school.

Higher education: South Korea—69 percent of adults finish college.

Workweek: Bhutan—the average worker toils for 54.3 hours per week.

Plastic pollution: China—37.6 million tons of plastic waste per year.

Billionaires: United States—735.

Divorce: Maldives—5.52 annual divorces per 1,000 people.

Rainfall: Colombia—127.6 inches of precipitation each year.

Sugar consumption: United States—126.4 grams per day per person.

Michelin stars: France—626 fine restaurants recognized with the prestigious award.

Potato chip consumption: United States and France—86 percent of people in both countries regularly eat them.

Sleeping in: Saudi Arabia—8:27 a.m. is the average wake-up time.

Cancer: Australia—462.5 cases (mostly skin cancer) per 100,000 people.

Smokers: Nauru—48.3 percent of the population smokes tobacco.

Belief in elves: Iceland—54 percent of people think elves are real.

Coffee consumption: Maldives—49 pounds per person each year.

Yams: Nigeria—two-thirds of the world's supply comes from the African country.

Lawyers: Israel—694 per 100,000 people.

Soccer players: Brazil—home country of 1,043 professional soccer players.

Women: Nepal—there are 84.55 males per every 100 women, and women make up 54.19 percent of the total population.

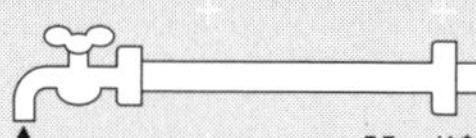

No #$@%ing joke: the symbol substitutes for profanity are known as *grawlix* or *obscenicon*.

ANSWERS

Wordplay Q&A *(Answers for page 139.)*

1. All three words have two y's: yoyo, yolky, and yay.
2. Add an e to fast to make a feast—the opposite of the fast meaning of "going without food."
3. "Empty orchestra" is karaoke in Japanese. "My own fault" is mea culpa in Latin. "Body-eating spirit" is from the Arabic word for alcohol.
4. Asthma.
5. Alone—which contains the synonyms a, lone, and one.
6. Minute—which means "60 seconds" and also a "miniscule amount."
7. An island and the letter t can both be found in the middle of water.
8. Forty is the only number whose letters are in alphabetical order.
9. Small.
10. Vowels. Louisiana and South Carolina have six, and four states have five: California, North Carolina, South Dakota, and West Virginia.
11. Estonia.
12. Catchphrase.
13. Seventy-seven.
14. Are becomes area.
15. Eat and ate.
16. Alphabet. It comes from the Greek letters alpha and beta.
17. "New York Giants" and "Towering Yanks" are anagrams of each other (meaning they contain all the same letters).

The Japanese Art of... *(Answers for page 227.)*

1. f; **2.** x; **3.** u; **4.** v; **5.** j; **6.** i; **7.** m; **8.** g; **9.** a; **10.** l; **11.** w; **12.** t; **13.** n; **14.** c; **15.** p; **16.** o; **17.** b; **18.** e; **19.** k; **20.** s; **21.** d; **22.** q; **23.** r; **24.** h

We are pleased to offer over 150 ebook versions of Portable Press titles—including Bathroom Readers available only in digital format! Visit *www.portablepress.com* to collect them all!

- ❒ The Best of the Best of Uncle John's Bathroom Reader
- ❒ The Best of Uncle John's Bathroom Reader
- ❒ Uncle John's Absolutely Absorbing Bathroom Reader
- ❒ Uncle John's Action-Packed Bathroom Reader
- ❒ Uncle John's Actual and Factual Bathroom Reader
- ❒ Uncle John's Ahh-Inspiring Bathroom Reader
- ❒ Uncle John's All-Purpose Extra Strength Bathroom Reader
- ❒ Uncle John's Awesome 35th Anniversary Bathroom Reader
- ❒ Uncle John's Bathroom Reader Attack of the Factoids
- ❒ Uncle John's Bathroom Reader Book of Love
- ❒ Uncle John's Bathroom Reader Cat Lover's Companion
- ❒ Uncle John's Bathroom Reader Christmas Collection
- ❒ Uncle John's Bathroom Reader Dog Lover's Companion
- ❒ Uncle John's Bathroom Reader Extraordinary Book of Facts
- ❒ Uncle John's Bathroom Reader Fake Facts
- ❒ Uncle John's Bathroom Reader Flush Fiction
- ❒ Uncle John's Bathroom Reader For Kids Only!
- ❒ Uncle John's Bathroom Reader For Kids Only! Collectible Edition
- ❒ Uncle John's Bathroom Reader Germophobia
- ❒ Uncle John's Bathroom Reader Golden Plunger Awards
- ❒ Uncle John's Bathroom Reader History's Lists
- ❒ Uncle John's Bathroom Reader Horse Lover's Companion
- ❒ Uncle John's Bathroom Reader Impossible Questions
- ❒ Uncle John's Bathroom Reader Jingle Bell Christmas
- ❒ Uncle John's Bathroom Reader Nature Calls
- ❒ Uncle John's Bathroom Reader Plunges into California
- ❒ Uncle John's Bathroom Reader Plunges into Canada, eh
- ❒ Uncle John's Bathroom Reader Plunges into Great Lives
- ❒ Uncle John's Bathroom Reader Plunges into History
- ❒ Uncle John's Bathroom Reader Plunges into History Again
- ❒ Uncle John's Bathroom Reader Plunges into Hollywood
- ❒ Uncle John's Bathroom Reader Plunges into Michigan
- ❒ Uncle John's Bathroom Reader Plunges into Minnesota
- ❒ Uncle John's Bathroom Reader Plunges into Music
- ❒ Uncle John's Bathroom Reader Plunges into National Parks
- ❒ Uncle John's Bathroom Reader Plunges into New Jersey
- ❒ Uncle John's Bathroom Reader Plunges into New York
- ❒ Uncle John's Bathroom Reader Plunges into Ohio
- ❒ Uncle John's Bathroom Reader Plunges into Pennsylvania
- ❒ Uncle John's Bathroom Reader Plunges into Texas
- ❒ Uncle John's Bathroom Reader Plunges into Texas Expanded Edition
- ❒ Uncle John's Bathroom Reader Plunges into the Presidency
- ❒ Uncle John's Bathroom Reader Plunges into the Universe
- ❒ Uncle John's Bathroom Reader Quintessential Collection of Notable Quotables
- ❒ Uncle John's Bathroom Reader Salutes the Armed Forces
- ❒ Uncle John's Bathroom Reader Shoots and Scores
- ❒ Uncle John's Bathroom Reader Sports Spectacular
- ❒ Uncle John's Bathroom Reader Takes a Swing at Baseball
- ❒ Uncle John's Bathroom Reader Tales to Inspire
- ❒ Uncle John's Bathroom Reader Tees Off on Golf
- ❒ Uncle John's Bathroom Reader The World's Gone Crazy
- ❒ Uncle John's Bathroom Reader Tunes into TV
- ❒ Uncle John's Bathroom Reader Vroom!
- ❒ Uncle John's Bathroom

Reader Weird Canada

- ❒ Uncle John's Bathroom Reader Weird Inventions
- ❒ Uncle John's Bathroom Reader WISE UP!
- ❒ Uncle John's Bathroom Reader Wonderful World of Odd
- ❒ Uncle John's Bathroom Reader Zipper Accidents
- ❒ Uncle John's Book of Fun
- ❒ Uncle John's Canoramic Bathroom Reader
- ❒ Uncle John's Certified Organic Bathroom Reader
- ❒ Uncle John's Colossal Collection of Quotable Quotes
- ❒ Uncle John's Creature Feature Bathroom Reader For Kids Only!
- ❒ Uncle John's Curiously Compelling Bathroom Reader
- ❒ Uncle John's Did You Know...? Bathroom Reader For Kids Only!
- ❒ Uncle John's Do-It-Yourself Diary for Infomaniacs Only
- ❒ Uncle John's Do-It-Yourself Journal for Infomaniacs Only
- ❒ Uncle John's Electrifying Bathroom Reader For Kids Only!
- ❒ Uncle John's Electrifying Bathroom Reader For Kids Only! Collectible Edition
- ❒ Uncle John's Endlessly Engrossing Bathroom Reader
- ❒ Uncle John's Factastic Bathroom Reader
- ❒ Uncle John's Facts to Annoy Your Teacher Bathroom Reader For Kids Only!
- ❒ Uncle John's Fast-Acting Long-Lasting Bathroom Reader
- ❒ Uncle John's Fully Loaded 25th Anniversary Bathroom Reader
- ❒ Uncle John's Giant 10th Anniversary Bathroom Reader
- ❒ Uncle John's Gigantic Bathroom Reader
- ❒ Uncle John's Great Big Bathroom Reader
- ❒ Uncle John's Greatest Know on Earth Bathroom Reader
- ❒ Uncle John's Haunted Outhouse Bathroom Reader For Kids Only!
- ❒ Uncle John's Heavy Duty Bathroom Reader
- ❒ Uncle John's Hindsight Is 20/20 Bathroom Reader
- ❒ Uncle John's How to Toilet Train Your Cat
- ❒ Uncle John's InfoMania Bathroom Reader For Kids Only!
- ❒ Uncle John's Legendary Lost Bathroom Reader
- ❒ Uncle John's Lists That Make You Go Hmmm...
- ❒ Uncle John's New & Improved Briefs
- ❒ Uncle John's New & Improved Funniest Ever
- ❒ Uncle John's Old Faithful 30th Anniversary Bathroom Reader
- ❒ Uncle John's Perpetually Pleasing Bathroom Reader
- ❒ Uncle John's Political Briefs
- ❒ Uncle John's Presents: Book of the Dumb
- ❒ Uncle John's Presents: Book of the Dumb 2
- ❒ Uncle John's Presents: Mom's Bathtub Reader
- ❒ Uncle John's Presents the Ultimate Challenge Trivia Quiz
- ❒ Uncle John's Robotica Bathroom Reader
- ❒ Uncle John's Slightly Irregular Bathroom Reader
- ❒ Uncle John's Smell-O-Scopic Bathroom Reader For Kids Only!
- ❒ Uncle John's Supremely Satisfying Bathroom Reader
- ❒ Uncle John's The Enchanted Toilet Bathroom Reader For Kids Only!
- ❒ Uncle John's Top Secret Bathroom Reader For Kids Only!
- ❒ Uncle John's Top Secret Bathroom Reader For Kids Only! Collectible Edition
- ❒ Uncle John's Totally Quacked Bathroom Reader For Kids Only!
- ❒ Uncle John's Triumphant 20th Anniversary Bathroom Reader
- ❒ Uncle John's True Crime
- ❒ Uncle John's Truth, Trivia, and the Pursuit of Factiness Bathroom Reader
- ❒ Uncle John's 24-Karat Gold Bathroom Reader
- ❒ Uncle John's Ultimate Bathroom Reader
- ❒ Uncle John's Uncanny Bathroom Reader
- ❒ Uncle John's Unsinkable Bathroom Reader
- ❒ Uncle John's Unstoppable Bathroom Reader
- ❒ Uncle John's Weird Weird World
- ❒ Uncle John's Weird Weird World: Epic
- ❒ Uncle John's Weird, Wonderful Bathroom Reader

THE LAST PAGE

FELLOW BATHROOM READERS:

The fight for good bathroom reading should never be taken loosely—we must do our duty and sit firmly for what we believe in, even while the rest of the world is taking potshots at us.

We'll be brief. Now that we've proven we're not simply a flush-in-the-pan, we invite you to take the plunge: Sit Down and Be Counted! To find out what the BRI is up to, visit us on the web and take a peek!

GET CONNECTED

Find us online to sign up for our email list, enter exciting giveaways, hear about new releases, and more!

Website: www.portablepress.com

Facebook: www.facebook.com/UncleJohnsBathroomReader

Pinterest: www.pinterest.com/portablepress

And visit Uncle John's Blog for fun throughout the year!
www.portablepress.com/blog

Well, we're out of space, and when you've gotta go, you've gotta go. Tanks for all your support. Hope to hear from you soon.

Meanwhile, remember...

Keep on flushin'!